GLOBAL JUSTICE AND INT[...]

Since the beginnings of the Gen[...]
ton Woods institutions, and on [...]
states have continued to develop institutions and legal [...]
global interdependence. International economic law, a field dominated by legal
regimes to liberalize international trade but that also includes international financial law and international law relating to economic development, has become
a dense web of treaty commitments at the multilateral, regional, and bilateral
levels. International lawyers are experts in understanding how these institutions
operate in practice, but they tend to uncritically accept comparative advantage as
the principal normative criterion to justify these institutions. In contrast, moral
and political philosophers have developed accounts of global justice, but these
accounts have had relatively little influence on international legal scholarship
and on institutional design. What is needed is a multidisciplinary approach to
understanding the economic fairness problems that societies face as they become
increasingly interdependent, and the solutions that international economic law
and institutions might facilitate. This volume reflects the results of a symposium
held at Tillar House, the American Society of International Law headquarters in
Washington, DC, in November 2008. This symposium brought together philosophers, legal scholars, and economists to discuss the problems of understanding
international economic law from the standpoints of rights and justice, in particular from the standpoint of distributive justice.

Chios Carmody is an Associate Professor of Law at the University of Western
Ontario Faculty of Law, where he has taught since 1999. He also serves as Cana-
dian Director of the Canada–United States Law Institute. He has been a visiting
professor at Georgetown University Law Center and an Emile Noël Fellow at the
Jean Monnet Center for Regional and International Economic Law and Justice,
NYU Law School.

Frank J. Garcia is a Professor of Law at the Boston College Law School. A Fulbright
Scholar, he has lectured widely on globalization and international economic law
in Europe, South America, and Asia. He has served on the executive boards of
the International Economic Law and International Legal Theory Interest Groups
of the American Society of International Law, and on the editorial board of the
Journal of International Economic Law.

John Linarelli is Professor of Law and Head of School at Swansea University School
of Law. He has held positions in both American and British law schools. He has
written extensively on international economic law, transnational commercial law,
and legal theory. He has served on the executive board of the International Legal
Theory Interest Group of the American Society of International Law and currently
serves as its Chair.

ASIL Studies in International Legal Theory

General Editors

Mortimer N. S. Sellers, *University of Maryland*
Elizabeth Andersen, *American Society of International Law*

The purpose of the *ASIL Studies in International Legal Theory* will be to clarify and improve the theoretical foundations of international law. Too often the progressive development and implementation of international law have foundered on confusion about first principles. This series will raise the level of public and scholarly discussion about the structure and purposes of the world legal order and how best to achieve global justice through law.

The idea for this series grows out of the International Legal Theory project of the American Society of International Law. The book series *ASIL Studies in International Legal Theory* will deepen this exchange by publishing scholarly monographs and edited volumes of essays considering subjects in international legal theory.

Global Justice and International Economic Law

Opportunities and Prospects

Edited by

CHIOS CARMODY
University of Western Ontario Faculty of Law

FRANK J. GARCIA
Boston College Law School

JOHN LINARELLI
Swansea University School of Law

CAMBRIDGE
UNIVERSITY PRESS

32 Avenue of the Americas, New York NY 10013-2473, USA

Cambridge University Press is part of the University of Cambridge.

It furthers the University's mission by disseminating knowledge in the pursuit of education, learning and research at the highest international levels of excellence.

www.cambridge.org
Information on this title: www.cambridge.org/9781107438514

© Cambridge University Press 2012

First published 2011, 2012
Second Edition 2012
Reprinted 2013
First paperback edition 2014

A catalogue record for this publication is available from the British Library

Library of Congress Cataloguing in Publication data

Global justice and international economic law : opportunities and prospects / [edited by] Chios Carmody, Frank J. Garcia, John Linarelli.
   p.   cm. – (ASIL studies in international legal theory)
Includes bibliographical references and index.
ISBN 978-1-107-01328-5 (hardback)
1. Law – Economic aspects – Congresses.   2. Distributive justice – Congresses.
3. Globalization and law – Congresses.   4. Foreign trade regulation – Congresses.
I. Carmody, Chi.   II. Garcia, Frank J.   III. Linarelli, John.
K246.G58   2011
343′.07–dc22   2011011644

ISBN 978-1-107-01328-5 Hardback
ISBN 978-1-107-43851-4 Paperback

Contents

PART III. CRITICAL RESPONSES TO CONTEMPORARY THEORIZING
ABOUT JUSTICE AND INTERNATIONAL ECONOMIC INSTITUTIONS

Contributors

Daniel Butt is Lecturer in Political Theory, University of Bristol.

Chios Carmody is Associate Professor of Law, University of Western Ontario Faculty of Law.

Jeffrey L. Dunoff is Professor of Law, Temple University Beasley School of Law.

Frank J. Garcia is Professor of Law, Boston College Law School.

Carol C. Gould is Professor of Philosophy, CUNY Hunter College.

Robert C. Hockett is Professor of Law, Cornell Law School.

Aaron James is Associate Professor of Philosophy, University of California Irvine.

Jonathan Klick is Professor of Law, University of Pennsylvania Law School.

Chin Leng Lim is Professor of Law, University of Hong Kong Faculty of Law.

John Linarelli is Professor of Law and Head of School, Swansea University School of Law.

Barbara Stark is Professor of Law and John DeWitt Gregory Research Scholar, Hofstra University School of Law.

Fernando R. Tesón is Tobias Simon Eminent Scholar, Florida State University College of Law.

Chantal Thomas is Professor of Law, Cornell Law School.

Joel P. Trachtman is Professor of International Law, Tufts University Fletcher School of Law and Diplomacy.

Acknowledgments

The contributions to this book started as presentations at the American Society of International Law (ASIL) International Legal Theory Interest Group symposium in November 2008 at Tillar House, the American Society of International Law headquarters in Washington, DC. The symposium has become an annual event. The symposia papers have begun to appear in books in the ASIL Studies in International Legal Theory, published by Cambridge University Press. The editors are gratified to see the ASIL International Legal Theory Interest Group play a significant role in fostering research and publications in this important series.

The editors owe debts of gratitude to many. The editors extend their sincere thanks to the authors in this book. It was an honor and a pleasure to work with a group of distinguished philosophers, legal scholars, and economists who worked diligently to produce the highest quality and innovative work.

The editors would like to thank Mortimer "Tim" Sellers of the University of Baltimore Law School for his vision and encouragement in promoting the symposia and the ASIL Studies in International Legal Theory series. Tim's tireless efforts, along with those of ASIL Director Elizabeth Andersen, to bring about the book series, are to be commended. We also need to thank Elizabeth Andersen and her staff at ASIL, in particular Sheila Ward, for their assistance in making our symposium a success. Sheila Ward is a great asset to ASIL and we continue to count our blessings that she is always there to help the Interest Group.

The editors would like to thank Brian Lepard of the University of Nebraska College of Law, who was then Chair of the International Legal Theory Interest Group. Brian was steadfast in his support for our symposium and was instrumental in securing funding from the University of Nebraska College of Law. We should also extend our thanks to Dean Steven Wilborn of the University of Nebraska College of Law for funding for the symposium.

Other law schools provided funding for the symposium as well. The editors wish to thank Dean John H. Garvey of the Boston College Law School, Dean Allen Easley of the University of La Verne College of Law, the University of Baltimore School of Law, and the University of Baltimore Center for International and Comparative Law for funding for the symposium.

The editors express their sincere gratitude to John Berger, commissioning editor for Cambridge University Press, for his support of this project. John is always helpful and responsive and we see him as an innovator in publishing on international legal theory. The editors would also like to thank Shana Meyer for her assistance in the copyediting phases of this project. Shana's patient attention to detail kept us all on track. The editors would like to thank the anonymous referees for the book, who provided excellent comments that helped us improve the book.

Chios Carmody would like to thank his fellow editors for their assistance at a time of considerable personal and professional difficulty and his research assistant, Ms. Michelle Dekens, for her help in the final phase of the project.

Frank J. Garcia would like to thank his students at the Boston College Law School and abroad for the many interesting conversations on trade and justice, from which he has learned a lot. Particular thanks go to his research assistant, Ms. Lindita Ciko, for her hard work and substantial intellectual commitment to this project. He would also like to thank his coeditors for the pleasure and privilege of working with them on this book. Finally, he would like to thank his wife Kim for her steadfast support for an interdisciplinary conversation about justice.

John Linarelli would like to thank his coeditors for the excellent teamwork and cooperative spirit in getting the book finished. He would also like to thank his very talented research assistant, Ms. Malalai Farooqi, for her work on the book. Finally, he would like to thank his wife Lina and son John Shih Shin for their patience as we planned the transatlantic move to Swansea while this book was being completed.

Introduction

Chios Carmody, Frank J. Garcia, and John Linarelli

Global justice, as both an idea and as a practice followed by countries and institutions, has faced many obstacles in its realization. Consider the difficulties a cosmopolitan might have in Washington, D.C. or any other capital city. A suggestion to anyone in the Washington, D.C. trade policy elite that the world should be governed by cosmopolitan notions of global justice in which states should not matter would be met with a blank stare, but only if the official were being polite. States matter in practical affairs. Theories that put states in tension, such as cosmopolitan theories of global justice, are difficult for states to accept. In the nationalist contexts in which officials of national governments perform their duties and in which people live their lives, justice is understood as a duty of the state, if it is understood as a duty at all. With states at the center of action on matters of justice, domestic institutions within a state provide justice to the state's citizens, and national borders determine who gets justice and who does not. Justice is political and political systems are domestic.

After World War II, the progression of international law into the area of human rights helped spread the notion that human rights are properly the subject of international law and that states may be called to account for failing to respect human rights. Still, the central case of human rights in international law is that states owe human rights to their own citizens.[1] International human

---

[1] This is changing as the connections between international human rights law and international humanitarian law are becoming less distinct. For example, human rights law is increasingly applied to military conduct in armed conflicts. In other words, states have a duty to respect the human rights of citizens of other states when their military is employed in other states. In addition, states likely must apply principles of fundamental human rights in general to noncitizens within their jurisdiction. See Mark Osiel, *The End of Reciprocity: Terror, Torture, and the Law of War* (New York: Cambridge University Press, 2009); Paul Eden and Matthew Happold, "Symposium: The Relationship between International Humanitarian Law and International Human Rights Law," *Journal of Conflict and Security Law* 14(3) (2009): 441–447.

rights law depends on the notion that states are the primary providers and enforcers of human rights. If the source of human rights is something distinct from positive law, such as the moral equality of all persons or the rights that persons possess in a state of nature apart from what any institution might grant, then human rights just might be cosmopolitan, but their dependence on national political communities makes their practical realization without states and domestic state law problematic. Regardless of one's views on the justification for human rights, positive law sources for human rights seem to be necessary to avoid Onora O'Neill's criticism that human rights are simply manifestos.[2]

The ideas that have influenced international law do not come from normative theories about justice, and certainly not from cosmopolitanism. International relations realism, Hobbesian notions of state sovereignty and the state of nature, and Grotian natural law accounts of international law have all had significantly more traction in influencing international law and international relations than theories of global justice.[3] John Rawls, the most prominent political and moral philosopher in our contemporary period, rejected the notion of global justice. Instead, his "Law of Peoples" set forth a limited set of basic rights and duties for well-ordered societies at the international level, distinct from his full-blown account of justice for the basic structure of domestic society.[4] In sum, it is sovereign equality of states, not the moral equality of persons, that has informed international law. Sovereignty is a political and not a moral concept.[5] It is conceivable, then, that international law might be fundamentally unjust. Add to this the unexamined assumption by many international economic lawyers that progressive trade liberalization based on Ricardian comparative advantage is the basic operating *grundnorm* for the World Trade Organization (WTO) legal system, and the results are predictable. The normativity of

---

[2] O'Neill's worry is about "putting rights first" in any question of global justice. Her view is that the discussion should start with obligations:

> The most questionable effect of putting rights first is that those rights for which no allocation of obligations has been institutionalized may not be taken seriously. When obligations are unallocated it is indeed right that they should be met, but nobody can have an effective right – an enforceable, claimable or waiveable right – to their being met. Such abstract rights are not effective entitlements. If the claimants of supposed "rights" to food or development cannot find where to lodge their claims, these are empty "manifesto" rights.

See Onora O'Neill, *Bounds of Justice* (Cambridge: Cambridge University Press, 2000), 126.
[3] Thomas Christiano and John Christman (eds.), *Contemporary Debates in Political Philosophy* (West Sussex: Wiley-Blackwell, 2009), 17.
[4] John Rawls, *The Law of Peoples* (Cambridge, MA: Harvard University Press, 1999).
[5] David Luban, "Just War and Human Rights," *Philosophy and Public Affairs* 9(2) (1980): 160–181.

international law operates from a core set of assumptions in need of serious reexamination.

This book deals with two fields that we believe are in great need of closer contact with one another, for the good of these fields but also for a more just world. One is international law, in particular the international law of economic relations, which needs to have more contact with theories of justice. The other is political theory on the problem of global justice, which needs to have more contact with international law and the design of actual institutions. Work is needed in two distinct domains, international law and practical philosophy. In his Storrs Lecture at Yale Law School in October 2004, Thomas Nagel started with reflections on the state of moral and political theory: "[C]oncepts and theories of global justice are in the early stages of formation, and it is not clear what the main questions are, let alone the main possible answers."[6] He also said that he believed "that the need for workable ideas about the global and institutional case presents political theory with its most important task, and even perhaps with the opportunity to make a practical contribution in the long run, though perhaps only the very long run."[7] Nagel's arguments easily extend as a critique of international law.

Let us first consider international law and how it might more concretely connect with theories of justice. It is by now a truism to say that the move in legal scholarship, at least in North America, has been toward interdisciplinary inquiry in the postlegal realist period of the past fifty years.[8] Legal scholarship, however, tends to lag behind in bringing the innovations of other disciplines to bear on the law.[9] International law scholarship lags even further, with most of

---

[6] Thomas Nagel, "The Problem of Global Justice," *Philosophy and Public Affairs* 33 (2005): 113–147, esp. 113.

[7] Ibid.

[8] The interdisciplinary turn in North American legal scholarship has prompted the claim by Judge Richard Posner that the law is no longer an "autonomous discipline." See Richard A. Posner, "The Decline of Law as an Autonomous Discipline: 1962–1987," *Harvard Law Review* 100 (1987): 761–780.

[9] Francis Mootz describes the relationship between legal scholarship and other disciplines as follows:

> In recent years, trends in legal theory generally have followed the intellectual movements within English departments and have lagged even further behind the developments emerging from philosophy departments. Although legal theorists sometimes resemble pathological necrophiliacs – rushing to embrace the latest Paris fashion without stopping to engage in careful, independent, and critical thinking – it would be incorrect to conclude that the interdisciplinary character of contemporary legal scholarship is entirely detrimental. Admittedly, legal theorists have, in the past, joined intractable debates that already had worn out their contestants in other disciplines, arriving too late to garner any intellectual energy. However, legal theorists have also brought new life to ongoing debates by culling the careful thinking and research that precedes them in other disciplines and

the interdisciplinary work being done with international relations theory.[10] To be fair, there has been a rise in law and economics accounts of international law, some of which have been the subject of significant controversy.[11] We are, however, only at the beginning of thinking how moral and political theory might be brought to bear on international law.[12]

> then advancing the debate within a new context. It would be as senseless as it is impossible to try to insulate legal theory from broader intellectual currents. Jurisprudence is not just an analytical tool for assessing the legal system; it is a critical gesture lodged within the concrete setting of legal practice that draws from and contributes to developments of our various political, ethical, epistemological, and ontological traditions.

Francis J. Mootz III, "Legal Classics: After Deconstructing the Legal Canon," *North Carolina Law Review* 72 (1994): 977–1038.

[10] In an empirical study of international legal scholarship, Marci Hoffman and Katherine Topulos found the following:

> Among international legal academics, at least those trained in American law schools, it is increasingly a truism that "we're all interdisciplinary scholars now." That is, most international lawyers would accept the claim that international law is not an autonomous discipline; rather, international law is increasingly understood as a discipline that is itself interdisciplinary. Our data shows a growing interest in interdisciplinary research by international law scholars, as measured by the increased use of terms prevalent in other disciplines (such as economics, political science, and most especially international relations) in the international law literature. However, these measures indicate international law scholarship still lags behind legal scholarship generally in its use of interdisciplinary methodologies.

See Marci Hoffman and Katherine Topulos, "Tyranny of the Available: Under-Represented Topics, Approaches, and Viewpoints," *Syracuse Journal of International Law and Commerce* 35 (2008): 175–200, esp. 180.

[11] Joel P. Trachtman, *The Economic Structure of International Law* (Cambridge, MA: Harvard University Press, 2009); Andrew T. Guzman, *How International Law Works: A Rational Choice Theory* (Oxford: Oxford University Press, 2009). Works that have generated controversy include Eric A. Posner, *The Perils of Global Legalism* (Chicago: University of Chicago Press, 2009), and Eric A. Posner and Jack L. Goldsmith, *The Limits of International Law* (Oxford: Oxford University Press, 2006).

[12] In the late 1990s, the American Society of International Law held a Symposium on Method in International Law. See Steven R. Ratner and Anne-Marie Slaughter, "Appraising the Methods of International Law: A Prospectus for Readers," *American Journal of International Law* 93 (1999): 291. There has been considerable progress in interdisciplinary inquiry about international law since that symposium. Notably, moral and political theory in general and theories of justice in particular apparently were not covered in the symposium. Most of the focus of interdisciplinary inquiry in international law relies on international relations theory. See Jeffrey L. Dunoff, "Why Constitutionalism Now? Text, Context and the Historical Contingency of Ideas," *Journal of International Law and International Relations* 1 (2005): 191 (on the interdisciplinary turn of international law and international relations theory scholarship), and Anne Marie Slaughter, "International Law and International Relations Theory: A Dual Agenda," *American Journal of International Law* 87 (1993): 205. Recently there has been a turn toward the approaches of law and economics.

This presents something of a paradox. As Fernando Tesón, a contributor to this book, said at the American Society of International Law Annual Meeting in 1987,

> [t]he marriage between international law and ethical theory has a long and venerable tradition. Grotius, the father of international law, conceived of the law of nations as an integral part of the law of nature. By the 19th century, however, the joint rights of nationalism, positivism, and relativism have all but destroyed references to the philosophical underpinnings of the discipline in international legal scholarship.
>
> While moral philosophy is now routinely part of the debates in areas such as constitutional or criminal law, international law lags behind in this respect. With few exceptions, current international legal scholarship is mired in a theoretical framework formed by a mix of so-called realism and old-fashioned positivism, both of which exclude independent philosophical analysis.
>
> Moral philosophy is necessarily part of the articulation of international legal propositions. For example, in attempting to define the concept of custom, are instances of state practice to be perceived as a violation of international law, creating a new rule of law, or simply an exception to the existing rule? I would submit that state practices are, and must be, interpreted in the light of their value or purpose, in short, in light of explicit or implicit normative moral political theory.[13]

More recently, Jeremy Waldron, in discussing the need for an analytical jurisprudence of international law, said,

> the neglect of international law in modern analytical jurisprudence is nothing short of scandalous. Theoretically it is the issue of the hour; there is an intense debate going on in the legal academy about the nature and character of customary international law, for example. Analytic legal philosophers seem mostly to have missed this, even when it is evident that they might have a substantial contribution to make.[14]

Although the series in which this book appears has begun to address Waldron's concerns with its publication of Brian Lepard's *Customary International Law: A New Theory with Practical Applications*,[15] the more general points that Tesón and Waldron raise still remain true. International law has had little

---

[13] Fernando Tesón, "Remarks," in Robyn Lipsky, "Ethical Foundations of International Law," *American Society of International Law Proceedings* 81 (1987): 415–445, esp. 416.

[14] Jeremy Waldron, "Hart and the Principles of Legality," in Matthew Kramer, Claire Grant, Ben Colburn, and Antony Hatzistavrou (eds.), *The Legacy of H.L.A. Hart: Legal, Political and Moral Philosophy* (Oxford: Oxford University Press, 2008), 67–84, esp. 69.

[15] Brian D. Lepard, *Customary International Law: A New Theory with Practical Applications* (Cambridge: Cambridge University Press, 2010).

contact with contemporary practical philosophy, and almost none with philosophical accounts of justice.[16]

Turning to political theory, we see that if Nagel is correct and moral and political theorists have a long way to go on global justice, then we may be some distance from the point where theories of global justice can even influence international law. There are a number of ways of understanding the contemporary state of global justice theory, although our task is not to survey these accounts.[17] Philosophical accounts of global justice are often not easily demarcated or entirely distinct. As a simple framework for understanding the questions that this book deals with, we may usefully distinguish between cosmopolitan and communitarian accounts.[18]

Communitarian and cosmopolitan accounts of global justice can be distinguished according to the different relationships they posit between norms of justice and social relationships. Perhaps the voice most closely identified with global justice is the cosmopolitan one, arguing that justice *precedes* social relations and should structure social relations.[19] Cosmopolitanism is ideal theory at its purest. It requires us to ignore actual institutions and ask what kinds

---

[16] For a panel discussion of the lack of contact, see Joost Pauwelyn, Frank Garcia, Christian Barry, and Susan Esserman, "Just Trade under Law: Do We Need a Theory of Justice for International Trade Relations," *American Society of International Law Proceedings* 100 (2006): 375–386. In a review of Frank J. Garcia, *Trade, Inequality and Justice: Towards a Liberal Theory of Just Trade* (Leiden: Brill, 2003), Joost Pauwelyn says this:

> It says a lot about the current U.S. perspective on international law that the first 144 of a 213-page book entitled *Trade, Inequality, and Justice: Toward a Liberal Theory of Just Trade* are spent convincing the reader that "trade law inescapably involves questions of justice." This is . . . a sobering remark on the prevailing realist approach to international law in the U.S. academy, an approach that explains international cooperation as the mere pursuit of self-interest and power and disavows any normative value to international law.

See Joost Pauwelyn, "Just Trade," *George Washington International Law Review* 37 (2005): 559–571.

[17] Recent works that provide comprehensive treatments include Gillian Brock, *Global Justice: A Cosmopolitan Account* (Oxford: Oxford University Press, 2009); Simon Caney, *Justice beyond Borders: A Global Political Theory* (Oxford: Oxford University Press, 2005); and Kok-Chor Tan, *Justice without Borders: Cosmopolitanism, Nationalism, and Patriotism* (Cambridge: Cambridge University Press, 2004).

[18] This classification is from Caney, *Justice beyond Borders*, at 15. He borrows the cosmopolitan–communitarian distinction from Chris Brown, *International Relations Theory: New Normative Approaches* (Hemel Hempstead: Harvester Wheatsheaf, 1992) and Janna Thompson, *Justice and World Order: A Philosophical Inquiry* (London: Routledge, 1992). Caney disaggregates communitarianism into realism, society of states, and nationalism.

[19] By saying justice precedes social relations, we mean to say that justice as an obligation is owed to individuals because of their moral status as human beings, independent of whatever social relations and institutions they find themselves in. See Charles Jones, *Global Justice: Defending Cosmopolitanism* (Oxford: Oxford University Press, 2001), 15–16.

of institutions we should have if we were starting from the very beginning. Thus, although the realization of global justice is necessarily constrained by political relations as we find them, its normative possibility is not established, or vitiated, by such relationships – it just *is*. The cosmopolitan view, as is well known, holds that we owe obligations of justice to one another because of our moral status as human beings, regardless of the nature or extent of social bonds between us.[20] In essence, justice precedes society; our social bonds grow out of and are structured by our obligations of justice.

From the point of view of a cosmopolitan, global justice as a concept is not a problem. We owe human beings justice in our social relations, wherever they are found, simply because they are human beings. The problem, of course, and it is still a considerable one, is determining what this justice consists of, and how to deliver it. One can distinguish between moral cosmopolitanism, which advocates individual cosmopolitan duties to be realized through existing institutional structures, and institutional cosmopolitanism, which advocates reform of existing institutions along cosmopolitan lines.[21] The bottom line for either view is that the possibility of global justice is rooted in the nature of individual duties to one another, expressed in and through global institutions.

The leading alternative view in this debate is communitarianism, objecting to global justice on the ground that justice is a virtue *within* political communities, not *between* them. Thus the very idea of global justice is incoherent because of the absence of the requisite global community. For communitarians, justice depends on the prior existence of certain kinds of social relationships, or "society," but it requires a deeper level of interaction that we call "community," usually identified politically with the nation and generally expressed in terms of shared traditions, practices, and understandings.[22] It is within communities that people create obligations of justice, through an intense level of social interaction that defines its principles, subjects, and objects.[23] In other words, social relations are more than the field of

---

[20] There is a rich cosmopolitan literature. See Simon Caney, "International Distributive Justice," *Political Studies* 49 (2001): 975–979, and Jeremy Waldron, "What Is Cosmopolitanism?," *Journal of Political Philosophy* 8 (2000): 227–243 (surveying cosmopolitanism). The strength and institutionality of such social bonds does, of course, affect the degree to which we can realize our obligations of justice, as do instrumental and practical concerns. Nevertheless, the obligations are asserted on this view to exist, independent of such concerns.

[21] Charles Beitz, "Social and Cosmopolitan Liberalism," *International Affairs* 75 (1999): 515–529.

[22] Communitarian theorists differ on the precise nature of these necessary relations, and in general this aspect of communitarianism is undertheorized. See Allen E. Buchanan, "Assessing the Communitarian Critique of Liberalism," *Ethics* 99 (1989): 852–882, esp. 867.

[23] See, e.g., David Miller, *On Nationality* (Oxford: Clarendon Press, 1995), and Michael Walzer, *Spheres of Justice* (New York: Basic Books, 1983). The communitarian critique of cosmopolitan global justice is only part of its larger critique of liberal justice, and liberalism generally.

application for justice: In a community, they create justice itself. No community, no justice.

Thus for communitarians it is this need for *community*, as something "deeper" than mere society, that prevents us from reaching anything like global justice. Communitarians maintain that although at the global level we may share a common humanity and mutual interests, we do not share obligations of justice because we do not reach community at the global level. Put another way, communitarians might grant the existence of some kind of global society, consisting of associations for mutual self-interest but distinguishable from true "community," which requires something more, reserving "justice" for the latter. Alternately, some communitarians might argue that an "international community" is under construction, but that it remains too embryonic and too ill defined to create true justice on a regular basis.[24] If we seek international justice, we need to look at specific international "communities" or their proxies in the shape of institutions, like the International Criminal Court or the WTO, to get some sense of what is involved.[25]

Although contractarian or contractualist accounts figure prominently in any discussion of justice, global or otherwise, they do not necessarily have to be identified as distinct accounts in the manner of cosmopolitan and communitarian accounts. This is because they can be understood not as justification for political obligation but as meta-ethics, as accounts of the form of moral argument or the idea and structure of morality and justice.[26] A contractualist as a moral philosopher, working in the moral version of contractualism identified by T. M. Scanlon, just might, in terms of the issues we are framing here, be a cosmopolitan, a communitarian, or a liberal nationalist, depending on

See Buchanan, "Assessing the Communitarian Critique of Liberalism," 852–882 (summarizing this critique).

[24] Michael Walzer, *Thick and Thin: Moral Argument at Home and Abroad* (South Bend, IN: University of Notre Dame Press, 2006).

[25] See Bruno Simma, "Bilateralism and Community Interest in the Law of State Responsibility," in Yoram Dinstein (ed.), *International Law at a Time of Perplexity* (Dordrecht: Springer, 1989), 821; also see Alan Boyle and Christine Chinkin, *The Making of International Law* (Oxford: Oxford University Press, 2007), 17, who note that "the concept of international community is an artificial construct and both its constitution and the content of the values derived therefrom are contested." For a more confident view of international community, see David J. Bederman, *The Spirit of International Law* (Athens: University of Georgia Press, 2002), 49–54. For an intermediate account arguing that globalization has brought about limited yet relevant elements of community in key areas of global social relations, see Frank J. Garcia, "Globalization and the Theory of International Law," *International Legal Theory* 11 (2005): 9.

[26] For this distinction see Samuel Freeman, "Moral Contractarianism as a Foundation for Interpersonal Morality," in James L. Drier, *Contemporary Debates in Moral Theory* (Hoboken, NJ: Wiley-Blackwell, 2006), 57.

how one works out general principles from Scanlon's notion of reasonable rejection.[27]

For contractualists such as Rawls, principles of justice are rooted in social association, specifically cooperative associations for mutual benefit.[28] In other words, it is the nature of their social interaction that brings about the need for agreed principles of allocation and that gives rise to the process of agreement concerning what such principles should be. This should not be confused with an actual historical agreement on first principles; rather, "they are the principles that free and rational persons concerned to further their own interest would accept in an initial position of equality as defining the fundamental terms of their association."[29] Absent the requisite social interactions and resulting agreements, there is no need for justice, and no opportunity for it. Thus a contractualist who accepts Rawls's *Law of Peoples* would be a liberal nationalist in the framework we are adopting.

Whatever the account of justice, in the end it all comes down to institutions and conditions on the ground. Moral and political theorists have long struggled with the notion of bringing their ideas to bear on the actual design of institutions. Much has been said about how the question of justice is fundamentally about institutional design. It is basic to the idea of justice itself that justice requires, in Charles Beitz's words, "efforts at large scale institutional reform."[30] Rawls's theory of justice is about the basic structure of society as that structure is reflected in social institutions, a tradition going at least back to his intellectual forbearers Rousseau, Kant, and Hobbes.[31]

Although philosophers have argued over and again that justice is about duties of social institutions, they have not gone very far in specifying how the requirements of justice might operate in practice. Their focus is almost wholly

---

[27] See, e.g., Michael Blake, "Distributive Justice, State Coercion, and Autonomy," *Philosophy and Public Affairs* 30(3) (2001): 257–296.
[28] For more on Rawls and these points, see, e.g., Norman Daniels, "Introduction," in Norman Daniels (ed.), *Reading Rawls* (New York: Basic Books, 1975).
[29] See John Rawls, *A Theory of Justice*, rev. ed. (Cambridge, MA: Harvard University Press, 1999), 10; also see John Charvet, "International Society from a Contractarian Perspective," in David R. Mapel and Terry Nardin (eds.), *International Society: Diverse Ethical Perspectives* (Princeton, NJ: Princeton University Press, 1999), 115. For a criticism of hypothetical nature of Rawlsian contractarianism, see Ronald Dworkin, "The Original Position," in Daniels, *Reading Rawls*, at 17–18.
[30] Charles R. Beitz, "Justice and International Relations," *Philosophy and Public Affairs* 4(4) (1975): 360–389.
[31] For accounts that claim that individuals owe duties of justice, see Gerald A. Cohen, *Rescuing Justice and Equality* (Cambridge, MA: Harvard University Press, 2008), and Liam B. Murphy, "Institutions and the Demands of Justice," *Philosophy and Public Affairs* 27(4) (1998): 251–291.

on *whether* institutions should be just and on what sorts of requirements justice might impose, but not on *how* institutions might go about implementing justice. In other words, philosophers have only reluctantly departed from the ideal view of "the forest" to look at "the trees" of how justice might work in practice.

Michael Blake, a Scanlonian contractualist, offers a promising approach. He suggests an institutional theory for moral and political theorists along the following lines:

> Another sort of attitude would prompt one to ask not what institutions we ought to have, but what the institutions we currently have would have to do to be justified. This sort of theory – which I call institutional theory – would take much more of the world as a pretheoretical given for purposes of analysis. It would include, I think, both the fact of state power and the division of territorial jurisdiction found in the world today. It would ask not whether we ought to have developed such a world, but what the various states we have now must do for their powers to be justifiable.[32]

Thomas Pogge advocates something similar for cosmopolitans. He makes the case for a distinction between a legal cosmopolitanism and a moral cosmopolitanism. Pogge's legal cosmopolitanism is "committed to a concrete political ideal of a global order under which all persons have equivalent legal rights and duties" and requires that everyone stand in relation to one another as "fellow citizens of a world republic."[33] This is not the sort of theory connected to practice to which Blake refers, nor do we endorse it. Nonetheless, Pogge's moral cosmopolitanism offers an account that connects more closely to this project in terms of approach, though we make no overriding claims in this book for cosmopolitanism. Pogge says that the moral equality that moral cosmopolitanism demands "imposes limits on . . . our efforts to construct institutional schemes" and provides "standards for assessing the ground rules and practices that regulate human interactions."[34]

More recently, Amartya Sen's *The Idea of Justice* offers the distinction between transcendental institutionalism and realization-focused comparison. According to Sen, transcendental institutionalism has two key features. First, it focuses on identifying "perfect justice" and not on relative comparisons of justice and injustice. Second, it concentrates on identifying ideal institutions needed for perfect justice and not directly on actual institutions in

[32] Blake, "Distributive Justice, State Coercion, and Autonomy," at 262.
[33] Thomas Pogge, "Cosmopolitanism and Sovereignty," *Ethics* 103(1) (1992): 48–75.
[34] Ibid.

actual societies.[35] In contrast, realization-focused comparison is concerned with societies that already exist or could "feasibly emerge" and with comparative analysis of actual institutions and actual behavior to understand how improvements in these actual institutions might affect people in those societies. Sen identifies Rawls, Rousseau, Kant, Hobbes, and Locke as transcendental institutionalists and Smith, Condorcet, Bentham, Wollstonecraft, Marx, and Mill as realization-focused comparativists.[36]

Economists have also had their struggles in making their approaches more institutionally sensitive, but they seem to have made substantial progress in examining institutional design when it comes to examining the problems faced by developing countries.[37] Building on Coase, Nobel Laureate Douglass North and others have pioneered the school of economics known as new institutional economics, the mantra for which seems to be "institutions matter."[38] New institutional economics is of particular relevance to the work of intergovernmental organizations devoted to developing countries and poverty alleviation, such as the World Bank.[39] However, although the new institutional economists bring a great deal to the discussion, they still might be

---

[35] Amartya Sen, *The Idea of Justice* (Cambridge, MA: Harvard University Press, 2009), 5–6.

[36] Ibid.

[37] Mainstream neoclassical economists treat institutions as "black boxes" exogenous to their models. In his Nobel Lecture, Ronald Coase criticized prevailing economic methods:

> What is studied is a system which lives in the minds of economists but not on earth. I have called the result "blackboard economics." The firm and the market appear by name but they lack any substance. The firm in mainstream economic theory has often been described as a "black box." And so it is. This is very extraordinary given that most resources in a modern economic system are employed within firms, with how these resources are used dependent on administrative decisions and not directly on the operation of a market. Consequently, the efficiency of the economic system depends to a very considerable extent on how these organizations conduct their affairs, particularly, of course, the modern corporation. Even more surprising, given their interest in the pricing system, is the neglect of the market or more specifically the institutional arrangements which govern the process of exchange. As these institutional arrangements determine to a large extent what is produced, what we have is a very incomplete theory.

See Ronald H. Coase, "The Institutional Structure of Production," *American Economic Review* 82(4) (1992): 713–719, 714.

[38] Douglass C. North, "Institutions Matter," *American Economic Review* 84(3) (1994): 359–368, 359.

[39] It is telling that the branch of economics most devoted to dealing with poverty alleviation has institutions as its central focus. North gave this explanation in his Nobel Lecture: "Neoclassical theory is simply an inappropriate tool to analyze and prescribe policies that will induce development. It is concerned with the operation of markets, not with how markets develop." Douglass C. North, "Economic Performance Through Time," in Torsten Persson (ed.), *Nobel Lectures: Economics 1991–1995*, 112–123 (Singapore: World Scientific, 1997).

seen to have an incomplete normative framework for understanding justice or injustice.[40]

For all of these reasons, Nagel's challenge to political theory resonates equally for international law, and his aims, as extended, capture well the aims of this book. The editors and the authors have made a serious attempt, in Nagel's words, at a practical contribution. The papers in this volume were presented in November 2008 at a symposium held at Tillar House, the headquarters of the American Society of International Law.[41] The symposium brought together four categories of key thinkers: philosophers who are working out advances in global justice, legal scholars who are sensitive to theories of global justice and who bring actual institutions to the beginning of the discussion, scholars who use economics as the primary tool for understanding the effects of international economic law, and at least one critical legal theorist who brings a good measure of skepticism to both the projects of global justice and international economic law. The animating purpose of the symposium was to assemble a disparate group of scholars who otherwise might not meet in the same room on the same day and to attempt to cross-fertilize and to advance thinking on the relationship of global justice theories to international economic law and institutions.

We see such multidisciplinary projects as necessary for the improved understanding of international economic law and institutions, and perhaps eventually to changes in the treaty framework for international economic law. Economics dominates the normative side of the WTO and its treaties. If you were to walk into any meeting of international economic lawyers and were sensitive to questions of justice, you would discern an uncritical assumption at work in the discussion, namely that Ricardian comparative advantage is the appropriate *grundnorm* or constitutional principle for trade law and policy. Such discussions usually start from the unexamined premise that liberalization is always good, no matter how it is accomplished, and the normative analysis ends there.

A doctrinal analysis of trade rules in themselves assumes a neutrality in the global economic order that we believe should be put under scrutiny. Although comparative advantage is a powerful idea and trade liberalization

---

[40] Efficiency in markets leading to economic growth and growth in GDP per capita remains their primary focus. A new institutional economic approach to development places law and government in the role of setting the basic background conditions for facilitating market exchange, so that poor countries can eventually participate in the neoliberal economic order that includes a world trading system designed to liberalize markets across borders. Justice is not something to measure in the economic toolkit, so it gets short shrift.

[41] The symposium is now an annual autumn event of the International Legal Theory Interest Group of the American Society of International Law.

can serve to alleviate poverty and improve the welfare of many people, we must avoid an uncritical dogmatism about these ideas that seems pervasive in inquiry about international economic law. As Paul Krugman has said about recent Buy American provisions in U.S. legislation intended to stimulate the U.S. economy in the wake of the global economic crisis of 2008–2009, "[d]on't say that any theory which has good things to say about protectionism must be wrong: that's theology, not economics."[42] We do not want to dismiss economics, but we do want to be reflective in our engagement with it and aware of its limits.

The chapters in this book all make progress on the difficult questions of how justice is to be accomplished in international economic law and on the limitations that prevailing accounts of global justice face in actually accomplishing justice in international economic relations. The book is divided into three parts. The first part deals with questions, broadly understood, in the philosophical tradition. The second part gives voice to legal scholars on how principles of justice actually might be applied or operate within the web of existing institutions that constitute the global economic order. The third part offers critique from the perspective of Ricardian comparative advantage and economic measures of welfare, from the standpoint of law and economics, and critical theory. The chapters cover areas in which the structure of moral and political theory is relatively open and flexible when compared to the moral and political theory relating to indisputably political societies governed by domestic constitutions. So too for the legal scholarship of international economic law, which, though constrained, still has a relatively open texture compared with settled areas of municipal law.

I. THEORIZING JUSTICE IN INTERNATIONAL ECONOMIC INSTITUTIONS

Carol Gould's contribution frames the themes for Part I of the book. Gould argues for a strongly egalitarian principle of justice of equal positive freedom to govern our relations to one another. To Gould, the grounds for equal positive freedom as a principle of justice derive from a conception of human agency that does not focus only or principally on self-determination but on the social interconnectedness one has with others. It is the person in relations of social interdependence with others that creates the recognition respect that equal positive freedom demands.

---

[42] Paul Krugman, "The Conscience of a Liberal: Protection and Stimulus (Wonkish)," *New York Times*, February 1, 2009.

Gould's conception of human agency has its roots in the work of Karl Marx and in her work on Marx, in particular her seminal book, *Marx's Social Ontology*, in which she argues that Marx combined social theory and political philosophy to develop a social ontology or metaphysical theory on the nature of social interaction.[43] As an account influenced by Marx (as well as Aristotle, Hegel, and the British Hegelians), Gould's account can be distinguished from most accounts of global justice, which are often extensions from Kantian notions of the moral equality of persons, whose autonomy, rationality, and consciousness endows them with the capacity to choose, which makes them subject to moral demands. To Gould, the capacity for choice is only part of the story; we must also look to the capabilities of persons to realize their life plans over time in a social context.

For Gould, the conditions for making equal positive freedom effective are through a broad and robust notion of human rights, which includes economic and social rights. Human rights are the conditions for human agency. Equal positive freedom and its connection to human rights allow Gould to bypass the problems associated with current accounts, which she finds involve two conundrums. One is the problem of moving from the priority for citizens of nation-states to global claims of universal personhood, and the other is what she characterizes as the "demandingness" of cosmopolitan egalitarian accounts. With its reliance on human rights, which are the subject of international law, Gould's contribution seems to align with Sen's notion that there can be an account of justice that engages in a realization-focused comparison, in Gould's case, through the realization of human rights. At the end of her contribution, Gould offers a number of concrete institutional reforms.

Whereas Gould's focus is on equal positive freedom as a principle of justice and the substantial human rights that follow from it, in the next contribution, Daniel Butt argues that international economic institutions should be guided by a cosmopolitan global equality of opportunity principle, requiring that individuals of equal talent, regardless of nationality, should have access to opportunity sets of equivalent values. Butt distinguishes his account from those of "sufficientarians," who argue for a minimal degree of intervention only so far as necessary to raise individuals in other countries to some minimal level of well-being. Butt carefully distinguishes between ideal theory and how principles of justice might be implemented in actual social and institutional contexts. The difficulty a global equality of opportunity principle might face in implementation is that it is transformative; it might ask us to make substantial

---

[43] Carol C. Gould, *Marx's Social Ontology: Individuality and Community in Marx's Theory of Social Reality* (Cambridge, MA: MIT Press, 1978).

changes to the status quo. Butt examines three aspects of a transformative move to global equality of opportunity: normative desirability, practicality, and popular legitimacy.

As for the normative desirability of a global equality of opportunity principle, Butt explores the idea of global equality of opportunity in some detail. He distinguishes between formal and substantive versions of global equality of opportunity, both of which are "profoundly challenging to current international practice," and how substantive versions explore more deeply into how social conditions bring about inequalities. In broad agreement with Gould, he explains how advocates of global equality of opportunity might draw on the Sen–Nussbaum capabilities account to determine what global equality of opportunity requires.

As for the practicality of a global equality of opportunity principle, Butt identifies six reasons that may be offered to oppose the principle. Here, Butt goes substantially beyond ideal theory and into how, in practice and implementation, global equality of opportunity might encounter substantial obstacles. His final reason for concern about whether global equality of opportunity can be implemented is that of popular legitimacy, which he connects to the democratic legitimacy of the principle. In this last section, Butt explores the question of what international institutions should do when "normative argumentation" and "popular sentiment" diverge. To determine what action should be taken, he suggests institutional analysis – that we examine the nature of the institution in question. For example, a legislature with a democratic mandate may have a wider range of actions that it could take than a court that is constrained by rule of law. Intergovernmental organizations may have less room to maneuver but they can nevertheless work to secure basic needs and campaign to change popular sentiment. For Butt, popular legitimacy may be a factor to consider but is not decisive in relation to the actions of institutions.

Robert Hockett's contribution, like those of Gould and Butt, is broadly egalitarian, but Hockett's focus is on the well-understood distinction in economics between efficiency and distribution. Hockett's contribution focuses on two claims. First, he offers a critique of economic and utilitarian maximization methodologies. If we maximize utility, which we do in either the case of economics or utilitarianism, but in quite different ways, we count something as important in the decision procedure for maximization while eliminating something else as unimportant. When we maximize, we cannot help but distribute. Maximizing utility means we reduce persons to one attribute and maximize that one attribute, but we do not maximize any other attribute. We might redistribute other things to maximize utility. When we distribute, explains Hockett, we also engage in producing or perpetuating inequality among persons.

Hockett contends that we need to take distribution seriously by dismantling maximization formulae and coming to understand what he calls their internal structures. Hockett wants us to get clear that all law and policy are both distributive and aggregative and that law and policy effectively identify persons as equals in some respect and nonequals in others. What we want, according to Hockett, is for law and policy to treat us as equals (or not) in the ways that we value. Hockett's is a conceptual model. What we fill in as "fair" or "fair allocation," Hockett explains, is an appropriate distribution based on maximizing "equal-opportunity-grounded welfare." Hockett's theory is, when taken through to its logical course, a robust egalitarian account. It has the potential to change the way we value and understand international economic law and institutions.

In his contribution, Aaron James focuses on how we might go about morally assessing international economic institutions by using internal as opposed to external moral principles. An external principle is one that is independent of how social relations structure the global economic order. Humanitarian principles, for example, are external principles; they are used to evaluate the morality of global economic arrangements and do not depend on these arrangements for their content. According to James, a problem with external principles is that they "rely on passing illustrations from the global economy without considering in any great detail what its legal and social institutions are like and how they might – or might not – fit together." James's internal principles derive their content from global economic arrangements themselves. James argues that internal principles of fairness exist in international economic relations and that they form around a more fundamental notion he calls "structural equity," which in turn depends on a particular social practice that James finds to be a practice among states of mutual market reliance. Like the accounts offered by Gould, Butt, and Hockett, James's account is egalitarian.

To test whether a principle is internal, James asks whether a particular aspect of social reality, such as a WTO ruling, (a) is part of the explanation why the principle applies and (b) is "not necessarily in question" from the point of view of the principle itself. According to James, through these "explanation" and "neutrality" conditions we can evaluate the "general structure or very existence of a legal system as fair or unfair." James identifies three further principles of structural equity: (a) "harms from trade" principles, such as that one's life prospects should not be worse off as a result of trade than they would have been if one's society remained closed; (b) "gains from trade" principles that apply within societies, such as that gains from trade are to be distributed equally among affected members of society unless inequality of gain is reasonably acceptable to everyone; and (c) "gains from trade" principles that apply across societies, such as that gains from trade are to be distributed equally across societies, as adjusted by relevant endowments, unless unequal gains benefit poor societies. From here, a number of further principles can be worked out, including principles of fair bargaining, fair competition, and fair wages.

II. HOW JUSTICE GETS DONE IN INTERNATIONAL ECONOMIC INSTITUTIONS

The three chapters in the second part of the book all deal with the *application* of justice in international economic law. In particular, they examine *legal* and *moral* obligation as expressions of justice, the legal being grounded in normativity and coercive force, the moral grounded in generally accepted conduct and observed behavior. As a result of these differences, the legal and the moral do not always mix well. A further element of complexity is introduced into the analysis by the nature of international economic law, which is a mix of sovereignty, a political concept, and interest, an economic concept. The total combination of legal, moral, political, and economic aspects in the practice of international economic law is something that each of these contributions examines.

To begin with, Chin Leng Lim's chapter, "The Conventional Morality of Trade," is concerned with the kinds of moral and political arguments that developing countries have made in the name of global justice. In the main, Lim argues that these have been about what lawyers call "substantive" as opposed to "formal" equality. This is evidently a moral question, Lim asserts, and one that he examines both through claims to fairness by developing countries and the pioneering work of the late Robert Hudec, who recognized the importance of studying the claims made by some trading nations as claims about fairness, but who expressed general skepticism about them.

Lim's argument is that theories about the development principles of the General Agreement on Tariffs and Trade (GATT)–WTO are necessarily deficient if they account only for ideal theories about the normative justification for alternative distributive arrangements. This is partly due to the fact that although the overarching most favored nation principle (MFN) is widely accepted today as a general governing principle in the WTO, it is observed largely in the breach. As a result, Lim maintains that we do not know where the principle ends and what sorts of normative justifications have been considered adequate in creating exceptions to it. Economic or moral theories that simply presuppose the reflective acceptability of the most favored nation principle presuppose a world that does not exist. Theory must therefore do better.

To illustrate his position, Lim draws on the Appellate Body's conclusion in *EC – Tariff Preferences*, a case involving a challenge by India to a preference program maintained by the European Communities, or EC, for some developing countries but not others. In taking an intermediate position, Lim maintains that the WTO Appellate Body was correct in treating differentiation between developing nations as legitimate, provided that the Appellate Body itself retains the right to scrutinize differential treatment to ensure conformity with the developmental, financial, and trade needs of individual country recipients. The Appellate Body's ruling in *EC – Tariff Preferences* upholds a substantive conception of equality, or at least rejects identical treatment as the default trade law rule, thereby going some way to vindicate underlying moral claims of states.

By singling out the actual historical claims of developing countries, Lim maintains that the "middle-level" theorizing attempted in his contribution is aimed against the tendency of economic analyses to efface these claims. Nevertheless, top-down moral theories tend to do the same. They proceed directly to the reflective acceptability of alternative arrangements. The core argument in Lim's contribution is that understanding the actual claims of developing nations – as Robert Hudec first tried to do – requires us to recognize the persistence, if not the centrality, of claims to equality. It requires us to accord such claims theoretical and critical attention, instead of treating them as mistaken from the outset.

A counterpoint to Lim's position is offered by Jeff Dunoff in his contribution, "The Political Geography of Distributive Justice." Dunoff suggests that although global inequality and poverty are stark facts, the landscape of our current understanding about it is heavily conditioned by ways of seeing that are moral. In contrast to Lim, however, Dunoff suggests that a moral explanation for nations' positions in the GATT and the WTO is inaccurate and rests "upon a mistaken reading of the history of the trade system." Briefly tracing the history of the contentious debates over extending preferential tariff treatment to developing states in the GATT, Dunoff suggests that developing state arguments in favor of preferences reflected contingent policy preferences that were driven by practical and pragmatic judgments in light of specific strategic and economic realities, rather than enduring commitments resulting from philosophical or moral imperatives. In contrast, Dunoff suggests that because the justification for preferences is rooted in specific economic and political conditions, these programs should be understood circumstantially and pragmatically. He then shows how, evaluated on such pragmatic terms, preference programs have contributed disappointingly little to developing states' development goals. Dunoff goes on explore how undue focus on preferences and developed state trade policy has diverted attention from alternative policies necessary to enhance developing state growth and development.

Dunoff concludes that although it appears trade can play an important role in development, we should not focus on trade policy in a way that diverts attention from other policy interventions – such as infrastructure, education, basic health care, good governance, and the rule of law – that can be more helpful, and that are necessary prerequisites for preferential treatment to be economically meaningful. In so concluding, Dunoff seeks to advance a comparativist approach to global distributive justice in the spirit of Amartya Sen, one which shares a common interest in making comparisons between ways in which development actually occurs in the process of attaining justice rather than in identifying perfectly just social arrangements.

Finally, Chantal Thomas's chapter, "The Death of Doha? Forensics of Democratic Governance, Distributive Justice, and Development in the WTO," explores the idea that distributive justice in the multilateral trade regime might be best served, at the moment, by democratizing its governance procedures. Rather than promote substantive equality, Thomas suggests that a procedural equality may be all that is reasonably achievable given the *political* realities of a state-centered legal system and the continuing, and very profound, differences among states over the nature of equality.

Thomas begins her exploration by examining why the relatively democratic framework of the WTO has had difficulty concluding the most recent round of multilateral trade negotiations. Using both "economistic" and "constructivist" approaches, Thomas shows why differentiation among developing countries has become such a challenge by drawing attention to recent examples in trade negotiations on intellectual property and agricultural trade. Here, she details the evident coordination challenges, the fact of economic differentiation among developing countries, and the fragmentation in the trading system into bilateral and plurilateral subsystems, to show how complexity is making trade governance problematic. This complexity, however, is precisely why a proceduralist account remains necessary. In the absence of universal policy directives, Thomas maintains that an open-ended dialogue may allow for the greatest possible consideration of disparate views and varied sources of information. Although a democratized negotiation procedure in the WTO may be far from ideal, it may nevertheless provide the surest path to decisions that reflect some semblance of distributive justice for developing countries.

To buttress her conclusion, Thomas goes on to examine why substantive arguments also lead back to the need for a proceduralist account of distributive justice. Drawing on the work of John Rawls, Thomas recounts that optimal social arrangements for justice are still too uncertain and unknown to constitutionalize them in any form. The indeterminacy analysis carries over into a study of emerging "equality jurisprudence" in the GATT–WTO. Thomas maintains that the "legalization" of the trade regime has resulted in the adoption of an equality, or nondiscrimination, doctrinal foundation for the judicialized decision making of the dispute settlement wing of the WTO, over and above the "reciprocity" model that characterizes WTO negotiations. Unlike Lim, however, Thomas concludes that the rise of equality jurisprudence in the WTO cannot by itself answer important questions about the parameters of development policy in the WTO, for example in the context of applying preferential treatment.

What is the solution? Thomas suggests that between the ideal of a fully inclusive deliberative community and existing reality, of course, many gradations exist. Short of one-state, one-vote procedural equality, greater support may be required for government negotiation coalitions to assert their interests effectively in negotiations and for a broader range of states to be included at earlier stages in negotiations. Thomas concludes that the traditional model of interstate democratic governance remains sufficiently out of reach in the WTO to constitute a worthy goal, and sufficiently conducive to reshaping WTO policies in the direction of egalitarian redistribution. As a consequence, proceduralist justice in the form of democratic governance presents itself as the approach that may be relatively most attainable, and most productive, in the foreseeable future.

III. CRITICAL RESPONSES TO CONTEMPORARY THEORIZING ABOUT JUSTICE AND INTERNATIONAL ECONOMIC INSTITUTIONS

The chapters in this third part challenge, in one way or another, the basic premises and aspirations of the global justice project as defined by normative political theory and international economic law. In "Global Justice and Trade," Fernando Tesón and Jonathan Klick argue strenuously that free trade is itself the preeminent vehicle for delivering the social welfare goals associated with the global justice project. Although this thesis is widely supported by mainstream economic theory, free trade remains a taboo among many philosophers, whose positions directly or indirectly support protectionist measures that further harm the world's poor, according to Tesón and Klick. Their aim in "Global Justice and Trade" is not simply to show that free trade is a more efficient means of alleviating world poverty, but to dispel the hostility of global justice scholarship toward free trade as unfounded and hasty.

Tesón and Klick differentiate between poverty and inequality. For them, improving the life of the world's poor "as a class," not as individuals, is morally more urgent than addressing inequality problems. Consistent with orthodox trade theory, they find that trade liberalization increases wealth for both trade partners, in the aggregate and individually. Further, this growth reaches down to the poor within each trade partner. Although they do not claim that trade liberalization reduces inequality between or within trade partners, in their view inequality does not present a moral problem and is of secondary importance, if any, to the discussion. It is free trade's wealth-creating capacity that confers its normative significance to the global justice debate.

Tesón and Klick argue that, although it is necessary, free trade is not a sufficient condition to alleviating poverty. Countries need domestic institutions, such as property and contract law, and government programs ensuring that some benefits from the open market are going to reach the poor. Further, trade liberalization does not necessarily mean abolishing all trade barriers, but eliminating protectionist measures. Nevertheless, trade liberalization, according to Tesón and Klick, is the most efficient way to alleviate world poverty. In contemporary economic theory, trade is a positive-sum game.

Tesón and Klick are not concerned with the ethics of international trade because their project is to dispel the shades of mercantilism clouding many aspects of the global justice debate. In their view, philosophers writing about distributive justice suffer from a mercantilist bias that trade is a zero-sum process in which the party that gets away by liberalizing less of its market wins. For this reason, Tesón and Klick maintain that many of these theorists disregard contemporary economic theories and, directly or indirectly, espouse protectionist theories that aggravate world poverty. Chastising philosophers and academic lawyers alike for being drawn into misleading normative debates, they urge scholars and architects of international economic law to stay close to the core prescriptions of trade economics if they are sincere in their desire to alleviate poverty.

Barbara Stark is equally skeptical of the capacity of contemporary international economic law to contribute to global distributive justice, but for different reasons. Drawing on postmodernism and on Marx's political theory (as well as on *Alice in Wonderland*), she argues in "Jam Tomorrow: A Critique of International Economic Law" that international economic law is too much the creature of the global elite to ever be able to seriously address the needs of the world's poor. Stark first shows that the neoliberal economic order, as presently construed, is ideologically opposed to wealth redistribution. She next shows that international economic law lacks the capacity to contribute to distributive justice because, much like the neoliberal economic order, it is a product of and works in the interest of economic elites who oppose distributive justice.

Stark focuses on the neoliberal ideology of development, arguing first that it primarily serves the interests of developed countries and not least developed countries, and second that the very concept of development is flawed. Using the Marxist concept of ideology, Stark discusses three eras in which the Western neoliberal ideology of development has aided the West rather than the developing countries it purports to help: the Cold War, when aid was used by Western liberal democracies to buy political opposition to the Soviets; the 1980s and 1990s, when stringent lending plans of the International Monetary Fund put all risk with the borrowers; and the present time, in which today's system of global reserves disfavors development in poorer countries by moving income *from* least developed countries, and not the other way around. In short, the neoliberal ideology of development perpetuates the exploitation of poorer countries.

Employing a postmodernist critique, Stark challenges the neoliberal ideology of development – the "meta-narrative of development" – as inherently flawed because of its reliance on a Western-centric argument. Further, in an era in which charity and philanthropy are commodities, distributive justice is not feasible because "[t]he real purpose of late capitalism is most glaringly revealed . ... in the notion that global poverty can be constructively dealt with by *shopping*, that is, by the very overconsumption that perpetuates it." Stark's criticism and rejection of the neoliberal ideology of development aims to "create space for local alternatives."

Finally, in "Doing Justice: The Economics and Politics of International Distributive Justice," Joel Trachtman offers a detailed analysis of the limits of philosophical inquiry into justice but concludes that, rather than abandon the project altogether, the way forward is through interdisciplinary inquiry. Such an approach will overcome the limitations of the present distributive justice discourse as Trachtman sees them: limited consensus, limited knowledge of causation, limited knowledge of remedies, and limited inducement.

Trachtman argues that philosophical inquiry into distributive justice is inherently limited because philosophy is confined to the realm of theoretical debate and there is often no consensus on the results of its investigations. His worry is that philosophical prescriptions also seldom lead to tangible policy measures. To overcome these limitations, and thus move from debate to policy implementation, Trachtman argues that the work of philosophers must be supplemented by the work of lawyers, economists, political scientists, and psychologists. Each of these disciplines supplements, and to an extent compensates for, the limitations of its sister disciplines. None of this, however, eliminates or reduces the need for sound philosophical inquiry at an early stage in the process. Despite their being empirical disciplines, economics, law, and political science have their own inherent limitation: They require a basic consensus on what justice is – a quintessentially philosophical preoccupation – before prescribing policy.

In the final part of his chapter, Trachtman uses this interdisciplinary framework to examine five problems in global justice: the HIV epidemic, the Bhopal disaster, Special and Differential Treatment at the WTO, the International Monetary Fund, and World Bank, and regulation of foreign and direct investment. Each of these examples shows that not one discipline can effectively solve these problems, and they reinforce the need for an interdisciplinary approach to distributive justice.

Thus Trachtman offers an important prescription that brings us back to the foundational aims of this book: It is only through "a coherent interdisciplinary program" that efforts to address as complex a social problem as global justice can have significant effect. It is the editors' hope that this volume contributes to such a program. Returning to Nagel's contention at the beginning of this Introduction, we are at the early stages of the project of understanding global justice and how it might affect us all in the interdependent world in which we live our lives.

PART I

THEORIZING JUSTICE IN INTERNATIONAL ECONOMIC INSTITUTIONS

1   Approaching Global Justice through Human Rights:
     Elements of Theory and Practice

Carol C. Gould

INTRODUCTION

Philosophers operating within a cosmopolitan framework have recently made
powerful claims regarding what global justice requires of us. Beginning from
the premise of the fundamental equality of persons, whether understood primarily in terms of interests, agency, or dignity, they argue that there are strong
requirements to more equally distribute wealth, resources, or opportunities so
as to alleviate poverty, or to meet basic needs, or to develop people's capabilities so they can be relatively equally agential in the course of their lives.[1]
Although drawing on different philosophical frameworks – consequentialist,
contractarian or contractualist, capabilities and positive freedom based – these
approaches can be highly demanding in requiring massive aid to the poor,
or else comprehensive redistributive schemes at the global level, or at the
very least intensified forms of development assistance. They also may call
for the introduction of institutional frameworks to effect these distributions
and to promote development, and they may contain innovative proposals

---

[1] See, e.g., Peter Singer, "Famine, Affluence, and Morality," *Philosophy and Public Affairs* 1(3)
(Spring 1972): 229–243; Charles Beitz, *Political Theory and International Relations* (Princeton,
NJ: Princeton University Press, 1979); Thomas Pogge, *World Poverty and Human Rights* (Cam-
bridge: Polity Press, 2002); Darrel Moellendorf, *Cosmopolitan Justice* (Boulder, CO: Westview
Press, 2002); and Simon Caney, *Justice beyond Borders* (Oxford: Oxford University Press,
2005).

This chapter was originally presented at the Conference on Global Egalitarianism, Institute
for Ethics and Public Affairs, San Diego State University, San Diego, CA, April 10–11, 2008
and in revised versions as the Keynote Address, Australian Society of Legal Philosophy Annual
Conference, University of Melbourne Law School, June 13, 2008; at the Research School of Social
Sciences, Australian National University, June 23, 2008; and at the Symposium of the International
Legal Theory Interest Group of the American Society of International Law, Washington, D.C.,
November 7, 2008. I thank the participants in those sessions and especially Michael Howard and
Darrel Moellendorf for their helpful comments.

for changes to the international system. Among the prominent approaches is Peter Singer's call for affluent people to donate a substantial percentage of their income to poverty relief,[2] more institutionally oriented calls for the implementation of a global difference principle, as in the early work of Charles Beitz,[3] or Thomas Pogge's proposals for a global resource dividend.[4] Again, cosmopolitan luck egalitarians who aim at equality in global contexts may propose achieving genuinely equal opportunity by correcting for the unchosen features of people's circumstances, such as the availability of natural resources, because these so affect their life chances.[5]

These various approaches have in common a commitment to cosmopolitanism along with calls for strongly redistributive schemes in global contexts, at least in terms of what justice requires normatively. Many of the objections to such schemes – where they do not simply reassert the prerogatives of contemporary capitalist neoliberalism – consist in objecting to their exclusively cosmopolitan premises and insisting instead on the priority or importance of one's fellow co-nationals or of other particularistic obligations (for example, to family or community), or of the right of national self-determination.[6] Alternatively, the objections may focus on the excessively ideal and (putatively) unrealizable character of these demanding approaches. To this, the theorists in question sometimes respond by showing how their conclusions are required by even much weaker assumptions about justice. One such example is Pogge's claims that his view follows from elementary libertarian requirements to avoid causing preventable harm to others.[7]

In terms of normative commitment, I side with the cosmopolitans, at least in the ethical domain. Indeed, I argue for a strongly egalitarian principle of justice, namely what I have called equal positive freedom.[8] However, I propose

---

[2] Singer, "Famine, Affluence, and Morality"; Peter Singer, *Practical Ethics*, 2nd ed. (Cambridge: Cambridge University Press, 1999), 246; Peter Singer, *One World: The Ethics of Globalization*, 2nd ed. (New Haven, CT: Yale University Press, 2004), 187–189.

[3] Charles Beitz, *Political Theory and International Relations* (Princeton, NJ: Princeton University Press, 1979), Part III; and Thomas Pogge, *Realizing Rawls* (Ithaca, NY: Cornell University Press, 1989), Part III.

[4] Pogge, *World Poverty and Human Rights*, chapter 8.

[5] Kok-Chor Tan, *Justice without Borders* (Cambridge: Cambridge University Press, 2004).

[6] See, e.g., David Miller, "National Self-Determination and Global Justice," in David Miller (ed.), *Citizenship and National Identity* (Cambridge: Polity Press, 2000), 161–179; and "Against Global Egalitarianism," *The Journal of Ethics* 9 (2005): 55–79.

[7] Thomas Pogge, *World Poverty and Human Rights*; and "Severe Poverty as a Violation of Negative Duties," *Ethics & International Affairs* 19(1) (2005): 55–83.

[8] For a discussion of this principle, see Carol C. Gould, *Rethinking Democracy: Freedom and Social Cooperation in Politics, Economy, and Society* (Cambridge: Cambridge University Press, 1988), esp. chapters 1 and 5; and *Globalizing Democracy and Human Rights* (Cambridge: Cambridge University Press, 2004), chapter 1.

here that when understood in its connection to human rights (on a certain interpretation of them), we get an approach that can provide practical and realizable guidance for moving toward global justice. I then suggest that approaching global justice in terms of human rights can avoid the sometimes excessively utopian character of some of the other views while still adhering to a firmly egalitarian framework. Moreover, I believe that this approach makes room for diverse and particular communities while at the same time arguing for strengthened global commitments (although I will not be able to develop this particular feature of the approach in much detail in this essay).

In what follows, I lay out some of the key theoretical elements of this framework, which privileges human rights, including economic and social ones, noting in passing its difference from Pogge's conception of such rights.[9] I then indicate some of the main practical directions by which such rights can be institutionalized in more effective ways than they are at present. It will be apparent that both the theoretical and practical conceptions of human rights presented here go beyond their current interpretations in international law and practice, but I suggest that they constitute plausible developments of these conventional understandings. In the course of this analysis, I will also address a few of the key objections that can be posed to this philosophical approach and some of the main difficulties that confront it in practice.

1. EQUAL POSITIVE FREEDOM, SOCIAL ONTOLOGY, AND A PHILOSOPHICAL CONCEPTION OF HUMAN RIGHTS

Without attempting to present an entire philosophical justification, we can say that the account of justice recommended here emerges from what can be called the positive freedom tradition, associated, for example, with the work of C. B. Macpherson,[10] following earlier accounts by Karl Marx, the British Hegelians, and some American pragmatists like John Dewey and more recently elaborated in a distinctive way by Amartya Sen and others.[11] As we shall see, however, the account I propose is a synthetic one centering on a conception of agency that brings together several features often treated discretely in various

---

[9] For an analysis and critique of Pogge's approach, see Carol C. Gould, "Coercion, Care, and Corporations: Omissions and Commissions in Thomas Pogge's Political Philosophy," *The Journal of Global Ethics* 3(3) (December 2007): 381–393.

[10] C. B. Macpherson, *Democratic Theory: Essays in Retrieval* (Oxford: Oxford University Press, 1973).

[11] Amartya Sen, "Equality of What?," in S. McMurrin (ed.), *Tanner Lectures on Human Values* (Cambridge: Cambridge University Press, 1980), 195–220; "Well-Being, Agency, and Freedom: The Dewey Lectures of 1984," *Journal of Philosophy* 82 (April 1985): 161–221; and "Capability and Well-Being," in Martha Nussbaum and Amartya Sen (eds.), *The Quality of Life* (Oxford: Oxford University Press, 1993), 30–53.

modes of thought. Moreover, it seeks to interpret agency in a way less strongly
tied than usual to liberal individualist premises, so that the understanding here
remains open to multiple cultural interpretations.

To explain some of these various claims, in a series of books and articles
dating from *Marx's Social Ontology*, I have argued for a conception of agency
as involving not only the capacity for choice but also a process of the development of capacities and the realization of long-term projects over time.[12] Such
agency centrally presupposes freedom from domination, but it is not limited
to this negative notion. In this way the account differs from some recent
republican theories. My theory takes a quasi-Aristotelian turn in conceiving
agency as not only requiring the absence of this sort of constraining condition,
along with freedom from interference with basic liberties, but also requiring
the availability of positive or enabling conditions if people are to be able to
transform or develop themselves effectively. The character of this agency can
be either individual or collective, as what I have called common activity or
joint activity.[13] In these cases, the activity is oriented to shared ends or goals,
and the social group is understood as being constituted by individuals in their
relations rather than as existing holistically above or beyond them.[14]

When characterized in these ways, the freedom of agents, understood as not
only negative but also positive, and as involving transformation over time in
social as well as individual contexts, can be distinguished from classical liberal
conceptions of autonomy, even when the latter are interpreted in terms of
newer ideas of relational autonomy. Along these lines, it is interesting to note
in passing that the term "positive freedom" is finally coming back into its own,
after falling into unjustified disrepute because of Isaiah Berlin's rejection of it,[15]
which presupposed his giving it a strangely statist interpretation. Furthermore,
from the standpoint of the account here, the focus on capabilities in Sen
and Nussbaum,[16] though important and included in my view by way of the
notion of the development of capacities, cannot in fact be the entire story with
respect to positive freedom. As noted, the realization of long-term projects also
has a place in this conception, and even the notion of basic interests can be
brought in, though this account eschews the conception of a person as simply a

---

[12] Carol C. Gould, *Marx's Social Ontology* (Cambridge, MA: The MIT Press, 1978).

[13] Gould, *Rethinking Democracy*, chapter 1.

[14] Carol C. Gould, "Group Rights and Social Ontology," *The Philosophical Forum*, Special
Double Issue on Philosophical Perspectives on National Identity, XXVIII (1–2) (Fall–Winter,
1996–1997): 73–86.

[15] Isaiah Berlin, "Two Concepts of Liberty," in Isaiah Berlin, *Liberty*, ed Henry Hardy (Oxford:
Oxford University Press, 2002), 166–217.

[16] For Nussbaum's account, see Martha Nussbaum, *Women and Human Development: The
Capabilities Approach* (Cambridge: Cambridge University Press, 2001).

"bundle" or aggregate of interests, a notion that often afflicts interest-centered approaches.

The social ontology operative in this conception is one that takes as its basic entities what I have called *individuals-in-relations*,[17] in recognition not only of the importance of agency but of the fundamental fact of social interdependence. This sociality plays a role in the centrality of common activities, as well as in the reciprocal recognition of each one's agency, as a core notion, along with the need for institutional and associational frameworks of social cooperation in economic, social, and political life. The idea of reciprocal recognition here, though derived partly from the Hegelian and Marxist traditions (especially in the Kojévian interpretation that privileges the master–slave dialectic), does not take such recognition to be constitutive of agency or of people's rights. Instead, it sees recognition as required by the equality of people as agential beings. Although human agency takes a great variety of forms and is elaborated variously, nonetheless it evidences a fundamental equality in the capacity for self-transformation – again, whether taken in a collective sense as in the production of culture or in an individual sense in the phenomenon of choice and self-development.

Observe the importance here of the conditions of agency, both negative and enabling. If each person is equally an agent and if agency requires access to conditions for it to be effective at all, as well as for the person to flourish, where such self-transformation constitutes the full meaning of freedom and is a normative imperative posited in activity itself, then it follows from the recognition of this fundamental equality that people should have prima facie equal access to the conditions of their agency. I have called this the principle of equal positive freedom, and it serves as an egalitarian principle of justice. The approach I take thus starts with the fundamental recognition of people's equality as agents but goes on to argue that their agency is empty or purely formal without access to the conditions that can make it effective. People's equality therefore extends to their access to a range of conditions necessary for their transformative activity.

When agency is taken relationally in these ways, as operating in conditions and as in many ways socially constituted, we can derive a powerful emphasis on the availability of material and social conditions, in addition to the absence of some constraining conditions. Some of these conditions are basic in that they are required for any human life activity whatever, for example, means of subsistence, security, and basic liberty, along with freedom from domination, while some of these are enabling conditions for people's fuller flourishing.

[17] Gould, *Marx's Social Ontology*, chapter 1; *Rethinking Democracy*, chapter 2.

Even the basic conditions are understood as required for distinctively *human* life activity, that is, as free life activity.[18]

In my view, these various conditions are specified in human rights, both basic and nonbasic. Because everyone needs access to these conditions for their agency, the recognition of people's equality in the situation of interdependence requires that we cooperate to provide for their fulfillment. People have mutually valid claims on these fundamental conditions of agency and development, where the notion of a valid claim is equivalent to the idea of a right. This account is reminiscent in some ways of Alan Gewirth's, but in fact it differs in important ways from his.[19] I am not arguing that we can reason from the importance of the conditions of agency for ourselves to their importance for others, but that the normatively required recognition of others as equal agents and the fact of our fundamental interdependence establish the validity of each of our mutual claims to the fundamental conditions of agency.[20]

Here the claims are not understood as in the first place *legal* claims on others, but as social and moral claims, and only derivatively as legal ones. It is in virtue of our interdependence that we make these social claims on each other for cooperation in meeting basic needs. In principle, then, human rights hold on all others. In practice, however, they must be satisfied through more delimited forms of social, economic, and political institutions. Nevertheless, such human rights, in this philosophical interpretation of them, have only contingently come to be seen as holding against states in the first instance. Human rights in fact have a more general, interpersonal significance, to use Pogge's terms,[21] as well as an institutional one. They are institutional because they are interpersonal claims that can only be realized institutionally.[22] Moreover, the institutions that they hold against are not only the state but also economic, social, and cultural institutions as well. Note how suitable this approach is for the current development of globalization, in which transnational communities are coming to prominence, along with new institutions of global governance. The view I present is consonant as well with feminist approaches that seek to "bring rights home," as it were, and to see them as extending to the private and

---

[18] See also the discussion of human rights and their relation to equal positive freedom in Gould, *Rethinking Democracy*, chapter 8 ("What Are the Human Rights?") and *Globalizing Democracy and Human Rights*, esp. chapter 1.

[19] Alan Gewirth, *Reason and Morality* (Chicago: University of Chicago Press, 1980).

[20] See also the discussion of Gewirth's view in Gould, *Rethinking Democracy*, chapter 1.

[21] Pogge, *World Poverty and Human Rights*, chapter 2.

[22] See also the discussion in Gould, "Coercion, Care, and Corporations: Omissions and Commissions in Thomas Pogge's Political Philosophy."

not only the public sphere.[23] It also supports the new ways in which human rights are being applied to a range of nonstate actors in current developments in international law.

A final ingredient of this philosophical account can be pointed out. From the principle of equal positive freedom, strong rights of democratic participation can also be seen to follow. These pertain not only to participation within political institutions but in the range of institutions in economic, social, and cultural life. The argument is that taking part in common activities is one of the main conditions for freedom, as we have seen in this social account. However, if people are not to be dominated by others within these common activities, then they have equal rights to codetermine these activities. That is, they have rights to democratically determine the goals and the course of the activities. Obviously, this presupposes a substantive and not only procedural conception of democracy in which deliberation plays an important role, and where majority voting, although usually required in large organizations, does not exhaust the meaning of the concept.

II. HUMAN RIGHTS AND GLOBAL JUSTICE

In this second part of my chapter, I suggest that this account, which foregrounds human rights in a certain interpretation of them, provides a way to break through two of the conundrums that have afflicted most discussions of global justice. I also elaborate the elements of the approach somewhat further and consider certain objections to it at the theoretical level. In the third section that follows, I briefly sketch some more specific practical directions for institutionalizing human rights, particularly those closely relevant to achieving justice.

As noted at the outset, the global justice discussion has often been framed as an opposition between cosmopolitan egalitarian views that require global aid or redistribution and alternative conceptions that privilege national political societies as the appropriate arena for redistribution.[24] Such antithetical formulations pose for us the first conundrum: between the global claims of

---

[23] See, e.g., Hilary Charlesworth, "What Are 'Women's International Human Rights'?," and Celina Romany, "State Responsibility Goes Private: A Feminist Critique of the Public/Private Distinction in International Human Rights Law," in Rebecca J. Cook (ed.), *Human Rights of Women* (Philadelphia: University of Pennsylvania Press, 1994), 58–115; and Donna Sullivan, "The Public/Private Distinction in International Human Rights Law," in Julie Peters and Andrea Wolper (eds.), *Women's Rights, Human Rights* (New York: Routledge, 1995), 126–134.

[24] It should be noted that cosmopolitans can accept that there are duties that apply at levels or associations below the global order. But the problem of reconciling these with the global ones remains, I suggest, insofar as it is a matter of which sort of duty or obligation should be privileged

universal personhood or global interconnectedness on the one hand and the nation-state or compatriot priority for economic distribution and redistribution on the other. The global claims can be understood in rigorously cosmopolitan terms founded in a notion of the equal consideration or redistribution owed to each person worldwide, or instead may be rooted in the increasing social interconnections that are in fact emerging with globalization, where these interconnections themselves are regarded as a basis for newly global or at least transnational social responsibilities of justice. The first option is illustrated in some individualist global difference principle accounts, certain human rights approaches, and in luck egalitarian views applied globally. The second variant is exemplified in Iris Marion Young's social connections model,[25] and to a degree in Pogge's account of the obligations resulting from the West's coercive imposition of exploitative systems on developing countries, although Pogge's commitment to human rights to a degree pulls in a more strictly cosmopolitan direction. The alternative emphasis on political society as a basis for redistribution is found in Thomas Nagel's reliance on systems of reciprocity as sources of obligation and in the accounts of David Miller and others that emphasize national ties or civic solidarity.[26] These latter views do not require that there be no duties of assistance or aid abroad, but they may well be compatible with such duties, as is evident in Rawls's account,[27] and Nagel's as well.[28]

The second conundrum is what may be characterized as the "demandingness" of egalitarian cosmopolitan approaches. Approaches such as luck egalitarianism or a difference principle applied globally pose this problem not only practically but also theoretically. How are people's situations to be compared across national and cultural borders and what mechanisms are to be used to affect the redistributions, presumably without making use of excessively coercive devices? Should these redistributions focus on resources, or goods, or opportunities, or the development of capabilities? What weight is to be given to people's own contributions to the production of the goods to be redistributed? (One would think that such contributions should count for something, after all.) And what about the various disutilities that global transfers can produce? How should these be put in the balance?

and also inasmuch as the contrasting approaches may involve different presuppositions about the priority of individuals globally or instead of nation-state groups.

[25] Iris Marion Young, "Responsibility and Global Justice: A Social Connections Model," *Social Philosophy and Policy* 23(1) (January 2006): 102–130; and "Responsibility and Global Labor Justice," *Journal of Political Philosophy* 12(4) (2004): 365–388.

[26] Thomas Nagel, "The Problem of Global Justice," *Philosophy & Public Affairs* 33(2) (2005): 113–147; David Miller, "Against Global Egalitarianism."

[27] Rawls, *The Law of Peoples* (Cambridge, MA: Harvard University Press, 1999).

[28] Nagel, "The Problem of Global Justice."

To begin with this second conundrum, we can observe that problems of demandingness would also affect the full implementation of the principle of justice that I have proposed, that is, the principle of equal positive freedom, understood as requiring prima facie equal access to the conditions of self-transformation or self-development. Nonetheless, I would suggest that this principle, along with the theory that frames it, has advantages over some of the others in several respects: in putting the focus on both the negative and positive (or enabling) conditions for agency, in building difference into its understanding of people's expressions of agency in various cultural contexts, in its openness to both capacities and projects, and in the space it makes for collective or shared activities. Further, the principle in question already qualifies strictly equal access with the notion of "prima facie," in recognition of the weight that sometimes should be given to other, perhaps consequentialist, considerations and principles of contribution or desert. These come into play when this sort of principle is applied in actual political economies, where there may well be the need for some differential rewards for special skills and cultivated abilities. Despite these qualifications and putative advantages, it must be admitted that this principle would also be subject to a charge of demandingness if applied globally, inasmuch as it would require the achievement of substantial levels of equality across nation-states and cultures, in the difficult context of economic globalization.

Even granting its "demandingness" in this sense, however, I believe that the principle of equal positive freedom can nonetheless serve as a useful goal or *heuristic* for the evolution of national and global institutions toward greater equality over time. Most significant, in distinction from other approaches, this one has the advantage of providing a *principled* way of prioritizing certain claims of global justice over others and thus provides the basis for a strategy for making progress in this domain. It does so by privileging human rights as those conditions most in need of being available to people worldwide. Further, among these rights, it distinguishes between basic and nonbasic ones, and in this way posits the fulfillment of the basic rights and needs as realizable goals for the nearer term. It thus takes a more practical, through not minimalist, approach to the realization of the more maximalist requirements of strongly egalitarian principles.

Clearly, among the basic conditions for any human activity whatsoever is access to means of subsistence. As noted, however, human rights are not to be taken as claims on others for direct provision but rather as goals and guides for the development of institutional frameworks that would realize them for everyone. Given the centrality of work to human existence, both as necessary for the provision of these means of subsistence and as a central source of

meaningful activity in itself, this economic right gives rise in the first instance
to a requirement that people be able to work so as to meet their basic needs.
If they cannot do so, then other ways have to be found to make these means
available to them, presumably through a system of welfare or of basic income.[29]
I will point to some of the complexities in the implementation of such rights
in the third section.

For now, we can note that aside from its philosophical strengths, a great
advantage of a human rights approach is that it is already recognized in international law, including the economic and social rights. It was a great step forward,
I think, for human rights to be enunciated in 1948 in the Universal Declaration
of Human Rights and subsequently elaborated in the various United Nations
(UN) covenants and other agreements. These practical recognitions of their
importance make the philosophy of human rights less of a pipedream, and
they provide a basis for sketching a path to their fuller realization. Of course,
a great deal remains that is problematic in these international formulations.
Several of the covenants have been ratified only by a subset of states. Notably,
the United States is mostly absent with regard to economic and social rights,
the Convention on the Elimination of All Forms of Discrimination Against
Women, and other important agreements. The list of rights covered is somewhat haphazard (there is the questionable right to a paid vacation[30]), and
the doctrine of the interdependence of all the rights makes it very difficult
to prioritize basic from nonbasic ones. Moreover, these rights have largely
been given a statist interpretation, which they are only now slowly beginning
to lose. That is, human rights were held to apply within states and, in some
sense negatively, against the state. Thus their original designers called for their
constitutionalization exclusively at the level of nation-states.[31]

Despite these drawbacks, we can see the great advantage in the recognition
of basic human rights in international law. Economic rights are included in
Article 25 of the Universal Declaration as a person's "right to a standard of
living adequate for the health and well-being of himself and of his family,
including food, clothing, housing, medical care and necessary social services,
and the right to security in the event of unemployment, sickness, disability,
widowhood, old age or other lack of livelihood in circumstances beyond his

[29] For a proposal on basic income, see Philippe Van Parijs, *Real Freedom for All* (Oxford: Oxford
University Press, 1995), chapter 2.
[30] International Covenant on Economic, Social and Cultural Rights, Art. 7(d). Of course, this is
primarily to be understood as a means toward the availability to persons of some sort of leisure
time and a break from constant work.
[31] I later consider the new moves to regionalize human rights, and I have noted the fact that
increasingly they are held to apply to nonstate actors.

control." A right to work is included among the provisions of the Universal Declaration in Article 23. These rights are incorporated in international law in the International Covenant on Economic, Social and Cultural Rights, and specified in several articles there, especially Article 11. Of course, these rights are often honored in the breach, but at least they are reasonably clear in principle and in law.

Before turning to questions of interpretation and implementation of human rights notions, along lines that could advance global justice, we can comment on the first conundrum noted earlier, between global claims of universal personhood or global interconnectedness on the one hand and nation-state priority for economic distribution and redistribution on the other. The view developed here is clearly on the cosmopolitan side, in insisting on the recognition of the claims of all people to the basic conditions of life activity. Nonetheless, we need to give some weight to what is due to people in virtue of their participation in cooperative processes of production and also what is due to the legitimate claims of political communities more generally, where these claims may include also economic and cultural factors. The social connections model, in particular, recognizes these sorts of ties but sees them as extending more globally as contemporary economic relations expand across borders.

The overall theory I have developed attempts to incorporate all three of these factors in a coherent fashion – the cosmopolitanism of human rights, the claims of (democratic) political and other more local communities, and the growing social relatedness given globalization. Here, we can more narrowly frame the issue in terms of the sort of human rights approach the theory entails and its implications for global justice. First, human rights not only hold against states, but as goals they require the development of a range of economic, social, and political institutions that would realize them. There is no reason to restrict these to institutions within the nation-state; transnational institutions and networks are required as well. Moreover, without going so far as to use human rights to cover all laws and rules of whatever sort, we can see that such rights are increasingly being taken, correctly, to hold against institutions below as well as across the level of nation-states. Correlatively, we can propose that the redistributive effects we seek, aimed at alleviating global poverty and the elimination of exploitation, will require the development of solutions that are not exclusively statist in their focus but engage this variety of cross-border associations and networks.

Political and other communities also come into play when we recognize that democracy is itself a human right. Although the Universal Declaration of Human Rights and the International Covenant on Civil and Political Rights use the language only of political participation and free elections, a right to democracy is increasingly being recognized in international law.[32] Moreover, self-determination is recognized in the covenant in its first article.[33] In addition, as I have argued in *Globalizing Democracy and Human Rights*, there are other important interconnections between human rights and democratic participation, beyond that these rights can serve to constrain democratic decisions.[34] As Henry Shue already argued in his early work *Basic Rights*, democratic participation importantly works to implement and preserve economic rights.[35] Moreover, I have argued that to determine what the effects of policies are on people's human rights, we need to hear from them and not only imagine these impacts, in a way that implicates forms of democratic input, if not full-scale democratic participation.[36] As I will note again in the final part of this chapter, this supports new requirements of democratic accountability in the institutions of global governance and of transnational representation, if we are to fulfill people's human rights.[37] In general terms, I propose that wherever decisions or policies prospectively impact the possibilities for people to fulfill their basic rights, they ought to be able to provide input into these decisions.

The emphasis on democratic participation suggests a role for political communities within global distributive processes, a role that moderates a thoroughgoing cosmopolitanism. Moreover, from the standpoint of economic justice, some recognition is required of the work and other contributions to productive processes that are made by members of a given economic community. Thus we cannot view the results of such production as simply open to redistribution to meet human rights criteria without considerable qualification.

Finally, to frame the issue of implementing these principles, it is important to emphasize the way in which nonstate actors can themselves support the achievement of global justice in such a human rights approach. This would involve the usual emphasis on civil society organizations such as international nongovernmental organizations in their role in influencing the institutions of

---

[32] See Gregory H. Fox and Brad R. Roth, *Democratic Governance and International Law* (Cambridge: Cambridge University Press, 2000).

[33] While differing in meaning from democracy, self-determination is itself increasingly being understood in terms of democratic self-determination. For a discussion, see Carol C. Gould, "Self-Determination beyond Sovereignty: Relating Transnational Democracy to Local Autonomy," *Journal of Social Philosophy* 37(1) (Spring, 2006): 44–60.

[34] Gould, *Globalizing Democracy and Human Rights*, chapters 8 and 9.

[35] Henry Shue, *Basic Rights* (Princeton, NJ: Princeton University Press, 1980).

[36] Gould, *Globalizing Democracy and Human Rights*, chapter 9.

[37] Carol C. Gould, "Structuring Global Democracy: Political Communities, Universal Human Rights, and Transnational Representation," Special Issue on Global Democracy and Political Exclusion, *Metaphilosophy* 40(1) (January 2009): 24–46.

global governance and in representing people from the Global South, but it equally emphasizes the role of social movements oriented to global justice, such as the World Social Forum. Besides this, I argue that solidarity networks of a new transnational sort can play a crucial role in working to eliminate oppression and aid others at a distance. These particularistic networks and associations, arising from social empathy with the situation of distant people and oriented to justice, importantly supplement a human rights approach, based on the universalist recognition of people's equality and dignity.[38]

III. SOME PRACTICAL DIRECTIONS FOR IMPLEMENTATION

In the final part of this chapter, I propose, by way of a list, some suggestions for innovations in public policy and institutional reforms that would advance global justice through a human rights approach. The first three of these directions specifically concern human rights implementation, and the last set concerns what could be regarded as conditions for fulfilling human rights more globally. A full answer to the question of how to realize economic and social rights worldwide would require addressing the current political economy in ways that are beyond the scope of this essay. Strategies would have to be devised to deal not only with the financial and other economic crises that are more global than heretofore, but also with the growing inequalities that globalization is engendering, and to figure out how to implement access to basic income or other modes of provision for subsistence needs globally. I will not be able to consider that here; instead I limit myself to the elements of a human rights approach. Further, in the list that follows, I emphasize only those directions that supplement existing ones such as foreign aid in innovative ways, bypassing those that are stressed in the existing literature.

The first and easiest reform would be the introduction of what I have elsewhere called *human rights impact assessments*.[39] These can be required of all important actors in the global arena, including the institutions of global governance and multinational corporations. Such human rights assessments

[38] See Carol C. Gould, "Transnational Solidarities," Special Issue on Solidarity, ed. Carol Gould and Sally Scholz, *Journal of Social Philosophy* 38(1) (Spring, 2007): 146–162; and "Recognition in Redistribution: Care and Diversity in Global Justice," *Southern Journal of Philosophy* 46 (2007, Supplement): 91–103.

[39] Gould, "Structuring Global Democracy"; see also Ronald K. Mitchell, Bradley R. Agle, and Donna J. Wood, "Toward a Theory of Stakeholder Identification and Salience: Defining the Principle of Who and What Really Counts," *Academy of Management Review* 22 (1997): 853–886; Robert A. Phillips, "Stakeholder Legitimacy," *Business Ethics Quarterly* 13(1) (2003): 25–41; and the discussion of these views in Bert van de Ven, "Human Rights as a Normative Basis for Stakeholder Legitimacy," *Corporate Governance* 5(2) (2005): 48–59.

can be modeled on current environmental impact or technology assessments, but they would focus instead on the expected consequences of a decision, policy, or activity for the human rights (or at least the basic human rights) of those likely to be importantly affected. This would require that efforts be made to determine these impacts and, to the degree possible, enlist in this process those affected or their representatives to provide the needed input. The assessments would have to show how basic human rights are not violated and instead protected, or enhanced if possible. This constitutes a rather minimal requirement in comparison with the scope of the global justice problem, but it can be implemented immediately, at least on a voluntary basis. It could be expected to help establish human rights standards – including the critical economic and social rights – as directly applicable to corporate conduct and to policy making by global institutions.

A second direction would encourage the further constitutionalization and more general juridification of human rights, including economic and social rights. Economic and social rights, known as second-generation rights, have already been incorporated into some constitutions, most notably that of South Africa, which has also taken the lead in their judicial enforcement. These moves represent a promising direction that other states can emulate, and some have. Of course, this is not to say that constitutionalization is sufficient without actual efforts to promote the realization of human rights through legislative action and decisions by other policy-making bodies.

Third, regional human rights agreements need to be developed; they need to be adopted where they currently do not exist, and implemented where they do exist. Regionalization is an important current trend in global politics, and not only in its main exemplar, the European Union. Economic regional arrangements are already well advanced. Such regionalism has much to commend it in terms of human rights protections as well. Given the emergence of new cross-border local communities, broader region-wide human rights agreements can protect the rights of the members of such communities, especially in regard to new forms of cross-border activity and cooperation.[40] Furthermore, regional agreements on human rights allow some scope for diversity in the interpretation of these rights. For example, property rights can be subject to considerable variation in interpretation in this way. However, we should also note the dangers in such variability, particularly in regard to women's rights. Europe, and more recently the European Union, constitutes the most prominent regional arena for human rights protection and, increasingly, provision. Its courts of human rights have been path breaking in allowing citizens

[40] See also Gould, "Structuring Global Democracy."

to appeal even against the laws and decisions of their own governments. Africa and the Americas also have regional agreements in place.[41] We can propose the development of such human rights agreements in other regions and also try to find new ways to make them really effective.

Turning now to the broader political economic context for the reduction of global inequalities and the provision of means of subsistence, we can propose, fourth, the need for new forms of global taxation, as well as measures to reform the existing tax system. This is clearly a major area for further research and of course would be challenging to implement. As Gillian Brock notes, good arguments can be given for carbon taxes, Tobin-type taxes on global financial transactions, taxes on arms trades, and air-ticket taxes, as well as aviation fuel taxes.[42] She also argues effectively for multinationals to pay their fare share of taxes, with attendant requirements to eliminate tax havens, tax evasion, and deceptive transfer-pricing schemes, along with requiring transparency in regard to the revenues paid for resources in developing countries.[43]

A fifth direction is the need to make international labor standards effective rather than merely enunciated. The human rights connection is given in the right to work and in the requirement of Article 23 of the Universal Declaration of Human Rights for "just and favorable conditions of work," among other provisions of the declaration and the International Covenant on Civil and Political Rights. These provisions call for the elimination of exploitative working conditions. Thus far, however, the International Labour Organization establishes only requirements of "good practices" and has little enforcement capacity. Voluntary efforts by corporations as in the UN Global Compact are useful to a degree but are far from sufficient. I suggest that new regulatory mechanisms have to be devised in this domain.

The final directions for human rights implementation are tied to the key role played by democratic participation in the approach I have laid out. Thus, sixth, we need to increase democratic accountability in the institutions of global governance. Although most international relations theorists seem satisfied with aiming at lesser forms of accountability for such institutions, denying

---

[41] These regional instruments include the European Convention on Human Rights (1950) with its five protocols, along with the European Court of Human Rights; the American Convention on Human Rights (Pact of San Jose, adopted by the OAS in 1969), supervised by the Inter-American Commission on Human Rights and the Inter-American Court of Human Rights; and the African Charter of Human and Peoples' Rights of the African Union (1981).

[42] Gillian Brock, "Taxation and Global Justice: Closing the Gap between Theory and Practice," *Journal of Social Philosophy* 39(2) (Summer 2008): 161–184.

[43] Ibid.

the relevance of democratic accountability in this context,[44] I believe that new ways have to be found to enable input into the policy making of these institutions by those people affected by these policies. There are numerous proposals along these lines, for example by Joseph Stiglitz, Peter Willetts, and others, and these often focus on requirements of transparency as well as the representation of these affected people by international nongovernmental organizations.[45] Beyond this, I think we can look to Internet forums that would open the deliberations of the "epistemic communities" within these institutions to contributions from credentialed representatives of broader publics.[46] There is also probably a role for even more open participation through wikis and other means.

Finally, we can mention two additional directions regarding democratization that are more far reaching but that are important for undergirding the proposals about human rights considered here. The first is the long-term need to devise new forms of transnational representation, extending even beyond the current institutions of global governance. Such forms of democratic representation would be important in order to provide the input into those institutions as just proposed. In addition, although it is possible to adopt the various measures presented here by way of agreements among nation-states, in the longer run the growth of transnational communities and the enhancement of regionalization will require some procedures to ensure the legitimacy of transnational regulation and law, including human rights law. This requires that we start thinking about new forms of transnational governance, perhaps primarily focusing on the regional rather than the global level.[47]

The second democratic innovation, which I can only mention here, is perhaps the most difficult, though it is also one that can be implemented in the near term. Effective respect for and fulfillment of the range of human

---

[44] Ruth W. Grant and Robert O. Keohane, "Accountability and Abuses of Power in World Politics," *American Political Science Review* 99(1) (February 2005): 29–43.

[45] Joseph E. Stiglitz, *Globalization and Its Discontents* (New York: Norton, 2002) and "Globalization and Development," in David Held and Mathias Koenig-Archibugi (eds.), *Taming Globalization* (Cambridge: Polity, 2003), 47–67; and Peter Willetts, "Remedying the World Trade Organisation's Deviance from Global Norms," in P. Griffith and J. Thurston (eds.), *Free and Fair: Making the Progressive Case for Removing Trade Barriers* (London: Foreign Policy Centre, 2004), 131–140.

[46] See also Carol C. Gould, "Global Democratic Transformation and the Internet," in John R. Rowan (ed.), *Technology, Science and Social Justice, Social Philosophy Today*, Vol. 22 (Charlottesville, VA: Philosophy Documentation Center, 2007), 73–88.

[47] See Carol C. Gould, "Regional vs. Global Democracy: Advantages and Limitations," forthcoming in *Global Democracy: Normative and Empirical Perspectives*, ed. by Daniele Archibugi, Mathias Koenig-Archibugi, and Raffaele Marchetti (Cambridge: Cambridge University Press, 2011).

rights requires, I think, the democratization of the institutions of economic and social life, as well as the range of political associations and institutions. If human rights are to be recognized by nonstate actors and if the list of human rights itself includes a right to democratic participation, then it is reasonable to expect that such opportunities for participation be introduced very generally, and not only at the level of nation-states. This, however, is a theme I have stressed elsewhere and cannot develop further at this point.[48]

Although the new practical directions sketched here may seem like something of a grab bag, I hope it can be seen that they are in fact based in a coherent philosophical approach to human rights and global justice. I have also proposed that this philosophical approach itself will only work as a guideline for practice if it is a reasonably open conception in its account of agency and its conditions and if it provides adequate space for diversity in interpretation and implementation. Moreover, I suggest that such a philosophical approach has to be responsive to current developments and to the real possibilities and challenges embedded in contemporary social reality.

[48] See the arguments in Gould, *Rethinking Democracy* and in Carol C. Gould, "Economic Justice, Self-Management, and the Principle of Reciprocity," in K. Kipnis and D. T. Meyers (eds.), *Economic Justice: Private Rights and Public Responsibilities* (Totowa, NJ: Rowman & Allanheld, 1985), 202–216. Cf. David Schweickart, *After Capitalism* (Lanham, MD: Rowman & Littlefield, 2002).

2   Global Equality of Opportunity as an Institutional Standard of Distributive Justice

Daniel Butt

We live in a world with a broad range of institutions whose actions affect the distribution of benefits and burdens both between and within particular political communities. As cooperation and interdependence between communities increases, so there is a greater need for overbridging institutions that regulate and control international interaction. We can expect both increases in the powers of existing international institutions and the development of significant new international institutions. Examples include international governmental bodies such as the General Assembly and Security Council of the United Nations and the Council of Ministers and European Parliament of the European Union (EU); international judicial bodies such as the European Court of Justice and the Inter-American Court of Human Rights; international trade organizations such as the World Bank, International Monetary Fund, and the World Trade Organization; and nongovernmental organizations, such as Oxfam or the Red Cross. By what standards should the decisions and actions of such institutions be assessed?

This chapter argues that international institutions should be guided by a cosmopolitan principle of global equality of opportunity (GEO), which holds that individuals should have access to opportunity sets of equivalent value regardless of their nationality. The central idea is that international justice requires international institutions to go further than the degree of intervention required by "sufficientarians," who accept only that we possess duties to raise those in other countries to some minimal level of well-being. The chapter defends a more demanding principle of global equality that seeks to remove egregious international inequalities of opportunity even when they apply to

This chapter was originally given at the Symposium of the International Legal Theory Interest Group of the American Society of International Law, in Washington, D.C. I am grateful to the participants at this event, and to the editors of this volume, for their very helpful feedback.

persons above the minimal sufficientarian threshold of well-being. This is a contentious claim. Global egalitarianism is controversial even on an abstract level – many deny that there is any sense in which justice requires an international redistribution of resources in keeping with the principle of equality. Things get even more difficult when we come to real-world policy claims: Here the advocate of GEO must confront skepticism as to the principle's practicality, both in terms of the desirability and the possibility of its implementation, and doubts as to the legitimacy of institutional intervention in its favor. This chapter does not respond to all such objections in detail, but it does sketch a version of GEO in which it could plausibly be said that it should – in an all-things-considered sense – be promoted by existing international institutions.

I. WHAT DOES IT MEAN TO SAY THAT INSTITUTIONS "SHOULD" IMPLEMENT PRINCIPLES OF DISTRIBUTIVE JUSTICE?

The question whether and how political institutions should be guided by principles of distributive justice is a complex and contested one. It does not necessarily follow from the claim that, in an ideal world, individuals would have particular entitlements as a matter of distributive justice that agents in the real world should seek to make actual holdings closer to these ideal holdings. This is true both of individual agents and of political institutions. As an egalitarian, I may believe that society would be more just if some of my rich neighbor's property was redistributed to me. However, it does not necessarily follow from this that I am entitled to help myself to her possessions, or that others – be they everyday citizens, agents of the state, or representative legislative bodies – are morally entitled or required to transfer some of her property to me, or that my neighbor herself is morally required so to act. There are a number of different reasons why one might maintain that action seeking to bring the world closer to its ideal state should or need not be undertaken by any or all of the agents listed. Specifically, a claim that a given principle of distributive justice should or should not be implemented at the political level may be a response to one of three distinct questions:

1. What is the best philosophical account of principles of distributive justice?
2. Is it desirable, in practical terms, that these principles should be implemented?
3. Do political institutions act legitimately in seeking to implement these principles?

Much contemporary philosophical writing about distributive justice relates to the first question. Some writers think that the answer to the first is connected to the answer to the second;[1] others see these as separate.[2] One dispute concerns the status of justice. Some argue that justice is simply one desideratum of political activity. As such, a claim that a given course of action would lead to a more just outcome may give us a reason to perform the action but does not settle the issue, because there may be other competing reasons, derived, from example, from overall utility, or the needs of the worst-off members of society, which also need to be assessed. For others, considerations of justice should be formulated in such a way as to take such considerations into account; hence Rawls's claim that "justice is the first virtue of social institutions, as truth is of systems of thought."[3] Regardless of how much pragmatism or pluralism one builds into one's principles of distributive justice in terms of Question 1, one will always have to consider the practical effects of their implementation before maintaining that they should be pursued in real-world, nonideal contexts.

The third question has sometimes been bracketed by political philosophers focusing primarily on questions of justice, though it has been extensively addressed by legal philosophers and democratic theorists. It can take two forms. The most familiar arises when we are confronted with a situation in which there appears to be a gap between what we believe to be the best course of action for society to follow, taking account of both normative requirements and considerations of practicality, and what a majority of the population believes the best course of action to be.[4] When should those individuals charged with making decisions on behalf of society pursue their own favored alternative, and when should they defer to the views of the majority? The question's alternative form arises for those who believe that certain forms of political action should not be justified by reference to a single comprehensive account of the good, but should instead appeal to a wider range of different approaches to life. So Rawls's later work placed an emphasis on the justification of political action that affects constitutional essentials and questions of basic justice in terms of

---

[1] See Rawls's account of his work as "realistically utopian," in John Rawls, *The Law of Peoples* (Cambridge, MA: Harvard University Press, 1999), 6–7.

[2] See G. A. Cohen, *Rescuing Justice and Equality* (Cambridge, MA: Harvard University Press, 2008).

[3] John Rawls, *A Theory of Justice* (Oxford: Oxford University Press, 1972), 3.

[4] See Richard Wollheim, "A Paradox in the Theory of Democracy," in P. Laslett and W. G. Runciman (eds.), *Philosophy, Politics and Society: Second Series* (Oxford: Blackwell, 1962), 71–87.

public reason, understood in terms of an overlapping consensus of reasonable comprehensive conceptions of the good.[5]

A claim that institutions should pursue distributive outcomes in an all-things-considered sense must, then, engage with questions of normative desirability, of practicality, and of legitimacy. All questions need not be answered in the same way – it is quite coherent, for example, to maintain that a given institutional action is justified in an all-things-considered sense even though it is not legitimate. Nonetheless, it must be shown why the action is of sufficient value to trump concerns of legitimacy. All of this can easily amount to a bias in favor of the status quo. Typically, it is harder to make such an argument in relation to transformative, as opposed to conservative, accounts of distributive justice. This is the type of hurdle that faces GEO. The cosmopolitan account of distributive justice upon which the account rests is controversial on three different levels. First, it is philosophically contentious as even an account of ideal-type justice. Second, it is often portrayed as impractical in the real world. Third, it appears to be radically divorced from the majority of real-world beliefs about how international institutions should act. We live in a world that is still predominantly characterized by the significance of state sovereignty over resources and borders. This principle of state sovereignty seems to have widespread popular support, and it is strongly rooted in contemporary understandings of international law. Is it really the case that cosmopolitan political theorists believe that international institutions in the real world should, here and now, be acting so as to promote global equality of opportunity? In what follows, I speak to each of these three concerns: first outlining GEO as an element of an ideal-type account of international distributive justice, second addressing concerns relating to its practical desirability and possibility, and finally briefly addressing the question of the legitimacy of institutional egalitarian interventions.

II. WHAT IS THE BEST PHILOSOPHICAL ACCOUNT OF INTERNATIONAL DISTRIBUTIVE JUSTICE?

The basic idea behind GEO is that we should show the same substantial concern for equality of opportunity at a global level as within a domestic context. Insofar as GEO maintains that boundaries between different peoples do not

---

[5] John Rawls, *Political Liberalism* (New York: Columbia University Press, 1995). For discussion, see T. M. Scanlon, "Rawls on Justification," in Samuel Freeman (ed.), *The Cambridge Companion to Rawls* (Cambridge: Cambridge University Press, 2002), 157–166.

have moral significance, it is cosmopolitan; insofar as it maintains that individuals should have equal opportunities, it is egalitarian. Thus, GEO is a variant of cosmopolitan egalitarianism, but it only maintains that distributions should be equal to the extent that is necessary to ensure that different individuals have, in some specified sense, equal opportunities for flourishing. Just as there are different conceptions of equality of opportunity at a domestic level, so one might develop a range of different forms of GEO. A common distinction is between "formal" and "substantive" equality of opportunity.[6] According to the former idea, equality of opportunity requires that desirable positions be open to all, and be filled on the basis of aptitude, so that the positions are allocated to those who are best able to perform the associated duties. This requirement does not scrutinize how different individuals come to possess the relevant aptitude, and so is seemingly compatible, for example, with an inegalitarian education system that provides a better education for some than others, making it relatively easier for some to gain desirable positions. Formal equality of opportunity is the approach that is most typically invoked in real-world contexts in relation to employment disputes, particularly in judicial contexts.

Substantive equality of opportunity goes further; it looks at the process by which the relevant aptitude is acquired. Insofar as this reflects factors for which the individual agents in question cannot be held responsible, substantive equality of opportunity judges ensuing inequalities to be unfair. So, for example, Rawls's account of fair equality of opportunity in *A Theory of Justice* rests upon a simple idea that many have taken to have immediate intuitive plausibility – that it is unfair if one's social circumstances, encompassing factors such as race, sex, and social class, affect one's ability to succeed in life. Richard Arneson describes the prescribed outcome of such an account as follows:

> [I]f Smith and Jones have the same native talent, and Smith is born of wealthy, educated parents of a socially favored ethnicity and Jones is born of poor, uneducated parents of a socially disfavored ethnicity, then if they develop the same ambition to become scientists or Wall Street lawyers, they will have the same prospects of becoming scientists or Wall Street lawyers if [fair equality of opportunity] prevails.[7]

---

[6] See Richard Arneson, "Equality of Opportunity," in Edward N. Zalta (ed.), *The Stanford Encyclopedia of Philosophy*, Fall 2008 edition (available at http://plato.stanford.edu/archives/fall2008/entries/equal-opportunity/).

[7] Ibid.

It should be understood that even the substantive account of equality of opportunity only goes a limited distance down the egalitarian road. As Samuel Freeman notes:

> The idea of fair equal opportunity is rather narrow; it concerns the opportunities people have to compete for social positions and the legal powers they involve. We might, then, say it involves equal opportunity for powers and positions among "those who are at the same level of talent and ability, and have the same willingness to use them." This is quite different from the much broader distributive idea of equal opportunity for welfare endorsed by some luck egalitarians.[8]

Equality of opportunity argues that desirable positions should be allocated fairly according to some idea of merit, but we still need an account of the extent to which there should be a hierarchy of social positions, which confers benefits and prestige upon their bearers. A concern for substantive equality of opportunity will limit the degree of material inequality in society insofar as doing so is necessary to prevent some individuals from gaining an unfair advantage over others in the competition for desirable positions. Such an approach is likely to place restrictions on the extent to which individuals can transfer advantages to their children, either by direct transfers such as the inheritance of wealth or by providing privileged access to education or health care – Rawls argues that it places an obligation on the state to prevent "excessive accumulations of property and wealth" and to maintain "equal opportunities of education for all"[9] – but it is still compatible with a range of more or less hierarchical ways of organizing the social order.

This is not to say that the advocate of substantive equality of opportunity need *condone* particular models of social hierarchies and unequal reward distributions. Equality of opportunity need not be viewed as a complete theory of distributive justice; instead it can be seen as placing constraints on justifiable distributions – *if* there are to be inequalities, they should be attached to offices and positions open to all under conditions of fair equality of opportunity. A full account will have to refer to further principles of distributive justice to determine to what extent inequalities in the social order are to be permitted. Whereas some people will be willing to organize society as to maximize efficiency, for example, others may wish to trade off overall efficiency for equality, and so restrict or eliminate more and less desirable social positions.

---

[8] Samuel Freeman, *Justice and the Social Contract: Essays on Rawlsian Political Philosophy* (New York: Oxford University Press, 2007), 117n.

[9] Rawls, *A Theory of Justice*, 73.

For Rawls, the difference principle answers this question: Inequalities are permitted, but only insofar as they benefit the least advantaged members of society. The point is that very different models of social hierarchy can accept the fair equality of opportunity principle. Rawls's second principle of justice, regulating inequalities, is as follows:

> Social and economic inequalities are to be arranged so that they are both:
>
> (a) to the greatest benefit of the least advantaged, consistent with the just savings principle, and
> (b) attached to offices and positions open to all under conditions of fair equality of opportunity.[10]

Significantly, (b) is lexically prior to (a) here, so the fair equality of opportunity principle has priority over the difference principle. This leaves open the possibility that other principles could replace (a) in this formulation without infringing upon (b). So, for example, one could replace (a) with one of the following: (a1) to the greatest benefit of society as a whole in terms of aggregate utility; (a2) only permitted when necessary to prevent some members of society from falling below a threshold level of minimal well-being; or (a3) only permitted when necessary to protect the security of the community. Given the lexical priority of (b) over (a), all three of these replacements respect fair equality of opportunity.

Substantive equality of opportunity, then, only requires distributive equality insofar as the distribution of resources affects competition for desired positions. In broad terms, the advocate of equality of opportunity will be concerned with three categories of goods. In some cases, equality of opportunity will require equal distributions of goods. In others, it will require that all individuals have access to a sufficient degree of resource provision. Finally, in some cases equality of opportunity will allow inequalities, insofar as they do not affect competition for desirable positions. A commitment to substantive equality of opportunity limits the range of acceptable complete theories of distributive justice, and it means that one must be more egalitarian than a person who adopts a straightforward sufficientarian approach, which looks only at absolute and disregards relative levels of advantage, but its acceptance of distributive egalitarianism is limited.

Turning to the global level, we find that it is possible to put forward either formal or substantive variants of GEO. Both appear to be profoundly challenging to current international practice. The claim that careers should be

---

[10] Ibid., 302.

"open to talents" seems antithetical to contemporary restrictions on immigration, which typically afford priority in employment to citizens of the country in question, or selected countries who are members of reciprocal agreements, as in the case of the EU. Substantive GEO goes even further, seemingly requiring significant material redistribution between different states if those persons of equal talent and motivation are to have equal chances of success in life. Both variants of GEO crucially rest upon what is perhaps the most powerful weapon is the cosmopolitan armory – the idea, which many find intuitively compelling, that there is something unfair about the fact that one's nationality – which is clearly, in Rawls's terms, arbitrary from a moral point of view – has such a critical impact on one's life prospects. The basic idea of substantive GEO in particular is that, at a global level, nationality is analogous to social class at a domestic level. The idea is put forward powerfully by Joseph Carens:

> Citizenship in the modern world is a lot like feudal status in the medieval world. . . . To be born a citizen of an affluent country like Canada is like being born into the nobility (even though many belong to the lesser nobility). To be born a citizen of a poor country like Bangladesh is (for most) like being born into the peasantry in the Middle Ages.[11]

Many find the claim that there is something unjust about such a situation plausible, but it is important to appreciate that it does not follow automatically from an acceptance of fair equality of opportunity at a domestic level. Strikingly, Rawls himself does not extend the reach of his principles of distributive justice globally. He argues not for an international difference principle, but for a sufficientarian minimal duty of assistance to other peoples, with a cutoff point that comes into play when the people in question become self-sufficient.[12] The key question here concerns what is sometimes called the "circumstances of justice." When do questions of distributive justice actually arise? For "nonrelational" theorists, the answer is straightforward – principles of distributive justice apply to any and all moral persons, regardless of the nature and extent of interaction between them.[13] Such a conclusion is undoubtedly controversial. Many writers argue that it is only when persons stand in a particular type of interactional relation with one another that questions of distributive justice,

[11] Joseph H. Carens, "Migration and Morality: A Liberal Egalitarian Perspective," in B. Barry and R. Goodin (eds.), *Free Movement: Ethical Issues in the Transnational Migration of People and of Money* (Hemel Hempstead: Harvester Wheatsheaf, 1992), 26.

[12] John Rawls, *The Law of Peoples*, 119.

[13] The terminology of relational and nonrelational theories is taken from Andrea Sangiovanni, "Global Justice, Reciprocity and the State," *Philosophy and Public Affairs* 35 (2007): 6.

and so concerns of equality of opportunity, arise. "Relational" theorists have put forward a range of different accounts of how people can come to owe one another duties of distributive justice: possible candidates include regular interaction through politics or commerce,[14] common subjection to coercive authority,[15] and joint authorship of coercive law,[16] among many others. Any relational theorist must answer two questions in connection with international justice. First, what is the form of relation between persons that would give rise to internationally applicable duties of distributive justice? Second, do we find such a form of relation in the real world? Answering the second question affirmatively commits one, at a theoretical level, to distributive cosmopolitanism. There are, then, multiple routes to distributive cosmopolitanism. One may advocate a nonrelational account of distributive justice, whereby the moral equality of persons leads to egalitarian distributive principles between persons regardless of whether there is any interaction between the persons in question. Alternatively, one may put forward a relational account whereby distributive principles only apply between persons who interact in a certain kind of way. The critical question for such accounts is therefore whether contemporary (or potentially historic)[17] global interaction meets the specified relational threshold. If so, the door is open to an argument for GEO.

This, then, is the ideal lying behind GEO. Quite what it means in practice for GEO to obtain is a contentious issue. The most straightforward account is given by Darrel Moellendorf, and it directly relates to the Rawlsian account of fair equality of opportunity:

> If equality of opportunity were realized, a child growing up in rural Mozambique would be statistically as likely as the child of a senior executive at a Swiss bank to reach the position of the latter's parent.[18]

This reference to the need for equal opportunity to achieve specific jobs has been much criticized, and the point is more generally expressed in terms of individuals having equal opportunity sets, so that they have access to comparably valuable opportunities, even if they do not possess identically the same

[14] Darrel Moellendorf, *Cosmopolitan Justice* (Boulder, CO: Westview Press, 2002), 32.
[15] Michael Blake, "Distributive Justice, State Coercion, and Autonomy," *Philosophy and Public Affairs* 30 (2002): 258.
[16] Thomas Nagel, "The Problem of Global Justice," *Philosophy and Public Affairs* 33 (2005): 128–129.
[17] See Daniel Butt, *Rectifying International Injustice: Principles of Compensation and Restitution Between Nations* (Oxford: Oxford University Press, 2009), 115–117.
[18] Moellendorf, *Cosmopolitan Justice*, 49.

set of opportunities.[19] So, for example, Simon Caney summarizes GEO as follows:

> Global equality of opportunity requires that persons (of equal ability and motivation) have equal opportunities to attain the positions valued in every society.[20]

Sylvie Loriaux's conception is broadly similar:

> [A] plausible version of global equality of opportunity can be constructed, which demands that equally talented and motivated persons who participate in the global economic order should have a roughly equal chance to benefit from this order if they so choose, irrespective of the society to which they belong.[21]

Much more could be said about the differences between these accounts; for now, it will suffice to note that an advocate of GEO must maintain that, in some sense, individuals of equal talent should have access to equal opportunity sets, regardless of their nationality. Such advocates typically draw on the capabilities approach of writers such as Amartya Sen and Martha Nussbaum to assess what is needed for GEO to obtain.[22] Again, we might differentiate between three categories of capabilities: those whose provision needs to be provided equally if opportunity is to be equal; those whereby a minimal level of provision is necessary for opportunities to be equal; and those where international inequalities seem largely insignificant. The crucial point is that GEO does not require that international redistribution be so extensive as to leave all states equally well off in terms of, for example, per capita GDP. For some capabilities, such as education and health, it does seem necessary that provision in different states be of a comparable standard if opportunity sets are to be equivalent.[23] For other capabilities, such as access to shelter and housing, what is most important is that each individual has access to a sufficiently good

---

[19] See David Miller, *National Responsibility and Global Justice* (Oxford: Oxford University Press, 2007), 62.

[20] Simon Caney, "Cosmopolitan Justice and Equalizing Opportunities," *Metaphilosophy* 32 (2001): 120.

[21] Sylvia Loriaux, "Global Equality of Opportunity: A Proposal," *Journal of International Relations and Development* 11 (2008): 2.

[22] Martha C. Nussbaum, and Amartya Sen (eds.), *The Quality of Life* (Oxford: Clarendon Press, 1993).

[23] This builds upon, but goes beyond, the approach to the right to the highest attainable standard of health articulated by the UN Committee on Economic, Social and Cultural Rights in General Comment 14. See Paul Hunt, "The Millennium Development Goals and the Right to the Highest Attainable Standard of Health," *The John D. and Catherine T.*

level of provision. GEO thus combines egalitarianism and sufficientarianism, depending on the good in question. Finally, the approach allows for resource differentials between different states, in relation, for example, to luxury goods, if (and only if) these differentials do not have an impact on GEO.

iii. FROM THEORY TO PRACTICE: SHOULD INSTITUTIONS IMPLEMENT GLOBAL EQUALITY OF OPPORTUNITY?

Although GEO rests upon a claim about fairness that many will find intuitively plausible, it is deeply controversial. One may oppose GEO for a number of reasons, six of which are listed here.

1. Unequal opportunities are not unfair even in a domestic context.
2. Unequal opportunities are unfair domestically but are not unfair internationally.
3. Although international inequalities are unfair, pursuing GEO would conflict with other morally valuable goals.
4. Although international inequalities are unfair, pursuing GEO would have undesirable effects in practice.
5. Although international inequalities are unfair, pursuing GEO would be impossible in practice.
6. Although international inequalities are unfair, there is little international public support for GEO and so pursuing GEO would lack democratic legitimacy.

These objections cover a wide range of different responses to GEO. Some stand as direct repudiations of the judgments at its heart; others are sympathetic to the project in some ways but are skeptical as to its costs, possibility, practicality, or legitimacy. Points 1 and 2 belong to the former category. With reference to Point 1, some writers have denied that justice requires that equality of opportunity obtain in a domestic context: Libertarians, for example, might argue that the pursuit of equality of opportunity infringes on the rights of employers or property owners; consequentialists might argue that it leads to inefficient outcomes or does not maximize the good, however understood.[24] This is clearly a profound difference of view. The case for GEO is unlikely to be persuasive to those who firmly reject equality of opportunity within particular

MacArthur Foundation International Lecture Series on Population Issues, Abuja, Nigeria (available at http://www.macfound.org/atf/cf/%7BB0386CE3–8B29–4162-8098-E466FB856794%7D/HUNT_POPULATION.PDF).

[24] See Richard Epstein's argument that antidiscrimination laws are unjustified on consequentialist grounds: "[T]here is no reason to believe that this antidiscrimination system generates

communities. The debate concerning the circumstances of justice is at the heart of Point 2; as the previous discussion suggests, an affirmation of this item may represent a normative or an empirical dispute with the advocates of GEO. There is room for debate between defenders and opponents of GEO when disagreement hangs upon different empirical interpretations of the nature of international interaction, but in cases in which different parties simply affirm different models of the circumstances of justice, backed up, ultimately, by their deeply settled intuitive judgments, there is likely to be only so much that each side can do to persuade the other of the force of its argument.

What, then, of the objections made in Points 3 through 6? These remaining objections are more sympathetic to the ideal of GEO, in that they at least admit that there is something unfair about unequal international opportunity sets. Points 3 and 4 are related and will sometimes overlap in practice, insofar as the lack of pursuit of a valuable goal is in itself an undesirable effect. They are separated here to point out that one may advance a version of Point 3 at the abstract level of what justice or morality would require in a perfect world, without necessarily worrying about the concerns of practicality that arise in relation to Point 4.

The different types of argument that different approaches employ can be seen by considering the following argument from Rawls's *The Law of Peoples*. Rawls describes two imaginary societies, which begin from equal starting points and choose to follow divergent paths: One decides to industrialize and increase its rate of (real) saving; the other prefers a more pastoral and leisurely society. The result of this is that, decades later, the first country is twice as wealthy as the second. Rawls asks this question:

> Assuming, as we do, that both societies are liberal or decent, and their peo-ple free and responsible, and able to make their own decisions, should the industrializing country be taxed to give funds to the second? According to the duty of assistance there would be no tax, and that seems right; whereas with a global egalitarian principle without target, there would always be a flow of taxes as long as the wealth of one people was less than that of the other. This seems unacceptable.[25]

As this stands, it is not clear why Rawls believes that such an outcome is unacceptable. He is advocating a world whereby peoples are held responsible for their actions across time, but this could be defended from a range of

additional benefits that exceed its costs, social or economic." Richard A. Epstein, *Forbid-den Grounds: The Case against Employment Discrimination Laws* (Cambridge, MA: Harvard University Press, 1992), 27.

[25] John Rawls, *The Law of Peoples*, 117.

different perspectives. One could, for example, simply maintain that it is right for communities to be held responsible for the choices they make on the grounds that it would be unfair to tax others so as to ensure any kind of egalitarian distribution, even though it is justifiable to tax individuals within a given polity to ensure domestic equality of opportunity. Such a position would, for Rawls, be a version of Point 2, denying the unfairness of international inequalities specifically. Such a position might have a degree of plausibility if we conceive of the world in terms of a single generation, but it is much harder to maintain that fairness prohibits the taxation of later generations, who were not even born at the time of the economic decisions in question. Objections 3 and 4, however, accept that there is something unfair about allowing one's holdings to be determined by the actions of one's ancestors, but they deny that the unfairness in question is sufficiently important to require GEO. One might, for example, maintain that there is a particular value associated with national self-determination, possibly in similar fashion to how autonomy is deemed valuable for individuals. Such a claim is best expressed in terms of Objection 3: The idea is that the value of self-determination is sufficiently great to trump the value of the fairness achieved by GEO. Alternatively, one might simply maintain that such an international taxation scheme would be undesirable in practical terms, because, for example, there would seemingly be little or no disincentive against expensive consumption. Thus, one might couch Rawls's argument in terms of the value of fairness, autonomy, or efficiency.

These are familiar concerns that typically also arise in domestic contexts. However, as in domestic contexts, they do not automatically trump arguments in favor of GEO, given an acceptance that international inequalities are unfair. The key point here is that, domestically, many people seem willing potentially to trade off efficiency for the degree of egalitarianism embodied in equality of opportunity. The idea is that although we may wish to hold particular individuals responsible for the choices that they themselves make, we nonetheless feel that we should structure society so as not to allow their choices to significantly affect the life chances of their children. This has obvious implications with regard to policy areas such as health care and education. The advocate of GEO need not deny that efficiency or national self-determination are valuable goals; the question is how valuable they are relative to the value of equality of opportunity. A full answer to this question would involve a complicated assessment of the costs and benefits of particular policy interventions, but for current purposes it is sufficient to see that one could coherently affirm that institutions should promote equality of opportunity despite Objections 1 through 4 if one was willing both to hold that international inequalities in relation to capabilities such as health care and education are unfair and to maintain that this unfairness is sufficiently serious as to outweigh other valuable goals that international institutions might seek to pursue.

Concern 5 is rather different – and seemingly poses a more fundamental challenge to the claim that GEO could operate as an institutional standard of distributive justice. Might it be the case that the comparison of opportunity sets in different countries and across different cultural contexts is actually impossible in practice? David Miller has pressed hard upon this point in seeking to oppose GEO. He argues that when seeking to assess different opportunity sets within a domestic context, we rely upon particular cultural understandings as to the value of different packages of opportunities. This is not possible, he argues, at a global level, where we struggle both to compare opportunities in relation to a particular dimension, such as education, given differing understandings of what education is, and particularly when we attempt to devise general metrics to compare overall opportunity sets. He uses the example of a comparison between the opportunity sets available to the inhabitants of Iceland and Portugal. Suppose we were to conclude that there were better leisure opportunities available in Portugal, but better educational opportunities in Iceland. Is this as far as the comparison can go, meaning that we can only say that they are each better according to two different metrics? Or can we make some kind of all-things-considered claim about whether the citizens of one country or the other are better off? Miller argues that the latter course of action is not available to us, because in attempting to make such a claim "we run into serious difficulties created by the fact that we can no longer rely on a common set of cultural understandings to tell us which metric or metrics it is appropriate to use when attempting to draw cross-national opportunity comparisons."[26]

Is it really the case that we can therefore never say that opportunity sets are unequal? Miller anticipates a response to his position: "Global egalitarians . . . will probably respond that the most urgent cases are cases of *gross* inequality where no reasonable person could doubt that the resources and opportunities open to members of A are superior to those available to members of B."[27] Thus the real issue is not one of comparisons between countries such as Iceland and Portugal, but between, for example, developed EU member states and sub-Saharan African countries. In such cases, it appears that we can plausibly make the claim that opportunity sets are unequal without having to resolve the more difficult issues raised by the Iceland–Portugal comparison.

[26] Miller, *National Responsibility and Global Justice*, 66.
[27] Ibid., 67.

Miller makes two observations in relation to this claim. The first is that the possibility of an identification of unequal opportunity sets in such cases "does not mean that in general we are in a position to make such inter-societal comparative judgments, either within the group of rich societies or within the group of poor societies, and so although we might be able to identify the most egregious forms on inequality, we remain unable to specify what *equality* (of opportunity) would mean." Second, in such cases we are typically looking at situations in which sufficientarians would agree that disadvantaged persons are victims of injustice, because they lack access to minimal conditions for decency and flourishing. In this way, it may be the absolute levels of disadvantage that are doing the work in terms of our judgment of injustice. There is a practical point here, in that the judgment of injustice is overdetermined, meaning that there can be broad agreement that remedial action is necessary, but also a normative point that, in extreme cases, "what seems at first sight to be a concern about inequality may well turn out on closer inspection to be a concern about absolute poverty or deprivation, a concern which suggests a quite different general understanding of global justice."[28]

Need advocates of GEO oppose these claims? This depends upon whether GEO is merely being defended as an element of the best ideal-type theory of international distributive justice or is being advocated as a goal that should guide real-world policy makers. The idea that it is unfair that different individuals have access to unequal opportunity sets is compatible with the claim that in some cases we will not be able to tell which individuals are advantaged relative to others. This will be so where we simply lack sufficiently nuanced data to make a meaningful comparison, and we may even concede that it is so when the different cultural meanings that are attached to goods by different societies make some kinds of comparison between opportunity sets impossible or meaningless. So, in fact, it would be possible both to defend GEO as the best philosophical account of what global distributive justice is, but also maintain that it is not possible, in practice, to determine to what extent the world is actually just or unjust, based on the difficulty of making international comparisons. However, this would be an extreme conclusion to draw from the acknowledged fact that *in some cases* making comparisons is likely to be problematic. There are two ways in which one might maintain that it is possible to identify gross inequalities, but that judgments are not possible when different opportunity sets are less manifestly unequal.

The first is the possibility considered by Miller, in considering citizens of Niger and France, where he suggests that the opportunity sets available to

---

[28] Ibid., 68.

citizens of the former may be "strictly smaller" than the sets available to citizens of the latter, in the sense that there may be no basic dimension of, for example, the Human Development Index[29] in which citizens of Niger outscore citizens of France. In such a case, we do not have to consider how to trade off one dimension against the other, as in the leisure versus educational opportunities case: The suggestion is that there may be *no* plausible dimension in terms of which the average Niger citizen outscores the average France citizen. Miller is only committed to accepting that inequality obtains in such cases.

We should also maintain, however, that it is possible to make comparisons even when some balancing of dimensions is required. The suggestion that in some cases it will not be possible to say which opportunity set is better because of the difficulty of comparing different dimensions does not necessarily lead to the conclusion that it is always impossible to make overall comparisons between different opportunity sets. The Iceland–Portugal comparison seems troubling to us because there seems to be a real danger that we will go wrong in attempting to maintain that the citizens of one country or the other are better off in an all-things-considered sense. But imagine, instead, that we are comparing two countries with manifestly different degrees of economic development. In all but one dimension, say leisure opportunities, Country A is clearly much more advantaged than Country B, whereas Country B is marginally better off in this single dimension. We might further stipulate that all the members of A and all the members of B regard the opportunity sets of Country A's citizens as superior to those of Country B's citizens. In such a case it does seem clear that there is inequality of opportunity and the advocate of GEO will be able to point to redistributive policies that will make the situation more just. It should be stressed that this claim is perfectly compatible with the claim that it may not be possible to pursue such policies to the point where injustice no longer obtains. The key point here is that as a regulative ideal, GEO can be interpreted in a positive and a negative fashion. The positive approach would claim that institutions should actively seek to bring about GEO. The negative approach instead maintains that institutions should seek to minimize or remove identifiable inequalities in opportunity sets between the citizens of different states. The difference is that the negative approach can accept that institutions should only act in response to what appear to be obvious inequalities in opportunity sets. Thus, it may be better to maintain that international institutions should *oppose*

---

[29] The Human Development Index ranks states by a formula that includes three dimensions: life expectancy at birth; knowledge and education; and standard of living. See http://hdr.undp.org/en/media/hdr_20072008_tech_note_1.pdf (accessed April 4, 2009).

global *inequality* of opportunity, rather than seeking to *achieve equality* of opportunity. This is how institutions concerned with domestic equality of opportunity typically operate. In an employment context, the ideal of equality of opportunity requires that jobs be awarded to the most meritorious candidate, without reference to attributes that do not relate to job performance. Bodies, such as courts, which seek to uphold this ideal cannot expect or be expected to be able to scrutinize all hiring decisions to ensure that this ideal is achieved; instead the judgments of those responsible for hiring are generally respected unless there is evidence of an egregious breach of equality of opportunity, on grounds, for example, of race or sex. No doubt in many hiring cases it will be impossible to say definitively that one candidate is better qualified than another specific candidate, either because those responsible for hiring lack sufficiently nuanced data upon which to make their judgment, or because different candidates have different strengths and weaknesses, meaning that there is no fact of the matter as to which is the most meritorious. This does not mean, however, that there will not be cases in which it is obvious that those responsible for employment decisions have violated the principle of equal opportunity, and, in such cases, we often feel it is appropriate for judicial institutions to intervene.

To be clear, none of this is to deny that comparing opportunity sets between different cultures will often be a problematic business. Given the very real variation we find in different cultures as to the meaning and values of particular social positions, assessing when equality of opportunity is and is not being achieved will be difficult in practice. Gillian Brock, for example, has stressed the dangers involved:

> Either we must articulate a version of equality of opportunity that mentions particular social positions that are favored and opportunities to occupy these positions are equalized, or we allow much cultural variation about what counts as a favored social position and it is now the standards of living or levels of well-being that they enable that are to be equalized. If we go with the first option, we are vulnerable to charges of being insufficiently attuned to cultural difference. If we go with the second and try to equalize standards of living, we may end up with an account of equality of opportunity too weak to rule out disadvantage and discrimination on morally arbitrary grounds.[30]

It is quite right to note that advocates of GEO need to be attentive to these considerations. It is not at all clear, though, that they should lead us to abandon a concern for GEO. A coherent account of GEO will have to

---

[30] Gillian Brock, *Global Justice: A Cosmopolitan Account* (Oxford: Oxford University Press, 2009), 61–62.

be sensitive to the fact that different jobs have different meanings in different cultures, but will also have to have at least some kind of external critical analysis of the value that different positions actually afford to individuals within the culture. This is a familiar problem within political theory. The proliferation of different cultures across the world certainly makes intercultural judgments and comparisons difficult, and it reminds us that we need to take careful account of different cultural understandings. Nevertheless, short of withdrawing into a fully fledged model of cultural relativism, it is unclear what else we can do other than to combine respect for other ways of doing things with an acknowledgment that the mere fact that a culture believes something to be right or good does not automatically make it right or good.

Thus it is not clear that advocates of GEO really do face a dilemma whereby they must either ride roughshod over different cultural understandings or give in to relativism as to the good. There will certainly be difficult questions to be answered when particular cultural traditions seemingly afford a different weight to opportunity sets than that attributed to them by externally derived schedules of capabilities, and any solution is indeed likely to be criticized from the external or internal perspective, if not from both. The challenge for the advocate of GEO is to defend the answer she or he gives to this question – but this is not to say either that the question is unanswerable, or that it emerges in all international comparison of opportunity sets. In particular, we might consider one crude way to track gross inequality between opportunity sets by looking at the extent to which people in one country seek to migrate to other countries.[31] In a world characterized by GEO, where the state where one resides does not make a difference to the value of one's opportunity sets, we would expect that people would want to move in and out of particular states to a roughly equal extent. This is not to say that the presence of such an equilibrium would mean that GEO had been obtained, as there are many reasons why people may not wish to leave the state where they grew up and where most of their family and friends reside, even if they know that by migrating they would have access to superior opportunity sets.[32] However, the absence of such an equilibrium would provide at least prima facie evidence for the claim that opportunity sets are not equal in different communities. There is nothing in such an analysis that involves disrespect for different cultural traditions. The claim is rather that inequality obtains according to the evaluations of the members of the

---

[31] Note that this is not the same as the extent to which people do in fact migrate in the real world, because of the presence of immigration restrictions.

[32] It is for this reason that removing immigration controls would not be sufficient for the realization of GEO. See Kieran Oberman, "Immigration and Freedom of Movement" (Oxford D. Phil. thesis, 2009).

disadvantaged cultures in question. The advocate of GEO should be troubled both by the inequality of opportunity sets that this disequilibrium indicates, and by the extent to which existing immigration controls prevent those living in disadvantaged areas seeking to improve their prospects by relocating.

Finally, although Miller is surely right to note that, in some cases, the immediate intuitive response to cases of deprivation will be grounded in concern for absolute rather than relative levels of well-being, this is not to say that this is the only normatively powerful concern in play in cases of global inequality. The advocate of GEO can insist that inequalities are troubling even when they operate above the threshold level of sufficientarian concern. The point is that for such a person the reaction is overdetermined. GEO advocates need not dismiss sufficientarianism altogether: As Paula Casal has argued, it is possible to maintain that sufficiency thresholds have a part to play in questions of distributive justice without maintaining that they tell the full story of distributive justice.[33] GEO advocates need not deny that the most troubling and pressing problems of distributive justice are those in which individuals lack access to basic resources; their claim is simply that the level of absolute deprivation is not solely constitutive of the situation's injustice, even if it is its most pressing part. It may well be that, in the current world, both sufficientarians and GEO advocates would agree on what measures should be taken in the short term to remedy the world's most serious injustices.

What advocates of GEO should not do is to give up on the idea of equality of opportunity and fall back on sufficientarian accounts that focus on absolute rather than relative disadvantage (bolstered, perhaps, by alternative egalitarian principles, such as that of democratic equality). The advocate of GEO can concede a certain amount to her or his critics without forsaking the deep egalitarian intuition that it is unfair if the place of one's birth makes a difference to how well one's life goes. She or he can accept that addressing the urgent needs of the world's poorest people is the most important task we face. The advocate can accept that this need not rest upon any kind of idea of equality to be normatively compelling, and that we should not pursue equality if such a pursuit in any way involves a trade-off of the interests of those in desperate need. She or he can further accept that perfect GEO is unrealizable in practice, that its practical pursuit will be limited to intervening to prevent the most obvious instances of inequality, and that many of these interventions could, for the foreseeable future, be justified by reference to sufficientarianism. Nonetheless, this advocate should reject vehemently the idea that the achievement of this task would result in a just world order. Many people care desperately about

[33] Paula Casal, "Why Sufficiency Is not Enough," *Ethics* 117 (2007): 296–326.

equality of opportunity at a domestic level, even in affluent states with reasonably well-working welfare states, and find it deeply unjust if, for example, the existence of a two-tier education or health care system means that those who have richer parents have better prospects in life. For the cosmopolitan, such inequalities should be just as troubling on a global level. Pursuing GEO may be more difficult in practice than pursuing its domestic counterpart, but there is nonetheless much that can be done to reduce international inequalities for equality's sake. The difficulty of doing so is not sufficient reason to accept sufficientarianism alone.

IV. COSMOPOLITANISM AND LEGITIMACY

What, then, of Objection 6, which queries the democratic legitimacy of GEO? For those who oppose GEO and seek to uphold noncosmopolitan accounts of international distributive justice, even if they accept sufficientarian duties of assistance, this question is much less problematic. Insofar as they advocate conservative principles of distributive justice, their prescriptive claims typically approximate to contemporary settled norms of international justice, as embodied in international law and mainstream international rhetoric, if not in actual international practice. In this way, it appears as if the justification for their position is backed by both normative argumentation and democratic consensus. The difficult question, then, comes for those who believe that the best philosophical principles of international distributive justice are transformative in nature. What should be done if normative argumentation points in one direction, but popular sentiment in another? This raises two questions:

1. Do international institutions act legitimately in seeking to implement global equality of opportunity?
2. Even if we deem such action to be illegitimate, should international institutions, in an-all-things considered sense, act to implement GEO?

Answering Question 1 negatively does not answer Question 2, because there might be cases in which the injustice of not intervening trumps concerns of legitimacy. This can be seen in relation to interventions to protect basic rights: There is no inconsistency in thinking, for example, that international bodies lack legitimacy in intervening in the affairs of sovereign states in order to uphold such rights, but maintaining that they should nonetheless so intervene. Question 2 might be answered negatively for one of two reasons, either based on the wrongness of illegitimacy, with reference to democratic principle, or on the practical effects of illegitimacy, such as, for example, in relation to the future capacity for intervention of the institution in question. A full consideration of either question largely lies beyond the scope of this chapter. However, as an initial response, the following points may be made.

First, the nature of the international institution in question is clearly significant. We might, for example, separate governmental and nongovernmental institutions, and we might note that particular questions of legitimacy obtain in relation to the former, because they operate, in some sense, at the behest of a demos, or of multiple demoi. This is not to say that no questions of legitimacy arise in relation to the nongovernmental organizations (NGOs); much has been written of the propriety of interventions by Western NGOs in the affairs of less developed countries,[34] and there are also issues relating to how their actions relate to the views of their members and supporters. Nonetheless, there is prima facie plausibility to the idea that NGOs should generally be free to promote GEO, particularly in cases where doing so is in accordance with views of their membership and does not involve unwanted interference.

The case of governmental institutions is more complicated. Is it justifiable for such bodies to base their decisions in politically controversial accounts of justice, which, let us say for the sake of argument, are not endorsed by a majority of their demos? A straightforward populist account of democratic legitimacy would give way on all occasions to the majority, but most accounts are rather more nuanced than this and pay attention to the particular office of the agent charged with decision making – be they elected legislator, appointed judge, bureaucrat, or soldier. For example, Cass Sunstein argues that the rule of law constrains official decision making, and so "tries to prevent people in particular cases from invoking their own theories of the right or the good so as to make decisions according to their own most fundamental judgments."[35] Thus, the rule of law rules off limits "deep ideas of the right or the good," and it holds that such ideas ought not usually be invoked by judges and officials. But the claim that these sorts of agents should not act upon their best understanding of what should be done does not necessarily apply to all decision makers; "we might make distinctions between the role of high theory within the courtroom and the role of high theory in the political branches of government... in democratic arenas, there is no taboo, presumptive or otherwise, on invoking high level theories of the good or the right."[36] If this is accepted then it opens the way to a legitimate pursuit of GEO, at least to international institutions that can claim their own democratic mandate.

[34] See Terry Macdonald, *Global Stakeholder Democracy: Power and Representation Beyond Liberal States* (New York: Oxford University Press, 2008).

[35] Cass Sunstein, *Legal Reasoning and Political Conflict* (Oxford: Oxford University Press, 1996), 44.

[36] Ibid., 45.

The most notable are international legislatures such as the European Parliament, and bodies composed of different actors with their own national mandates, who come to possess legitimacy in an international context when acting collectively.

What, though, of the harder case of international institutions that are appointed by governments, and so are in this sense governmental, but that do not possess their own independent democratic mandates? Take, for example, international courts. It is often maintained that it is legitimate for courts to override majoritarian decision making when majorities threaten individuals' basic rights. However, it is far more controversial to argue that courts should intervene in such a way as to further a contentious principle of distributive justice, such as, for example, egalitarianism. This is not to say that courts should never act in such a way. A striking recent example of a justification for the courts acting in such a manner comes from South Africa, where Chief Justice Pius Langa has argued that the South African courts should be guided by a principle of "transformative constitutionalism" whereby the courts are committed to creating a substantively equal society, defined both in terms of the prevention of discrimination and also, strikingly, the promotion of distributive justice. He speaks explicitly of "the leveling of the economic playing fields that were so drastically skewed by the apartheid system," and he claims that the constitutionally required transformation of South African society "does not only involve the fulfillment of socio-economic rights, but also the provision of greater access to education and opportunities through various mechanisms, including affirmative action measures."[37] It may be noted, however, that the South African context is highly unusual. Langa's defense of transformative constitutionalism rests not solely upon a philosophical defense of egalitarianism, but also on both South Africa's particular political history of apartheid and on the extraordinarily extensive process of public consultation that fed into the new South African constitution. To argue that a judicial institution, without a comparable democratic mandate, should act in such a fashion is certainly controversial.

Two points, then, may be made in relation to the legitimacy of the pursuit of GEO by international institutions that lack their own direct mandate. First, as has already been noted, it may well be that in practice sufficientarians and egalitarians agree as to the first moves that such institutions should be making to secure individuals' most basic needs. We are still a long way from the realization of sufficientarianism, and this creates a window of opportunity for political campaigns to build popular majorities in favor of GEO. It may

[37] Pius N. Langa, "Transformative Constitutionalism," *Stellenbosch Law Review* 17 (2006): 352.

well be that given the philosophically controversial nature of GEO, it will
not be possible to reach a point where support for GEO is consensual in
the same way that is increasingly the case for basic rights claims, but there
is still the potential for an agonistic approach to international democracy,
whereby cosmopolitans seek to win over a sufficient portion of popular opinion
to implement their principles through majoritarian means.[38] In this view,
cosmopolitans should focus on building popular majorities in favor of equal
access to those capabilities such as health care and education that are critical
to GEO. International institutions can legitimately intervene to implement
GEO when backed by popular majorities of this kind.

Second, and potentially more radically, it was previously noted that the
question of the legitimacy of an institutional intervention is not the same
as the question of whether such an intervention is justified.[39] A belief that
a given action is illegitimate does not necessarily lead to the view that that
action should not be fulfilled if legitimacy is seen as a desideratum, rather
than a sine qua non, of institutional action. Thus it would be possible for
an advocate of GEO to accept that furthering GEO is not legitimate but
nonetheless maintain that, in an all-things-considered sense, it ought to take
place. The readiness of such an advocate to argue in this way will depend
upon the amount of weight he or she affords to institutional legitimacy, and in
particular to whether this is seen as intrinsically good for reasons of democratic
principle or simply instrumentally valuable for the achievement of particular
good outcomes. Thus domestically, one might oppose judicial activism on
the grounds that it is wrong for courts to assume a law-making function that
properly belongs to legislatures as a matter of democratic principle, or on the
grounds that courts damage their ability to bring about other good outcomes
by risking losing popular support in acting without legitimacy. The more
critical the interests being served by transformative institutional action, the
more justifiable it is for institutions to disregard public opinion.

It might be noted, by way of conclusion, that we should not assume that
the same considerations that are taken to be compelling in a domestic context
will necessarily apply in an international setting. Questions of legitimacy are
easier to settle in state-centered democracies, where elected officials possess
relatively straightforward mandates from a given demos. To be sure, a host of
problems arise when we try to speak meaningfully of the way in which such a
mandate corresponds realistically to the will of the people given the real-world

[38] Chantal Mouffe, "For an Agonistic Model of Democracy," in Noel O'Sullivan (ed.), *Political Theory in Transition* (London: Routledge, 2000), 113–130.
[39] See A. J. Simmons, "Justification and Legitimacy," in *Justification and Legitimacy: Essays on Rights and Obligations* (Cambridge University Press, 2001), 122–157.

circumstances of contemporary representative democracies, and such reasons may well lead us to query whether illegitimate action is wrong for reasons of democratic principle even in state-centered contexts. According to this perspective, the legitimacy-based concerns facing international institutions are largely pragmatic and prudential in nature. Such problems are amplified in an international context, where law making and governance emerges from a much more complicated process of decision making, involving a wide range of both elected and unelected bodies, with seriously disputed democratic legitimacy.

For many, the value of democracy in real-world contexts lies not in the way it translates the will of the people into public policy, but in the way it authoritatively settles the question of who should wield political power. From such a perspective, domestic illegitimacy may be problematic in a way that does not arise in the same fashion in an international context. An international institution that seeks to further GEO may be going against public opinion, but this does not threaten to challenge or undermine socially beneficial democratic institutions in the same way that similar action could in the domestic sphere. It may still be that reasons of prudence and pragmatism may counsel institutions against the promotion of GEO – but the point here would not necessarily be that such action would be illegitimate and thus wrong, but rather that bad outcomes would result from a popular perception that the institution in question was acting illegitimately. Such a judgment would obviously be particular to the case in question, and it leaves open the possibility of a conclusion that given institutions should indeed, in an all-things-considered sense, promote global equality of opportunity.

3 Human Persons, Human Rights, and the Distributive Structure of Global Justice

Robert C. Hockett

INTRODUCTION

Let us start with an example:[1] Beatrice and Benedict each have enough resources to subsist upon. "Global society" has an additional three units at its disposal of what we can call "benefit stuff" – resources available to direct toward Beatrice and Benedict.[2] Let us assume that Benedict derives marginally more utility from benefit stuff than does Beatrice, until he has received two units.[3] Thereafter, Beatrice receives marginally more utility from benefit stuff than does Benedict. If we are utilitarians and accordingly wish to maximize feasible global utility under the circumstances, we will give the first two available units of benefit stuff to Benedict and then give the final available unit to Beatrice.

Call the benefits, *after* they are distributed in this way, "aggregate-maximizing" units, or "maximizers."[4] Call the benefits, *prior* to distribution,

---

[1] We can also render it more abstract and formal. A summary rendition of this kind is provided in note 9.

[2] These units could be money or some other resource transformable into utility such as wealth and opportunities more generally.

[3] I rescind worries about interpersonal comparability here, as do utilitarians themselves.

[4] They are accordingly characterized not just in terms of their ex ante material attributes but in terms of their aggregate ex post utility effects when distributed over a given population of individuals. These effects, that is to say, are internal to, or constitutive of, the things as thus

Thank you to Matt Adler, Kaushik Basu, Jagdish Bhagwati, Brian Bix, Robin Boadway, Kevin Clermont, Mike Dorf, Dan Farber, Marc Fleurbaey, Frank Garcia, Alon Harel, Aristides Hatzis, John Linarelli, Jerry Mashaw, Trevor Morrison, Eduardo Peñalver, Jeff Rachlinski, John Roemer, Larry Solum, Alexander Somek, Chantal Thomas, and Joel Trachtman. Thanks especially to Frank Garcia, John Linarelli, and Chi Carmody for organizing the November 2008 American Society of International Law Symposium on Global Justice and International Economic Law, held at the Tillar House in Washington, D.C., and inviting this contribution to it. Particular thanks go to Lindita Ciko of the Boston College Law School for significant editorial assistance in preparing this chapter for publication.

"generic benefit" units. Then there are three or even four distinct ways to characterize the aforementioned distribution:[5] We can say that we have maximized global utility. We can say we have distributed generic benefit units unequally ex ante, two to one in favor of Benedict over Beatrice. Alternatively, we can say we have distributed aggregate-maximizing units equally ex post over Beatrice and Benedict, and in that sense treated Beatrice and Benedict, whom we take for no more than their utility functions, as equals. In sum, we have distributed benefits unequally in a manner that treats Beatrice and Benedict as equals in respect of the utility functions with which we identify them – though in no other respect.[6] In so doing we have maximized aggregate global utility.

There is thus an intertranslatability between maximization, distribution, equalization, and identification formulations, because maximization language and formulae tend to lead us toward *thinking* in terms of maximization.[7] In addition, speaking *exclusively* in such terms leads us to thinking exclusively in those terms as well.[8] We are apt to lose sight of the fact that in maximizing we are also distributing, and likewise in distributing we are equalizing some things while "disequalizing" other things over our fellow persons. Then we are apt not to notice that we are reducing those fellow persons to some single attribute of themselves – for example, their utility functions – in respect of which we exclusively maximize.[9]

---

individuated. Thank you to Matt Adler and Jeff Rachlinski for pushing me to make this point more clearly. I hope I have succeeded.

[5] There are three ways if we *assimilate* equalization to identification, or four ways if we attend to these as distinct characterizations in their own rights.

[6] The "in no other respect" qualifier proves important for reasons that emerge presently.

[7] They bear, to employ the increasingly popular idiom, "framing effects."

[8] You likely know the word "maximandum" or its elliptical rendition, "maximand." Do you know the words "equalisandum" or "equalisand"? They are in the same dictionaries as their maximizing counterparts.

[9] Here is a summary rendition of the point in formal terms: Maximization imperatives typically are expressed as injunctions to "Max" the global aggregate of something called "W," the aggregate measure of which varies with something experienced by individuals called "u." W is accordingly, in the typical case, said to be a "function" of individuals' summed u-measures. Hence $W = W(u_1, u_2, u_3, \ldots um)$, where the numeric subscripts index the u-functions of the m individuals who constitute the citizenry. And the imperative is to Max $W = \sum ui$, where the Greek letter sigma indicates that we are summing, and the "i" subscript indicates that we are to count each individual i's u-measure in the sum. (This summing of course requires interpersonal comparability to take into account for differences among persons are both partly causative of their differential faring and yet "arbitrary from a moral point of view.")

Each individual's u-measure, in turn, is itself typically viewed as a function of benefits and burdens received or experienced by, hence distributed to, the individual. So for each individual i, $ui = ui(b_1, b_2, \ldots bn)$, meaning simply that the individual's u-measure is a function of a vector (or "basket") of n distinct benefits and burdens. (A positive function of the former, and a negative function of the latter. Comparative contributions and detractions made by distinct b's to the

These potential blind spots present us with a normative problem. The tendency to cast transnational legal and policy inquiry exclusively in maximizing terms is potentially problematic, first because it is as individuals – as recipients of distributions of various kinds – that our fellow persons engage our collective concern in the first place. Second, this tendency is problematic because most of us wish to accord one another *equal* concern of some appropriate type – a type keyed to some politically appropriate conception of who or what we are – in our always inherently distributive transnational legal and policy decisions. We would do well, then, to crack open our "maximization-speak" and maximization formulae systematically, in order to lay bare their inherently distributive, equalizing, and ultimately individual-characterizing internal structures. Moreover, once we have done the dismantling and then turn to querying how we ought, if at all, to amend or restructure our formulations in light of what we find, we should adopt a policy of addressing the maximization, distribution, equalization, and individual-characterization components of the inquiry in reverse order.[10] There is a critical sense in which the question of what we take ourselves to be for transnational legal and policy purposes is normatively prior to the others.[11] However, none of this is fully transparent until we open the internal structures of our maximization norms to systematic inspection.

u-measure of course imply commensurability, hence something like "price ratios," among the b's.) W is accordingly, in the final analysis, a composite function $W \circ ui \circ bj$, or $W(ui(bj))$, meaning that W is a function of aggregated u-measures, which are themselves functions of aggregated b-measures.

A quick formal way of putting the points made over the previous few pages, then, is that maximizing W generally entails distributing b's to individuals i, who are "counted" and treated as equals for policy purposes solely in virtue of their u-functions.

[10] Thank you to Trevor Morrison for suggesting that I emphasize this point.

[11] Why? In short, because our principal care is what we are and whether we are treated accordingly. Plausible answers to the question in what respects we are properly regarded as equals then proceed immediately from answers to the identification question. Plausible answers to the question of what ought to be distributed in what patterns and measures, in turn, proceed at once from our answers to the equalization question. In turn, the appropriate form of maximization takes care of itself: Distribute the right things to the right people in the right measures, and you will have maximized that which it makes sense to maximize.

Note also that many of those who seem most wedded to maximization formulae seem ironically if nevertheless unwittingly to be logically committed to precisely this claim. The so-called individualist global welfare functions they champion acquire whatever intuitive attraction they carry from an inarticulate understanding that it is by reference to the individuals who constitute it that a society fares well. Where the articulation peters out for these people is at the point where we note that there are *many* different *respects* in virtue of which individuals can be individuated for transnational legal and policy purposes, some of which are normatively arbitrary and others of which are not. The term "individualism" used in connection with global welfare functions appears to originate with Paul Samuelson, *Foundations of Economic Analysis* (Cambridge, MA: Harvard University Press, 1948), 310–334.

To attend systematically to the internal structure of maximization language and maximization formulae, I shall argue, is a way to "take distribution seriously."[12] This means to *frame and thus aim our attention* correctly in law and policy evaluation. It is ultimately a way of taking our fellows more seriously when we are engaged in those forms of evaluative activity. It is therefore also a way of taking ourselves more seriously, both as co-persons and as mutually responsible transnational legal and moral agents, when working to ascertain what we ought to be doing collectively.

The aim of this chapter is to lay out what it might look like to take distribution seriously in normatively oriented transnational legal and policy analysis.[13] This would afford a means of bringing systematic moral-conceptual clarity to transnational legal and policy analysis bearing normatively assessable distributive import. The key is to focus on what I call "distributive structure," the structure that is manifest not only in all fully analyzed global welfare functions but also in the grammar of a less formal distributive language itself. I shall accordingly be attending to both.

The remainder of the chapter proceeds as follows: Section I preliminarily characterizes the conditions under which a normative distributional assessment is called for. These are the circumstances under which "who holds what" can intelligibly be, and thus ethically ought to be, evaluated as globally right, wrong, better, or worse. Though these conditions are foundational and ought to be evident, their brief enumeration serves both to ground, and to facilitate fuller assimilation of, the more detailed discussion that follows. They also appear to be often forgotten in much of the theoretical literature.

Section II then systematically examines five classes of questions to which transnational law and policy-bearing distributive consequences potentially give rise. These classes of questions jointly constitute what I am calling a

---

[12] Ronald M. Dworkin, *Taking Rights Seriously* (Cambridge, MA: Harvard University Press, 1977). Others on whose shoulders I would be standing include Richard Crasswell, "Taking Information Seriously: Misrepresentation and Disclosure in Contract Law and Elsewhere," *Virginia Law Review* 92 (2006): 565; Jon D. Hanson and Douglas A. Kysar, "Taking Behavioralism Seriously: The Problem of Market Manipulation," *New York University Law Review* 74 (2000): 45; Daniel Farber, "Taking Slippage Seriously," *Harvard Environmental Law Review* 23 (1999): 1; George A. Berman, "Taking Subsidiarity Seriously: Federalism in the European Union and the United States," *Columbia Law Review* 94 (1994): 1; and Michael Bratman, "Taking Plans Seriously," *Social Theory & Practice* 9 (1983): 271. More waggish forays include Mark Kelman, "Taking Takings Seriously: An Essay for Centrists," *California Law Review* 74 (1986): 1829; William E. Forbath, "Taking Lefts Seriously," *Yale Law Journal* 92 (1983): 1041; David A. J. Richards, "Taking Taking Rights Seriously Seriously," *New York University Law Review* 52 (1977): 1265.

[13] And hence, among other things, what an ethically intelligible welfare or economic analysis of law might look like.

"distributive structure." They also prove neatly tractable by reference to what linguists will recognize as the cognitive grammar of "to distribute" and cognate infinitives – verbs such as "to allocate," "to apportion," "to mete out," and so on.[14] The gaps opened up by this grammar – in effect, "variables" for those who distribute, those to whom they distribute, what they distribute, per what pattern, and by what means they distribute – afford helpful bearings for purposes of systematically structuring simultaneous attention to the *full range* of normative questions that legally determined distribution invariably implicates. It is precisely this form of plenary attention that I believe we must now make a practice of employing, if we are to avoid so-called framing blind spots of the kind over which I have been raising red flags.[15]

Section III then shows how readily the conception of appropriate distribution (hence identification, equalization, and maximization) derived in Section II lends itself to practical realizability, in view of transnational legal and institutional design considerations on the one hand and correlative feasibility constraints on the other. Indeed, as this section shows, the correct conception of appropriate distribution looks to be much more readily realizable than are its chief competitors – welfare and wealth-maximizing views on the one hand and prioritarian views such as "maximizing" Rawlsian justice theory on the other. Moreover, much if not most of our law and the principles that animate it prove to be best interpreted as aimed at vindicating the distributive ethic upon which the lines of Section II converge. That bears obvious practical consequences for transnational legal interpretation on the bench as well as for future law making in the legislatures. It also bears critical theoretic consequences for those who debate the comparative merits of "law and economics," "welfarism," "Rawlsianism," and competing normative approaches to law and transnational legal theory.

Not surprisingly, then, I conclude the chapter with some suggestions as to its implications for the future agendas of a more ethically intelligible, as well as more conceptually and formally rigorous, mode of transnational legal and policy analysis.

---

[14] More on this grammar is given in Section II. It should not be surprising, on reflection, that the structure of distribution would be mirrored in the language in which we communicate about it.

[15] One might draw an analogy here to the general equilibrium analysis favored by more sophisticated economic theorists. The founding idea in both that case and this is that when items figuring into analysis are interdependent and in that sense constitute a system, the system itself is the appropriate unit of analysis. In the present case the system in question is the set of variables carried by "to distribute" and cognate infinitives, all of which must be filled before a distributive claim can be determinate, and each of which must be filled in a manner compatible with the manners in which the others are filled.

I. GLOBAL DISTRIBUTIVE CIRCUMSTANCES

Normatively evaluable transnational *legal* arrangements and public policies have the effect of distributing not simply tables and chairs over floors, but perceived goods and ills over persons. Transnational legal rules and rulings, statutory enactments, government programs, and policies of various sorts all tend to yield so-called winners and losers – recipients of benefits and burdens at the receiving end. Patterns of policy-wrought wins and losses amount, relative to each status quo ante they displace, to redistributions of perceived goods and ills. These redistributions, like each status quo ante they supplant, are subject to normative critique because they implicate the ethical propriety of how we are treated.

The minimal conditions for a distributive-ethical assessment to be apt are these: First, there must be things that *can* be variably distributed or "distribuenda." Second, there must be beings to whom these things can be distributed, "distribuees." Third, those to whom things can be distributed must hold *preferences* or *interests* in respect of their receiving or not receiving them: The items must be regarded as beneficial or burdensome by their prospective recipients. Fourth, the recipients of items who hold preferences or interests in respect of the same must hold transnational legal or ethical *claims to our regard*. They must be entitled to our consideration of their preferences or interests as we distribute. We for our part must reciprocally be under obligation to consider the claimants' preferences or interests. It is this entitlement and its correlative obligation that render our assessment of distributions to the preference or interest holders normative, or ethical, in nature. It means we are dealing with rights held by the distribuees.

Fifth, all items the distribution of which would be subject to ethical assessment must be scarce: There must be potential for interests or preferences to diverge or conflict. Distributions to some subclass of the full class of claimants must entail the nonsatisfaction of another subclass of claimants' preferences. This prerequisite, combined with the previous one, entails a need for adjudication in order to balance the distribuees' potentially conflicting rights-claims against one another.

II. GLOBAL DISTRIBUTIVE STRUCTURE

To take distribution seriously in normative transnational legal and policy analysis, we do well to attend to distributive structure, as tracked by the grammar in which it is manifest.

A. *Global Distributors*

Law and policy typically bear distributive consequences. That means that those who enact and then act upon law and policy effectively distribute things. In a derivative sense, so do or would do those who assess or evaluate law and policy. In the act of assessing or evaluating laws and policies bearing distributive consequences, one says in effect how she or he would distribute.

The distributors are "the people" – the citizenry or humanity at large, all who bear rights to take part in deciding what is right from the standpoint of distribution. Conversely, they are "the policy community" – judges, legislators, advocates, analysts, academics, and others assumed to be thinking and acting on behalf of that broader constituency. The latter constituency in such case includes us as its proxies or representative members. In either case, then, we are effectively distributing over ourselves so far as transnational legal and policy debates are concerned. Thus, the class of distributors, particularly in modern polities, typically converges with that of distribuees.

B. *Global Distribuees*

Where there are distributions, there are distribuees. Just as there must be a "fit" between our distributive-ethical norms and how we characterize distributors, so too must there be fit between those norms and how we characterize the distribuees whose rights those norms vindicate. How, then, do we or should we construe the recipients of distributed benefits and burdens? How should we characterize or identify them, and what should we take them to be?

The fact that "they" are in fact "we" here affords us a critical clue: Our being the distributors, and our being accordingly *responsible* in the final analysis for the distribution that concerns us, says something important about us as distribuees. Curiously, however, not everyone seems to have caught the hint. Many transnational legal and policy theorists and analysts effectively commit themselves to a view of distribuees that conflicts with the view that their likewise being distributors would seem to entail. It is tempting to hope we might end this conflict simply by bringing it to light. I will begin with the gradually emerging consensus view of distribuees – the one on which most people seem to agree when the question of how to construe them is explicit. Then I turn to the view that is implicitly held only when analysts fail to examine the presuppositions to which their proffered distribuenda and distribution formulae effectively commit them.

1. Responsible Agents

The gradually emergent consensus view of distribuees among those who concern themselves explicitly with the ethics of distribution is that which is in harmony with their simultaneous role as the would-be distributors. In this view distribuees are best considered "boundedly responsible agents."

Boundedly responsible agents largely, though not completely, determine their own well-being. Nonetheless, boundedly responsible agents also are constrained, to not fully determinable degree, in affecting their welfare by the environments into which they are born. That is what "boundedness" means in this context. Our inherited capacities, incapacities, advantages, and disadvantages – themselves features of our environments – permit us wide, and yet limited, latitude in altering or exiting our environments. We experience ourselves and others both as freely choosing and as constrained to a vaguely determinable degree in the choosing. That experience is reflected in our capacities to experience guilt, shame, ambition for and frustration with self, and resentment of and gratitude to others. It is also reflected in cognate "reactive attitudes" we often experience, attitudes that are intelligible only under conditions of relative freedom

The construal of distribuees as boundedly responsible agents carries a cluster of interlinked consequences for normative distributional assessment: First, to the degree that distribuees can choose freely, they are responsible for what they choose. This is not merely a matter of punitive attitude, nor even of incentives-sensitive productive efficiency, though of course such considerations can sensibly underwrite the view. It is, more compellingly, a matter of human dignity and respect. It is part of what it is to view persons as agents – as practical forgers of fate – rather than simply as patients or addicts – mere passive objects of fate, akin to children who "do not know any better" or "couldn't help it."[16] Second, an often-ignored corollary of this form of respect is the imperative that all agents be viewed as *equally* dignified and *equally* deserving of most forms of respect.

Another consequence that stems analytically from the view of distribuees as boundedly responsible agents is this: To the degree that we hold

---

[16] It is tempting to suppose that some such commitment is what ultimately underwrites the Kantian idea of a "right to punishment," as P. S. Greenspan does in "Responsible Psychopaths" (available at http://www.philosophy.umd.edu/Faculty/PGreenspan/Res/rp.html; accessed December 28, 2009). Another example is Randy E. Barnett and John Hagel III's "Assessing the Criminal: Restitution, Retribution and the Transnational Legal Process" (available at http://www.randybarnett.com/assessing_the_criminal_.html; accessed December 28, 2009).

agent-distribuees largely responsible for authoring their own lives, we com-mit ourselves to those conceptions of appropriate distribuenda, distribution formulae, and distribution mechanisms that give latitude to the operation of responsible agency. Appropriate distribuenda will be conceived as ex ante inputs to individual welfare or utility functions. Appropriate distribution for-mulae, for their part, will speak to the ex ante distribution of such responsibility-exogenous inputs. Our formulae will not be directly concerned with ex post, responsibility-endogenous welfare outcomes as such. Instead they will treat these as by-products, mediated and endogenized by distribuees' responsible agency as brought to bear in transforming resource and opportunity inputs into deserved, because individually produced, welfare outputs. Preferred distribu-tion mechanisms, in turn, will accordingly be those that give most effective expression to these ideals.

2. Patients and Addicts

The residuum left by incomplete agency – the "boundedness" portion – might be called "patienthood." To the degree that one *really* "cannot help himself," he or she is a patient – an object of fate or of others, acted upon rather than acting. Or he or she is an addict – one who quite literally "cannot resist."[17]

To the degree that our agency is bounded, we are all patients. We may feel disgust or contempt for those who are too quick to admit limitation. Because of this, along with the indeterminacy of the boundary between choice and chance in the many borderline cases each of us experiences each day, we tend generally to let the boundary take care of itself.

Because welfare or utility draw attention to outputs rather than inputs, for example, it is difficult, absent a Byzantine distribution formula, to be unambiguously welfarist or utilitarian without effectively treating distribuees as not being responsible for outcomes – hence as patients. Similarly, because resources and wealth are readily viewed as welfare inputs – inputs to distribuees' welfare functions – advocates of ex post egalitarian resource or wealth distribu-tion even apart from the working of distribuees' responsible choices likewise treat distribuees effectively as patients.

---

[17] I intend "patient" as used here, like "agent" before, in its grammatical sense – as the recip-ient of rather than the initiator of an action. John Lyons, *An Introduction to Theoretical Linguistics* (Cambridge: Cambridge University Press, 1968), 350; Bernard Comrie, *Language Universals and Linguistic Typology: Syntax and Morphology*, 2nd ed. (Chicago: University of Chicago Press, 1989), 42–43, 58–61; Ronald Dworkin, *Sovereign Virtue: The Theory and Practice of Equality* (Cambridge, MA: Harvard University Press, 2000), 303 ("addicts"); Daniel Markovits, "How Much Redistribution Should There Be?," *Yale Law Journal* 112 (2003): 2295 ("patients").

Finally, insofar as any distribution mechanism might fully instantiate some distribution principle such as that just mentioned, it too treats distribuees as mere patients.[18] Insofar as it *fails* to be egalitarian *prior* to or *apart* from the operation of distribuees' responsible choices, by the same token, it violates ethical equality and respect for agency. It does so by effectively treating some distribuees as deserving of less than others even when what is being considered is prechoice, action-antecedent claims to material opportunity upon which action and choice are to operate.

C. Global Distribuenda

In addition to the subjects and indirect objects that implicate distributors and distribuees, distribution and its infinitives take direct objects as well. There are always distribuenda – distributed things.

1. Welfare or Well-Being

A particularly venerable family of proffered distribuenda have gone by such names as "utility," "welfare," "well-being," "happiness," "satisfaction," and cognate expressions. Although there are subtle distinctions from one author to the next in construing the terms, all of the terms share distinct family resemblances rooted in one guiding idea: Faring well is what matters to people. Indeed this is trivially so, in view of the meanings of words such as "good" and its adverbial form, "well." Indeed these terms, like "utility," "satisfaction," "happiness," and related terms of art, are often *defined* as being simply what ever is effectively "produced" by people's being satisfied. Law and policy, then, or so this line of thinking concludes, should aim at enhancing these magnitudes, for to do so is simply to satisfy people.

Nothing as yet is implied here as to what such "enhancing" or "satisfying" would look like. Things remain pitched at a high level of abstraction. Attending to welfare and cognates as thus counseled accordingly seems unobjectionable – again, trivially so. One might then wonder why anyone would propose anything *other* than welfare as distribuendum. I think what is objected to is not welfare as abstract normative distributional touchstone; rather, what people protest is either (a) "welfare" as construed by some of its more eccentric or irresponsible advocates;[19] (b) related to the first objection, welfare as mere output that is

---

[18] This prospect of course suggests that distribution mechanisms might be composite in nature: Market allocations followed by taxation and redistribution would constitute a familiar case in point. The suggestion is borne out in Section III.

[19] One such group is utilitarians, for example. See Louis Kaplow and Steven Shavell, *Fairness versus Welfare* (Cambridge, MA: Harvard University Press, 2002), 421–422 ("The idea of an

aggregated and globally "maximized," without regard to the way in which it is produced;[20] or (c) welfare as literal, direct distribuendum.[21]

2. Resources or Wealth

The principal competitors to welfare as proposed distribuendum have histori-cally been material resources or wealth of one sort or another. The simplest and most abstract characterization is simply as *wealth* – some index-tied medium of exchange or scalar "stuff" that recipients can transform into the welfare purchasing and consuming of more variegated goods and services.[22] More complex and concretely particularized characterizations include Rawlsian "primary goods," among others.[23]

The advantages and disadvantages of resources as prospective distribuenda can be viewed as the inverse image of the disadvantages and advantages of

analyst substituting his or her own conception of what individuals should value for the actual views of the individuals themselves conflicts with individuals' basic autonomy and freedom.") The short answer is that imprisonment, too, "conflicts" with basic autonomy and freedom – that of convicts. Few, if any, disapprove of autonomy and freedom, just as few disapprove of welfare or well-being. However, the question has always been how we are to demarcate individuals' *legitimate* spheres of autonomy satisfactorily, and that question of satisfactory demarcation is part of the question of fair allocation. The "we don't want to judge" disclaimer accordingly avails nothing. Determining fair allocation is judging, period. All law and policy require such determinations. Use of the ethically loaded terms "welfare" or "well-being" rather than less deck-stacking terms such as "preference satisfaction," moreover, registers precisely such judgment.

[20] Non-construal-based objections to welfare as distribuendum are rooted in the fact that welfare is not a directly measurable or distributable substance. The physical distribution problem is the most immediately apparent. Whether understood as endorphins, preference satisfactions, idealized or fully informed or ethically laundered preference satisfactions, welfare just is not directly doled out. It is, rather, at best "produced" by distribuees, from physical things that are doled out.

[21] There are also familiar measurability concerns occasioned by welfare as proposed distribuen-dum: On most present-day construals, welfare lends itself no more to practicable quantifiability or interpersonal comparability in the holding than it does to direct distributability. Commensu-rability is the one measurement task for which welfare does not present difficulties, because in theory it serves as a numéraire in terms of which more concrete items might be comparatively valued. The trouble, of course, is that in view of its unamenability to actual quantification or interpersonal comparison, it can serve as numéraire *only* in theory. It is of no *practical* use at all.

[22] These include risk-bearing services, the fuller significance of which emerges in the Rawlsian Justice subsection of Section III. This rough characterization of wealth, incidentally, is cognate with but not identical to that offered by Posner in the 1980s, as discussed in Mechanisms, Laws, and Governments subsection. A suitable synonym for my usage would be "purchasing power."

[23] John Rawls, *A Theory of Justice*, rev. ed. (Cambridge, MA: Harvard University Press, 1999), 54–55, 78–81, 358–365; J. Rawls, *The Law of Peoples* (Cambridge, MA: Harvard University Press, 2000). I prescind from those complexities here. They are not germane to present purposes and bracketing them accordingly does no harm. Fuller discussion is found in Robert Hockett and Mathias Risse, "Primary Goods Revisited" (under revision for *Economics & Philosophy*).

welfare. First, as for advantages, resources are directly distributable. Second, they are readily measurable, at least in respect of simple quantification and interpersonal comparability in the holding. Third, they provide space for the working of distribuees' at least partial responsibilities for affecting their own well-being: What satisfactions distribuees enjoy will ride partly upon what they *do* with their resource allotments. That seems to most people both ethically right and, in terms of incentives, efficient.

The disadvantages of resources as a distribuendum are straightforward functions of the degree to which considerations of the propriety of their spread are detached from considerations of welfare. Where the severance is complete and entire, resourcism devolves into fetishism. In such case the stuff that is spread is best viewed as – though surprisingly not observed in the literature to be – not even so much as *cognizable* as "resource," "wealth," or the like.

3. Opportunity or Access

One perceived difficulty attending resources as proposed ditribuenda is a counterpart to the objectionable preference problem attending many construals of welfare. It has in consequence occasioned a distribuendum candidate that differs in the articulation, but at bottom amounts to a mere fuller naming, of resources.[24] Because welfare, or "advantage," is what matters to people, material stuff in itself is not ethically salient. Moreover, because material resources are variegated and accordingly in need of commensuration if they are to be spread under one distribution formula, some common denominator is required: That is again welfare, or advantage. Accordingly, the item whose spread can intelligibly engage our distributive-ethical concern or assessment, even if material in nature, must be understood as "opportunity for welfare," or "access to advantage."[25]

---

[24] The difficulty was just flagged: It is the danger of fetishism. The sense in which it is counterpart to objectionable preferences in welfare construal is this: The danger that afflicts welfare is that *all* preferences – even admittedly antiethical ones – might illicitly be counted, when satisfied, as affording normatively cognizable "welfare." The danger that afflicts resources is at the other extreme: It is that *no* preferences will be considered when labeling ethically inert, nonvalued substances as "resources." "Resource," like "welfare," is an ineluctably value-laden term. It is worth noting that "resource" is subject to objectionable overinclusive construal as well, just as "welfare" is subject to objectionable underinclusive construal: Just as it is philistine to treat welfare as solely hedonic, it is grotesque to claim that all things the possession of which might afford pleasure can be counted as "resources." Slaveholders and some husband seem often to have viewed human beings in this way, for example.

[25] R. J. Arneson, "Equality and Equal Opportunity for Welfare," *Philosophical Studies* 56 (1989): 77; R. J. Arneson, "Liberalism, Distributive Subjectivism, and Equal Opportunity for Welfare," *Philosophy & Public Affairs* 19 (1990): 158–194; Cohen, "On the Currency of Egalitarian Justice," 906. An analogue in the case of welfare would be someone's suggesting we use

III. GLOBAL DISTRIBUTION MECHANISMS

In turning to distribution mechanisms we move from *grundnorms* to specifically transnational legal norms – the stuff of statutes, regulations, and judicial decisions. One might imagine many means by which to effect distributions of benefit and burden. Such means might be specified, in turn, at varying levels of abstraction. The possibilities here run from the microdetailed description of existing institutions on up to the quite broadly schematized, variably instantiable designs contemplated in axiomatic mechanism theory.[26] Surprisingly, most normatively oriented transnational legal and policy analysts have been quiet on the subject of feasible distribution mechanisms. That is regrettable for at least two reasons. For one thing, "can" limits "ought," as is commonly recognized. Hence "ought" claims that *ignore* "can" limitations risk being merely idle. For another thing, *some* "cans" render *some* "oughts" particularly attractive. They do so not merely by rendering option menus more manageable by means of elimination of nonfeasible alternatives. They do so also by highlighting ways we can sidestep even some theoretic conundrums, as I shall demonstrate.

One distribution mechanism that I shall specify appears to fit the most acceptable conceptions discussed in Section II of distributor, distribuendum, distribuee, and distribution formula very gracefully and, as it happens, uniquely. That renders those conceptions more attractive on feasibility grounds, of course. But it also does more than that. The process of schematizing and justifying this mechanism further illuminates why those conceptions are independently attractive in the first place.

A. *Mechanisms, Laws, and Governments*

Most who speak normatively in respect of distributive questions take the following for granted: First, that most of the material things that matter to people – "resources" or "material opportunities" – are distributed by various forms of private bequest and exchange. Second, that the latter presuppose antecedently defined private law rights sounding in civil obligation – property, contract, and

"ethically compatible preferences" instead. Just as the term "welfare" already connotes such conditions (in contrast to "satisfaction" or "utility"), the word "resources," I am claiming, already connotes the conditions I note here.

[26] L. Billera and R. Bixby, "A Characterization of Pareto Surfaces," *Proceedings of the American Mathematical Society* 41 (1973): 261; E. Kalai and M. Smorodinsky, "Other Solutions to Nash's Bargaining Problem," *Econometrica* 43 (1975): 513.

tort – that are vindicable in courts. Third and finally, that these rights are in turn subject to occasional amendment or alteration by centralized legislative action. Things seldom grow more finely grained than this.[27]

1. All Dressed Up with No Place To Go: Utilitarianism

Consider first utilitarianism – that is, naïve welfare maximization. Collecting the information assembled in Section II, we know that a utilitarian polity will wish to aggregate its patient-distribuees' unweighted welfare outputs and maximize the resultant sum. It will, moreover, be willing to do so by any means necessary. The utility aggregate is the sole normative touchstone guiding utilitarian policy, both as a matter of personal and of political morality.

But now consider the following. First, in view of the difficulties noted in Section II to afflict direct welfare measurement, it is indeterminate what means *would* suffice or be necessary. If you cannot know when utility is maximized, can you know what to do in order to maximize it? Notwithstanding that inconvenient question, the utilitarian will regard a high degree of centralized government action as warranted and probably even required. She or he will consider such authority to be necessary both for the regular collection of utility data and for the regular redistribution of holdings to maintain a maximal aggregate utility reading. She or he will also take the utilitarian planner to be unconstrained by any rights held antecedently by persons.[28] The latter are utility factories, not autonomous rights-bearing agents.

What is one to make of so dystopian and incoherent a picture? A government stunningly empowered in principle, which for theoretical reasons nevertheless literally could not actually perform the function upon which that surprising degree of power is predicated: It is all dressed up with no place to go. In view of such difficulties as these, which are not merely about implementation but are also foundational, utilitarianism looks to be a nonstarter where determinate distributive-ethical prescribing is concerned. Its noninstantiability does not point toward a so-called second best. Rather, the *reasons* why it cannot be implemented reveal a sense in which it is not even a merely accidentally nonimplementable first best – or even so much as a specified "good": It is

---

[27] For example, not one of the sources cited herein describes or prescribes any distribution mechanism in more detail than just sketched.

[28] This is not even to mention redistribution's effects on effort expense, hence goods and services production, and hence the size of the utility aggregate itself. In view of utility's functioning as a fetish, incidentally, the need of an extensive governmental apparatus should not be surprising. In effect, the utility aggregate is a contemporary analogue to the pyramids of Egypt and the ziggurats of Mesopotamia and Mesoamerica. Societies organized around such monistic and inhuman pursuits have historically been both theocratic and autocratic.

prescriptively sterile or stillborn au fond, a fact that its advocates have sought to conceal by leaving the mechanism variable unvalued.

2. More Tastefully Dressed but Still No Destination: Rawlsian Justice

Observations reminiscent of those made in connection with utilitarianism hold for Rawlsian justice theory as well. Rawls himself was refreshingly candid about this. He admitted that his concern was solely with what he called "the basic structure" of a just society. The problem, alas, is that the structure he seems to have had in mind is so basic that we do not know what Rawlsian principles have to say about matters as basic as a society's constitutional order itself, let alone subsequent legislation and private law doctrine.

Rawls left such matters for what he called "later stages" of polity constitution, with which his work was said not to be immediately concerned. There seems to have been a rough expectation that there would be property rights and market exchange.[29] We are accordingly left to wonder how Rawls's principles might so much as even begin to be operationalized. This raises a worry that the principles as articulated impart no determinate prescriptive information. Note further that this is a worry that had already arisen earlier, in connection with the indeterminacy of "the worst off class" in Rawls's prescribed distribution formula.

As in the case of utilitarianism, then, here we find that the lack of attention paid to questions of mechanism do not simply leave implementation and "second best" questions unanswered: Rawls allows even the matter of "first bests" to remain undetectably underspecified. We are left wondering whether there is any "here" here. The theory so underdetermines its own implementation that we do not know what to make of the theory itself – or, perhaps better put, what to make *with* it. How much is it actually telling us if it is equally realizable in any number of possible polities with radically divergent property, tort, contract, and other transnational legal arrangements? Put differently, how do we recognize a Rawlsian society upon seeing one?

3. Locally Determinate, Globally Indeterminate Prescription: Normative "Law and Economics"

The only serious mechanism-proposals one finds in the distribution-concerned transnational legal and policy literatures is that of normative economists of law.[30] Unlike utilitarians and Rawlsians, these analysts attend carefully to

---

[29] Rawls, *A Theory of Justice*, 52.

[30] That is, these are practitioners of normative "law and economics." For another mechanism, refer to Robert Hockett, "Human Persons, Human Rights, and the Distributive Structure of Global Justice," 40 COLUM. HUM. RTS. L. REV. 343, 404 (2009).

micro-institutional detail. Indeed, their bailiwick is precisely the Kaldor–Hicksian wealth-aggregate effects wrought by alternative choices available at the simplest unit of institutional structure – the rule. Nevertheless, by what might at first blush seem a curious irony, this is precisely their undoing from a distribution mechanism point of view. The problem stems ultimately from a gap between macro-objective and microdetail akin to that which I have just noted in Rawls.[31]

The foundational mechanism problem for mainstream economics of law is rooted in a fallacy of composition: Suppose that each of n rules $Ra/1$, $Ra/2$, ..., Ra/n tends, within the confines of its particular domain 1, 2, ..., or n, to be wealth maximizing in comparison to its envisaged competitors b, c, d, and so on in that domain.[32] It does not follow from this that the full vector of rules $Ra/1$, ..., Ra/n will be wealth maximizing as compared, say, to some other vector $Rb/1$, ..., Rb/n that would come to the theorist's mind only were he or she to contemplate a fuller institutional backdrop. The latter is a backdrop that simply is not on the agenda when all that is being asked is which of $Ra/1$, $Rb/1$, ..., $Rm/1$ is wealth maximizing in domain 1 considered in isolation. And this is what practitioners of normative economics of law do: They consider domains one at a time, without reference to other domains or to interactions between domains.

Realistically speaking, choices in nominally distinct domains 1, ..., n cannot reasonably be expected to be linearly independent, as any student of general equilibrium theory – or, for that matter, of the proverbial "seamless web of the law" – will recognize.[33] Rules within one domain will affect the distributive consequences wrought by rules in other domains. It will accordingly again be illicit to conclude from $Ra/1$'s dominating $Rb/1$ in domain 1 that the full vector

---

[31] Rawls ignored micro for macro, at macro's expense. Normative economics of law ignores macro, as we will see, at micro's expense.

[32] Think of a "particular domain" as, for example, the question of what kinds of damages ought to be available for a particular tort, or what rules should constitute the "consideration" regime in contract, or what should be required of pleadings in suits brought in fraud, and so on. I designate such domains here with numerals, that is, 1, 2, 3, and continuing up to n. I am then designating alternative proposed rules within domains by lowercase letters commencing with a. If 1 is the domain of contract remedies, then, and a is specific performance, b is liquidated damages, c is compensatory damages, and so on in that domain, then the rules to that effect are here designated $Ra/1$, $Rb/1$, and so on. Shift to another domain 2, for example, \ remedies for battery, and lay out another menu of options a, b, c, and so on, and there will be rules with names $Rb/1$, $Rb/2$, and so forth.

[33] Indeed normative "law and economics," like much of the Marshallian–Pigouvian (as distinguished from Walrasian) welfare economics from which it descends, is confined to partial equilibrium modes of analysis.

$Ra/1, \ldots, Ra/n$ dominates $Rb/1, \ldots, Rb/n$, let alone any other available vectors Rm/n.

There is, then, a foundational gap in mainline economics of law between normative ideal – that is, wealth maximization – in macro, and mechanism-evaluative practice – that is, rule evaluation – in micro. The gap here, more-over, is inherently unbridgeable because the normative economics of law's guiding ideal – Kaldor–Hicksian "wealth maximization" – is itself normatively indeterminate in macro.[34] One simply cannot prescribe an initial distribution of entitlements on the basis of that distribution's effect upon total "wealth."

Why? Because "wealth" as the name of a putative mechanism-maximizable maximandum cannot be so much as defined until *after* an assignment of transnational legal entitlements has already been carried out. This is not an empirical accident; it is a conceptual truth. There is no concept of wealth that is understandable apart from an antecedent distribution of entitlements.[35] Hence there is no wealth aggregate to employ as a normative touchstone in deciding how best to distribute those entitlements.[36] Normative economics of law cannot prescribe a macrodistribution of transnational legal entitlements.[37] It is, in the end, as prescriptively sterile as are utilitarianism and Rawlsianism.

B. One Satisfactory Mechanism

There is a mechanism that determinately realizes the best vector of values proffered in Section II to fill the distributive variables. Intriguingly, moreover,

[34] The seminal articles from which the pseudo-normative concept of Kaldor–Hicksian "wealth" derives are Nicholas Kaldor, "Welfare Propositions of Economics and Interpersonal Compar-isons of Utility," *Economic Journal* 49 (1939): 549; and John R. Hicks, "Foundations of Welfare Economics," *Economic Journal* 49 (1939): 696. The legal theoretic rendition of such wealth is that recommended by Posner in the first edition of his *Economic Analysis of Law*, pursuant to which wealth is that which is maximized when all goods are in the possession of those who most value them. Richard A. Posner, *Economic Analysis of Law* (Boston: Little, Brown, 1973).

[35] The matter is ably treated in J. L. Coleman, "Efficiency, Utility and Wealth Maximization," *Hofstra Law Review* 8 (1980): 509.

[36] This is, in effect, normative economics of law's manifestation of welfare economics' so-called Scitovsky Paradox – the possibility for two states of the world to be Kaldor–Hicks superior to one another. Tibor Scitovsky, *The Joyless Economy: An Inquiry into Human Satisfaction and Consumer Dissatisfaction* (Oxford: Oxford University Press, 1976). Note that utility, were it measurable, would not be vulnerable on this score, even though it would be fetishist for reasons given in the Global Distribuenda subsection of Section II.

[37] Posner, to his credit, accepted criticism to this effect early on. He then went on blithely to observe that the problem did not afflict what I am calling here the "micro" choice problem of selecting between possible rules within a single, more limited domain. But that is pre-cisely what I am claiming here to *be* the problem for normative economics of law from a mechanism-prescriptive point of view. If the macro backdrop must be normatively evaluated but is literally unevaluable by one's normative theory, then one's microcritiques have not been made normatively intelligible. See the ensuing paragraphs.

this fact does not seem to be mere happy accident: The "hows" of this mechanism's vindicating the best valuations illumine yet further the independent attractiveness of those valuations themselves. That is an additional attraction over and above the practical advantages offered by this mechanism's capacity to realize the best valuations. What is more, our laws, policies, and institutions appear to be animated at least inchoately by a shared societal commitment to realizing precisely this mechanism.

1. One Fully Specifiable Mechanism: Real Opportunity Spreading

Here, first in idealized form, is the mechanism that I have in mind: Begin by assuming, for heuristic purposes, a "complete" market. That is a forum in which all and only desired voluntary trading occurs.[38] Assume that this trading is in, first, all goods and services that can practically be made available and that anyone values. These, then, would be all things that are intelligible as normatively interesting distribuenda.[39] Assume that the trading is in, second, "arrow securities." These are contingent claims to compensation upon the occurrence of such eventualities as distribuees might *dis*value. The compensation is payable by anyone willing to take the opposite side of what amount to "bets" on the disvalued contingencies.[40] In effect, then, they are "mini-insurance policies."

Assume next that the market I describe also is neutral in two ways: First, each participant enters it with an initial endowment of ethically exogenous

---

[38] Market "completeness" in this sense includes trading in contingent claims, more on which I will cover over the course of the next several paragraphs. I will also argue that completeness in this sense is a function, in part, of what I shall presently label "neutrality," a fact that appears to go largely ignored. The classic sources on the role of contingent claims in completing markets are John R. Hicks, *Value and Capital* (Oxford: Oxford University Press, 1940); Maurice Allais, "Généralisation des Théories de L'Equilibre Economique Général et du Rendement Global au Cas du Risque," *Econometrie, Colloques Internationaux du Centre National de la Recherche Scientifique* 11 (1953): 81; Kenneth J. Arrow, "Le Rôle de Valeurs Boursières par la Répartition la Meilleure des Risques," *Econometrie, Colloques Internationaux du Centre National de la Recherche Scientifique* 11 (1953): 41; and Gerard Debreu, *Theory of Value* (New Haven, CT: Yale University Press, 1959). Completeness is more precisely characterized by formal means. Its presence bears many ramifications, only some of which can be treated here. For fuller treatment, see Robert Hockett, "Just Insurance Through Global Macro-Hedging," *University of Pennsylvania Journal of International Economic Law* 25 (2004): 107. For state-of-the-art plenary treatment, see Michael Magill and Martine Quinzii, *Theory of Incomplete Markets I* (Cambridge, MA: MIT Press, 1996).

[39] Assume also, for obvious reasons, that valued "goods" and "services" do *not* include among them the nonconsensual expropriation of others' entitlements, which would violate the neutrality conditions I next describe. I will also explain how to apportion and determine entitlements, and hence what counts as expropriation.

[40] Robert Hockett, "Gaming as Micro-Insurance: How and Why to Regulate, Not Eliminate, Online Gambling" (manuscript under review, on file with the author).

assets – that is, the "material opportunities" of the Resources or Wealth subsection – equal in value to that with which everyone else enters it. Call this form of
neutrality "entry neutrality." Second, the market is neutral because regulatory
norms prevent such collusively, strategically, or expropriatively opportunistic
behaviors as can yield a particular consequence, namely some participants'
coming to possess greater or lesser holdings, or price-affecting effective demand
powers, than are traceable solely to (a) the participants' ethically exogenous
initial endowments, and (b) their ethically *endogenous* – that is, responsible –
transaction histories. Call this form of neutrality "process neutrality."[41] It is
the sort of neutrality that so-called European competition law and American
antitrust law are meant to maintain.

This mechanism straightforwardly instantiates a particular set of valuations
of the distributive variables discussed in Subsections II.A through II.C. It also,
simultaneously, sidesteps the three critical measurement concerns discussed
in II.C, in a manner that no other mechanism even begins to attempt.

First, with respect to those valuations of the distributive variables, note that
the mechanism honors distribuees as boundedly responsible agents, that is, as
agents who are largely, but not completely, responsible for their well-being.
Distribuees transact voluntarily pursuant to their own autonomous relative
valuations of material goods, ills, and contingencies that they do and do not
prefer. What they hold or enjoy at any given moment is, moreover, a function
of those same autonomous valuational and transacting decisions.

The mechanism treats as distribuenda whatever non-neutrality-violative
goods or services, including risk-bearing services, the agent-distribuees themselves value or disvalue. These goods and services are the resources or material
opportunities already countenanced in the Resources or Wealth and Opportunity or Access subsections. They are that from which, in conjunction with
their choices, agent-distribuees' welfares derive.

The mechanism, by means of the entry neutrality imposed upon it at the
outset and the process neutrality retained throughout, equalizes what is ethically exogenous – that which is not traceable in the holding directly to a
responsible choice. At the same time, it allows holdings over time to vary with
ethically endogenous – in other words, responsible – transactional and other
decisions. The distribution formula to which the mechanism gives expression,
then, is an opportunity-egalitarian formula.

Now the measurement challenges: First, the mechanism sidesteps, in
an ethically satisfactory way, the problem of cardinal welfare measurement

---

[41] Please set aside, just for the moment, the questions of means by which endowments would be
measured and endowment equalization effected. We will get to those shortly.

discussed in the Welfare or Well-Being subsection. It does so by enabling agent-distributees, by means of their voluntary trading activity, to maximize welfare in a manner consistent with two conceptually equivalent, normatively required conditions: first, ethically exogenous endowment equality among market participants; second, by way of corollary, an equally shared scarcity of the exogenously given resources from which agents "produce" their own welfare.[42] The maximization of this normatively intelligible form of welfare[43] is effectively guaranteed to occur – that is a straightforward entailment of the "first fundamental theorem of welfare economics."[44]

Similarly, the mechanism unobjectionably sidesteps the problem of interpersonal welfare comparison. So long as the material opportunity components of welfare manufacture[45] are counted[46] among the exogenous endowments that must be equalized over participants, the following will hold true: Whatever the absolute or comparative quanta of welfare enjoyed by distributees, these will be the "highest" that they can be and still be consistent with the opportunity-egalitarian distribution formula and the consequently equally shouldered constraints posed by the exogenously given environment.

Finally, the mechanism "automatically" *commensurates* distribuenda, per the discussion in the Resources or Wealth subsection, in the only way that ethically matters: by means of the implicit comparative valuations of autonomously

---

[42] In essence, we are describing an economy characterized by so-called equal division Walrasian equilibria, or "EDWEs." The technical literature on the theory of EDWEs and fair allocation more generally is vast, though curiously ignored by economically oriented transnational legal academics. A canonical sampling would include the following: T. E. Daniel, "A Revised Concept of Distributional Equity," *Journal of Economic Theory* 11 (1975): 94; Duncan Foley, "Resource Allocation and the Public Sector," *Yale Economic Essays* 7 (1967): 45–98; E. A. Pazner and David Schmeidler, "Egalitarian-Equivalent Allocations: A New Concept of Economic Equity," *Quarterly Journal of Economics* 92 (1978): 1; Elisha Pazner and David Schmeidler, "A Difficulty in the Concept of Fairness," *Review of Economic Studies* 41 (1974): 441–443; H. R. Varian, "Equity, Envy and Efficiency," *Journal of Economic Theory* 9 (1974): 63–91; H. R. Varian, "Two Problems in the Theory of Fairness," *Journal of Public Economics* 5 (1976): 249. The work from which these studies take departure is Leon Walras, *Elements of Pure Economics*, trans. William Jaffé (1844). Walras appears to have anticipated, indeed even inchoately to have intended, precisely such developments as these. See William Jaffé, *William Jaffé's Essays on Walras*, ed. Donald A. Walker (Cambridge: Cambridge University Press, 1983), 17–52, 326–442.

[43] For reminder of the contrasting, normatively unintelligible form of welfare, see the Introduction and the Welfare and Well-Being subsection in Section II.

[44] Kenneth J. Arrow, "An Extension of the Basic Theorems of Classical Welfare Economics," *Proceedings of Second Berkeley Symposium* (1951): 507.

[45] This includes physiological determinants.

[46] These would be, for example, in the form of drugs, prostheses, or contingent claims to those and other forms of compensation.

transacting agent-distribuees.[47] We need not, that is to say, concern ourselves with how much of some good G_2 "would" or will compensate person P_1 for a deficit of good G_1, let alone seek to construct a "perfectionist" index of *all* such goods and ills.[48] Our distribuees themselves will, in effect, autonomously and with equal voice construct the only normatively *salient* index – in effect, a spontaneously emergent price index. As long as entry and process neutrality are maintained, this latter amounts to the ethically relevant "global" valuation of goods and ills. That is a valuation in the construction of which each participant has exercised, by dint of neutrality itself, an equal "vote."[49] Prices, then, in a market bearing the completeness and neutrality attributes discussed herein, will be what medieval scholars long sought but never found: They will be "just prices."

2. Instantiability Challenges and Ordered "*n*th Bests"

The opportunity-egalitarian market mechanism, then, insofar as it can be instantiated, simultaneously assists in realizing what looks to be the most plausible vector of Section II distributive values, while meeting or neutralizing each of the principal measurement challenges. The ways in which it does so, moreover, serve to reinforce the independent normative-theoretic attractiveness of the indicated Section II values themselves – distributors and distribuees as boundedly responsible agents, distribuenda as material opportunities, and distribution formula as opportunity egalitarian.

Among the things worthy of notice are the following: First, the mechanism actually amounts to a normative refinement and completion of the mechanism unsatisfactorily and incompletely specified by mainline economics of law. Second, the mechanism is progressively instantiable over time, in a manner that ordinally replicates a normative scale from *n*th best to first best. Third, our laws, policies, and institutions appear to be actuated by the implicitly shared goal of ascending that scale.[50] Fourth and finally, there are means by which to

---

[47] Hockett and Risse, "Primary Goods Revisited."

[48] Ibid. The claim that the need to index commits one to perfectionism – the proposition that some goods are inherently more worthy of collective pursuit than others – figures into a prominent criticism of Rawlsian primary goods leveled by Arneson. Richard J. Arneson, "Primary Goods Reconsidered," *Nous* 24 (June 1990): 429. The criticism is addressed in Hockett and Risse, "Primary Goods Revisited."

[49] Again, provided that market completeness and neutrality exist in the senses already explicated. Trading here is voting, and voting rights are equally spread in the only sense that ethically matters – equal bargaining power involving the apposite form of equality, namely equality of ethically exogenous endowments.

[50] Hence we will see reason to displace even "positive" economics of law with a more convincing picture.

ascend further – hence by which more fully to realize the mechanism – that we have yet to employ.

The first challenge arises in connection with market neutrality, in particular with entry neutrality. If we are to equalize holdings of the material opportunity endowments with which agent-distribuees enter the market, then we must presumably commensurate those endowments. But how are we to do that *prior* to the operation of the equal-endowment grounded market mechanism, when it is that mechanism itself that affords the ethically satisfactory method of commensuration? Is there not a pragmatic indeterminacy here ultimately just as vitiating as the foundational indeterminacies found in the Mechanisms, Laws, and Governments subsection to afflict utilitarianism, Rawlsian justice theory, and normative economics of law?

The answer is no. To show why not, let us proceed in three steps. First, we demarcate certain classes of material opportunity endowment that are unambiguously ethically exogenous in the holding; call these "core endowments." Second, we indicate means by which holdings of those can be readily equalized. Third, we show that any forward movement in these directions is unambiguous movement toward the ethically optimal distribution. The upshot is that the ideal mechanism is straightforwardly approached in a continuous upwardly sloped fashion. (This means we will corroborate the second and fourth noteworthy facts mentioned a moment ago.)

First, then, are core endowments: At least four classes of endowment are uncontroversially ethically exogenous in the holding, beginning with the genetic determinants and obstacles, so far as we are able to determine them at any given time, of and to successful welfare pursuit. Many handicaps are obvious and incontestably undeserved; many talents are likewise incontestably unearned. With the advance of empirical science we grow ever more able to sort out, at least probabilistically, what is predisposed and what is not. Second, childhood health care and education: Children do not earn or deserve greater or lesser access to such assets, particularly when the children are very young. Their degrees of responsibility gradually grow as they move toward adulthood. Third, inherited nonhuman capital, that is, money-valued wealth: Like other forms of inheritance, this one is morally arbitrary. Moreover, it does not grow less so with time and maturation. Fourth and finally, there is the opportunity to shed or share unforeseeable risk through trade or collective risk-pooling action. This is best seen as nonconfiscatory compensation for deficits in other resources or material opportunity.[51]

---

[51] Some seek to include the presence of counter-traders in the opportunity set here, such as Colin M. MacCleod, *Liberalism, Justice, and Markets: A Critique of Liberal Equality* (Oxford:

Core endowments of these types are not only manageable in number, but with the advance of empirical science are also growing more readily quantifiable, directly allocable, and indeed allocable equitably. They are also in little if any need of commensuration inter se. If we distinguish between beneficial and burdensome endowments, moreover, we see that this is particularly so of the beneficial ones: early education, health care, and inherited nonhuman capital. The burdensome endowments are somewhat more difficult, because they disproportionately include physiologic resources. But they too are far from unmanageable.

The hardest of the latter is genetically poor health or handicap. Some such deficiencies can be valued by reference to current prices affixed to their mitigation – prostheses, medicines, and so on. There seems no harm in beginning to address such deficits with compensation equal to the going rates. Other such deficits are not so readily mitigated. There the best that we can do is to estimate the compensation afforded by insurance policies that typically are, or perhaps "would," be purchased against such contingencies were they available.[52]

The second challenge to mechanism instantiability concerns completeness as the first concerns neutrality. It runs thus: Is it reasonable to require that "all and only desired trading" occur? Is that possible, and should we even wish it? Would not we have to abandon our market-inalienability norms and "commodify" everything?[53] And if we do not do that, can the opportunity-egalitarian market mechanism that I have described discharge the tasks I have assigned it?

This challenge is more easily addressed than that directed to neutrality. First divide it into its desirability and feasibility halves, and then dispatch the first of these first. To begin with, consider the core opportunity endowments again:

Clarendon Press, 1998); Daniel Markovits, "How Much Redistribution Should There Be?," *Yale Law Journal* 112 (2003): 2291. I think this position is mistaken – in effect, a retreat from the position from which one treats distribuees as responsible agents – by dint of its treating co-persons and their responsible tastes as resources. Thus I count only infrastructure.

[52] See Hockett, "*Whose Ownership?* Which Society?," 217–237; Dworkin, *Sovereign Virtue: The Theory and Practice of Equality*, 307–50. Real, rather than "hypothetical" such insurance, is proposed in Hockett, "Just Insurance through Global Macro-Hedging"; Alexander Tabarrok, "Trumping the Genetic Tarot Card," *Contingencies* 9 (1997): 20. See also J. H. Cochrane, "Time-Consistent Health Insurance," *Journal of Political Economy* 103 (1995): 445.

[53] The classic contemporary objection to commodification is Margaret Jane Radin, "Market-Inalienability," *Harvard Law Review* 100 (1987): 1849. See also Michael Sandel, *Public Philosophy* (Cambridge, MA: Harvard University Press, 2005). Contemporary protests of commodification revive concerns raised repeatedly in the past. Two classic Victorian-era objections are Thomas Carlyle, *Past and Present*, ed. Robert Thorne (1890); John Ruskin, *Unto This Last and Other Writings*, ed. Clive Wilmer (New York: Penguin Classics, 1985), 155–228.

All of these are subject, in principle, to unobjectionable market valuability already. We have already commodified what most needs commodifying here.

Next consider what *else* might be traded – in the earlier idiom, "all that enters into responsible agent-distribuees' welfare pursuit." It is easy enough simply to bracket out of market transactions such things as we might adjudge should not be commodified – babies, blood, or human organs, for example – and still approximate to distributing goods and services as best as we thereby permit ourselves to do. For again, as I will show, there are second clear down to *n*th bests that are ordered equivalently to ordered degrees of neutrality and completeness.[54]

That is the desirability side of the so-called completeness challenge. The feasibility side comes in the transaction- and information-cost barriers to market completion in the technical sense. Is it reasonable to suppose that all parcelings of ownable and tradable goods, and that payment claims defined in terms of all specifiable contingencies, might be made tradable? Can we really "complete" markets in the sense required?[55] Here the problem, the guise of which is more technical than the alienability guise, can be handled in three ways.

The first way is to note that it is by now a well-established theorem of general equilibrium- and stochastic-calculus-rooted financial theory that complete markets can be simulated through a comparatively small number of hedging strategies.[56] Moreover, many more contingent claims markets can be provided than are currently provided. Further, the number of such claims that can be made tradable is growing almost by the day. I exploit those facts elsewhere.[57] Thus we can do a lot more completing than we have done so far.

---

[54] The baby allusion is of course to Elisabeth M. Landes and Richard A. Posner, "The Economics of the Baby Shortage," *Journal of Transnational Legal Studies* 7 (1978): 323, one of the bugbears that prompted Radin, "Market-Inalienability," *Harvard Law Review* 100 (1987): 1849. The blood and human organ allusion is of course to Richard Titmuss, *The Gift Relationship: From Human Blood to Global Policy* (New York: Pantheon Books, 1971).

[55] Thank you to Henry Hansmann for first pressing me on this score.

[56] Robert C. Merton, "Lifetime Portfolio Selection Under Uncertainty: The Continuous-Time Case," *Review of Economics & Statistics* 51 (1969): 247; Robert C. Merton, "Optimum Consumption and Portfolio Rules in a Continuous-Time Model," *Journal of Economic Theory* 3 (1971): 373; Robert C. Merton, "Continuous-Time Portfolio Theory and the Pricing of Contingent Claims," Working Paper No. 881–76 (Cambridge, MA: A.P. Sloan School of Management, MIT, 1976).

[57] For an analysis of these facts see Hockett, "Just Insurance Through Global Macro-Hedging," *George Washington Law Review* 37 (2005): 167; Hockett, "Gaming as Micro-Insurance: How and Why To Regulate, Not Eliminate, Online Gambling" (manuscript on file with author); Hockett, "What Kinds of Stock-Ownership Plans Should There Be? Of ESOPs, Other SOPs, and 'Ownership Societies,'" *Cornell Law Review* 92 (2007): 1.

The second and third ways of addressing the completeness challenge are more immediately satisfying. Note, for one thing, that greater entry neutrality itself yields greater completeness. First, completeness rides in part upon all desired tradings being available. Second, more trades per unit of wealth occur at lower levels along personal wealth curves. Third, entry neutrality accordingly opens market doors to larger numbers of participants who enter at the low end. Hence greater entry neutrality results in more trade.

The completeness-feasibility problem has no more than an illusory "bite" here. As my answer to the third, final challenge will show, more complete and more neutral always means more consistent with an opportunity-egalitarian allocation. There is an ordered set of nth bests that is ordinally equivalent to the set of "more" complete and "more" neutral markets. Let me, then, turn to the third challenge.

The third challenge is this: Suppose you cannot achieve full completeness and neutrality of the sort that characterizes the ideal mechanism. In such a case, might you not, in seeking merely more completeness and neutrality than you presently have, ironically end up farther from your ideal end state? Has not Hart, for example, proved that the move from less to more complete markets short of full completeness can incur Pareto losses?[58]

The suggestion, then, is that ascending degrees of completeness and neutrality might not be ordinally equivalent to a scale of nth bests. This suggestion happens to be false. The argument turns crucially on a normatively uninteresting conception of efficiency. "Efficiency," in the everyday sense of the word, connotes the maximization of output given a stipulated input, or the minimization of input given a stipulated output. It means roughly "more" or "the same," respectively, for "the same" or for "less." The more technical understandings of "efficiency" familiar to welfare economists and normative economists of law amount to variations on that theme.

Pareto-efficient distributions of goods or ills to persons are best understood, intuitively, as distributions the quasi-aggregated preference satisfactions deriving from which cannot be raised without lowering the individual preference of at least one person. That is the sense in which it amounts to a form of efficiency, the one sense in which it can warrant the use of that word. Pareto efficiency is the maximization of aggregate preference satisfaction as constrained by a polity-conferred "veto" wielded by any distribuee.

Kaldor–Hicks efficiency is yet closer to the workaday understanding of "efficiency." The reason is that it is unapologetically aggregative rather than

[58] Oliver D. Hart, "On the Optimality of Equilibrium When the Market Structure Is Incomplete," *Journal of Economic Theory* 11 (1975): 418.

quasi-aggregative. Distributions are efficient in the Kaldor–Hicks sense if there is no departure from them that would render some parties' aggregated gains greater than other parties' aggregated losses. The guiding intuition, then, is that the scalar welfare output of a given wealth-distributive input vector is, given the individual welfare functions (input vector components) that we have to work with, the "highest" it can be.[59]

But now consider what this means. It means that Pareto and Kaldor–Hicks efficiency alike are forms of "naïve maximization." They are in consequence normatively inert. Their maximanda, that is, distributive-ethically unfiltered preference satisfaction in the one case, opportunity-indifferent "wealth" in the other, are ethically irrelevant magnitudes.

Efficiency, then, in either the Paretian or the Kaldor–Hicksian sense is devoid of normative interest. The only form of welfare that matters is equal-opportunity-grounded welfare. The only form of efficiency that matters, accordingly, is that form which maximizes this form of welfare. Furthermore, the maximization of this form of welfare takes care of itself as we work to equalize the distribuendum that is material opportunity over the distribuees who are boundedly responsible agents.[60] The upshot is that the third challenge facing the opportunity-egalitarian market mechanism evaporates.[61]

3. The Role of Transnational Law

I mentioned in the Instantiability Challenges and Ordered nth Best subsection that, among the advantages offered by reflecting upon how to instantiate that distribution mechanism which gives best expression to the most plausible distributive ethic, is this: We notice in doing so that the laws, policies, and institutions typically encountered in the advanced political economies seem intended in large part to foster and buttress some such mechanism as that which I have just sketched and defended.[62] If this is so, then thinking along the lines of that subsection and the one before it offers further advantages.

[59] One "produces" welfare, in the Pareto and the Kaldor–Hicks senses, by distribution operations. Those are the variable inputs, so to speak, whereas persons' utility functions are the fixed inputs.

[60] The opportunity-egalitarian distribution formula requires not only that ethically exogenous holdings of that from which ethically endogenous wealth and welfare are derived – material opportunity – be equalized; it also requires that ethically *endogenous* such holdings be left to *vary* with the responsible choices that produce them.

[61] The third challenge should not be confused with another possible challenge – that some means of affording more completeness or neutrality in one sphere of activity might lessen the degree of completeness or neutrality in another. To what extent such interactions occur is an empirical question, not one of "high theory." I will address it later in connection with the matter of comparative institutional competencies.

[62] We might say, then, that early normative economics of law was positively incorrect in a manner precisely analogous to that in which it was normatively incorrect.

First, it will enable us to better interpret our own legal traditions, and thus to extend the tradition in a manner more in keeping with its own animating ideals. Second and relatedly, it will position us well to improve the laws, policies, and institutions that we have, with a view to rendering the resultant mechanism both more complete and more neutral, hence more fully in keeping with its own opportunity-egalitarian ideal. Third, by way of theoretic side benefit, it will enable us to better see what mainline economics of law has got right and got wrong, and thus to better fashion that discipline itself in a manner that leaves it less prescriptively mute than it is presently. Let me, then, at least preliminarily bear out the interpretive claim.

Much familiar private law doctrine across modern jurisdictions seems to be transparently opportunity egalitarian and responsibility vindicating in character. In connection with the latter, consider the centrality of the concept of diligence across property, contract, and tort, for example, in common law, civil law, and modern hybrid legal traditions. Likewise consider adverse possession in most property regimes, mitigation of damages in most contract regimes, and comparative negligence in most tort regimes. Even the presumption in favor of contractual freedom found in most modern legal systems seems rooted in respect for autonomy, that is, responsible agency.

As for equality of opportunity, consider the treatment of bargaining power and capacity in contract and testament. In remedies, concern for "making the plaintiff whole" per the compensatory damages regime looks straightforwardly actuated by considerations of corrective justice: It is a matter of equalizing present circumstances to a status quo ante. Furthermore, the many doctrines of equity jurisprudence that pervade our law are, of course, transparently exogenous circumstance equalizing and responsibility vindicating in nature, as both the term "equity" and the doctrines' Thomist–Aristotelian roots would have led one to anticipate.

Turning from private to public law, we see that the best interpretation of most market-regulatory norms in advanced political economies is as attempts to afford something like greater neutrality and completeness of the sorts I have just assayed. Laws prohibiting invidious discrimination on the basis of racial, gender, and other ineluctable or morally arbitrary traits, for example, look to be straightforward cases of process-neutrality promotion. Public education and sundry forms of government-facilitated global insurance for their parts are aimed at promoting entry neutrality. They work to equalize ethically exogenous material opportunity. Moreover, for reasons noted earlier, such neutrality-boosting measures tend to enhance market completeness as well.

There are other completeness-enhancing measures that advanced political economies have taken steadily over the past several decades and even centuries.

The trend in respect to commodification, for example, seems by and large to have been to permit, and indeed in many cases even to foster, the trading of more and more goods and services, including contingent claims. Witness the government's fostering of secondary debt "securitization" markets in the United States since the 1930s, for example, as well as its funding of much research that has led to the design of derivative securities.[63]

The trend in commodification also has been to "unbundle" more and more once-conjoined items into separately traded items. Conspicuous cases of such market fostering include government regulatory and start-up support for active markets in securities, derivatives, and, more recently, pollution rights trading, for example. Conspicuous cases of *mandated* unbundling – which incidentally show again the linkage between neutrality and completeness – include antitrust action against large telecommunications concerns in the 1980s and software manufacturers in the 1990s.

The fact that such measures can often be argued to enhance aggregate global welfare, wealth, or consumer surplus should not surprise us. Nor should it be taken for unalloyed indication that legislatures or common law judges do, let alone ought, to craft law, doctrine, or policy with a view to such goals. All the less should it be taken for encouragement to conceive "improvements" we think likely more fully to effect aims of that sort – for we have seen now that opportunity-indifferent aggregate maximizing is normatively empty. *And* we have seen that equal-opportunity-grounded maximizing nevertheless overlaps in part, short of full coextension, with other forms of maximizing.

That fact itself explains how "positive" economists of law in the past were able to suppose common law judges subconsciously actuated by Kaldor–Hicksian wealth-maximizing aims. We would effectively fine-tune mainline economics of law, then, by interpreting our transnational legal arrangements as being aimed at edging us closer to the responsible agency, equal opportunity ideal, and framing our own efforts at improvement in keeping with the same.

If I am correct in what I suggest here, then a substantial new research agenda is opened for what might be called an "ethically intelligible economics of law." Some actual or proposed rules thought to be wealth maximizing in ethically inert ways, for example, will prove suboptimal in light of the opportunity-egalitarian ideal. Responsive amendments to such rules might accordingly carry us further along in the direction of realizing the ideal mechanism

---

[63] Hockett, "Just Insurance Through Global Macro-Hedging," and Hockett, "Gaming as Micro-Insurance: How and Why TO Regulate, Not Eliminate, Online Gambling." Also see Hockett, "What Kinds of Stock-Ownership Plans Should There Be? Of ESOPs, Other SOPs, and 'Ownership Societies'"; Hockett, "A Jeffersonian Republic by Hamiltonian Means," *Southern California Law Review* 79 (2006): 45.

I have schematized. Of course, parallel remarks hold for our efforts to interpret and extend the rules that we have, as well as to formulate, legislate, and
administratively implement the best new policies and programs we can.

4. Comparative Transnational Legal and Institutional Competencies

I should, in closing, say a few words about what I am *not* claiming. Certainly
I do not mean to suggest that domestic or transnational courts should attempt
to make general determinations of litigants' overall material opportunity allotments in deciding cases. Even less do I mean to imply that they should allow
such determinations to enter into decisions as to whom should prevail in lit-
igated cases, as if courts were engines of non-case-specific compensation or
distribution more generally. Nor do I even intend here to recommend that
legislators, policy makers, or treaty negotiators as a general rule amalgamate
spheres of human activity in their thinking so as to prescribe, say, that persons
who fare unjustifiably poorly in one sphere of activity be held to different
standards in other spheres of activity, in order that they may be "compensated
overall."

It is, rather, the case that the integrity and long-term stability of institutions
operating in the many different domestic and transnational "spheres" of activity
that jointly constitute a pluralist global society require that we *not* typically
determine individuals' outcomes in one sphere by reference to their outcomes
in other spheres.[64] Full equality of opportunity among persons requires our
working severally – but simultaneously – toward this equality sphere by sphere.
We must work simultaneously, because the opportunity-egalitarian ideal is best
realized in each when well realized in all.[65] Alas, this is not the place either
to commit to or argue for these provisional judgments.

My claim here is accordingly more modest. It is simply that, where domestic
or transnational rules or regimes or programs or policies are crafted or drafted,
the crafting and drafting ought to be done with equal regard for persons
conceived as boundedly responsible agents. That is the first, fundamental
right that every person on the globe should be regarded as bearing. It is the
secular legal analogue to that "sacredness" that most of us regard as inherent
in each of us.

---

[64] Others who seem to think so include Jon Elster, "Local Justice," *European Journal of Sociology*,
31 (1990): 117; Alistair McIntyre, *After Virtue* (Notre Dame, IN: University of Notre Dame Press,
1984); David Miller, *Principles of Global Justice* (Cambridge, MA: Harvard University Press,
1999); Michael Walzer, *Spheres of Justice* (New York: Basic Books, 1983); H. Peyton Young,
Equity in Theory and Practice (Princeton, NJ: Princeton University Press, 1996).

[65] These are for reasons discussed in the Normative "Law and Economics" subsection in Section
III, in connection with the nonindependence of domains.

My more modest claim here is that treating one another as equal-rights-endowed boundedly responsible agents in turn requires that judges, legislatures, executives, administrative agencies, and transnational institutions view their roles in a specific way. First, they are to *equalize* such benefits and burdens as both (a) they are themselves institutionally authorized to be effectively bestowing, and (b) are *ethically exogenous* in the holding by the persons in regard to whom they are acting. Second, and at the same time, they are to dispense in proportion to differential *responsibility* such ethically *endogenous* benefits and burdens as they are institutionally authorized to be effectively bestowing. One entailment of this latter claim, in light of the foregoing subparts, is that transnational legal doctrine and legislative policy ought generally be elaborated with a view to broadening the reach and improving the operation of the distribution mechanism I have schematized.

These observations bear some possible implications for a thus far inconclusive discussion on institutional roles taking place in the transnational legal-economic literature. One strand of this discussion has it that courts are better suited to maximizing aggregate wealth in the incremental crafting of transnational legal doctrine, whereas distributional concerns are more efficiently (more deadweight-loss-avoidingly) handled through tax policy.[66] I must defer fuller discussion of such matters to another venue. Two comments, however, can be offered in light of the foregoing discussion.

First, in light of what has emerged over the previous pages, the "efficiency" appealed to in these debates will simply not be of normative interest if decoupled from the responsible agency, equal material opportunity ideal. Second, assigning distributional tasks on the one hand and naïve maximizing tasks on the other to separate institutional spheres raises considerable and possibly inescapable risk. One is that the normatively intelligible maximandum itself cannot be identified *apart* from the equal material opportunity backdrop against which normatively relevant maximizing activity on the part of responsible agents takes place. Another is that the institutional decoupling of welfare or income reward from discrete transactional settings tends to undermine the continued practice of responsible agency itself.

---

[66] For recent discussion of this long-contested claim, see Chris W. Sanchirico, "Taxes versus Transnational Legal Rules as Instruments for Equity: A More Equitable View," *Journal of Legal Studies* 29 (2000): 797; Louis Kaplow and Steven Shavell, "Should Transnational Legal Rules Favor the Poor? Clarifying the Role of Transnational Legal Rules and the Income Tax in Redistributing Income," *Journal of Legal Studies* 29 (2000): 821. Fuller consideration would require a discussion of the sizeable optimal taxation literature, in particular the contributions of Hammond, Mirrlees, and Vickrey. Regrettably I must pass this over in silence for now.

A practical corollary implied by the more finely grained nature of the mechanism we have argued best instantiates the responsible agency, equal opportunity ideal is a principle of subsidiarity. Rewards to responsible agency should follow as proximately to particular exercises of such agency as possible.[67] Tying minute-by-minute distributive changes as closely as possible to the voluntary transactions that immediately produce them is itself part of what recommends a more microdetailed distribution mechanism.

IV. CONCLUSION

We have covered much ground here, and it is clear that much more has to be done. Indeed, if I am right in what I have been arguing, there is more to be done than we have hitherto realized: For it seems we have been on the wrong track now for years as far as the normative theory of law's links to economy is concerned. We have been fixated upon end states that are not only in the end unmeasurable but are normatively uninteresting even as aims. All the while, we should have been looking toward ethically salient opportunity "inputs" whose right distribution allows rightful "outputs" to take care of themselves, just as our deep opportunity-egalitarian commitments have been found here, upon distributive structure-sensitive analysis, to counsel.

If collective action affects the distribution of benefits and burdens to our fellow persons, we cannot *help* but think through the ethics of distribution: We *must* "take distribution seriously." If we find, on analysis, that distributive ethics call out for the growing and spreading of material opportunity, we must think through how that can be done. What are the real determinants of real, equal-opportunity-grounded well-being – the real material opportunities? What means can we develop for more accurately limning the boundary between ethically exogenous and ethically endogenous such opportunities? How might we best design means of spreading the former, so that the latter – the sole ethically intelligible maximand – might be maximized? What institutions are better at what in that project, and how much functional specialization of the sort rendering institutions less visibly part of just wholes can endure? All of these questions and others press upon us urgently, the moment we see that we cannot really dodge them.

For far too long now – just over a century, in fact – Paretian complacency and its bedfellow, Kaldor–Hicksian wealth fetishism, have worked as a mere ball and chain. They have conferred vetoes upon beneficiaries of morally

---

[67] The want of precisely this form of proximity is one of the flaws that vitiates veiled-choice distribution scenarios, including those of Vickrey, Harsanyi, and Rawls.

arbitrary distributions, for literally no normatively cognizable reason whatsoever. Now that we see they are not only unnecessary but in fact incompatible with prescription itself, it is high time we tossed them.[68] Thus transnational law and international economics can be reconciled again to their origins – ethics – and both will again be what once they were admitted to be: moral sciences.[69]

---

[68] Hockett, "Why Paretians Can't Prescribe: Preferences, Principles and Imperatives in Law and Economics," *Cornell Journal of Law and Public Policy* 18 (2008-09): 391-476; also Hockett, "The Impossibility of a Prescriptive Paretian," Cornell Legal Studies Research Paper No. 06-027, http//ssrn.com/abstract=930460.

[69] Ethics and economics were of course once united under the Cambridge "Moral Sciences Tripos." For an example see Robert Skidelsky, *John Maynard Keynes* (New York: Penguin Books, 1983). And of course Adam Smith, seemingly the patron saint of Chicago, lectured and wrote not only on political economy but upon ethics and jurisprudence as well.

4   Global Economic Fairness: Internal Principles

Aaron James

Now more than ever, it is clear that the global economy should be assessed and governed from a moral point of view. Such moral assessment can, however, come in at least two quite different forms. Political philosophers have tended to focus on a range of issues (e.g., poverty, human rights, or general distributive justice) whose basic moral importance is "external" to and wholly independent of how the global economy is socially organized. The result has been relative neglect of a quite different class of "internal" moral issues, which *do* in various ways depend on the complex legal and social relations that now organize the global economic scene. These include a dizzying array of politically important but poorly understood fairness concerns – concerns such as nondiscrimination, special and differential treatment, fair trade, fair play, fair competition, level playing fields, equitable growth, fair wages, and exploitation. My aim in this discussion is to suggest a framework for understanding how several such fairness notions might be systematically connected and have an internal rather than external character. Specifically, I suggest that the content and internal nature of several such fairness notions can be explicated in terms of a more fundamental idea of what I call "structural equity."

From the point of view of political philosophy, the issue turns on the sorts of *principles* that might ground a moral assessment of the global economy. External principles are justified and apply quite independently of what the global economy and its social organization happens to be like. Humanitarian

For comments or relevant discussion, I thank Ben Alaire, Bruce Brower, Frank Garcia, Varun Gauri, Ruth Kelly, Chin Leng Lim, John Linarelli, Sophia Moreau, Douglas Portmore, Wayne Sumner, Sergio Tenenbaum, Fernando Tesón, Chantal Thomas, and Ernest Weinrib, as well as audiences at the University of Toronto, at Tulane University's Murphy Institute, and at the Symposium associated with this volume at the American Society of International Law, Washington, D.C. I also thank Tim Sellers and editors Chi Carmody, Frank Garcia, and John Linarelli for their work on the present volume.

principles are a natural example: In asking whether or not the current global economy is set up so as to bring as many people as possible out of poverty, the assumed goal of poverty reduction can be seen as important and morally necessary quite independently of how the global economy is institutionally organized, and indeed independently of its very existence. Internal principles, by contrast, are not justified, and do not apply, independently of the global economy and its organizing institutions. They have the shape and content they have precisely *because* the global economy is socially organized in a particular way – because the international systems of trade, finance, and money, and the underlying state system and its rules of sovereignty, property, and labor mobility, are of a certain general sort or have certain central features.

The global justice literature has by and large focused on external humanitarian, human rights, or distributional principles,[1] or else on principles whose status as internal or external is not especially clear.[2] The latter trend is exemplified by accounts that take an existing "global basic structure" to explain, in a general way, the applicability of certain principles of distributive justice.[3] Such accounts tend to rely on passing illustrations from the global economy without considering in any great detail what its legal and social institutions are like and how they might – or might not – fit together. Usually it is thought to suffice that the various cited realities are broadly coercive, or that they together pervasively influence life prospects, or that they meet some other highly abstract criterion of relevance. The unfortunate result is that the status of the proposed principles as internal principles remains obscure. One could easily instead conclude that the principles are external principles that require a global institutional scheme for their implementation, but not their very applicability.[4]

---

[1] Carol Gould and Daniel Butt each endorse versions of such external principles in their respective contributions to this volume.

[2] One important exception includes work on systemic economic consequences of the current state system's property rules, e.g., that they partly cause a "resource curse." See Thomas Pogge, *World Poverty and Human Rights: Cosmopolitan Responsibilities and Reforms* (Cambridge: Polity Press, 2002), 155–158; Thomas Pogge, "Recognized and Violated by International Law: The Human Rights of the Global Poor," *Leiden Journal of International Law* 18 (2005): 717–745; Leif Wenar, "Property Rights and the Resource Curse," *Philosophy and Public Affairs* 36 (2008): 2–32.

[3] Charles R. Beitz, *Political Theory and International Relations*, rev. ed. (Princeton, NJ: Princeton University Press, 1999); Pogge, *World Poverty and Human Rights: Cosmopolitan Responsibilities and Reforms*; Allan Buchanan, "Rawls's Law of Peoples: Rules for a Vanished Westphalian World," *Ethics* 110 (2000): 697–721; Kok-Chor Tan, *Justice without Borders: Cosmopolitanism, Nationalism, and Patriotism* (Cambridge: Cambridge University Press, 2004).

[4] Noteworthy in this connection is Beitz's shift away from the specifics of the existing global economy and toward the more general idea that "*some* type of basic structure" will always be "required and inevitable." See the Afterward of "Political Theory and International Relations," pp. 203–204. Though it is perhaps not Beitz's intent, one could read this as a general claim

This poses my main question: To what extent, if at all, are the principles applicable to the institutions of the global economy of an internal kind? In other words, let us adopt the working stipulation that there are no external principles. Is any basis for moral evaluation of the global economy left? Do we have any basis in internal principles for assessing how the institutions of the global economy are arranged? Of course, this does not entail that the global economy has no external principles. Once we have seen whether and to what extent internal principles do apply, we can relax our working stipulation and see internal and external principles as having distinct though perhaps related roles.

My answer is that that various internal principles of fairness do indeed arise, and that these can be organized around an underlying idea of "structural equity." As I will explain, I take the global economy to be fundamentally constituted and shaped by a particular kind of social practice: an international practice of mutual market reliance. Once we see how this social practice generates its own internal demands of structural equity, we can in turn explicate several further "dependent" fairness issues with reference to this underlying fairness idea. We thereby characterize how various applicable fairness ideas hang together, in a way that preserves their distinctive features, and we see how the family of notions is of an internal rather than external sort. The resulting framework hardly amounts to a theory of global economic internal fairness, but it may be seen as setting the stage for one.[5]

I. THE INTERNAL–EXTERNAL DISTINCTION

Before turning to examples from international economic law, I should first say more about the crucial distinction between so-called internal and external principles. Among the principles that apply to a form of human activity (for example, some social relationship, practice, or institution),[6] a principle is

---

about what would be required simply for the implementation of principles, rather than their very applicability. Beitz also says that principles for a world with minimal economic relations would be of no "practical interest," not that currently applicable principles simply would not apply.

[5] The present discussion is perhaps something of a précis for my forthcoming book, *Fairness in Practice: A Social Contract for a Global Economy* (Oxford University Press), which develops a theory of this kind. I draw from previously published papers on the subject, including Aaron James, "Distributive Justice without Sovereign Rule: The Case of Trade," *Social Theory and Practice* 31 (2005): 533–560 and "Equality in a Realistic Utopia," *Social Theory and Practice* 32 (2006): 699–724.

[6] The stated definition includes individual conduct (e.g., one-off encounters between persons), but I generally focus on regularized forms of interaction such as ongoing, temporally extended social relationships, practices, and institutions. My concern is with institutional and not interpersonal morality, though I do briefly remark in later text on how economic transactions might relate to institutions.

internal relative to the activity just in case it is *justified under an independent conception of what that form of activity is*. Otherwise, an applicable principle is *external* relative to the form of activity in question.[7]

This abstract conception divides standard theories of political philosophy. The most prominent examples of internal principles are John Rawls's principles of justice, which he takes to apply to the major institutions of society and nowhere else.[8] Rawls is not a state-of-nature theorist on the model of Hobbes or Locke; his argument takes as given societies of the sort familiar from the modern world. The question of distributive justice is what it would take for the major institutions of a modern society to constitute a fair scheme of cooperation. That is to say, the principles of justice, and the "original position" reasoning that supports them, are justified under what I an calling an "independent conception" of how modern societies are to be understood. By contrast, utilitarianism and most forms of consequentialism are usually defended as external relative to all human activity. The specified general goal (maximized utility, equality of distribution, and so on) is supposed to be important and morally necessary quite independently of the forms of action or institution that might promote it. No "independent understanding" or conception of those activities has a role in the argument.[9]

To illustrate the internal–external contrast by way of example, consider the fact that global market relations are largely organized by, and exist because of, the underlying state system and the policies and rules adopted by different countries. The global economy is fundamentally structured by a set of international relations. As far as external principles are concerned, this fact is simply not relevant to what principles require, though it of course might bear on how they are best implemented in practice. External principles (for example, requiring the elimination of absolute poverty) would equally apply "anyway," even if the systems of lending, money, and trade were of a radically different,

---

[7] The general internal–external distinction thus represents a form of argument, rather than the truth of the matter about what principles do in fact apply. A principle that is *proposed*, on the basis of some proposed justification, may or may not ultimately be applicable or justifiable.

[8] John Rawls, *A Theory of Justice* (Cambridge, MA: Harvard University Press, 1971).

[9] Most philosophers will nevertheless agree that internal principles can be less than fundamental "regulative principles" or principles of "non-ideal theory." Disagreement arises over whether they can *basic* principles. In this vein, Cohen has argued that all basic principles must be "fact-insensitive," in which case they cannot depend on social or other factual conditions and so be "internal" in my sense. G. A. Cohen, "Facts and Principles," *Philosophy and Public Affairs* 31 (2003): 211–245, and G. A. Cohen, *Rescuing Justice and Equality* (Cambridge, MA: Harvard University Press, 2008). I do take internal principles to be fundamental, but set the debate about fundamentalness to one side. I engage this more general debate in Aaron James, "Constructing Justice for Existing Practice: Rawls and the Status Quo," *Philosophy and Public Affairs* 33 (2005): 281–316 and my unpublished paper "Deflating Fact-Insensitivity" (available at http://www.faculty.uci.edu/profile.cfm?faculty_id=4884).

noninternational sort, and perhaps even in a global economic or political state of nature. If the principles apply independently of *any* social organization, as with utilitarianism, we may say they are *absolutely external* principles. If they nevertheless assume some background social organization, such as the state system, they may be called *relatively external* principles; they are then internal relative to the state system but external relative to the institutions of the global economy.[10] As for internal principles of the global economy, we do have to look at what the systems of trade, money, and lending are like. It potentially matters that these are fundamentally international systems – that the global economy is created and shaped by policies and rules adopted by different countries. It also potentially matters that such policies and rules have been adopted on the basis of certain understandings, including assumptions about the special responsibilities of each state for its own members, and the assumed purposes of the economic arrangements in question.

It is a difficult question *how* exactly such features of the social order matter, a question I will return to. For present purposes the crucial point is that, if the systems of lending, money, and trade were radically different than they are – if they were not of a fundamentally international kind, or if they simply did not exist – we could not assume that their internal principles apply. What internal principles do apply would be a fresh moral and interpretive question, to be answered in light of the distinctive situation being imagined.

My abstract characterization of the "internal" is quite inclusive as to *how* the requisite "independent conception" of an activity or practice might support an argument for a principle. Several different methodologies of justification might qualify. Consider three.

Pure interpretivism: Principles are justified *by purely interpretive argument* as constitutive of, or otherwise assumed within, an independently identified practice; without the putative principles, the practice would not be the kind of practice it is.[11]

[10] For example, both Walzer and Rawls understand human rights as internal to international law and practice, but external relative to the global economy. See Michael Walzer, *Just and Unjust Wars* (New York: Basic Books, 1977) and John Rawls, *The Law of Peoples* (Cambridge, MA: Harvard University Press, 1999). Similar approaches to human rights include T. M. Scanlon, "Human Rights as a Neutral Concern," in *The Difficulty of Tolerance* (Cambridge: Cambridge University Press, 2003), 113–123; James Nickel, *Making Sense of Human Rights* (Oxford: Blackwell, 2007); Charles Beitz, *The Idea of Human Rights* (New York: Oxford University Press, 2009).

[11] Examples of varying pure interpretivist approaches include Lon Fuller, *The Morality of Law* (New Haven, CT: Yale University Press, 1964); Ernest Weinrib, *The Idea of Private Law* (Cambridge: Harvard University Press, 1995); Michael Walzer, *Spheres of Justice* (New York: Basic Books, 1983); Martti Koskenniemi, *From Apology to Utopia: The Structure of International*

Pure moralism: Principles are justified by *purely moral argument*, for example, for an abstract form of human association, including cooperative human relationships. Although abstract principles must be applied in particular cases by interpretive judgments (that relevant applicability conditions are met), this does not affect their status as bona fide principles. They are full-fledged principles in the abstract.

Moralized interpretivism: Principles are justified by a *combination* of social interpretation and moral judgment. Our independent conception of a relevant practice comes from moralized "constructive interpretation" of the activity going on, and this conception shapes both the form of appropriate principles and what substantive moral considerations bear on, or are excluded from, justificatory argument. What principles are justifiable is ultimately settled by substantive moral reasoning.[12]

Although I favor the third approach, I will assume for present purposes that all three – and perhaps others – offer putative defenses of internal principles as I understand them. Each can potentially be said to share the crucial feature of arguing *from* and *for* an independently specified and defended conception of the activity or practice in question.

One might object that the choice of justificatory methodology is where the real action is, and so that my abstract conception of the internal–external contrast is inadequate simply because it is neutral among different approaches. Although I will return to my own favored approach, my argument strategy is not methodologically front loaded. I start out with the abstract conception I have offered and consider in an open-ended way the extent to which internal principle might seem to arise. This open-ended approach *would* be problematic if the internal–external contrast were so vague that our basic question (whether or not the global economy has internal rather than external principles) became empty or trivial. But in fact, in my characterization of the contrast, our basic question retains considerable force. Our working stipulation, again, is that a moral principle does not apply in the global economy unless it is justified under an "independent conception" of what its organizing institutions are like.[13] (More specifically, to focus on the global economy in particular, we should rule out principles that may be external relative to the

---

Legal Argument (Helsinki: Lakimiesliiton Kustannus: Finnish Lawyers' Publishing Company, 1989); and Alexander Wendt, "Anarchy Is What States Make of It: The Social Construction of Power Politics," *International Organization* 46(2) (1992): 391–425.

[12] I discuss the role of constructive interpretation in reasoning about justice in James, "Constructing Justice for Existing Practice: Rawls and the Status Quo."

[13] Notice that we do not test for internal principles by asking whether or not any external principles might make the same demands. We cannot, for instance, simply ask if the same requirements would equally apply in a state of nature and regard them as external if they would so apply.

global economy but internal relative to the state system. Thus we assume there
are no principles external to the internationally organized global economy.)
This stipulation has force, because it precludes many familiar humanitarian,
human rights, or general distributive principles, which are rarely justified
under an independent conception of how the global economy is organized.
Because it is not obvious whether or how anything is left, our basic question is
of significant interest, and neither empty nor trivial. Because it is as yet unclear
whether the global economy can be said to support internal principles at all,
it is a significant thesis to say that internal principles do indeed arise there. I
now turn to examples that suggest why and how this is the case.

ii. SUGGESTIVE EXAMPLES FROM INTERNATIONAL ECONOMIC LAW

As a model internal issue, consider the idea of an *unfair ruling*, perhaps
by a World Trade Organization (WTO) dispute settlement panel. Suppose
established principles of international economic law as found in the General
Agreement on Tariffs and Trade (GATT) Article XX or the WTO Sanitary and
Phytosanitary Agreement allow a WTO member to pass and implement legislation to protect public health or the environment and in so doing to restrict
international trade.[14] In deciding the case, a WTO dispute settlement panel
nevertheless rules erroneously that trade interests should prevail. The panel
might incorrectly rule that the legislation is a disguised form of protectionism.
In this case, the ruling may be said to be unfair, in the sense that a relevant
rule is improperly applied: The panel has not attended to considerations that
are clearly made relevant by standing law.

This is an *internal* issue because the principles that ground the judgment of
impropriety – the relevant canons of interpretation – are specifically concerned
with the rule in question and how it is applied. This is not to evaluate the rule
itself; one can be neutral as to its merits as law. It may be presumed legitimate,
but it can also simply be accepted, as it were, for the sake of argument. One
can even regard the rule as bad or even illegitimate law and yet coherently take

Even if they would apply, this is simply to say the demand is *overdetermined*, not that the
internal principle is really external or somehow less than fundamental.

[14] One might think here of the famous *Tuna/Dolphin* cases, decided by GATT panels prior
to the coming into existence of the current WTO dispute settlement system, which turned
on a balance between economic and noneconomic factors. *United States – Restrictions on
Imports of Tuna (Mexico v. U.S.)*, GATT Doc. DS21/R (September 3, 1991), reprinted in 30
International Legal Materials 1594 (1991); *United States – Restrictions on Imports of Tuna (EEC
& Netherlands v. U.S.)*, GATT Doc. DS29/R (January 16, 1994), reprinted in 33 *International
Legal Materials* 839 (1994). I of course mean to offer a stylized and so clearer-cut example.

issue with the panel's ruling as given. It is enough that the rule manifestly does provide for public health protection (and that the judge was indeed issuing a *ruling*, as opposed to, say, rebelling against the system).[15]

This suggests the following (methodologically neutral) test for whether a principle is internal. If a principle is, by the aforementioned definition, internal relative to some independently characterized aspect of social reality, then that aspect is (1) part of the explanation why the principle applies (call this the "explanation condition"), and (2) not necessarily in question, from the point of view of that principle (call this the "neutrality condition"). International economic law provides further examples of internal principles in this abstract sense.

Even if a rule is applied properly, we may wish to say that it is an unfair rule. For instance, many criticize the WTO's dispute settlement system on the grounds that WTO members that are developing countries are not in a position to effectively rely on the WTO Dispute Settlement Understanding (DSU). According to the DSU, only the wronged party has a right of retaliation if all other remedies, in particular compliance with the ruling and compensation, fail.[16] However, WTO members that are developing countries often have little capacity to effectively use such sanctions against WTO members with large developed economies – not to mention that they also have limited bargaining power to negotiate for compliance or compensation. Poorer WTO members therefore do not enjoy the "fair value" of their rights under the DSU, as compared with richer or larger WTO members, who can take full advantage of the system. Moreover, the rule could well be otherwise: Third-party or collective retaliation could instead be permitted, mitigating the inequality.

This can be seen as an internal issue even if the ground of argument is a substantial principle of equality under the law. The explanatory and neutrality conditions are met because the existence of the system is in part the basis for the objection and not itself necessarily up for review. One can object to the inequality in enforcement privileges, as long as the system exists, and yet coherently favor its abolition. The argument is internal in a still stronger sense if this substantial principle is attributed to the dispute settlement system itself; its aim, we may say, is precisely to provide effective legal privileges to all

---

[15] Here I bracket "hard cases" in which the line between application and judgment is less than clear. I also do not mean to deny a deeper Dworkinian conception of jurisprudence, which makes a lot of the fluid relation between these. Ronald Dworkin, *Law's Empire* (Cambridge: Belknap Press, 1986).

[16] WTO DSU Article 22.

member countries. Although reference to an aim of the system itself clearly meets the explanatory condition, the neutrality condition also holds, because this is not necessarily to open that aim itself for evaluation.

We may have a similar internal concern with an unfair system of rules. Consider trade law's guiding "nondiscrimination" norms, the idea that trade and trade-related policy is not to discriminate between different countries. Though the idea of same treatment (as expressed in the most-favored-nation rule and the rule of national treatment) has a kind of presumptive fairness, it is normally qualified by "special and differential treatment" provisions for developing countries, in part for fairness reasons.[17] Across a range of areas – including currently governed areas such as trade in goods and services and intellectual property, as well as proposed areas such as investment and competition – there are thought to be good reasons why discriminatory policies should be allowed, in specified circumstances. Otherwise, developing countries tend to incur special harms, or their development trajectories are impaired: They often need to take special measures to protect highly vulnerable groups, to nurture infant industries, or to sustain fiscal solvency (e.g., through tariff revenues), in virtue of their less developed infrastructure, institutional capacity, levels of poverty, and so on. To relate to developing countries under a blanket nondiscrimination norm, without giving them special privileges of protection, would be to unfairly ignore their special circumstances.

Although this concern of fairness applies across several areas of trade law, it can still be an internal issue. The basis of criticism could be an aim internal to the trading system, either as a matter of understood purpose or explicit provision: The aim might be that all participating countries benefit.[18] Reference to an internal aim means the explanatory condition is met, but the argument remains neutral in the required sense. To say that the trading system's aim requires special and differential treatment provisions is not necessarily to open that basic aim for evaluation. One can take it as given for purposes of internal argument and yet coherently reject it as too limited, or too demanding, on relatively external grounds.

The argument is also internal even if it directly appeals to a substantial principle, for example, a principle according to which the burdens of a blanket nondiscrimination rule to developing countries are excessively high. The explanatory condition is still met insofar as the relevant principle is justified

---

[17] Chin Leng Lim provides an enormously helpful history of this kind of moral argument in his contribution to this volume.

[18] GATT, Article XXXVI (3), mentions a "need for positive efforts designed to ensure that less developed contracting parties secure a share in the growth in international trade commensurate with the needs of their economic development."

specifically for the *trading system*, given a conception of what it is, of which more is discussed in later text. The neutrality condition is also met because, as already mentioned, the unfairness can be construed in conditional terms: If we have a functioning norm of nondiscrimination, then fairness requires special and differential treatment provisions. But this is compatible with also holding, on the basis of an external standard, that the presumptive nondiscrimination norm should be abolished in favor of a less restrictive default norm.

III. TRADE AS A SOCIAL PRACTICE OF MARKET RELIANCE

This last example suggests a further point of reference from which to internally evaluate the general structure or very existence of a legal system as fair or unfair. Trade as we know it is not simply a flow of transborder economic transactions or relations. It is not even a given country's unilateral decision to allow or encourage them. It is, rather, a *social practice* in which two or more countries mutually rely on a common market. They do so according to mutually understood roles, and for the sake of the common goal of mutual gain – especially the national "gains of trade" that are due to greater efficiency in the division of labor, to economies of scale, and to the spread of technology and ideas.

The minimum form of participation in this practice is the maintenance of trade policies, whether tariffs and quotas or "behind the border" measures such as subsidies, internal taxes, or preferential rules, which allow a common market to exist. If the trade barriers are high enough, business will (aside from the occasional so-called black market) all but cease. Beyond this, a country participates to different degrees, depending on the extent to which it adjusts its policies according to established policy expectations such as treaty rules, or according to more informal understandings of what it takes for the common market relations to be beneficial in the intended ways.

A given country participates *within* a larger pattern of ongoing coordination. The pattern of coordination can be structured in different ways, with different consequences for different countries or their respective members. This structure itself, quite aside from any member's quality of participation, can be appraised as fair or unfair, in the light of alternative ways it may be arranged, and how each possibility distributes different advantages and disadvantages to countries or their members. It is here, I take it, that the basic issue of fairness in trade arises, what we may call the issue of structural equity. Principles of structural equity in trade specify how advantages and disadvantages must be distributed, across societies and within their respective classes, if the structure that creates them is to be fair to everyone it affects.

Here I postpone hard questions about the scope of the most basic trade relationship. Does it include bilateral and regional trade agreements, or simply
the multilateral system? Are these sufficiently related (for example, because
"trade diverting"), but simply governed independently? Moreover, does the
basic trade relation include less-well-regulated capital markets and the monetary reserve system? Or are they a local state of nature, perhaps in need of
regulation but not yet subject to their own internal principles? I return to this
issue of scope in later text. It does not affect my basic claim that principles
of socioeconomic structural equity do apply to the existing trade relationship,
even if simply the multilateral system of trade.

I take these principles to be of the following three kinds.[19] The first principle concerns the harms of trade, such as unemployment, wage suppression,
and income volatility that diminishes lifetime savings: Trading nations are to
protect people against the harms of trade, either by temporary trade barriers
or safeguards, and similar protections, or, under free trade, by direct compensation or social insurance schemes. Specifically, no person's life prospects are
to be worse than they would have been had the person's society of origin been
a closed society. The second and third principles concern the gains of trade,
as specified by classical trade theory and as understood within the trading
system. According to the second principle, gains to a given trading society
are to be distributed equally among its affected members, unless inequality of
gain is reasonably acceptable to them all (for example, according to domestic
distributional principles). According to the third principle, gains to trading
societies, as adjusted according to the relevant endowments of each (for example, population size and level of development), are to be distributed equally,
unless unequal gains flow (for example, by means of special trade privileges)
to poor countries.

I will not offer further explication or defense of these principles here. What is
important for present purposes is that principles of this sort support evaluation
of international economic law in quite general yet fully internal terms. Any
part of the legal trading system, or its general design, or even its very existence,
will be unfair to the extent that it fails to promote outcomes that the relevant
principles require. This is not to say the current system is indeed fundamentally flawed. There are various reasons why codified or even enforced rules are
probably necessary. The current system has in fact been quite successful in sta-
bilizing otherwise conflict-prone relations; it has tended to provide assurance
that compliance will by and large be reciprocated, and so mitigated potential
grounds for caution, such as loss of relative political power, or costs to displaced

[19] I develop and defend these principles in my "A Theory of Fairness in Trade" (work in progress).

groups who cannot easily be compensated. Although such assurance has also been supported more informally by the "embedded liberalism compromise," an understanding which was based in mutual trust and shared social values.[20] There are also general reasons of political economy why the nondiscrimination norms, in particular, may be effective in this role; for example, they may facilitate a desirable balance of special interest groups. Nevertheless, there are many conceivable ways to arrange a trading system, both in its general structures and its many details. The present point is that all of these are, in principle, open for review according to general principles of structural equity.

But are these then internal principles? Principles of structural equity do meet our basic test, the explanatory and neutrality conditions. They meet the neutrality condition insofar as they are principles *for* a specific sort of cooperative relationship, which may or may not apply anywhere else. One can then appeal to them as a basis for evaluating the existing trade relation as fair or unfair without equally opening its existence for evaluation. Much as in earlier text, one can argue that fairness requires substantial reform, as long as the trading system remains in place, and yet coherently recommend its abolition as a route to a fundamentally different, more deeply "cosmopolitan" economic order. Principles of structural equity also meet the explanatory condition. The underlying international social practice partly *explains* their application. That is to say, the principles would not apply if countries instead existed in a state of relative isolation, as there would then be no harms or gains of trade to prevent or distribute. Other external or internal principles would presumably apply, including some that may require the establishment of a trade relation if it does not yet exist. But these principles, given our working stipulation, are not now at issue.[21]

As a way of developing this thought, we can ask the following question: If structural equity principles would not apply to countries in a condition of

---

[20] See John G. Ruggie, "International Regimes, Transactions, and Change: Embedded Liberalism in the Postwar Economic Order," *International Organization* 38 (1982): 379–415 and Robert Howse, "From Politics to Technocracy – and Back Again: The Fate of the Multilateral Trading Regime," *The American Journal of International Law* 96 (2002): 94–117.

[21] In other words, such principles are concerned only with the sorts of advantages and disadvantages that the *trade relation* creates. Preexisting or independent conditions are not being assessed, including conditions of poverty or levels of development as such. Special poverty or development-related privileges or benefits *are* often relevant, but this is because they are relevant to benefits of the general sort on offer in the trading relationship. Indeed, most every development success story has involved significant integration into the global economy (especially the cases of "export-led" growth in South Asia). Nevertheless, actually *being* fully developed and poverty free is not a result of trade in and of itself, because this state of affairs depends on other related but independent factors, such as the quality of domestic institutions or geography.

universal autarky, what would it take for them to kick in? It would not be enough, I take it, simply if various black markets came to straddle otherwise isolated societies despite all efforts to contain them, or if low-level transactional flows got going without state resistance. Under these conditions, the resulting outcomes in the world still cannot be attributed to an international social practice of the sort that constitutes trade relationship as we know it. They would not fall under the special responsibilities which that practice generates for what are, in the real world, quite substantial and pervasive market outcomes. Nor would it be enough, I take it, if still less isolated countries each unilaterally allowed substantial trade, for temporary or strategic reasons. If we cannot attribute the outcomes to a *common practice* of market reliance, the issue of structural equity still would not come up.

A version of this challenge is suggested by the standard economic case for free trade. As economists often emphasize, the basic argument is unilateral. The value of trade lies in imports, which allow greater productive efficiency and introduce new embedded technologies. Exports simply pay for imports. Thus there is no need to wait for export market access to gain from trade: A country benefits by dropping trade barriers of its own accord. In theory, all countries could see this and open their borders. No general practice of market reliance would be required. As Paul Krugman puts the point, "If economists ruled the world, there would be no need for a World Trade Organization. . . . [G]lobal free trade would emerge spontaneously from the unrestricted pursuit of national interest."[22] In this case, my appeal to the idea of structural equity might seem off the mark. A move from universal autarky to universal free trade would of course have dramatic consequences within and across societies – consequences of just the sort structural equity principles are concerned with. Would not such consequences be fair or unfair? If so, this shows they are not issues of structural equity in the sense characterized, because no "structure" is required.

Here it matters how exactly the imagined world is described. If we are to imagine a true coincidence of unilateral action, this would not necessarily display the sort of mutuality needed for a common practice. However, it would not necessarily raise issues of fairness, either. Perhaps we are imagining each country's move to free trade as something that pays no regard for potential consequences for others – perhaps as akin to its choice of how to manage good or bad weather. In that case, the policy choice itself might be unfair to the "losers" within each society (assuming compensation is not arranged), but there is no

---

[22] Paul Krugman, "What Should Trade Negotiators Negotiate About?," *Journal of Economic Literature* 35(1) (1977): 113–120.

unfairness in the trade relation with outsiders, such as it is. In contrast, if a uni-lateral choice to free up trade is taken in full awareness of the similar choices of other countries, perhaps based in a common understanding of its benefits, and this (perhaps implicitly) becomes an established arrangement that all in turn rely on, and are known to rely on, then we *do* have mutuality of the right kind. The organization and consequences of the resulting social practice can then be assessed according to principles of structural equity.[23]

Indeed, it is hard to imagine a realistic conception of existing trade that does not fit this basic description. To see this, consider some ways the economic argument for free trade is not as clear-cut as is often suggested. In fact, certain market barriers can be optimal in theory (terms of trade and strategic trade theory both imply this, for example). For this reason, the standard economic defense of free trade often turns to political-economic considerations. For one thing, it is suggested, the optimal trade barrier is usually quite difficult to set in practice. Because the costs of regularly getting it wrong outweigh the modest benefits of success, a standing policy of free trade is good political-economic practice. Moreover, it is sometimes added, such self-interested optimizing invites retaliation from other countries, and perhaps a mutually destructive trade war. It is therefore better to forgo temporary gains for the sake of mutually beneficial cooperation. Douglas Irwin explains this in his history of the free-trade debate:

> The analysis of strategic trade policy, like the terms of trade argument, illustrated the possible unilateral advantages of deviating from free trade to exploit one's trading partners. . . . But the real implication . . . is not so much that . . . trade interventions can be potentially beneficial. Rather, these theo-ries reinforce the notion that trade is a form of economic interdependence. If each country ignored others and pursued policies that were apparently to its unilateral advantage, most countries would likely be worse off in the end. Cooperative agreements between countries, in which all agree to forgo the use of such policies, could potentially make each of them better off.[24]

In fact, as I explain further in later text, it is precisely such reasoning that led countries to establish the multilateral trading system in the wake of the mutu-ally destructive interwar years. Trade as we know it is a cooperative practice of market reliance, and so utterly unlike our imagined world of spontaneous

---

[23] I do assume that practice must be governable, even if by informal means. I develop this further in "Distributive Justice Without Sovereign Rule: The Case of Trade."

[24] Douglas A. Irwin, *Against the Tide: An Intellectual History of Free Trade* (Princeton, NJ: Princeton University Press, 1996), 216.

free trade. It is, for that reason, the kind of social reality to which principles of structural equity apply.

Still, to say trade is a kind of cooperative practice is not yet to explain how exactly these principles are justified *for,* and so partly explained by, that practice's existence. It may seem that fairness issues arise only because we are illicitly assuming external principles. To more clearly explain why this is not the case, we need to turn from our abstract conception of the internal–external contrast to the methodology of justifying internal principles.

Though I will not argue for this here, I doubt that my proposed structural equity principles can be derived by purely interpretive argument, as "constitutive" of the trading system or otherwise assumed as part of trade practice, although some fairness principles are of course explicitly cited in positive trade law. The argument also requires more substantial reliance on a conception of morality and substantive moral considerations, in a way I presently explain.

In the broadest terms, my proposed principles are intended to specify "what we owe to each other" in the trade context, in the sense of T. M. Scanlon's contractualism.[25] The principles are those "no one could reasonably reject," given our relevant generic interests in both the benefits of life in an open society and in protection against its insecurities. The general framework of Scanlon's theory shows how principles can be tailored to activities of specified kinds. Our answer to the question of reasonable rejectability for a given kind of activity – that is, substantial regulative principles for that form of conduct – can be justified (based on reasoning about reasonable rejectability) without reference to principles applicable in other areas of human life. Being primarily devised for interpersonal morality, however, Scanlon's theory does not directly tell us how to address the large-scale patterns of economic interdependence we find in the current global economy – patterns beyond any individual person's control, and so largely beyond the scope of interpersonal morality. Nevertheless, they cannot be regarded merely as the workings of fate; the patterns are both created and substantially shaped by domestic and international social institutions, which include the trading system.

A central concern of Rawlsian theory, seen as one part of "what we owe to each other," is precisely of this sort: The special concern of *social* justice is the justifiability of collectively sustained social institutions and practices, in light of their large-scale distributive consequences. Specifically, a central Rawlsian preoccupation is with structural equity – the concern that a governed social practice treats all those it affects equitably, given the way it distributes the

---

[25] T. M. Scanlon, *What We Owe to Each Other* (Cambridge, MA: Harvard University Press, 1998).

benefits and burdens it creates among them. This is already a broadly egalitarian concern, in the sense that differences in treatment under the common structure are assumed to be arbitrary unless they can be justified as acceptable (not reasonably rejectable) to everyone affected. Although this is not yet to place substantial limits on inequality, it does indirectly support a presumption in favor of equality of distribution. Insofar as participants in the practice can be said to have the same presumptive claim to greater rather than lesser shares of the goods their participation helps to create, according to its generally understood purpose, equality of distribution is the default: Unless special reasons can be given why inequality is acceptable to all, anything short of equality would arbitrarily discriminate against those who receive lesser shares. Nonparticipants would lack this special claim, having had no hand in creating the cooperatively produced goods, yet could still raise other potentially reasonable objections, for instance, against harm done or their exclusion from the practice.

As I understand it, the argument for my three proposed principles of structural equity involves working out, *as both an interpretive and substantive moral matter*, how this general Rawlsian concern applies to trade. The principles are internal principles in the sense that they are justified *from* and *for* the trade relation, in the sense specified by moralized interpretivism. Although I cannot rehearse the full argument here, the relevant point for present purposes is the essential role of interpretive assumptions about the nature of trade in shaping basic principles of fairness. My proposed principles are not intended to represent the conclusions of purely abstract moral reasoning, quite aside from what actual economic relations are or can be expected to be like. An independent conception of the trade practice shapes what could qualify as principles for that practice.

To put the thought another way, even if one accepted the previously stated Rawlsian concern as so many abstract moral truths, this is not yet to say that they have any application as principles that should govern the trade relationship. It also has to be shown that and how the abstract notions do apply, because the trade relationship is of the appropriate kind. This further step of argument is *not* merely a matter of applying full-fledged fairness principles in particular cases (as according to pure moralism). According to both Scanlonian and Rawlsian theory, moral principles are essentially principles for the regulation of specifiable forms of conduct, by (individual or collective) agents in certain circumstances. An abstract moral truth therefore qualifies as a bona fide principle only when it is characterized *in a governing role*, within the relevant form of activity. Nonetheless, a characterization of this kind must be an interpretive: We need an independent characterization of the relevant activity, including its relevant aims. Earlier I suggested that actual world trade is an international mutual market reliance practice, for the presumptively legitimate goal of mutual national income gains. This moralized interpretive claim is thus a crucial step in the argument that my proposed structural equity principles are indeed bona fide principles of fairness in trade.

Without reviewing the full argument here, consider for the sake of illustration one way the distinctive structure of trade shapes the substantial content of fairness principles. According to the Rawlsian egalitarian concern just outlined, equality of distribution becomes the default requirement of equal treatment under a practice, because participants have the same presumptive claim to greater rather than lesser shares of the goods their participation helps to create, according to its generally understood purpose. Claims concerned with *relative* gains or losses among different participants are then essentially claims to the type of good the relevant practice is intended to create.[26] In the case of trade, we said that the ultimate aim of international market reliance is for countries to mutually increase national (aggregate or average) income, via productivity-enhancing specialization. It follows that the basic egalitarian issue of cross-national distribution in trade concerns the distribution of *national* gains (the relevant intended goods), and only secondarily with benefits to members of particular societies. That is, as far as cross-societal distribution is concerned, we are to compare how different countries fare in their relative gains, but not how individuals in different societies fare.[27] Principles of distributional fairness across borders thus have a strongly international rather than "global" or "cosmopolitan" form. (Or at least the present internal principles have this feature; the same may not be true of external principles which are not our present concern.)

IV. DEPENDENT ISSUES

I now explain how several other fairness issues can be viewed as internal issues. They count as internal on the grounds that, once adequately characterized, they make reference to, and so depend on, the notion of structural equity just characterized. This is not to say they cannot in theory be expressed

---

[26] Notice that this applies only to relative claims of the kind in question. I do not take this restriction to apply to noncomparative claims, and indeed my first principle of fairness (requiring compensation for harm) is not so constrained. The first principle still applies only to harm done by the trade practice, however, which is partly identified by the goods it aims to create.

[27] Relative benefits to individuals do matter under my second proposed principle of structural equity, but only among fellow members of the same society. Given a partially integrated world, cooperation within a society remains relevantly different from cooperation across societies.

abstractly in independent terms, but rather that their practical content, for the global economy, depends at least partly on structural equity principles; the best understanding of how the relevant issues apply in the global economy makes essential reference to the idea of structural equity, and so to whatever it demands. Insofar as structural equity involves internal principles, these further "dependent issues" are thus internal as well: Their associated principles are ultimately justified in light of an independent conception of what the global economy is like. I consider several such issues in turn: fair play, fair bargaining, fair versus free trade, fair competition, and fair wages.

A. Fair Play

Consider the idea of fair play, roughly the idea that one is to do one's part within a cooperative system when it comes time to do so.[28] At the level of routine policy administration, the basic responsibility of fair play is to follow established rules. However, trade rules are usually crafted in terms that require judgment to apply. What sort of judgment is required here? The basic responsibility, I suggest, is to make a good faith effort to apply given rules in the light of both their understood purpose and the principles that specify a structurally equitable trading practice.[29] So, for example, to set policy *simply* according to "national self-interest" would violate this basic responsibility. The interests of a given country or its members do matter, but structural equity principles concern how other countries and their members fare as well.

The same is true at the specifically *political* level of trade negotiations when there are established bargaining procedures. These can also be structurally fair or unfair, quite independently of the underlying structure of trade rules. Negotiators are to abide by them, even if their great bargaining power allows them to simply set them aside.

B. Fair Bargaining

As for what a trade negotiator should concede or demand in substantive bargaining *within* established procedures, the basic responsibility of so-called fair

---

[28] H. L. A. Hart, "Are There Any Natural Rights?," *Philosophical Review* 64 (1955): 175–191 and Rawls, *A Theory of Justice*, 112.

[29] My claim is not just that the good faith provisions of public international law require this, but that it is a moral obligation of fair play. Insofar as the morally required judgment is an interpretive one, one might add (perhaps on Dworkinian grounds) that interpretation should be morally sensitive in the suggested way. For examples (associated with "constructivism") from judicial rulings in international law see Koskenniemi, *From Apology to Utopia: The Structure of International Legal Argument*.

bargaining is to negotiate toward trade rules that, in the context of the larger system, are fair to all countries involved, according to the system's basic structural equity principles. This is not call for selfless altruism. Developing countries with limited bargaining power may fulfill the duty by zealously advocating for their own interests; this may be the only way structurally equitable rules will be adopted. When, by contrast, a rich country's bargaining power means it can have most any agreement it wants, its responsibility is to negotiate toward rules that favor its own *only* to the extent this is fair, again, as specified by principles of structural equity. To bargain *simply* for the "national self-interest," perhaps on the grounds that developing countries are doing so, is to derelict the duty one incurs by involvement in the trading system: negotiating toward and abiding by structurally equitable terms is the fair price of the system's significant benefits.

C. Fair versus Free Trade

"Free trade" can be fair, but only provided in an institutional background which ensures that the resulting advantages and disadvantages are appropriately distributed, according to the principles of structural equity. For example, rules that make trade freer, by reducing a trade barrier, are unfair to the people they may harm unless supplementary arrangements, such as social safety nets and transitional protections, are also in place. This may often be possible in developing countries provided sufficient support from developed countries. The cost of supporting countries is the fair price of involvement in the system: The benefits they receive are fair only when the system does others no harm, especially others who are already poor. When compensatory institutions cannot for whatever reason be put in place, then protective trade barriers are perfectly fair, though perhaps not wise except on a limited and specific basis.[30]

In a range of quite different cases, a country may prefer market protection because it takes objection to conditions present within its trading partner's jurisdiction, such as human rights abuses or environmental degradation. This kind of objection is beyond our discussion's purview insofar as it makes reference to principles *external* to the trade relation, even if internal to the underlying state system; our working stipulation is that there are no external principles. Setting that stipulation aside for the moment, it is plausible to think rules allowing protection on such moral grounds would be fair, even if not always

[30] Fernando Tesón, however, argues in his contribution to this volume that such grounds for protection rarely if ever arise.

wise – economics is not all that matters, after all.[31] In any case, the issue arguably *is* internal if the concern is not simply with the objectionable conditions in the partner country, but rather with the way members of a country may become *complicit* in those conditions through the trade relation. Then market protection may well be a condition of structural equity on internal grounds, though, again, whether or not it is wise is separate and often delicate question.

D. Fair Competition

People also sometimes object to conditions present within a trading partner's jurisdiction on more straightforwardly economic grounds. The fact that in many developing countries labor is cheap, environmental rules are lax, and rules of intellectual property are not established or weakly enforced is sometimes said to create unfair competitive advantages for developing-country economic actors. Developed-country actors have to compete with them in a common market environment while saddled with the economic burdens of high wages and strict environment or intellectual property rules. Even if this does not justify outright trade protection, rules that "harmonize" policy across countries, such as the Agreement on Trade-Related Aspects of Intellectual Property Rights, can be seen as a fair way to reduce the competitive disadvantage and level the playing field, so to speak, though this point is contestable.[32]

Though it is legitimate in principle, I believe that this line of argument lacks the significance often claimed for it.[33] We do not generally take competitive interactions to be subject to a demand of fairness for level playing fields in the sense that no player is allowed to have a competitive advantage over any other. The extent to which ex ante prospects of victory should be equalized depends entirely on the extent to which this would serve purposes assumed in the form of competition going on. The shape of competitive fairness thus depends largely on these sorts of *instrumental* considerations. Aggressive equalization (as in the handicap system in golf) is sometimes desirable, but only because it makes the game more competitive, interesting, and enjoyable, not because

---

[31] For a version of this claim, see Robert Howse and Michael Trebilcock, "The Fair Trade-Free Trade Debate: Labor, and the Environment," *International Review of Law and Economics* (1996): 61–79.

[32] Whether this agreement benefits developing countries has been the subject of considerable debate. See, e.g., Carsten Fink, *Intellectual Property and Development: Lessons from Recent Economic Research* (Washington, D.C.: World Bank, 2005); Peter Drahos and Ruth Mayne (eds.), *Global Intellectual Property Rights: Knowledge, Access and Development* (New York: Palgrave Macmillan, 2002).

[33] I develop the following argument in greater detail in *Fairness in Practice*.

equal ex ante chances of winning are somehow intrinsically fair. In a range of other cases – competitive horse racing, dog shows, tennis matches – we see no reason of fairness to hobble the ex ante superior competitor. In the trading game, differential advantages are indeed part and parcel of its basic mechanism for mutual benefit, and in that sense perfectly fair. According to classical economic theory, each country benefits as each trades to its respective comparative advantage. Although countries are not in competition, fierce competition between their respective economic actors is the normal way each country's comparative advantage is revealed.

As with any other practice making use of competitive interaction, I take it the specific terms of competition are or should be sensitive to what structural equity in that practice requires. Thus it is not inappropriate to ask, *in that sense*, why developing-country actors or countries should receive competitive advantages, instead of having the playing field leveled by harmonized environmental, labor, and intellectual property rules. However, the crucial point is that this cannot be the sort of demand for fair competition that thinly veils self-interested protectionism. What is fair depends entirely on what the basic principles of structural equity require, and so the issue of competitive fairness turns on what these general principles are. If anything, they seem to favor special privileges for developing countries, according to what will best advance their development goals. Insofar as such privileges include freedom from harmonization rules – even if the result is significant competitive advantages for developing-country firms – the advantages are then perfectly fair.

E. Fair Wages

A different fairness concern is more clearly concerned with the plight of people in developing countries. Developing countries have their comparative advantage in cheap labor. However, to simply leave wages and working conditions to the market seems tantamount to allowing systemic exploitation of third-world workers. Because the labor supply is abundant, multinational firms can ask people to work long hours, in unsafe conditions, doing menial tasks, for meager wages (the market wage rate). Economists often emphasize that, as Paul Krugman puts it, "bad jobs at low wages are better than no jobs at all," and that sweatshops create significant spillover effects, including rising standards of living for both urban and rural workers.[34] However, this does not clearly take the charge of *exploitation* seriously. One can be made better off and still be wrongfully exploited. In coming to your roadside rescue, for example,

---

[34] Paul Krugman, "In Praise of Cheap Labor" (available at http://www.slate.com/id/1918/).

I may make you better off by selling you a spare tire for $500 and reaping a $400 profit (perhaps your life was thereby saved). Nonetheless, I have still wronged you in charging so much. So if no other justification of sweatshop labor is forthcoming, it can indeed seem only fair to developing-country workers to make labor standards, perhaps including minimum wages, a condition for trade, and perhaps the subject of future WTO commitments.

There is, by contrast, a line of argument that does answer the charge of exploitation on its own terms.[35] Bartered transactions, outside of a market context, are usually thought to be subject to requirements of fair exchange, as decided and enforced by the transacting parties. According to one strand of the social contract tradition, the special role of modern market-oriented social institutions is to assume much of this responsibility for transactional fairness. The responsibilities of fair labor remuneration, in particular, are taken off of the labor negotiation table. Thus it is fair for the capitalist to "exploit" the worker, in Marx's technical sense of expropriating the surplus of his labor, as long as this is part of a larger fair system of cooperation, whose institutions return real and sufficient benefits to that worker over time. Thus if it turns out that the international institutions of trade, investment, lending, and aid, in conjunction with the worker's domestic institutions, *do* return appropriate levels of benefit to that worker over time, as specified by structural equity principles, then it would be fair if labor standards were never in enforced within the multilateral trading system established by the WTO or otherwise. It might equally turn out that enforced standards are necessary, of course.[36] They may be needed if the demands of structural equity are to be met. For present purposes, the central point is that the exploitation issue turns ultimately on the nature of general structural equity requirements.

v. THE ISSUE OF SCOPE: CAPITAL MARKETS

I have been explaining how several notions of fairness can be understood in terms of an underlying idea of structural equity – equity in an international practice of market reliance. In the remainder of my discussion, I consider further what this underlying practice encompasses, what I called the "issue of scope" in earlier text. This represents a further, more direct way that internal fairness issues can arise. Beyond the multilateral trading system, the underlying practice might sweep in social and market relations of other forms, including

---

[35] I develop the following argument in greater detail in *Fairness in Practice*.

[36] See Christian Barry and Sanjay Reddy, *International Trade and Labor Standards: A Proposal for Linkage* (New York: Columbia University Press, 2008).

bilateral or regional trade agreements and the global financial system. The "currency" of basic structural equity principles (i.e., the range of benefits and burdens they govern) would then be ever encompassing as well. To develop this possibility, I focus on financial globalization.

It is not inevitable that ostensibly similar market-oriented relations are all instances of one and the same general practice of market reliance. The relations may be of the same abstract type, but they may be quite distinct concrete instances of the kind. By analogy, suppose that the division of labor is unfair in my household, and that the same is true of the division of labor in your household. It does not follow that *we share an unfair labor practice in common*: We may live in different households, and our respective household arrangements may not otherwise be related (e.g., by common sexist gender expectations, or some such thing). In much the same way, the fact that one country engages in a practice of market reliance does not necessarily mean that it shares a common practice with any country that does so as well. Even in the case of a single society, one might regard its choice to rely on markets in goods and services as quite independent of its choice to liberalize capital. These might be said to reflect participation in wholly distinct market reliance practices, not a "common" practice in the relevant sense. In this way, "market reliance practices" could well proliferate.

Although all of this is true in theory, the question is what to make of the arrangements we actually find. I have focused on the multilateral system of trade. But liberalization of capital movements is a quite different sort of case. It is governed as much by informal bilateral negotiations as within multilateral organs such as the International Monetary Fund (IMF). Indeed, one might doubt the existence of a truly common practice in this area, in part because of the perceived failure of multilateral governance. In recent years, for example, developing countries have amassed huge dollar (and now euro) currency reserves, as savings to be used for currency stabilization or debt repayment, to "self-insure" against the numerous financial crises that the IMF cannot prevent, or, as some would argue, exacerbated or even created. If there is a common rule for staying afloat in the high seas of global capital markets today, one might say, it is "every country for itself." In the wake of the global economic crisis of 2008–2009, the G20 group of countries might pursue some form of international cooperation to avoid or mitigate global economic crises, through the scope of this cooperation remains uncertain and it is doubtful that it will rise to the level of the sorts of legal commitments that currently govern international trade.[37]

---

[37] See http://www.G20.org for recent efforts.

Nevertheless, I take it there is a long-standing common practice of reliance on foreign capital by many countries, which took shape well before relatively recent increases in capital flows. Developing countries now quite rationally take special privileges of self-insurance, despite recognized costs to themselves, *within* a larger practice that was intimately associated with the multilateral system of trade in goods and services from its inception.[38] Although it is the GATT that caught on and endured, ultimately becoming part of the WTO, its founding context suggests a practice of much broader scope. For one thing, its less successful precursor, the International Trade Organization (ITO), itself had a substantially broader purview, which included arrangements for employment policy, economic development, and commodity agreements. Yet even the ITO reflected only one part of still broader agreement on the need to address the delicate link between finance and trade, in part by the roughly concurrent establishment of the IMF. The ITO was based in a consensus to cooperatively avoid the mutually destructive behavior of the interwar years. The perceived problems turned on systemic links between finance and trade, which the IMF was supposed to address. Robert Hudec gives this explanation:

> Most of the inter-war restrictions on trade and payments had been justified as measures to deal with balance-of-payments problems. When payment deficits grew large enough to threaten a country's reserves of foreign currency and gold, governments usually had intervened in commercial transactions in order to reduce foreign expenditures and increase foreign receipts. The full catalogue of trade and monetary controls had been used to this end – tariffs, quantitative restrictions, export subsidies, and exchange controls. . . . The central idea of the IMF reform was to increase the reserves on which governments could draw in times of payment deficits. The increased reserves would allow governments to finance larger deficits and thus to avoid, or at least delay, restricting trade.[39]

If the specific aim was to segregate finance and trade policies, the point of doing so was that a larger practice of common market reliance would function, unlike in the interwar years, on cooperative and mutually beneficial terms. Even in the interwar years, the *shared idea* of general economic cooperation was reflected in a number of international conferences. As a then-influential, 1942 League of Nations report described the conferences and the period,

> trade was consistently regarded as a form of warfare, as a vast game of beggar-my-neighbor, rather than as a co-operative activity from the extension of

---

[38] What follows derives from Robert E. Hudec, *The GATT Legal System and World Trade Diplomacy* (New York: Praeger, 1975), chapters 1 and 2.
[39] Ibid., p. 10.

which all stood to benefit. The latter was the premise one which the post-war conferences based their recommendations – a premise accepted by all in theory but repudiated by almost all in practice.[40]

The problem was not lack of general agreement "in theory" on a general practice of economic cooperation, which many were willing to officially avow. The problem was rather that no functioning realization of that practice had emerged.

What does this mean for fairness issues? One implication is for the range of benefits and burdens covered by applicable structural equity principles. Along with the benefits and burdens of trade narrowly construed, we can add to the list any number of benefits and burdens created specifically by capital market reliance, including its effects on growth, standards of living, development, and employment. Thus structural equity principles can be internal principles and yet have quite significant purview.

The case of employment helpfully illustrates the point. Trade in goods and services alone does not clearly justify regarding employment *levels* as an issue of international structural equity, at least in normal times and among advanced countries. At least in theory, such trade does not change the overall number of jobs in an economy; jobs are instead simply distributed across import or export-oriented industries.[41] This does not mean that *a given worker* can follow his or her job to the industry where it goes, in which case transitional protections are still necessary. But at least in Keynes' founding view of the IMF, employment levels and trade are indirectly related in crucial respects. In the first instance, full employment is a central aim of fiscal and monetary policy. Instead of saving, money can and should be invested to stimulate demand and thus create jobs. Trade provides a further, external source of job-generating demand. However, it also fluctuates as foreign countries go through economic cycles. All countries therefore benefit from reliable external borrowing that would allow each to stabilize demand, for example, through countercyclical public investment. An intergovernmental organization such as the IMF thus should be designed to help create a global economic climate amenable for domestic economic stability and full employment.[42] If all of this is right, then a country's capability to sustain employment levels, given its terms of market

[40] League of Nations Report, quoted in ibid., 6.
[41] For discussion, see Douglas Irwin, *Free Trade Under Fire* (Princeton, NJ: Princeton University Press, 2002), chapter 3.
[42] This follows Stiglitz's account of Keynes' conception, which he contrasts with the less coherent, more recently dominant "market fundamentalist" one. Joseph Stiglitz, *Globalization and Its Discontents* (London: Penguin Books, 2002), 196–197.

integration, is an important aspect of the question whether those terms are fair.

Though practices of capital market reliance raise potentially large issues of fairness, these remain internal issues. Capital market reliance is one aspect of the same more general practice of market reliance that also underlies the system of multilateral system of trade. Insofar as its basic issue of structural equity is internal, as argued herein, issue of fairness in capital market reliance is internal as well. The specific principles and policy contexts vary, but the general issues and site of fairness are one and the same.

PART II

HOW JUSTICE GETS DONE IN INTERNATIONAL ECONOMIC INSTITUTIONS

5   The Conventional Morality of Trade

Chin Leng Lim

I. INTRODUCTION

This chapter is concerned with the kinds of moral and political arguments that developing countries have made in the name of global justice. Claims for the direct global redistribution of resources have not loomed large in international trade law and regulation. To be sure, they were raised during the failed negotiations for an International Trade Organization (ITO), but the principal tension that has come to the fore in trade law and policy debate is that between the formal rules of nondiscrimination under the General Agreement on Tariffs and Trade (GATT) and the developing countries' calls for exceptions to those rules. First, there was the argument against the developing countries having to make reciprocal concessions for developed country market access (or "nonreciprocity"). Developing countries argued for the lowering of tariffs by developed nations without asking for reciprocal concessions. Calls for unilateral liberalization by developed countries fell within that argument. The United States' Trade Expansion Act of 1962 is one example.[1] While the developing countries made progress between the Dillon and Kennedy Rounds culminating in the Generalized System of Preferences in 1971, they also advanced a second argument – that is, the argument for "new" tariff preferences that would be exempt

[1] Robert E. Hudec, *Developing Countries in the GATT Legal System* (Brookfield, VT: Gower, 1987; hereinafter *Developing Countries*), 44.

I am grateful to Frank Garcia, John Linarelli, Chios Carmody, and Tim Sellers for their warm hospitality and for inviting me to speak at the Symposium for which this chapter was originally prepared. Jeffrey Dunoff, Joel Trachtman, Chantal Thomas, Aaron James, and Fernando Tesón offered thoughtful comments on the chapter. Henry Gao read an earlier draft. I am grateful to them all. Finally, I acknowledge with gratitude Hong Kong University's Committee on Research and Conference Grants, and its Seed Funding Scheme for Basic Research for their financial support. All errors remain my own.

from the GATT's most favored nation (MFN) obligation.[2] The argument for developing nations to enter into regional arrangements for broader, preferential market access was made early during the ITO negotiations (ITO Charter Article 15)[3] but had lain fairly dormant until around 1961, when it resurfaced following the controversy over the establishment of the European Economic Community (EEC).[4]

At that time, the EEC had sought to make the case for preferences not only among its members but also in relation to preferences for various European colonies. This incursion into the MFN rule gave the developing countries cause to argue for their own customs unions and free-trade areas.[5] A good example was the Latin-American Free Trade Area, which, together with the colonial preferences of the European Community (EC), marked the increasing use of preferential tariffs as a development strategy by developing-country GATT members.[6]

By 1979, both nonreciprocity and new preferences had found a firm place in the GATT's Enabling Clause.[7] In contrast, broader debate over international economic law and policy was divided in the 1960s and 1970s by redistributionist calls for a new international economic order. Although that argument was central to certain historic General Assembly resolutions during this period,[8] many of the same countries entered the GATT Tokyo Round negotiations in 1973 by calling for "differential and more favorable treatment" instead – that is, exemption from having to make reciprocal concessions, and preferences exempted from the MFN obligation.

---

[2] General Agreement on Tariffs and Trade, Oct. 30, 1947, 61 Stat. A-11, T.I.A.S. 1700, 55 U.N.T.S. 194, Article 1. The argument for developing country preferences was characterized as one for "new" preferences because preferential tariffs existing before the establishment of the GATT, such as the British Imperial Preferences, were grandfathered or reserved under GATT Article 1(2)-(4).

[3] John H. Jackson, *World Trade and the Law of GATT* (Indianapolis: Bobbs-Merrill, 1969; hereinafter *World Trade*), 577–578. See, e.g., U.N. Doc. E/PC/T/C.II/7, 9 (1946) (Lebanon); E/CONF.2/11/Add.14 (1947); E/CONF.2/C.3/1/Add.28 (1947).

[4] Ibid., 50. See also GATT B.I.S.D. (7th Supplement), 70 (1959).

[5] See *Developing Countries*, supra note 1, 150–151.

[6] Kenneth Dam, "Regional Economic Arrangements and the GATT: The Legacy of a Misconception," *University of Chicago Law Review* 30 (1963): 615, 658; *World Trade*, supra note 3, 602.

[7] GATT B.I.S.D. (26th Supplement), 203–204 (1980).

[8] G.A. Res. 1803 (XVII), 17 G.A.O.R. Supplement (No. 17) at 15, U.N. Doc. A/5217 (December 14, 1962) (Permanent Sovereignty of Natural Resources); G.A. Res. 3201 (S-VI), S-6 G.A.O.R. Supplement (No. 1) at 3 (May 1, 1974) (Declaration on the Establishment of a New International Economic Order); G.A. Res. 3281 (XXIX), 29 G.A.O.R. (No. 31) at 50 (December 12, 1974) (Charter of Economic Rights and Duties of States).

Today, little has changed in relation to the basic developing-country position. The kinds of legal policy arguments that these countries have made in the GATT in the name of global justice have been about what lawyers call "substantive" as opposed to "formal" equality. My concerns in this chapter are empirical, having to do with claims that developing countries have actually made, how these claims have contributed to their institutional behavior in the GATT, and to the making and application of trade rules. Before we ask what theories of justice can tell us about actual situations, we would need to know something about the actual situation at hand. We would need to revisit the history of developing-country participation from the earliest days of the GATT. Asking about the nature of actual events could also bridge the gap between today's ideal theories of global justice and the international lawyer's preoccupation with how nations have conducted themselves in practice. This would include inquiry into the claims that trading nations make about justice and rules. Understanding such positive or conventional trade morality is an important part of understanding what theories of justice can ultimately bring to improvements in institutional and trade rule design instead of treating such moral claims which developing countries have made as irrelevant or mistaken from the outset.

II. STRUCTURE

We need to examine the views of the late Robert Hudec, who did important, pioneering work through first-hand interviews at the conference during which the GATT was signed and through a close study of the records of GATT debates. Hudec was among the first, if not the first, to treat actual developing-country claims as a form of moral argument. There is also another reason for his importance. Whereas his study of developing-country behavior became one of the most important works on GATT conventional morality, Hudec consistently criticized the resort to considerations of fairness in trade policy debate. This chapter explores the tension in Hudec's work, namely that between the importance of studying the claims made by some trading nations as claims about fairness, and Hudec's own general skepticism about such claims.

Section III introduces Hudec's views on the normative value of fairness claims; Section IV goes on to describe the moral claims made by developing nations during the formative years of the GATT. Readers who are already familiar with the history of developing-country claims for infant-industry protection, nonreciprocity, and new preferences might wish to skip this part and proceed directly to Section V, which discusses Hudec's rejection of any role for fairness as a concept in trade policy debate. Sections VI and VII critique Hudec's moral skepticism and Section VIII discusses the *EC – Tariff Preferences* case as the latest step toward "constitutionalizing" the developing-country argument. In this chapter, I argue against treating developing countries' claims to "reverse discrimination" as mistaken from the outset on grounds of efficiency, and I call for greater attention in our theoretical accounts to the sorts of claims made by the developing nations. I argue that theories that do not account for the question of conventional morality would be incomplete. Our theories about the development principles of the GATT–World Trade Organization (WTO) would be deficient if we accounted only for ideal theories about the normative justifications for alternative distributive arrangements, just as it would be an incomplete description of GATT–WTO practice to focus on WTO members' behavior without accounting for the normative claims they make about such behavior.[9] This is partly the case because, although the MFN doctrine is widely accepted today as a general governing principle, it is also observed largely in its breach. We do not know where the principle ends and what sorts of normative justifications have, in practice, been considered adequate in creating exceptions to it. Economic or moral theories which simply presuppose the reflective acceptability of the MFN principle presuppose a world that does not exist. Theory must do better.[10]

[9] I am suggesting that our theories about the developing country debate in the WTO should strive toward a fuller understanding of the forms of actual GATT behavior we are dealing with, and thus we should also look toward the reasons that are stated for such behavior – i.e., the "moral" reasons developing countries state for their claims – because we would be striving to "portray the rules for what they are in the eyes of those whose rules they are." See Neil MacCormick, *H.L.A. Hart* (Palo Alto, CA: Stanford University Press, 1981), 37–38 (hereinafter MacCormick).

[10] There are other reasons for taking developing country claims in the GATT seriously. As Aaron James argues in this book, whatever our ideal theories of justice about third-world development are, there are "internal principles" that matter. Fairness concepts (such as fair play, nondiscrimination, competitive fairness, level playing fields, and so on) arise for consideration in the context of institutional practice. This would include GATT and WTO institutional practice. On another significant front, Joel Trachtman has drawn our attention in his remarkable contribution to the behavioral aspects of fairness and in particular on the importance of inquiry into (a) the extent to which inadequate theories of justice may have played a historical role in ineffective forms of action to redress poverty, and (b) how a more appealing philosophical theory of justice could be translated into more effective transformative behavior or action. Focusing on what moral claims developing countries make and how such claims govern their actual (i.e., effective) practice within the institutional setting of the GATT and the WTO is closely related to these concerns. It does not require, however, that we treat national boundaries to be ethically significant in themselves in the construction of an ideal theory. In this regard see Daniel Butt's chapter in this volume. Our concern with the moral claims that developing countries make could simply go toward what fairness means within the WTO, or how fairness claims govern actual practice. My argument is simply that there may be strong reasons other than those that are solely concerned with the construction of the soundest ideal theory of justice that require us to address developing country claims in their own right. I also agree with

III. "THERE ARE NORMATIVE VALUES AT WORK"

We could start by taking the arguments of the developing countries seriously. We should accept, as a preliminary constraint, that the economic and moral claims and beliefs of the developing countries are potentially coherent. For example, developing countries may concede that preferential tariffs are trade distortive but also believe that they are justified on other grounds. For them, reciprocity – another cardinal notion - is an equally difficult concept when viewed purely in economic terms. If lowering tariffs is good from an economic viewpoint, then why ask for reciprocal concessions at all? The reply from political economy is that reciprocity helps to sell a deal to the domestic populace. Developing countries argue that just as there may be arguments in favor of reciprocity that have nothing to do with efficiency, there may be similar, equally weighty arguments against it.[11] Thus they argue that although special preferences might risk trade distortion, such preferences could nonetheless improve the developing nations' terms of trade; and that doing so is at least an equally worthy trade law and policy aim.[12]

There is nothing new in studying such claims as a species of moral claim. Robert Hudec's work remains an appropriate starting point.[13] Arguing against the view that fairness claims, generally, are merely rhetorical, he once wrote this:

> I believe that this political constraint involves more than a choice of words. There are normative values at work here. They do supply a certain force to laws which claim to advance them. The normative ideas may be wrong-headed and self-serving. They may also be capable of manipulation to justify purely protectionist goals. But they do give a general shape and direction to trade laws, and they will exert an influence on how such laws develop in the future.[14]

Hudec's other insight was that developing countries' claims for fair treatment require serious appraisal, even if these claims are ultimately deficient or mistaken. What follows is a description of developing-country arguments during

---

Butt that redressing global underdevelopment and poverty requires international institutional action.

[11] *Developing Countries*, supra note 1, 128.

[12] It is therefore not necessary to argue that "free trade hurts development." In this respect see Fernando Tesón's contribution in this book.

[13] Robert Hudec, "Mirror, Mirror on the Wall: The Concept of Fairness in U.S. Foreign Trade Policy," in Robert E. Hudec (ed.), *Essays on the Nature of International Trade Law* (London: Cameron May, 1999), 227, 230 (hereinafter *Essays*).

[14] Ibid.

that formative period when claims for "special and differential" (S&D) treatment were first fully articulated and heard.

IV. THE UNFOLDING OF SPECIAL AND DIFFERENTIAL TREATMENT

We have seen that the developing countries argued against reciprocity in trade
negotiations and for new trade preferences. Some countries had also argued
along the lines of resource transfer, but this argument never gained traction
and was probably never seriously argued in the ITO–GATT. Nonetheless,
there was also a fourth, infant-industry argument that was advanced, roughly
speaking, from 1947 to 1958. Although it was a short-lived argument, it provides
a useful contrast to the arguments that were eventually to succeed it.

A. *The 1947 Debate on Infant Industries: "Equality as Sameness"*

The GATT 1947, negotiated by Great Britain and the United States, was rightly
characterized as having created a "rich man's club."[15] It had introduced an
entirely new norm at the time, namely trade nondiscrimination.[16] Despite
its novelty, the GATT had a "network effect." The resultant trade diversion
compelled others, including the growing number of developing countries, to
seek membership.[17] On the side of the United States, the necessities of the Cold
War meant that it could not risk alienating the developing countries,[18] as well
as the European nations whose commitment to the MFN principle had always
been more mixed. We might have thought that, during this period, the debate

---

[15] John H. Barton et al. (eds.), *The Evolution of the Trade Regime* (Princeton, NJ: Princeton University Press, 2006), 2 (hereinafter *Evolution*).

[16] Certainly when viewed against the system of British Imperial preferences and the Smoot-Hawley tariff. See *Developing Countries*, supra note 1, 12. In truth, nondiscrimination's roots were deeper. By the eighteenth century, the MFN doctrine was considered an essential part of the commercial law of European nations. However, its strength and acceptance among the trading nations ebbed and flowed. Prior to 1923, the United States held to a conditional MFN clause in its treaty practice (i.e., according MFN treatment only upon receiving the same or similar concessions from the claimant as were received from a third state accorded such treatment). It was British practice that held unconditional MFN treatment in high esteem. Unconditional MFN treatment was revived in Woodrow Wilson's Fourteen Points, thereafter making its way into post-1923 U.S. treaties before the enactment of the Smoot-Hawley Tariff in 1930. The tariff prompted other nations to adopt discriminatory policies, such as the British system of imperial preferences.

[17] See *Evolution*, supra note 15, 2.

[18] Bernard M. Hoekman and Michel M. Kostecki, *The Political Economy of the World Trading System* (Oxford: Oxford University Press, 2001), 390 (hereinafter *Political Economy*). See also *Developing Countries*, supra note 1, 18.

over GATT Article XVIII – the clause on infant-industry protection – would have been relatively uncontroversial. Moreover, the number of developing countries was still relatively small. But this was not so. According to John Jackson, "the focal point was whether a developing country should be allowed to use quantitative restrictions to assist its development plan without prior permission from the organization, which the underdeveloped countries felt would be composed primarily of unsympathetic industrialized members."[19]

The developing countries felt that the very structure of international trade rules would freeze the existing international division of labor.[20] For them, the issue had to do with fairness. But what does that mean? According to Hudec, fairness in the U.S. domestic context means something different – that businesses should succeed on merit, and what it comes down to is that "one-sided government assistance" should not be allowed.[21] This disconnect was played out in 1947. Whereas the developed countries saw the developing nations' argument as amounting to no more than a thinly veiled excuse for governmental intervention, the developing countries saw themselves arguing instead for regulatory evenhandedness.[22]

Cuba, for example, had complained that what the developing countries sought was merely one further exception for infant industries to the one and a half pages of exceptions to the rule prohibiting quotas that the developed nations had already tabled in draft form. This, the Cuban representative said, was demonstrative of the developed world's immorality dressed up in legal garb.[23] It was all well and good to say that businesses should succeed on merit, but here were the developed-country governments making rules that would favor established businesses over the new industries in the developing countries. The Chilean delegate likewise observed that businesses in the developed countries and their governments were not representing the interests of fair competition at all; instead they feared competition and were seeking to suppress it.[24] Jackson sums up that debate as follows:

> The issues at Geneva in 1947 did not . . . seem to be free trade versus protectionism. . . . Each of the groups in the debate desired international control of

---

[19] See *World Trade*, supra note 3, 629.

[20] Ibid. See also Australia's stance in championing the cause of the developing countries at the time, as discussed in Ann Capling, *Australia and the Global Trade System* (Cambridge: Cambridge University Press, 2001), 23.

[21] See *Essays*, supra note 13, 231.

[22] As Hudec observed, this meant that the developing countries were looking for a clean start. See *Developing Countries*, supra note 1, 6.

[23] U.N. Doc. EPCT/A/PV.22, 37–45 (1947), reproduced in *World Trade*, supra note 3, 634.

[24] U.N. Doc. EPCT/A/PV.23, 6 (1947), reproduced in *World Trade*, supra note 3, 636.

some things and not of others. Both sides desired to use certain types of trade protective measures but wanted to limit or restrict others. . . . From the point of view of the less-developed country, the wealthy countries wanted freedom to use those restrictions that only they were most able to use effectively while banning those restrictions that less-developed countries felt they were more able to use.[25]

Essentially, the developing countries argued that what is sauce for the goose is sauce for the gander. If trade restrictive measures are allowed for developed countries, they too should be allowed for developing countries. No prior approval should be required for measures taken to protect infant industries. A decade later the developing countries would move away from this kind of equality argument. They began to argue, instead, that the developing countries required differential treatment precisely because they are in fact different.[26]

B. Havana to Tokyo: Winning Equal Treatment

Quotas were an especially hard case. As a result of the recent economic experience of the 1920s and 1930s, quantitative restrictions were viewed in 1947 as anathema – hence the inclusion of GATT Article XI prohibiting them. Unsurprisingly, the developing countries did not succeed in Geneva in 1947 in securing permission to impose quotas without the GATT's prior approval.[27] They were only a little more successful eight years later during the GATT Review Session of 1954–1955, at which Article XVIII:B, which contained the balance-of-payments exception, was inserted.[28] The significance of this, together with Articles XII and XIV, was that quotas would be justified on the alternative basis of balance-of-payment needs.[29] That route had emerged following the Havana Conference in 1947.[30] In addition, the 1955 Working Party report had pointed out that resort could also be had to GATT Article XIX's escape clause. For a time, then, the argument appeared to shift from fairness to necessity, with a focus on the kinds of exceptional triggering events that would necessitate the invocation of such exceptions. In reality both of these alternative measures were poor substitutes.[31]

---

[25] See *World Trade*, supra note 3, 637–638.

[26] Patricia Hughes, "Recognizing Substantive Equality as a Foundational Constitutional Principle," *Dalhousie Law Journal* 22 (1999): 5, 38–49.

[27] See *World Trade*, supra note 3, 636.   [28] *Political Economy*, supra note 18, 386.

[29] *World Trade*, supra note 3, 639. See further Raj Bhala, *International Trade Law: Interdisciplinary Theory and Practice*, 3rd ed. (Alexandria, VA: LexisNexis, 2008), 428–432.

[30] *World Trade*, supra note 3, 639.

[31] It should be noted, though, that until the conclusion of the Uruguay Round (1986–1994), safeguards were subject to compensation and this in time became a critical negotiating issue at

Something going beyond these eight years of debate from Geneva to the Review Session was needed.[32] By then, the relationship between the developed and the developing countries had reduced itself to quibbling over legal technicalities.[33] It was not until the Tokyo Round in 1979, more than thirty years later, that the developing countries would finally get what they wanted in permanent form – the right to take measures to protect infant industries without prior GATT approval.[34] In the meantime, the battle had moved elsewhere. Developing countries had themselves turned from import substitution to export-oriented policies. Correspondingly, their arguments shifted from a concern with equality in law making, rule design, and policy space to an overriding concern with market access.[35] With that shift, the outlines of the modern S&D doctrine began to take shape, bringing with it a shift from formal equality-based arguments to arguments about substantive equality.

C. The Haberler Report and Market Access

The equality debate lasted roughly from 1947 to 1979. The developing countries' arguments underwent transformation during that period. That transformative process commenced with the Haberler Report of 1958, which coincided with the shift toward export-oriented policies. The Report observed the different needs of the developing countries and the importance of the issue of preferential market for developing country products, an issue first raised during the 1947 Geneva meetings. As we saw, however, the arguments following the establishment of the GATT had, initially, become focused on infant-industry protection instead. But by 1958, having failed to secure the freedom to impose quotas without prior GATT approval, the developing countries shifted their focus to the need to promote exports. The campaign began in earnest with the preparations for the 1960 Dillon Round. Developing nations started out by asking for trade negotiations on a nonreciprocal basis but were turned down. This was ostensibly because GATT Article XXVIII (*bis*), which resulted from the earlier 1954–1955 GATT Review Session, already recognized the principle

that Round, leading to the present, more flexible regime. They were of arguably limited value to the poorer nations.

[32] *World Trade*, supra note 3, 628–638.   [33] *Developing Countries*, supra note 1, 32.

[34] Ibid., 179. See also *Safeguard Action for Development Purposes*, Decision of 28 November 1979, GATT B.I.S.D. (26th Supplement) 209 (1980).

[35] This is not to say that the issue of policy space had become irrelevant. To the contrary, see C. L. Lim, "Do International Financial Institutions Repress Development," paper presented at the 102nd A.S.I.L. Annual Meeting, Washington, D.C., April 9–12, 2008. Also see Dani Rodrik, "Rethinking Growth Policies in the Developing World," Luca D'Agliano Lecture, Torino, Italy, October 8, 2004 (available at http://www.ksghome.harvard.edu).

of nonreciprocity. The developing countries then asked for unilateral liberalization by developed countries, but the United States could not reach a consensus with the EEC on this in the run-up to the 1964 Kennedy Round.

The developing countries then pushed on a third front; namely developing-country special preferences. The corresponding provision in the ITO Charter (Article 15) had fallen through the cracks with the ITO's collapse.[36] However, the formation of the EEC had undermined the GATT MFN obligation. The EEC had argued, disingenuously, that its preferential trading arrangements with European colonies fulfilled the requirements of GATT Article XXIV. Debate in the GATT failed to yield consensus on the issue aside from a pragmatic wait-and-see attitude.[37] It was against this background that the developing countries saw their opportunity to revive an issue that Syria and the Latin American nations had first raised in 1946 during the drafting of Article XXIV. They had sought permission for developing countries to enter into regional preferential agreements among themselves.[38] The compromise reached during the drafting of GATT Article I was that whereas "new" trading preferences for developing countries would fall foul of the provision, existing colonial preferences would be preserved. That exception was also extended to the Syria–Lebanon Customs Union and its arrangements with neighboring Palestine and Jordan. Now the developing countries were trying to revive the Syrian and Latin American argument.

Economic debate has concentrated on the distortive effect of such preferences, but what is also important to notice is that the developing countries were advancing a normative argument – that is, an argument about right and wrong, not efficiency. Although GATT Article I prohibits preferential agreements justified solely on the basis of economic development, this was not how the developing countries saw it. Article XXIV, in their view, should have explicitly allowed for such preferences. The political impetus for that was only lost when preferential arrangements such as the Lebanon–Syria Customs Union and other Latin American preferences were specifically exempted from the MFN rule.[39] Now the issue had become one of general principle as opposed to the carving out of specific exemptions, namely whether GATT's nondiscrimination rule should allow for a development exception.[40]

---

[36] *Developing Countries*, supra note 1, 14.

[37] GATT B.I.S.D. (7th Supplement) 70 (1959); *Developing Countries*, supra note 1, 50–51.

[38] See U.N. Doc. EPCT/C.II/7, 9 (1946); *World Trade*, supra note 3, 577.

[39] *World Trade*, supra note 3, 578.

[40] I am grateful to Jeffrey Dunoff, who was the commentator to this contribution at the symposium. He asked whether this is the only reading available when one surveys the record of the GATT debates. In particular, he questions whether developing countries were in fact arguing on the basis of moral principle. Were they not simply intending to advance their individual national

As the MFN obligation would have it, like cases should be treated alike by treating all GATT contracting parties identically. The developing countries disagreed that they were in a like situation with developed countries. They considered that true equality required recognition of their developing status. Equality required developed countries to respect the differences between the developed and developing countries and not simply treat all GATT members formally in an identical fashion. This was the beginning of the modern era of GATT developmental discourse. Coinciding with a shift from import substitution to export orientation, developing countries were no longer saying that they should be "equally entitled to impose quotas" but that they should have differences in their developmental status recognized. GATT's formal equality rule had become the principal obstacle to development.

By treating all nations as sovereign equals, the classical Westphalian conception of the legal order that the GATT – unlike the Washington-based international financial institutions – embodied simply assumed its own political inclusiveness. This the developing countries challenged, and they did so in the GATT and elsewhere.[41] Two complementary trends were to coincide – the developing countries' arguments about status equality (i.e., that they were "different" from developed countries, and that difference is morally significant because it implicates our meaning of equality), and their search for preferential market access. True participation on an "equal" footing in the GATT required recognition of these principles. Robert Hudec once wrote that the "truth is that MFN tariff policy really doesn't give a damn about whether any particular country gets what it 'deserves'."[42] That may be so, but the developing countries do.

D. Deepening the Substantive Reading and the Argument for Status Equality: Debating Reciprocal Concessions

Status equality played out even more forcefully in the debate on reciprocal concessions. Trade talks have always been something of a contradiction.

---

interests? My answer is that they could do both. Arguing on the basis of state self-interest does not necessarily detract from the moral nature of the claims made.

[41] See further C. L. Lim, "Neither Sheep nor Peacocks: T.O. Elias and Post-Colonial International Law," *Leiden Journal of International Law* 21 (2008): 295, 301; Dan Danielsen, "Book Review," *American Journal of International Law* (2006): 757. For the impact of developing country GATT practice on the development of new international law rules, see *Developing Countries*, supra note 1, 104–106.

[42] He also wrote that the "true virtue of MFN tariffs is simply their ability to make the world's productive resources respond efficiently." See Robert Hudec, "Tiger, Tiger in the House: A Critical Appraisal of the Case against Discriminatory Trade Measures," in *Essays*, supra note 13, 281, 324.

Concessions are made in the GATT on the basis of concessions received. The trading nations are mercantilist beasts notwithstanding the economic benefits of MFN as a trade accelerator.[43] That is why, today at the WTO, negotiations cannot advance without the agreement of the "Big Four" (the United States, the European Union, India, and Brazil).[44] That other, lesser trading nations would get a "free ride" came to be viewed as a problem, not an ideal. The developing countries' retort was that if liberalization is good, then it should be pursued without asking for concessions.[45] That in part answers Hudec's criticism (detailed later) that because fairness lies in the eyes of the beholder, we should stick to the economics. Economics, for whatever reason, do not in any case govern how nations behave; the developing nations know that. The developing countries therefore sought to counter the demand for reciprocal concessions by turning nonreciprocity into a formal principle in multilateral negotiations. Whereas the demand for reciprocal concessions proved an embarrassment to the logic of MFN, calls for nonreciprocity presented both a strong economic argument and a plausible moral claim.

That argument developed in stages. Recall that nonreciprocity had emerged as a developing-country argument during the ITO negotiations,[46] and the developing countries' attempt to revive the issue during the Dillon Round. However, the 1962 Trade Expansion Act failed to encourage unilateral preferences and the developed nations continued to maintain reciprocity during the Kennedy Round.[47] Matters only came to a head when Uruguay brought a "show trial" type of complaint arguing an overall, resultant imbalance of benefits under GATT Article XXIII. Uruguay's message was that reciprocal trade concessions had brought the developing countries little.[48] This led to the creation of GATT Part IV, which entered into force on June 9, 1966. Unfortunately, Part IV also added little beyond what had been agreed upon during the

---

[43] See, e.g., John Linarelli, "The Economics of Sovereignty," in Christopher Harding and C. L. Lim (eds.), *Renegotiating Westphalia* (Dordrecht: Nijhoff, 1999), 351, 378. For counter-arguments against the allegation of developed-country mercantilist behavior, see *Developing Countries*, supra note 1, 17. Among these, however, are arguments that sound too much like "two wrongs do not make a right," and "do as I say, not as I do." As for the need to sell the deal at home, the obvious flip side is rent seeking and capture by special interests.

[44] See Larry Elliott, "Big Four Are Urged to Revive Doha Round," *The Guardian*, January 26, 2007.

[45] Paul Krugman, "What Should Trade Negotiators Negotiate About?," *Journal of Economic Literature* 35 (1997): 113.

[46] The argument failed when the EC refused to extend unilateral preferences. See *Developing Countries*, supra note 1, 44.

[47] Ibid., 44–47.

[48] Ibid., 46–47. See further Robert E. Hudec, *The GATT Legal System and World Trade Diplomacy*, 2nd ed. (Salem, NH: Butterworth, 1990), 240–242 (hereinafter *The GATT Legal System*).

Kennedy Round – that although there would be a special rule for developing countries, reciprocal concessions were still generally to be expected.[49]

In 1968 at the second United Nations Conference on Trade and Development, known as UNCTAD II, the United States finally reversed its position against developing-country preferences and called for a Generalized System of Preferences (GSP).[50] However, although the United States did persuade the EEC to abandon its demand for reciprocal concessions, it did not succeed in putting a stop to European selective treatment of developing countries.[51] In time, the GSP schemes of both the United States and the EEC became neither unilateral and nonreciprocal nor general in application. Instead, they require political payment in kind and even market access. Discrimination between various developing countries also became the norm.[52] The failure of the GSP meant that developing nations' attempt to advance status equality through the GSP had failed.[53]

E. The Turn to Preferential Trade, Assault on Formal Equality, and Erosion of the MFN Obligation

It became easier to create an exception to the MFN obligation instead. Two factors were particularly important. The first was the creation of the EEC. The second came when the United States reversed its stance against developing-country preferences. Both events were driven by Cold War necessity.

The emergence of the EEC in 1957 presented an opportunity to renegotiate the GATT. That, however, would have been both drastic and hazardous, and the GATT parties opted instead for ad hoc diplomacy above principle; pragmatism above legality.[54] The result was MFN erosion.[55] In reality, the MFN rule had always been a creature of compromise; it was never designed to prevent, but simply to regulate, discriminatory preferences.[56] As for the EC's Association Agreements with former European colonies, they too were never

---

[49] See *Developing Countries*, supra note 1, 45, 58.

[50] Ibid., 44, 112–113. See further Rachel McColloch, "United States Preferences: The Proposed System," *Journal of World Trade Law* 8 (1974): 216.

[51] See *Developing Countries*, supra note 1, 63.

[52] Ibid., 113–116. See further Gene M. Grossman and Alan O. Sykes, "A Preference for Development: The Law and Economics of GSP," in George A. Bermann and Petros C. Mavroidis (eds.), WTO *Law and Developing Countries* (Cambridge: Cambridge University Press, 2007), 255, 256–260 (hereinafter *WTO Law*).

[53] Edwini Kessie, "The Legal Status of Special and Differential Treatment Provisions under the WTO Agreements," in *WTO Law*, 12, 16 (hereinafter Kessie).

[54] *The GATT Legal System*, supra note 48, 212–213.

[55] Ibid., 214.   [56] Ibid., 221.

intended to become fully blown customs unions, just as the liberalization of substantially all the trade with those dependencies (as GATT Article XXIV would have required) was never intended. The EEC's preferences, in other words, were legally dubious but the EEC's Cold War strategic importance precluded any real demand for legal compliance. Other such agreements soon followed suit with the European Free Trade Area while EEC preferences grew in variety and number.[57] The developing countries too jumped on the bandwagon and the Latin-American Free Trade Area was one result. These agreements were justified only very loosely, if at all, under GATT rules.[58]

In short, the years 1957–1958 became a turning point. The Haberler Report had called for greater market access, the EEC was created,[59] and the developing countries shifted away from infant industry and import substitution toward export-oriented policies.[60] The developing countries also shifted from reliance upon an argument in favor of nonreciprocal concessions to an argument which favored the prospect of new, preferential concessions (i.e. concessions that would be accorded to them exclusively in view of their status). The two GATT ten-year waivers in 1971 (and subsequently, the Enabling Clause that put them on a permanent footing) embraced both principles, even if nonreciprocity was weakly stated when compared to the principle that developing countries should be accorded special preferences. Be that so, Resolution 21(ii) at UNCTAD II called for recognition of both principles. The price for developing-country participation in the GATT had gone up.[61] What was more important was that the United States had responded positively to the GSP scheme even though it found itself in the position of intermediary between developing-country complaints of European discrimination and its own felt need to support the Treaty of Rome on strategic grounds.[62]

v. FAIRNESS AS A GOVERNING CONCEPT: HUDEC REVISITED

Hudec's well-known analysis of these events reveals a tension. On the one hand, he criticized the developed countries (which simply considered GATT to be a "serious" forum for the exchange of trade concessions) for ignoring the developing nations' paper victories on important questions of principle.[63] On the other hand, he considered these developments in favor of the developing

---

[57] Ibid., 222–223.

[58] Ibid., 223.

[59] Ibid., 224.

[60] See also Kessie, supra note 53, 17.

[61] Ibid.

[62] *The GATT Legal System*, supra note 48, 222, 224.

[63] *Developing Countries*, supra note 1, 73–74.

countries to be a part of a period of general decline in GATT legality from 1963–1964 to 1975. Although he did not attribute the "delegalization" of the GATT to the developing countries as such, but to pressures resulting from the EEC's formation, there was an unmistakable nostalgia in his writings for a return to GATT legality. At the time he wrote, it was not clear which would prevail – the developing nations' attempt to forge new principles or the general decline of principled behavior; the emergence of developing-country preferences or a return to legality where such preferences would then be subjected to stricter scrutiny. Jackson, in comparison, saw that even before the Enabling Clause in 1979, the GATT's MFN obligation had been amended in all but name.[64] Recall the ITO Charter's Article 15 and the Syrian and Latin-American call for developing-country regional arrangements during the drafting of Article XXIV, which was dealt with pragmatically by creating specifically tailored exceptions for the Syria–Lebanon Customs Union and other Latin-American arrangements.[65] Nevertheless, the issue of developing-country preferences had remained and the developing countries pushed for individualized, case-by-case treatment of their regional arrangements under Article XXIV. For Jackson, the loosening of Article XXIV legal scrutiny in these instances signified a new kind of so-called law in action, not lawlessness.[66]

Hudec instead mounted a significant critique of fairness discourse in trade policy debate. He accepted that there were "normative values" involved,[67] and he acknowledged the behavioral significance of such talk of fairness at a time when international lawyers generally would not have paid much attention to such matters. Conventional international lawyering treats actual state claims as important mainly for the identification of legal rules.[68] Lawyers might concede, at best, that certain kinds of state practice that lead to nonbinding principles are only "more than non-law" but still "less than law."[69] In contrast, economic debate is not hamstrung by such rigid behavioral categories.

---

[64] *World Trade*, supra note 3, 591.   [65] Ibid., 578.

[66] Ibid., 590–591. My reference here to the "law in action" is taken from Karl Llewellyn, who drew a distinction between those "pure paper rules" to which officials paid no heed and "the accepted patter of the law officials." See Karl Llewellyn, "A Realistic Jurisprudence: The Next Step," *Columbia Law Review* 30 (1930): 431, 449–451.

[67] *Essays*, supra note 13, 230.

[68] See, e.g., Kessie's treatment of the "legal status" of special and differential treatment provisions; Kessie, supra note 53.

[69] G. J. H. van Hoof, *Rethinking the Sources of International Law* (Deventer: Kluwer, 1983), 187–189; compare O. A. Elias and C. L. Lim, *The Paradox of Consensualism in International Law* (The Hague: Kluwer, 1998), 230–232. Elsewhere, analytical jurisprudence is occupied with the question of a necessary or conceptual connection between law and morality. See, e.g., Joseph Raz, "Legal Positivism and the Sources of Law," in Joseph Raz, *The Authority of Law: Essays on Law and Morality* (Oxford: Oxford University Press, 1979), 38; John Finnis, "The Truth in

For the economist, it does not matter whether developing-nation practice in the mid-1960s amounted to law or not in light of the facts of such practice. It is no surprise that the terms of the debate on the justice of contemporary international economic arrangements have been set by economic theory about the detrimental, distortive effects of preferences.[70] I have chosen the somewhat cumbersome phrase "conventional" or "positive" morality to describe – however loosely – the elaborate behavioral category that Hudec did much to identify.[71] The term was borrowed by the Oxford legal philosopher, H. L. A. Hart, from the early English utilitarian philosophers,[72] and it denotes a "morality actually accepted and shared by a given social group" as distinguished "from the general moral principles used in criticism of actual social institutions," including criticism of positive morality itself.[73] For Hart, attention to positive morality improves our understanding of the social functions of moral rules and standards.[74] This is especially significant where it is also the normative legitimacy of social-moral rules that determines their efficacy. Like Hart, Hudec recognized that normative legitimacy contributes toward the

---

Legal Positivism," in Robert P. George (ed.), *The Autonomy of Law: Essays on Legal Positivism* (Oxford: Oxford University Press, 1996), 195, 206.

[70] Gardner Patterson, "Would Tariff Preferences Help Economic Development?," *Lloyd's Bank Review* 18 (1965): 76; Harry G. Johnson, "Trade Preferences for Manufactured Goods," in Harry G. Johnson, *Economic Policies toward Less Developed Countries* (Washington, D.C.: The Brookings Institute, 1967), 163. Both are reprinted in Bernard Hoekman and Çağlar Özden (eds.), *Trade Preferences and Differential Treatment of Developing Countries* (Washington, D.C.: The World Bank, 2006), 23, 33 (hereinafter Hoekman and Özden).

[71] I am not saying that Hudec would have seen it as such. He probably saw much of it from the viewpoint of the New Haven School. See Myres S. McDougal and Harold D. Lasswell, "The Identification and Appraisal of Diverse Systems of Public Order," *American Journal of International Law* 53 (1953): 1; Myres S. McDougal and W. Michael Reisman, "International Law in Policy-Oriented Perspective," in R. St. J. MacDonald and Douglas M. Johnston (eds.), *The Structure and Process of International Law* (The Hague: Nijhoff, 1983), 131.

[72] MacCormick, supra note 9, 47.

[73] H. L. A. Hart, *Law, Liberty and Morality* (Palo Alto, CA: Stanford University Press, 1963), 20.

[74] MacCormick describes Hartian positive morality as "[a] morality as so characterized is social rather than individualistic, and it is the morality of a group of people who live together and interact socially"; further, "[m]uch of it is learned, much from anyone's point of view a matter of imitation and going along with the herd, perhaps because one desires that there be a herd along with which to go"; MacCormick, supra note 9, 46. More recent debate has centered on the fact that as an explanation of positive morality, the Hartian method must therefore account for the existence of social rules as the reason for our acting in accordance with them (e.g., such as practice in the GATT following the Enabling Clause). However, individual and social morality need not depend in such a way on the existence of a social practice as a reason for – or as a standard of – behavior. Strict vegetarians criticize meat eating out of conviction instead, even assuming a hypothetical society inhabited exclusively by vegetarians. See further, H. L. A. Hart, *The Concept of Law*, 2nd ed. (Oxford: Oxford University Press, 1994), 256.

"compliance pull" of social rules.[75] His treatment of the concept of fairness in U.S. foreign trade policy gave recognition to these aspects of fairness talk. For example, Hudec addressed the fairness justifications for U.S. antidumping laws (AD laws) as something that lies in the "background" and "supplies normative legitimacy to the technical operation" of the law.[76]

Why then was Hudec so strangely bound to conventional legal analysis in his treatment of developing-country fairness claims? Having chosen to analyze two distinct movements in the GATT sometime between the mid-1960s and the 1970s – a "legalizing" and another "delegalizing" form of behavior – he characterized the establishment of the new S&D treatment norms as part of a larger, delegalizing move. Elsewhere, Hudec pointed out that the new S&D norms such as the GSP were only "permissive," not "mandatory" – in other words, his concern was with their precise legal nature.[77] The reasons for his legal conventionalism, as opposed to his moral conventionalism, are to be found elsewhere in his work.

vi. HUDEC'S "MORAL SKEPTICISM"

In a seminal paper, Hudec had also traced the origin of U.S. trade remedies rules to calls for fair competition. However, such calls are heard despite the fact that the foreign and domestic business competitors are regulated differently in different places. In the purely domestic context, fairness claims had at least a common history in the Interstate Commerce Clause and U.S. antitrust laws. In the domestic setting, fairness means "that businesses should succeed or fail according to their respective merit as competitors."[78] The "normative role of the fair competition concept is useful primarily in situations in which there is growing competition."[79] Not so with AD laws and countervailing duty (CVD) laws in the United States. These apply to the foreign trade policy sphere and possess no immediate domestic counterpart.[80]

Noting the political compromise underlying the Trade Agreements Act of 1979 – that is, the tightening of AD and CVD regulation in exchange for greater trade liberalization – Hudec saw the idea of fairness as essentially nothing more than a deal struck between government and business in the

---

[75] See also Thomas M. Franck, *The Power of Legitimacy among Nations* (Oxford: Oxford University Press, 1990).
[76] *Essays*, supra note 13, 240. [77] *Developing Countries*, supra note 1, 64.
[78] *Essays*, supra note 13, 231. [79] Ibid.
[80] This thought was to be played out on the Mexican side during the NAFTA negotiations. See Hermann von Bertrab, *Negotiating NAFTA: A Mexican Envoy's Account* (Westport, CT: Praeger, 1997), 68.

United States. Business would accept more competition provided it was "fair." Nonetheless, if fairness were to become a governing criterion, "the facts of the international market [would] still make the concept potentially limitless when applied to foreign trade. Any government-created advantage not available to outsiders [would be] a potential 'unfair advantage/subsidy'."[81]

In addition, because CVD laws protect manufacturing industries that benefit from tariff protection at home, talk of fairness makes sense only when the subsidy is considered in pure isolation.[82] In the foreign setting, the concept of fairness becomes therefore either unpersuasive or unadministrable because the global regulatory field can never be level. The same is true with AD. The idea of fair competition is therefore sound when that competition only concerns foreign manufacturers enjoying monopoly profits in their home market. It is persuasive in those instances in which home and export market price differentials are solely at issue. However, as with CVD, the fairness concept is not meant to apply to businesses that are governed differently in different places where any difference (e.g., in national tariffs) would complicate discussion about what is "fair."[83]

All this explains why Hudec was generally skeptical about moral (i.e., fairness) arguments in trade. Having identified the normative significance of trade fairness discourse, he ultimately rejected its usefulness. Fairness, although significant in explaining behavior because of its normative aspects in terms of positive morality, fails to fulfill its normative promise. In particular, it explains why he believed "reverse discrimination" (as he termed the developing-country argument) is penny gin, and that the developing countries' desire[84] "would be [for] something like a law proclaiming that concerns for the poor require giving them greater legal freedom to use narcotic substances."

In the final analysis, proof of the value of arguments about equality or fairness lies not in their normative soundness but in the soundness of their economic premises. Hudec questioned the economic assumptions of infant-industry protection and the call for new preferences. The infant-industry argument is economically unsound because governments are inept market interveners while businesses tend to misbehave and rent seek.[85] The new-preferences argument (i.e., that developed nations should offer new, non-MFN preferences to poor countries) is stronger in economic theory, but it too suffers because developed-country MFN tariffs are already low and there is widespread use of nontariff barriers instead.[86]

[81] *Essays*, supra note 13, 236.
[82] Ibid., 237–238.
[83] Ibid., 238–242.
[84] *Developing Countries*, supra note 1, 141.
[85] Ibid., 144–151.
[86] Ibid., 151–153.

Hudec's account misfires, especially his argument that S&D treatment must be tested not on the strength of its underlying equality claims but its underlying economic reasoning. What is the reason for ultimately choosing to test these claims against economic theory? His moral skepticism might have some role in this. However, in his influential *Developing Countries and the GATT Legal System*, Hudec advanced the argument that equality was not just meaningless but also deceptive and delusional. Putting aside his skepticism about fairness-based arguments in the AD and CVD contexts (what he called "offensive unfairness" claims), Hudec's skepticism extended to "defensive unfairness" claims – claims for the United States to do something about getting a more balanced or fairer deal. Defensive arguments are like the claims of developing-country nations; in his essay entitled "Mirror, Mirror on the Wall," Hudec concluded that the problem was *not* that of overinclusiveness, as in the case of offensive unfairness:

> Unfortunately, balance is not a measurable phenomenon. It is a crude per-ception, based on observations about what foreign governments are doing in comparison to one's own government. The perception is quite manipulable – in either direction.... Given the pressure of export interests behind claims of imbalance, attempts to correct imbalance in day-to-day operations must inevitably be corrupted and become simple power diplomacy under a veil of normative justification.[87]

Hudec's critique of the developing countries' arguments for S&D treatment is similar. Those arguments address poverty with the narcotic of mercantilist protectionism. The end result is self-deception or worse, a bald-faced lie, no more than "simple power diplomacy under a veil of normative justification."[88] The result is that Hudec's views ultimately left virtually no room for any moral argument about trade policy. His is a wholesale skepticism not based simply on spotting confusion at the level of individual arguments but based on an argument about the general incoherence of moral theorizing about trade policy. For Hudec, offensive unfairness claims were doomed. They were overinclusive in those cases in which they try to account for a world divided by states, and underinclusive in those in which they do not account for differences in sovereign regulation. They are unpersuasive because of sovereign regulatory differences or unadministrable in those instances in which they try to address

---

[87] Reprinted in *Essays*, supra note 13, 249.

[88] Clearly, the developing countries had and continue to have power measured in terms of num-bers, that is, "power divorced from force." See further Alan K. Henrikson, "Global Foundations for a Diplomacy of Consensus," in Alan K. Henrikson (ed.), *Negotiating World Order: The Artisanship and Architecture of Global Diplomacy* (Wilmington, DE: Scholarly Resources, 1986), 217, 238–239.

all those differences. Defensive claims, in contrast, are not doomed. They are deceptive or delusional because of their concealment of underlying export pressures, which are the real cause that such claims are made in the first place. In other words, defensive unfairness is unpersuasive because it is a disguise for mercantilism.[89] As such, defensive unfairness should be measured by the same economic arguments we would use to defeat mercantilism. Fairness claims seem to matter to trading behavior but cannot live up to their normative promise.

VII. EQUALITY AS A VALUE

In the account just given, equality has no value where it has no economic value. Formal equality in the form of the MFN doctrine is valuable because it acts as a worldwide tariff accelerator. The most efficient world economy is one based on MFN liberalization. But for developing countries, MFN alone may not be as useful.[90] Neither those who grant preferences to developing countries nor the developing countries that grant preferences to other developing countries should be compelled to grant similar concessions to third-party countries. This is what substantive equality is about. Developed countries argue the opposite – that MFN liberalization will benefit competitive industries in developing countries.[91] The developed-country argument is similar to saying that equality is an economic concept while the developing nations must deny this. For developing countries, the developed-country argument is not unlike having to challenge the nonadmission of women to the Virginia Military Institute in order to demonstrate not only that women are being discriminated against, but that not discriminating against them will also increase the efficiency of military college education.[92] It might be said that the analogy is inappropriate because the GATT–WTO *is* about efficiency. There are at least three responses to this.

---

[89] For a similar argument see Franklin A. Gevurtz, "An Essay on Teaching International Economic Law through a Corporate Perspective," in Colin B. Picker et al. (eds.), *International Economic Law: The State and Future of the Discipline* (Oxford: Hart, 2008), 171, 173.

[90] This is not to say that smaller, developing trading nations do not enjoy free riding through multilateral liberalization.

[91] *Developing Countries*, supra note 1, 152.000

[92] The complaint here would be the same as the argument that wealth is not a social value. See, e.g., Ronald M. Dworkin, "Is Wealth a Value?," *Journal of Legal Studies* 9 (1980): 191, 195. See contra Richard A. Posner, *The Economics of Justice* (Cambridge, MA: Harvard University Press, 1981), 107ff. (hereinafter *The Economics of Justice*). For another attempt to lend economic analysis normative foundations, see Jules L. Coleman, *Risks and Wrongs* (Cambridge: Cambridge University Press, 1992).

First, we could modify the analogy by treating this issue of admission to the Virginia Military Institute according to its proper military and educational purposes. It would still be like asking prospective female applicants to demonstrate that their admission to the Virginia Military Institute would advance military education – that is, that equality should not be valued for its own sake. Second, the developing country arguments we have seen actually precede the GATT's founding. Preferential agreements between developing countries were intended to have been included in the GATT 1947, and the position of the developing countries, including those that joined the GATT subsequently, has remained fairly consistent over time. It is therefore historically questionable to suggest that the GATT–WTO prizes efficiency only. At best, the pure efficiency rationale is no more than advocacy on the part of some, but not all, of the GATT's members. Third, as Hudec himself acknowledged, the various rounds of liberalization were justified to the populations of GATT members in mercantilist terms. Although his response was to accept this simply as a form of public posturing,[93] we could ask whether the most sensible interpretation of what GATT members have said about what they do is to treat it as an elaborate hoax.

After fifty years of making these kinds of moral claims about status equality, the developing countries are still trying to alter the constitutional norms of the GATT–WTO in a more comprehensive, systematic way. True, at different times in history they did manage to modify the GATT's formal norm of nondiscrimination by altering the constitutional balance during critical moments. Examples include the argument for developing-country preferences in the 1960s and 1970s at the height of the Cold War. This brings us to a noteworthy ruling of the latest participant in the WTO constitutional order – the Appellate Body.

VIII. THE *EC – TARIFF PREFERENCES* CASE

In the *EC – Tariff Preferences* case,[94] the Appellate Body drew on the actual, historical claims of developing nations in the face of textual ambiguity. India challenged the preferences that the EC accords to certain developing countries. At the heart of India's challenge was the view that GATT–WTO law

---

[93] *Developing Countries*, supra note 1, 142–144.
[94] *European Communities – Conditions for the Granting of Preferences to Developing Countries*, WT/DS246/AB/R (April 4, 2004).

requires that the EC's preferences should be accorded equally to all developing countries. The dispute turned on the proper legal interpretation of Articles 2(a) and 3(c) of the Enabling Clause. According to the EC, there was no obligation to treat all developing countries in an identical manner. The panel agreed with India instead and ruled out discriminating between the developing countries under the Enabling Clause. The EC therefore failed to convince the panel that, first, differential treatment is permitted provided the differentiating measure bears a reasonable relation to the developing, financial, and trade needs of the individual developing country (i.e., a "rational basis" rule), and second that not "all" developing countries should be entitled to preferences according to the terms of Articles 2(a) and 3(c).[95]

On appeal, the Appellate Body also found the text of the Enabling Clause to be somewhat inconclusive. But as Gene Grossman and Alan Sykes have noted, the Appellate Body adopted a "middle way" instead in ruling that preferences need not be identical, and nonidentical treatment need not be discriminatory. In effect, the Appellate Body – having found the Enabling Clause to be law – applied a "substantive" conception of equality. Nations are only treated equally when their legitimate differences are taken into account, especially where differences in their developmental, financial, or trade needs are in question. This is therefore similar, in broad terms, to the developing-country position that economic status does matter. The Appellate Body ruled, however, that the EC had failed to prove that its differentiating measures were sufficiently narrowly tailored toward such differences.[96]

Criticizing the Appellate Body's reasoning, Grossman and Sykes dismiss the explanation just offered. According to them, the deal struck between the developed and developing countries was that developed countries would put up with trade distortion if preferences were to avoid further differentiation between developing countries, much in the way that was suggested by the panel.[97] If this view is correct, then an economic rationale based on efficiency, or at least a "least distortive method" rule, should define the Enabling Clause. Grossman and Sykes therefore consider that the Appellate Body's ruling went too far. Their account fits with the economic interpretation of the GATT–WTO, but it does not fit with a historical understanding of the GSP scheme. The United States had wanted to dispense with discrimination between developing countries in a "generalized" scheme of preferences but because the EEC had refused to go along, that attempt failed to achieve a general, or nondiscriminatory, system. Put simply, the EEC never agreed

---

[95] See further *WTO Law*, supra note 52, 262–264.
[96] Ibid., 264–269.   [97] Ibid., 267–268.

to a "least distortive method" rule. So whatever we might think about the economic justifications for the Appellate Body's ruling,[98] the Appellate Body appears correct in treating differentiation between developing nations as legitimate provided that the Appellate Body itself retained the right to scrutinize such differential treatment to ensure their conformity with the actual developmental, financial, and trade needs of individual developing-country recipients. The Appellate Body's ruling upholds a substantive conception of equality, or at least rejects identical treatment as the default trade law rule. India "lost" its argument but the larger developing-country argument against a rigid, formal view of equality seems to have prevailed. How close will the Appellate Body's scrutiny be in the future? Perhaps there will be a fair degree of tolerance for differential treatment so long as such treatment bears a reasonable relation to the needs of the individual developing country, a test that in any event the EC failed to pass on the facts of the case. In my view, *EC – Tariff Preferences* was therefore a victory for India even if it lost the argument that there should be no developing-country differentiation. The GSP system as a thinly veiled system of trade conditionality now falls under the Appellate Body's equal treatment supervision,[99] and so it is that the Appellate Body is now institutionally entrusted with articulating the conventional morality of the majority of the world's trading nations.

IX. CONCLUSION

There are two matters I have not dealt with. First, arguments for S&D treatment promise to remain central to WTO debates. For a time during the 1980s, it seemed this would no longer be the case. The Uruguay Round's Single Undertaking indicated a new trend toward integrating the developing countries. S&D treatment had become "issue specific" or "agreement specific" instead.[100] But fueled by developing-country complaints of the Round's failed

---

[98] This occurred through the curbing of negative externalities on exporting nations that do not enjoy preferential treatment; see *WTO Law*, supra note 52, 271–274. The authors raise many of the usual arguments, however, against developing country preferences, such as whether preferences help to pick the right developing country manufacturers and industries for preferential treatment and the issue of compliance costs.

[99] I am grateful to Chantal Thomas for our exchanges during the symposium, which helped considerably to sharpen my thoughts on the issue. In her chapter she argues that Appellate Body intervention will be insufficient to address the problems of underdevelopment and distributive justice, that democratic reform of the WTO would be more advantageous, and that India "lost." I agree that Appellate Body intervention alone is insufficient, but it goes in the right direction and India and the developing countries "won."

[100] Hoekman and Özden, supra note 70, xxix.

promises, S&D has risen again with renewed vigor in the 1990s, together with calls for a rethinking of Uruguay.[101] I have not addressed the ongoing Doha Development Round negotiations. This is not to say that the negotiations are irrelevant to the concerns of this contribution, but simply that we have had the benefit of a longer historical perspective in relation to certain classic arguments that the developing countries have made in the past, and that continue to shape the S&D doctrine.

Second, and perhaps what is more important, I have not taken sides with any top-down or ideal moral theory, much less with moral over economic theory. I do not say, much less show, that equality ultimately matters more than economic reasoning. Simply, I mean to distinguish arguments based solely on fairness from those based on efficiency (or the role of GATT–WTO law in promoting efficiency). By singling out the actual, historical claims of developing countries, the middle-level theorizing attempted here is aimed against the tendency of economic analyses to efface these claims. Top-down moral theories tend to do the same. They proceed directly to the reflective acceptability of alternative arrangements. The argument in this contribution is that understanding the actual claims of developing nations – as Robert Hudec first tried to do – requires us to recognize the persistence, if not the centrality, of claims for equality. It requires us to accord such claims theoretical, even critical attention, instead of treating them as mistaken from the outset.[102] Failing to do so could lead us to theorize about a world that did not exist, perhaps never truly existed, and that in all probability will never exist.

[101] Ibid., xxx.

[102] Compare Posner's economic analysis of the U.S. Supreme Court's rulings on racial discrimination and affirmative action; *The Economics of Justice*, supra note 92, chapters 12–14. In trying to show that judicial balancing could result in the upholding of discrimination on efficiency grounds even where distributive effects are weighed in the balance, Posner at least seeks to address racial discrimination as something which is prima facie morally wrong in the mainstream morality of American society. Similarly, we need to address more seriously the developing countries' argument that inflexible MFN treatment is sometimes morally wrong even if these arguments would, if applied in practice, result in economically inefficient outcomes.

6 The Political Geography of Distributive Justice

Jeffrey L. Dunoff

The gruesome facts of global inequality and poverty are depressingly familiar. Nevertheless, the enormous disparities in wealth and power that mark our world still have the power to shock. Consider the following:

1. There are 1.4 billion people who live at or below the poverty line of $1.25 per day and over 3 billion people who live on less than $2.50 per day. At least 80 percent of humanity lives on less than $10 per day.[1]
2. The net worth of the three richest individuals in the world exceeds the aggregate gross domestic product (GDP) of the forty-eight least developed states,[2] and one-half of the world's population possesses less than 1 percent of its wealth.
3. The world's forty-nine poorest states account for 10 percent of the world's population, yet they account for 0.4 percent of world trade.
4. Each day, over 26,000 children die of hunger and other preventable diseases. This is equivalent to one child every three seconds, and almost 10 million deaths annually.[3] In addition, more than 500,000 women die in pregnancy and childbirth each year; 99 percent of these deaths are in developing countries.

[1] See *World Bank Development Indicators* (Washington, D.C.: World Bank, 2008).
[2] Jeff Gates, "Statistics on Poverty and Inequality" (available at http://www.globalpolicy.org/socecon/inequal/gates99.htm; accessed February 5, 2010).
[3] For additional statistics see UNICEF, *The State of the World's Children 2008 – Child Survival* (New York: UNICEF, 2008; available at http://www.unicef.org/sowc08/).

This is a revised and expanded version of a presentation given at the American Society of International Law–International Economic Law Group Symposium on Distributive Justice and International Economic Law in Washington, D.C., in November 2008. I am grateful to Chios Carmody, Frank Garcia, and John Linarelli for the opportunity to participate in this symposium; to Chin Leng Lim, Fernando Tesón, Chantal Thomas, and Joel Trachtman for stimulating exchanges over the relationships between international trade and distributive justice; and to symposium participants for challenging questions and comments.

5. Approximately 2.5 billion people do not have access to improved sani-
   tation, and roughly 1.2 billion lack access to clean water.
6. Gender inequality is endemic: Some 70 percent of the 1.3 billion people
   living in poverty are women, and women work two-thirds of the world's
   working hours yet earn only 10 percent of the world's income. They
   own less than 1 percent of the world's property.[4]

The brutal social and economic realities that lie behind these facts render
demands for distributive justice increasingly salient and urgent. Nevertheless,
meaningful response to the plight of the poor in general and in developing
countries in particular has proven to be both frustratingly inadequate and
extraordinarily challenging. Some difficulties result from the enormous diversity among developing states. For example, while some developing states have
been at the forefront of global economic growth, another group – much greater
in number, if smaller in population – is falling further behind.[5] Moreover, the
barriers to economic growth and development vary enormously across countries. As a result, generalized policies are unlikely to be effective, and more
nuanced approaches are needed.

The disparity and complexity is exacerbated by the fact that the global
economy has entered a period of extraordinary turbulence. Although these
economic difficulties first became apparent in the United States, they quickly
spread around the globe. Unemployment is rising quickly in Europe and the
once-sizzling economies in Asia and Latin America have begun to sputter.
Hence, the world economy is entering a wrenching downturn that is likely to
be both broad and deep, confronting global justice advocates with a difficult
empirical landscape.

As if these empirical difficulties were insufficiently challenging, reformers
also face significant conceptual difficulties. The economic and political causes
of structural global inequalities and the more current global downturn are
both complex and contested. Thus broad-based agreement on how to change
current realities remains elusive. As a result, addressing questions of global
distributive justice are as difficult as they are pressing.

The different contributions to this volume address various dimensions of
global justice debates: As a political matter, should our focus be on ending

---

[4] Figures culled from the Web site of the Millennium Development Goals campaign (available
at http://endpoverty2015.org; accessed February 5, 2010).
[5] Seven developing states account for 80 percent of high-technology exports and more than
70 percent of low-technology exports; see the *Human Development Report 2005* (New York:
United Nations Development Programme, 2005), 117.

global poverty, or on advancing a broader social justice agenda?[6] As a conceptual matter, is the relevant unit of analysis the state or the individual? As a normative matter, what are the justifications for arguing that individuals or groups in one part of the planet have justice obligations to individuals or groups in another part of the planet?[7]

These are large, important, and highly contested issues, and it is not possible to address all of them adequately in this short essay. Instead, I will explore the much narrower topic of how questions of distributive justice have historically arisen in the multilateral trade system. As we shall see, these questions have tended to focus on a small number of relatively discrete topics, and I will critique a recent line of scholarship suggesting that these topics have been addressed in moral terms. Although it is certainly true that the depressing empirical realities just summarized present compelling moral challenges – and that the structure and operation of the international trade system raises pressing moral concerns – I believe that the recent scholarship rests upon a mistaken reading of the history of the trade system. My interest, however, is not simply historiographical. As demonstrated more fully in the paragraphs that follow, the deeper concern is that misreading the history of the General Agreement on Tariffs and Trade (GATT) may have the effect of diverting our attention from some of the potentially most effective and pragmatic ways of addressing economic inequality and promoting global distributive justice.

To develop these claims, this chapter proceeds as follows. In Section I, I give a brief outline of two ways of orienting ourselves vis-à-vis questions of distributive justice. In Section II, I briefly trace the history of the contentious debates over extending preferential tariff treatment to developing states. I suggest that arguments by developing states in favor of preferences reflect contingent policy preferences driven by practical and pragmatic judgments in light of specific strategic and economic realities, rather than enduring commitments resulting from philosophical or moral imperatives. In Section III, I explore why understanding this history correctly is relevant to contemporary policy disputes. Those who argue that the argument for preferences rests upon moral claims

---

[6] Of course, even limiting our focus to poverty implicates a number of conceptual difficulties. See, e.g., Sudhir Anand and Joseph Stiglitz (eds.), *Measuring Global Poverty* (Oxford: Oxford University Press, 2008); Branko Milanovic, *Worlds Apart: Measuring International and Global Inequality* (Princeton, NJ: Princeton University Press, 2005).

[7] See, e.g., Thomas Nagel, "The Problem of Global Justice," *Philosophy & Public Affairs* 33 (2005): 215. The scholarship here includes a literature on cosmopolitanism exploring whether legal duties can or should exist outside the context of a meaningful political association such as a state. See, e.g., Kwame Anthony Appiah, *Cosmopolitanism: Ethics in a World of Strangers* (New York: Norton, 2006); Jeremy Waldron, "What Is Cosmopolitan," *Journal of Political Philosophy* 8 (2000): 227.

also argue that preference policies should be evaluated in moral, rather than economic or political, terms. In contrast, I suggest not only that the justification for preferences is rooted in specific economic and political conditions, but also that these programs should be evaluated on the basis of political and economic terms. I then show that, evaluated in these pragmatic terms, preference programs have contributed disappointingly little to developing states' development goals. In Section IV, I explore whether undue focus on preferences and developed-state trade policy has diverted attention from alternative policies necessary to enhance developing state growth and development. A brief conclusion follows.

I. TWO APPROACHES TO GLOBAL JUSTICE

In recent years, issues of global justice have moved from the periphery to the center of academic and political debate. Happily, the dialogue has moved beyond the important, although intellectually and politically limiting, debate between cosmopolitanism on the one hand and its statist or nationalist antithesis on the other. Instead the literature now spans topics as diverse as global governance, international humanitarian aid, military intervention, corporate social responsibility, and post-national citizenship, and global justice scholars employ a variety of theoretical and empirical perspectives. Just as importantly, global justice debates are no longer confined to the pages of scholarly journals but have also entered the world of diplomacy and international relations: "The debate about what justice demands beyond the state does not belong only to political philosophy; it is already part of the world of global politics."[8] Although the scholarly and diplomatic attention is both overdue and welcome, it poses difficult questions about points of entry into these debates. To contextualize the arguments set out more fully in Sections II through IV, I briefly set out two basic orientations toward questions of global justice.

A. *Macro and Micro Approaches to Global Justice*

In a recent book, Amaryta Sen argues that post-Enlightenment thinking about justice is characterized by two dominant approaches.[9] One, which he calls

---

[8] Joshua Cohen and Charles Sabel, "Extra Rempublicam Nulla Justitia?," *Philosophy & Public Affairs* 34 (2006): 149, 150.

[9] Amartya Sen, *The Idea of Justice* (Cambridge, MA: Harvard University Press, 2009; hereinafter Sen). Earlier version of Sen's arguments can be found in Amartya Sen, "The Idea of Justice," *Journal of Human Development* 9 (2008): 331; Amartya Sen, "What Do We Want from a Theory of Justice?," *Journal of Philosophy* 103 (2006): 215.

"transcendental justice," is associated with classical writers such as Hobbes and contemporary thinkers such as Rawls and Nozick. This approach looks at society as a whole, and it focuses on the structure and design of institutions designed to ensure a perfectly just society. Sen contrasts this with a second approach, which he calls a "comparative" approach to justice. The comparative approach focuses on social injustices in a comparative setting. Comparativists seek to remove or fix specific injustices. Hence, whereas the "transcendentalists" seek the completely just society, the "comparativists" are incrementalists. They seek not the achievement of a perfectly just society, but the more modest goal of producing as just a society as possible under a given set of circumstances. Sen argues that contemporary political philosophy has been preoccupied with exploring "the grand question" of "what is a just society," and that we should shift our focus to more pragmatic matters of achievable reductions in injustice.

To be sure, it is not entirely clear if these two approaches are or can be entirely unrelated. For example, a comparativist may only know that a certain reform increases the amount of justice (or reduces the amount of injustice) in the world by reference to a conception of a just society. In other words, even the most pragmatic approaches to justice may necessarily rest upon more comprehensive, even if inchoate, theories of justice.[10] And a transcendentalist might appreciate that, as a pragmatic matter, the achievement of justice more often occurs in an incremental, step-by-step manner, as opposed to through system-wide or revolutionary change. Nevertheless, I think that Sen's distinction captures two rather different orientations to the achievement of global justice, and these orientations have very different implications for both scholarship and reform efforts.

I read many of the contributions to this volume, including the contributions on international trade by Chantal Thomas and Chin Leng Lim, as falling into the second camp. To be sure, the contributions differ in many important respects. Each focuses on one of the two central dimensions of global justice. Lim focuses on the substantive dimensions of global justice, and in particular on the international trade rules that apply to developing states. In contrast, Thomas focuses on the procedural dimensions of global justice, and in particular on the mechanisms of the World Trade Organization (WTO) for reaching

---

[10] I am grateful to Maxwell Chibundu for elaborating the argument that there is a necessary link between these two approaches to justice. Indeed, there are glimmers of such a connection in Sen's references to a "conglomerate theory." See Sen, ibid. Nevertheless, Sen rejects the claim that a comparativist approach presupposes a grander theory of justice: "There would be something deeply odd in a general belief that a comparison of any two alternatives cannot be sensibly made without a prior identification of a supreme alternative." Sen, ibid., 338.

political decisions.[11] Her chapter raises the question of whether international and transnational regimes should meet standards of political justice, including inclusiveness, that apply on the state level.[12]

Despite these differences, I believe that Lim and Thomas share a common orientation to questions of global justice. Both are, in Sen's terms, comparativists. That is, neither seeks to construct or to reveal a transcendental or idealized vision of justice. Neither Thomas nor Lim begins "in the sky," as it were, but rather in concrete conditions, "on the ground." Both are rooted in and responsive to current realities. For current purposes, I share these methodological instincts; I will similarly offer arguments that are particularistic rather than universal, and that are grounded in current and historical realities.

B. Mapping Global Justice

Another other way of orienting ourselves toward justice debates is to consider what we might call the political geography of distributive justice. We typically associate geography with maps and other representations of physical space. However, maps can be used to communicate information about more than physical geography or political boundaries. Can maps be used to convey information about – and help shape policy responses to – global distributive justice?

This idea is not entirely fanciful. In recent years, the World Bank and other international bodies have devoted substantial intellectual and material resources to the development of poverty maps. An example is set out in Map 1.

According to a comprehensive World Bank review, poverty mapping can generate deeper understandings of the causes and incidence of poverty in a locale; engender dramatic shifts in the dialogue over poverty, including prompting new strategies and approaches; and foster the development of capacity and interest in evidence-based policy-making processes.[13]

---

[11] For another interesting effort to advance alternative forms of democratic decision making within the WTO, see Ilan Kapoor, "Deliberative Democracy and the WTO," *Review of International Political Economy* 11 (2004): 522.

[12] For important treatments of this question see Daniele Archibugi and David Held (eds.), *Cosmopolitan Democracy: An Agenda for a New World Order* (Cambridge: Polity Press, 1995); David Held, *Democracy and the Global Order* (Cambridge: Polity Press, 1995); William Smith and James Brassett, "Deliberation and Global Governance: Liberal, Cosmopolitan, and Critical Perspectives," *Ethics & International Affairs* 22 (2008): 69; James Bohman, "International Regimes and Democratic Governance," *International Affairs* 75 (1999): 499.

[13] Tara Bedi et al., "Poverty Maps for Policy Making: Beyond the Obvious Targeting Applications," in Tara Bedi et al. (eds.), *More than a Pretty Picture: Using Poverty Maps to Design Better Policies and Interventions* (Washington, D.C.: World Bank, 2007), 5.

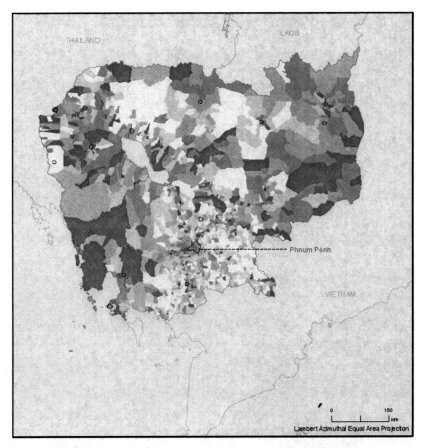

Map 1. Poverty map. This map illustrates income inequality in different regions of the country. The darker the color, the greater the role of income inequality among individuals living in that area.

What if we attempted to map other dimensions of global economic injustice? What would these maps look like? The size of a state might not be a function of landmass, but rather a function of GDP or of the number of people living in poverty. Alternatively, a state's size might reflect the percentage of public funds spent on public health, or the percentage of girls who attend secondary schools. Maps might convey information about per capita income, or the distribution of income or wealth inside states.

To be sure, efforts to map some factors relevant to global justice already exist. For example, the size of each state in Map 2 reflects the proportion of a state's population that lives on less than U.S. $1.00 per day.

In Map 3, the size of a state reflects its proportion of total worldwide wealth, measured in terms of GDP.

Map 2. The size of each state reflects the proportion of a state's population that is living on less than U.S. $1.00 per day (*source:* http://www.worldmapper.org/display .php?selected=179; copyright 2006 SASI Group, University of Sheffield, and Mark Newman, University of Michigan).

Of course, a comprehensive set of global justice maps would not concentrate exclusively upon wealth. Global justice maps could convey, for example, the differential contributions states make to global environmental degradation. In Map 4, the size of each state reflects the magnitude of that state's carbon emissions.

Map 3. The size of a state reflects its proportion of total worldwide wealth, measured in terms of GDP (*source:* http://www.worldmapper.org/display.php?selected=169; copyright 2006 SASI Group, University of Sheffield, and Mark Newman, University of Michigan).

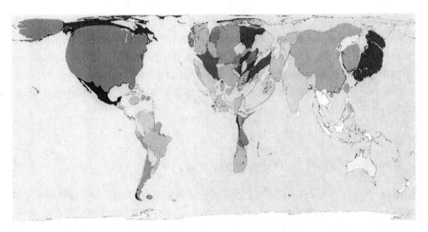

Map 4. Carbon emissions map.

Notably, each of these maps not only conveys different aspects of social reality but may also suggest very different approaches to the problem of global justice. There is every reason to believe that global justice maps of this sort can be as useful a tool in the global justice context as they have been in the poverty context.

However, for current purposes it is useful to consider not only physical maps but also the mental and conceptual maps that we employ when considering questions of global distributive justice. Just as physical maps can organize our understanding of spatial relations among different physical locations, conceptual maps help organize the relations among different ideas. All physical maps face a common challenge: How can one project the earth, a round object, onto a flat surface? There are literally thousands of ways to do so, each with certain strengths and weaknesses. Thus, the choice among maps is, in effect, a choice to privilege certain perspectives or values.[14] Similarly, there are numerous different conceptual maps one can use to analyze global justice. These various maps will both illuminate and obscure different parts of the problem, and they can point us in one or another policy direction.

The question I wish to explore in the remainder of this chapter is whether current conceptual approaches to global distributive justice do more to illuminate or obscure, and whether alternative approaches are available. Would

[14] For example, traditional Mercator projection maps are wildly distorting. These maps make the global North appear to be slightly larger than the global South, although the North covers 18.9 million square miles and the South covers 38.6 million square miles. Similarly, these maps make Europe's land mass appear to be relatively larger than it actually is.

different conceptual orientations more effectively build awareness, change perceptions, or open more fruitful dialogues over global justice? Stated more provocatively, I wish to consider whether the conceptual maps currently on offer in global justice debates are, in an important sense, upside down or backwards: Might we advance these debates by turning these conceptual maps inside out?

II. SHIFTS IN DEVELOPING STATE ADVOCACY FOR PREFERENTIAL TREATMENT: PRINCIPLED OR PRAGMATIC?

The contributions in this volume amply demonstrate the range and reach of contemporary debates over global justice. Given that international trade is simultaneously a driver of prosperity and of increasing global inequality, one might expect an equally rich set of debates over the ways in which the international trade system affects global justice. For example, one could imagine a rich dialogue over whether the international trade regime system organizes, extends, or legitimates global disparities of wealth or power. It is thus somewhat surprising that, as a historical matter, distributive justice debates among trade negotiators and scholars have been significantly narrower; they have tended to revolve around a small number of issues.[15] In general terms, the debates have centered upon whether developing states should be subject to the basic GATT–WTO concepts of nondiscrimination and reciprocity, or whether, in light of their economic conditions, developing states should receive various forms of differential treatment. In particular, for many years much debate has focused on whether goods from developing states enjoy "preferential tariff treatment" when they enter developed state markets (i.e., face a lower tariff rate than like goods from developed states).

A recent strand of scholarship reviewing these debates – exemplified by Chin Leng Lim's contribution to this volume – suggests that the developing-state positions in these debates have been *moral* claims.[16] This scholarship criticizes Western trade scholars for ignoring or overlooking the moral dimension of developing-state claims. It also suggests that developing-state moral claims are not fully answered by *economic* arguments about the relative (in)effectiveness

---

[15] Among those who do not specialize in trade, the debate over the effects of trade has tended to be wider. See, e.g., Kevin Danaher (ed.), *50 Years Is Enough: The Case against the World Bank and the International Monetary Fund* (Boston: South End Press, 1994); Thomas Pogge, *World Poverty and Human Rights* (Cambridge: Polity Press, 2002); Peter Singer, *One World: The Ethics of Globalization* (New Haven, CT: Yale University Press, 2002); Joseph E. Stiglitz, *Globalization and Its Discontents* (New York: Norton, 2002); George Monbiot, *Manifesto for a New World Order* (New York: The New Press, 2004).

[16] Chin Leng Lim, "The Conventional Morality of Trade," in this volume.

of preferential trading policies. Thus, this new strand of scholarship (1) points us toward a very different understanding of the history of North–South tensions in the trade regime, (2) urges Western scholars to take developing state arguments on their own terms, and (3) offers a very different metric for evaluating preference programs.

As noted, the key analytic move in this line of argumentation is the claim that developing states self-consciously understood and presented their claims concerning preferential treatment as *moral* claims. I read this analytic move as setting out a historical or descriptive claim about developing-state arguments. Regrettably, however, there is often little detailed discussion or analysis of the historical materials or practice that would support this claim. Paradoxically, the support for this historical claim is often strikingly ahistorical. Taking the claim on its own terms invites an examination of the available historical evidence to determine whether, as a historical matter, developing state arguments for differential treatment were rooted in *morality*.

To be sure, such an inquiry confronts formidable historiographical difficulties. A large number of official documents from various negotiating sessions exist. However, these documents are often sufficiently bureaucratic in tone and vague in content as to be of limited utility. Moreover, statements made in negotiating fora can serve to divert attention from hidden agendas, and they may or may not accurately reveal a party's motivation.

In addition, many official memoranda of important bilateral and multilateral discussions as well as diaries and memoirs of key participants are available. Although valuable, these sources can also prove problematic. Memos and memoirs are inevitably partial and frequently self-serving. These sources are often written with an eye to the future; they often are as much an effort to "create" history as to record it. Moreover, many of the readily available sources are often written by, or reflect, Western orientations, and they run the risk of misreading developing-state positions.

Finally, a growing number of detailed historical accounts are available.[17] These accounts often provide important insights into the contemporaneous

---

[17] Douglas A. Irwin et al., *The Genesis of the GATT* (Cambridge: Cambridge University Press, 2008; hereinafter Irwin – GATT); Thomas W. Zeiler, *Free Trade, Free World: The Advent of the GATT* (Chapel Hill: University of North Carolina Press, 1999); Robert E. Hudec, *Developing Countries in the GATT Legal System* (Brookfield, VT: Gower, 1987; hereinafter Hudec – *Developing Countries*); John H. Jackson, *World Trade and the Law of GATT: A Legal Analysis of the General Agreement on Tariffs and Trade* (Indianapolis: Bobbs-Merrill, 1969; hereinafter *World Trade*); Richard N. Gardner, *Sterling-Dollar Diplomacy* (Oxford: Clarendon Press, 1956; hereinafter Gardner); William Adams Brown, *The United States and the Restoration of World Trade: An Analysis and Appraisal of the ITO Charter and the General Agreement on Tariffs and Trade* (Washington, D.C.: Brookings Institute, 1950); Clair Wilcox, *A Charter for World Trade* (New York: Macmillan, 1949; hereinafter Wilcox – *Charter*).

concerns, and the personalities, of important historical figures. However, many of these accounts are written by Western observers or academics, and hence they may reflect the Western bias that some scholars from the developing world critique.

For current purposes, it may be possible to sidestep many of the difficult historiographical issues in play by focusing primarily upon the positions that developing states have taken over time with respect to preferences, and the arguments they have offered. As we shall see, developing states have evidenced a variety of shifting positions and offered self-serving claims with respect to preferences. This pattern of behavior is more consistent with the thesis that policy regarding preferences reflects contingent political and economic judgments than it is with the thesis that policy regarding preferences grows out of moral commitments.[18]

A. *The Run-Up to the GATT*

During the latter stages of World War II, the United States engaged its allies in a series of discussions concerning the shape of the postwar economic order. As part of these efforts, the United States began developing plans for a new International Trade Organization (ITO); in December 1945 it circulated to other

---

[18] Three important caveats are in order at this point. First, in setting forth this argument, I am not suggesting that states never advance moral claims or that moral claims have no relevance to international relations. Even scholars generally skeptical of the efficacy of moral and legal claims acknowledge that moral claims can serve important functions in international relations. See, e.g., Jack L. Goldsmith and Eric A. Posner, "Moral and Legal Rhetoric in International Relations: A Rational Choice Perspective," *Journal of Legal Studies* 31 (2002): S115 (moral claims play an important signaling role and help states coordinate to realize mutual gains). Similarly, I do not mean to suggest, as some realists do, that moral arguments are invariably used as pretexts to disguise pursuit of national interests. See, e.g., Hans Morgenthau, *Politics Among Nations: The Struggle for Power and Peace* (New York: Knopf, 1948), 61–62; Hans Morgenthau, *In Defense of the National Interest: A Critical Examination of American Foreign Policy* (New York: Knopf, 1951), 35. Second, to claim that developing state positions were rooted in political and economic, as opposed to moral, claims is not to maintain that no moral claims could be advanced in favor of preferential tariff treatment. For example, one could imagine a moral argument rooted in the need to redress historical injustices committed against developing states. For a sampling of the literature on whether historical wrongs give rise to contemporary duties, see, e.g., John Torpey (ed.), *Politics and the Past: On Repairing Historical Injustices* (Lanham, MD: Rowman & Littlefield, 2003); Lukas H. Meyer (ed.), *Justice in Time: Responding to Historical Injustice* (Baden-Baden: Nomos Verlagsgesellschaft, 2004). Third, to assert that moral claims did not drive developing state agendas is not to say that scholars and others should not engage in moral theorizing about global justice (or other issues). See, e.g., Jason Brennan, "Beyond the Bottom Line: The Theoretical Aims of Moral Theorizing," *Oxford Journal of Legal Studies* 28 (2008): 277.

governments its *Proposals for Expansion of World Trade and Employment.*[19] This document called for the creation of an ITO within the United Nations (U.N.) system to oversee and govern compliance with rules concerning a wide range of economic issues, including trade, restrictive business practices, commodity arrangements, and international labor issues. Other states were receptive to the idea of an international body, and plans to commence formal negotiations ensued. In February 1946, the United States successfully introduced a U.N. resolution creating a Preparatory Committee to draft an ITO Charter, which would then be adopted under a "United Nations Conference on Trade and Employment."[20] Thereafter, the United States circulated the *Suggested Charter for an International Trade Organization of the United Nations,* which helped frame the negotiations that followed. Between 1946 and 1948, a series of international negotiations produced the never-ratified ITO Charter[21] as well as the GATT.

During many of the early negotiations over what would eventually become the GATT, the disagreement between the United States and the United Kingdom over Britain's "imperial preferences" – preferential tariffs for goods from members of the British Commonwealth – were "the central issue."[22] Indeed, U.S. frustration with British "intransigence" on this issue led the United States to seriously consider breaking off negotiations.[23] Notably, the United States opposed these preferential tariffs largely for strategic reasons;

---

[19] The ideas contained in the *Proposals* had been discussed in the context of Anglo-American negotiations over U.S. loans to the United Kingdom. The United Kingdom expressed its "full agreement on all important points" in the U.S. *Proposals* when they were issued. See "Statement by President Truman and Prime Minister Attlee" (December 6, 1945), reprinted in XIII Department of State Bulletin, Vol. XII (December 9, 1945), 905.

[20] For an excellent discussion, which informs the analysis that follows, see Wilcox – *Charter,* supra note 17, 36–50. Wilcox served as chair or vice-chair of the U.S. delegation during much of the negotiations over the ITO Charter.

[21] The seminal discussion of the ITO's stillbirth remains William T. Diebold, Jr., "The End of the ITO," *Princeton Essays in International Finance* 16 (1952).

[22] See Irwin – *GATT,* supra note 17, 45. Thomas W. Zeiler, "Managing Protectionism: American Trade Policy in the Early Cold War," *Diplomatic History* 22 (1998): 337. Although less noted, France also sought to maintain existing preference programs. See Hudec – *Developing Countries,* supra note 17, 10.

[23] See Irwin – *GATT,* supra note 17, 196–197. The clashes between the United States and the United Kingdom over this issue, which included angry exchanges between Assistant Secretary of State Dean Acheson and John Maynard Keynes, representing the U.K. Treasury, and between President Roosevelt and Prime Minister Churchill, have received substantial attention. See, e.g., Leo Amery, *The Empire at Bay: The Leo Amery Diaries, 1929–45,* edited by John Barnes and David Nicholson (London: Hutchinson, 1988); Hugh Dalton, *The Second World War Diary of Hugh Dalton, 1940–1945,* edited by Ben Pimlott (London: Jonathan Cape, 1986).

the government believed that these preferences had an adverse effect on U.S. exports.[24]

Although developing states did not have significant influence in these negotiations,[25] several did articulate positions on the preference issue. For example, Latin American states also opposed the U.K. preference system – although not on moral grounds. Rather, Latin American objections rested upon the entirely pragmatic ground that permitting preferences between former colonies and their colonial powers would favor some developing states but discriminate against others. Moreover, as we shall see, Latin American states changed their position on the desirability of preference programs several years later. Once again, however, the position was not a principled or moral position in favor of (or, against) preferences for *all* developing states. Rather, the new position was the entirely strategic proposal that the United States provide preferential access to Latin American products, but not to products from other developing states.[26]

Lebanon was another original developing state party to the GATT. Like the Latin American states, Lebanon opposed the U.K. preference program. However, it did not take a consistent moral position for or against all preference schemes. Rather, it urged that certain forms of preferences, namely regional preferences, be permitted. This position was designed to permit Arab states to coordinate their economic policies while not extending the supposed benefits of preferential schemes to other developing states.

The leading account of developing state positions at the GATT argues that, in the development of their negotiating positions, developing states were responding to and reenacting the strategic "trade policy lessons" they had learned from developing states, rather than generating moral claims. The lesson, apparently, is that trading nations should seek rules that confer competitive advantage to their own producers and exporters at the expense of foreign competitors:

> Those that had been colonies had been taught by their parent countries that economic benefit was maximized by controlling trade and suppressing competition from alternative suppliers. . . . Those who traded with the United States has been taught a similar lesson when, in 1930, the United States had

---

[24] Thus, in testimony before Congress, Secretary of State Cordell Hull called Imperial preferences "the greatest injury, in a commercial way, that has been inflicted on this country since I have been in public life." See Gardner, supra note 17, 19.

[25] Hudec – *Developing Countries*, supra note 17, 23.

[26] Norma Breda dos Santos et al., "Generalized System of Preferences in General Agreement on Tariffs and Trade/World Trade Organization: History and Current Issues," *Journal of World Trade* 39 (2005): 637, 645 (hereinafter Breda dos Santos).

chose to protect itself by enacting what was believed to be the highest tariff in its history – the infamous Smoot-Hawley tariff.[27]

This understanding of states acting in highly pragmatic, as opposed to highly principled, ways is confirmed by Gardner Patterson, a prominent trade economist and GATT official, who summarized developing states' contemporaneous views on discrimination and preferences as follows: "If rapid economic development and industrialization requires, as we expect, many government controls and if this in turn means discrimination, then so be it. We do not now advocate discrimination, but neither are we willing to rule it out as undesirable."[28]

On balance, the available historical record on GATT's founding does not provide evidence that developing states understood their positions on preferences to be grounded in moral claims, or that they articulated their position in moral terms. Rather, developing states – like developed states – sought to mold GATT norms to their economic and political advantage. As John Jackson summarized debates between developed and developing states:

> The issues . . . [did not] seem to be free trade versus protectionism, or internationalism versus national sovereignty. Each of the groups in the debate desired international control of some things and not of others. Both sides desired to use certain types of trade protective measures but wanted to limit or restrict others. The controversy seemed to be over which trade restrictions would be subjected to greater international control and which not. From the point of view of the less-developed country, the wealthy countries wanted freedom to use those restrictions that only they were most able to use effectively while banning those restrictions that less-developed countries felt they were more able to use.[29]

B. Developments after the GATT's Founding

The practice of grounding arguments for preferential treatment on highly contextualized and contingent circumstances did not change after the GATT came into existence. For example, at the second session of GATT's Contracting Parties, in 1948, the United States sought a GATT waiver to permit it to extend

---

[27] Hudec – *Developing Countries*, supra note 17, 12.
[28] Gardner Patterson, *Discrimination in International Trade: The Policy Issues 1945–1965* (Princeton, NJ: Princeton University Press, 1966), 14 (hereinafter *Discrimination*).
[29] *World Trade*, supra note 17, 637–638. See also Hudec – *Developing Countries*, supra note 17, 10–13; Irwin – *GATT*, supra note 17, 78 ("the main goal of the developing countries . . . was to shift attention toward employment and economic development and to ensure that rules did not prevent them from using qualitative import quotas to promote those goals").

duty-free treatment to imports from Pacific Islands formerly under Japanese rule that the United States was administering under the U.N. trusteeship system. As Patterson observed, "the justification was cast primarily in political terms: the islands' exports had been accorded preferential treatment by Japan; to deprive them of something like equivalent treatment in the United States would hardly be in keeping in the spirit of the United Nations and the responsibilities of the Allies as victors."[30] Although this fact pattern involved a request for preferential treatment by a developed state, developing states were soon to enter the debate.

For example, in 1953, Australia – then considered a developing state – sought permission to extend duty-free treatment to goods from Papua New Guinea without extending this treatment to goods from other states or areas.[31] The request was not couched in moral terms but rather as a means to create incentives for investment. Although the waiver was eventually granted, several developing states expressed deep concerns over Australia's request. Again, this developing state concern was not grounded in morality but rather in the entirely pragmatic observation that the proposed waiver might negatively affect their exports.[32]

In 1957, the GATT Contracting Parties took note of the "failure of the trade of less developed countries to develop as rapidly as that of industrialized countries" and decided to create a "Panel of Experts" to examine "past and current international trade trends and their implications."[33] The resulting report, known as the Haberler Report, concluded that disappointing results for developing states were due in no small measure to developed state trade policies.[34] The report was a "turning point" in North–South relations at the GATT,[35] and thereafter the "demand for greater market access [would] become the first issue on the [trade] agenda."[36] However, the pattern of asserting arguments rooted in contemporaneous economic and political realties and perceptions of national economic interest – rather than lofty moral considerations – did not change.

For example, during the early 1960s, a group of twenty-one developing states proposed a Programme of Action urging developed states to reduce tariffs and other barriers that affected developing-state exports.[37] However, just

---

[30] See *Discrimination*, supra note 28, 325.   [31] GATT Doc. L/133 (September 19, 1953).

[32] See *Discrimination*, supra note 28, 330.   [33] GATT B.I.S.D. (6th Supplement) 18 (1958).

[34] See *Trends in International Trade* (Geneva: GATT, 1958).

[35] Diana Tussie, *The Less Developed Countries and the World Trading System: A Challenge to the GATT* (New York: St. Martin's Press, 1987; hereinafter Tussie).

[36] Hudec – *Developing Countries*, supra note 17, 41.

[37] For accounts see Kenneth W. Dam, *The GATT: Law and International Economic Organization* (Chicago: University of Chicago Press, 1970), 235; Tussie, supra note 35, 27–28.

as these states were calling for freer trade on an MFN basis, eighteen former African colonies were negotiating for preferential access to European markets. Significantly, these divergent policies did not reflect moral disagreement over appropriate treatment of developing states. Rather, as Tussie notes, "[t]hese dispersed moves merely reflected the dissimilarity of their circumstances."[38] Indeed, the developing states that issued the Programme of Action opposed the extension of preferences to African states out of a fear that African imports would displace imports from other developing states.

By the 1960s, thinking about the role of international trade in developing state economies had evolved, but even at this point in time the dominant justifications offered for preferential treatment were not moral arguments. Rather, as Paul Prebisch explicitly noted in his influential report to the 1964 U.N. Conference for Trade and Development, the justification was a variation on the familiar infant-industry argument[39]:

> [I]t was commonly believed by those speaking for the less-developed countries that their inability to produce goods at competitive prices very frequently stemmed from the fact that their unit costs during the early years would be high because they were not yet in a position to take advantage of the known economies of large-scale production. They argued that if markets could be provided to permit them to reach such a level of output, they could then successfully compete.[40]

The other justification that was frequently cited at this time grew out of a concern over deteriorating terms of trade between developed and developing states. The underlying theory, developed by Prebisch, rested upon the observation that the cost of manufactured goods produced by developed states tends to rise at a faster rate than the raw materials supplied by developing states. As a result, the gap between the "core" and the "periphery" tends to increase over time.[41] For example, India's delegate referred to this "terms of trade" argument in GATT proceedings.[42]

---

[38] Tussie, ibid., 28.

[39] United Nations Conference on Trade and Development, "Towards a New Trade Policy for Development," U.N. Doc. E/Conf. 46/3,65 (1964).

[40] See *Discrimination*, supra note 28, 344.

[41] See, e.g., Raul Prebisch, *The Economic Development of Latin America and Its Principal Problems* (1950); Hans Singer, "The Distribution of Gains between Investing and Borrowing Countries," *American Economic Review* 40 (1950): 473. This thesis has proven to be highly influential and highly controversial. For a recent overview of empirical research into the terms-of-trade problem, see United Nations Conference on Trade and Development, *Trade and Development Report 2005* (2005), 85–113.

[42] Irwin – GATT, supra note 17, 127.

Notably, even Prebisch's advocacy for preferences was shaped by strategic calculations. For example, to preempt potential opposition to preference programs, he acknowledged the political need to impose various types of limitations on preference schemes. Specifically, he argued that preferences need not be extended to developing state industries that were already internationally competitive, and that they could be limited to manufactures and semi-manufactures. In addition, he believed that developed states should be able to use safeguard mechanisms to protect against disruptive import surges.[43]

During this time, states continued to press for preference policies that would best advance their political and economic interests. This is perhaps best illustrated by Argentina, Brazil, and Chile, which pursued a two-track strategy during the early 1960s. First, they attacked the European Community's (EC's) limited extension of preferences to former colonies only. They argued that such preferences injured them, and they urged the EC to extend their preferences to all developing states. Simultaneously, they lobbied the United States to extend preferences to Latin American states – but not to extend preferences to other developing states. It is surely a curious form of morality that would critique one preference program for favoring some developing states at the expense of others, and at the same time urge another developed state to create a preference program that would favor certain developing states at the expense of others.

A similar pattern emerged during the World Trade Conference of 1964, when developing states were split on whether to recommend a generalized system of preferences. Once again, however, the motivations behind this divergence are better understood on pragmatic rather than moral grounds; the differing positions of various developing states grew out of "their varying levels of economic development."[44] For example, some developing states were concerned that a comprehensive Generalized System of Preferences (GSP) program would undermine preferential access that they already enjoyed to particular developed-state markets.[45]

These divergent interests continued to manifest themselves even after GATT parties agreed, in principle, to the idea of a GSP available to all developing states. Given that any new preference programs would violate GATT's MFN principle, it was clear that a waiver would be necessary. In

---

[43] See, e.g., Breda dos Santos, supra note 26, 637, 644, and n. 27.
[44] Abdulqawi Yusuf, *Legal Aspects of Trade Preferences for Developing States* (Dordrecht: Nijhoff, 1982), 21.
[45] See *Discrimination*, supra note 28, 366–369.

1971, GATT parties voted to approve a ten-year waiver authorizing developed states to establish "generalized, non-reciprocal and non-discriminatory preferences beneficial to the developing countries."[46] Notably, in the closed vote on this waiver, "many of the LDCs [least developed countries] that enjoyed preferential [tariff] arrangements voted against the [waiver]."[47]

Finally, similar fissures appeared during negotiations over what would eventually become Part IV of the GATT. Again, developing states pressed dramatically different positions regarding preferences, depending on local circumstances. For example, while Brazil argued that only nonprimary products should be covered, the United Arab Republic argued that semi-manufactured and manufactured goods should be covered; Ceylon argued that only specified goods should be covered; and Nigeria and Uganda argued that all goods should be covered.[48] In another set of debates, India and Chile argued that preferential treatment extended to products from one developing state should be applied immediately and unconditionally to like products from other developing states, while Nigeria argued against a "one size fits all approach" and urged that preferences be tailored to the development needs of the beneficiary states.[49] A similar range of disagreements emerged among developing states over the nature and duration of preference programs.[50]

Space considerations preclude a decade-by-decade analysis of debates over preferences, but the general pattern of shifting and self-serving developing state positions should by now be clear. Moreover, the pattern of adopting positions based on national interest, rather than moral concerns, persists. Consider, for example, the recent dispute among the EC, Thailand, and the Philippines involving EC tariffs on tuna. Under an agreement with former colonies known as the Cotonou Partnership Agreement, these states could export tuna duty-free to the EC, while tuna from Thailand and the Philippines were subject to a 24 percent duty. When the EC sought a WTO waiver for the discriminatory treatment under the Cotonou Agreement, the Philippines and Thailand refused to approve the waiver unless they received equivalent market access benefits for their tuna exports. Eventually, the EC significantly reduced the tariffs on tuna from the two Asian exporters, and the two countries withdrew its

---

[46] GATT, *Decision of the Contracting Parties of 25 June 1971*, GATT B.I.S.D. (18th Supplement) 24 (1971).

[47] Robert Rothstein, *The Weak in the World of the Strong: The Developing Countries in the International System* (New York: Columbia University Press, 1977), 146–147.

[48] Irwin – GATT, supra note 17, 129.   [49] Ibid., 127–128.

[50] Ibid., 129.

objections to the WTO waiver.[51] Of course, the recent GSP dispute,[52] which involved an Indian challenge to Pakistan's receipt of certain tariff preferences from the EC, also involved interesting splits among developing states that reflected pragmatic economic judgments.[53]

III. DO PREFERENCE PROGRAMS WORK?

The history reviewed herein suggests that developing-state positions in regard to preferences were based much more on expediency than principle, and that these arguments displayed far more mutability than predictability.[54] This history is relevant to current debates. Scholars who argue that developing-state arguments for preferences rest upon moral claims also argue that preference programs should therefore be evaluated on moral terms.[55] However, the historical overview just presented suggests that developing-state arguments for preferences in fact were (and are) largely strategic, contextual, and instrumental. It is thus entirely appropriate to evaluate preference programs on precisely these grounds. The moral claim, in short, points us in exactly the wrong direction, and we would do better to flip the historical argument right side up.

Doing so suggests the relevance, rather than the irrelevance, of inquiry into the real-world effects of preference programs. A substantial literature examines the empirical effects of preferences. Although no consensus exists in this large body of scholarship, it is fair to say that much of this literature is deeply skeptical about the effects of preferences. In particular, the weight of the econometric and simulation analysis performed to date suggests that preferential schemes are often underinclusive and underutilized, that the benefits generated by

---

[51] Jason Gutierrez, "Philippines Claims Victory over Europe Using WTO Mediation in Tuna Tariff Dispute," BNA *International Trade Reporter*, Vol. 20, p. 1015 (June 12, 2003); Daniel Pruzin, "Yerxa to Mediate EU, Thailand, Philippines Canned Tuna Dispute," BNA *International Trade Reporter*, Vol. 19, p. 1836 (October 24, 2002).

[52] See *European Communities – Conditions for the Granting of Tariff Preferences to Developing States*, WT/DS246/AB/R (April 7, 2004).

[53] I have discussed the doctrinal, institutional, and jurisprudential implications of this dispute in Jeffrey L. Dunoff, "When – and Why – Do Hard Cases Make Bad Law? The GSP Dispute," in George Bermann and Petros C. Mavroidis (eds.), *WTO Law and Developing Countries* (Cambridge: Cambridge University Press, 2007), 283.

[54] Again, I emphasize that to claim developing state positions were strategic and contextual rather than moral is not to deny that a moral claim for preferential policies is available. Nor does it suggest that powerful economic and political arguments against MFN and reciprocity are unavailable. For example, in a world where large industries with economies of scale dominate, it is possible that developing states' firms will not be able to acquire the scale effects to compete with first movers from developed states.

[55] See Chin Leng Lim, "The Conventional Morality of Trade," in this volume.

preferential schemes are often limited and narrowly focused, and that preferences have done disappointingly little to promote economic development in beneficiary states. As the limitations of preference programs have been ably discussed elsewhere,[56] I briefly summarize the arguments here.

One factor that significantly reduces the value of preferential schemes is the widespread exclusion of goods from sectors in which developing states enjoy comparative advantage from preference schemes. For example, labor-intensive industries provide developing states a base for industrialization and participation in the world economy. However, many developed-state preference programs exclude precisely these sectors. Particularly controversial examples of limitations on economically significant goods include the strict limitations on imports of sugar – which accounts for more than half of all foreign exchange earnings for some Caribbean states – from the original U.S. Caribbean Basin Initiative (CBI),[57] the exclusion of tuna, leather and footwear products, petroleum products, and apparel from the U.S.'s Andean Trade Preferences Act,[58] and highly complex rules regarding apparel found in the U.S.'s African Growth and Opportunity Act (AGOA).[59]

Many preferential programs have a number of other features that limit their reach. For example, many preference schemes incorporate the concept of graduation, whereby beneficiary states lose preferential treatment when exports reach a certain value,[60] or when a state reaches a certain level of economic development.[61] As states successfully export certain goods, or are dropped

---

[56] For an excellent summary, see Frank J. Garcia, *Trade, Inequality, and Justice: Toward a Liberal Theory of Just Trade* (New York: Transnational, 2003).

[57] The Caribbean Basin Trade Partnership Act is an extension of CBI; notably the bill extends eligibility for preferential tariff treatment to a number of sensitive products, including apparel and petroleum and petroleum products.

[58] As amended by the Andean Trade Promotion and Drug Eradication Program, preferences were extended to these goods, subject to restrictive rules of origin.

[59] Title I, Trade and Development Act of 2000, Pub. L. 106–200 (1970).

[60] Thus, under the U.S. GSP program, goods lose their eligibility for preferential treatment when they exceed a specified amount – $130 million in 2007, an amount that increases by $5 million every year – or when a beneficiary country captures more than 50 percent of the market share for imports of a particular good. Not surprisingly, research reveals that these "competitive need limitations" primarily benefit U.S. import-competing firms, rather than firms in beneficiary states. See James M. Devault, "Competitive Need Limits and the U.S. Generalized System of Preferences," *Contemporary Economic Policy* 14 (1996): 58.

[61] Thus, e.g., a number of states have been "graduated" from the U.S. GSP program, including Singapore, Hong Kong, Taiwan, Korea, Malaysia, Mexico, and Botswana. In addition, states can also be removed from preference programs for political reasons. For example, the Central African Republic, Eritrea, Cote d'Ivoire, and Mauritania were removed from AGOA following political events such as coups and failures to implement democratic reforms.

entirely from preferential programs, they may be left with overcapacity and a production structure that does not reflect comparative advantage.[62] Moreover, the U.S. and EC GSP programs also contain safeguards clauses that permit preferences to be suspended for certain products or states if those imports cause real or potential injury to domestic producers.

In addition, most preference programs are legislated to last a certain number of years and must then be reauthorized. Reauthorization is, of course, never guaranteed, and at times has occurred on a retroactive basis following expiration of the program. For example, the U.S. GSP program has been renewed nine times since its inception in 1974; eight of these renewals have been after periods of expiration ranging in length from two to fifteen months. This practice introduces substantial commercial uncertainties, and hence lowers the incentive to invest in eligible sectors. Simply put, investors and importing firms attracted by preferences are less likely to invest in or source from beneficiary states when the status of the preferences is in doubt.

Moreover, a number of factors tend to reduce developing states' ability to take advantage of the preferences that are potentially available. Perhaps most importantly, complex rules of origin and relatively high administrative costs result in the significant underutilization of available preferences.[63] In 1999, for example, only one-third of the imports to the EC that were eligible for preferences actually entered the EC with reduced tariffs, largely as a result of complex and restrictive rules of origin.[64] During the same year, excluding minerals, only 4 percent of dutiable imports into the United States from developing countries received preferential treatment.[65] A more recent study has found that the share of eligible exports to the EC that requested GSP treatment was only

---

[62] Alexander Keck and Patrick Low, "Special and Differential Treatment in the WTO: Why, When and How?," in Simon J. Evenett and Bernard M. Hoekman (eds.), *Economic Development and Multilateral Trade Cooperation*, 147–188 (London: Palgrave Macmillan, 2005; hereinafter Keck and Low).

[63] Rules of origin set out the conditions that a product must satisfy to be considered as originating from a beneficiary state. The classic work on rules of origin in preference programs is Jan Herin, "Rules of Origin and Differences between Tariff Levels in EFTA and in the EC," EFTA Occasional Paper No. 13 (1986). For more recent research, see, e.g., U.S. International Trade Commission, *The Economic Effects of Significant US Import Restraints: Fifth Update* (USITC Publication No. 3906, 2007); Patricia Augier, Michael Gasiorek, and Charles Lai-Tong, "The Impact of Rules of Origin on Trade Flows," *Economic Policy*, 20 (2005): 567–624; José Anson et al., "Assessing the Costs of Rules of Origin in North-South PTAs with an Application to NAFTA" (CEPR Discussion Paper No. 2476, 2003).

[64] Paul Brenton and Miriam Manchin, "Making EU Trade Agreements Work: The Role of Rules of Origin," *The World Economy* 26 (2003): 755, 757.

[65] Ibid.

6 percent.[66] Similarly, for the U.S. GSP program, the utilization rate of many tariff lines is zero, and the average for all lines is 25 percent.[67] Conversely, liberalization of restrictive rules of origin can produce significant results, as changes to the AGOA and Canada's GSP program demonstrate.[68]

Finally, the benefits from preferential tariff schemes tend to be narrowly concentrated.[69] Consider, for example, the United States' AGOA program. In 2003, approximately thirty-three sub-Saharan African states were eligible for preferential treatment under the AGOA. However, three states – Nigeria, South Africa, and Gabon – accounted for over 86 percent of total AGOA imports. Benefits were similarly highly concentrated in a few economic sectors. In 2003, energy-related products represented 79.5 percent of U.S. purchases from sub-Saharan states; the second largest sector, textiles and apparel, accounted for 8.5 percent of U.S. imports.[70] Moreover, within the apparel sector, the seven sub-Saharan states that accounted for 99 percent of exports to the United States before the AGOA also captured 99 percent of exports after the AGOA was enacted.[71] Similar results obtain for other preferential schemes; as a general matter "the top ten beneficiaries generally occupy[] a share of between 80 and 90 per cent of total imports receiving preferences under any individual scheme."[72] What is even more troubling is that an emerging

[66] Miriam Manchin, "Preference Utilisation and Tariff Reduction in EU Imports from ACP Countries," *The World Economy* 29 (2006): 1243, 1246. Manchin also reports that ACP states utilized Cotonou preferences (which are generally better than GSP preferences) close to 50 percent of the time. Another study found that utilization rates for preferences granted by Canada, the EU, Japan, and the United States are 61, 31, 46, and 67 percent, respectively. World Trade Organization, "Market Access Issues Related to Products of Export Interest Originating from Least-Developed Countries," WTO Doc. WT/COMTD/LDC/W/31 (2003).

[67] Daniel Lederman and Çaglar Özden, "U.S. Trade Preferences: All Are not Created Equal" (Central Bank of Chile Working Paper No. 280, 2004).

[68] Aaditya Mattoo, Devesh Roy, and Arvind Subramanian, "The Africa Growth and Opportunity Act and Its Rules of Origin: Generosity Undermined?," *The World Economy* 26 (2003): 829; Denis Audet, "Smooth as Silk? A First Look at the Post MFA Textiles and Clothing Landscape," *Journal of International Economic Law* 10 (2007): 267.

[69] United National Conference on Trade and Development, "Trade Preferences for LDCs: An Early Assessment of Benefits and Possible Improvements," UNCTAD/ITCD/TSB/2003/8 (2004; hereinafter "Trade Preferences"). See also Drusilla K. Brown, "General Equilibrium Effects of the US Generalized System of Preferences," *Southern Economic Journal* 54 (1987): 27, 47.

[70] U.S. International Trade Commission, *U.S. Trade and Investment with Sub-Saharan Africa: Fifth Annual Report* (USITC Publication No. 3741, 2004).

[71] See Marcelo Olarreaga and Çaglar Özden, "AGOA and Apparel: Who Captures the Tariff Rent in the Presence of Preferential Market Access?," *The World Economy* 28 (2005): 63 (hereinafter Olarreaga and Özden). On the other hand, these states enjoyed dramatic increases in their exports to the U.S. following AGOA's enactment. Ibid., 67.

[72] Keck and Low, supra note 62, 158.

literature suggests that a substantial share of the "benefits" generated by preferential market access may accrue to importers, rather than to firms in the beneficiary state.[73]

In the aggregate, the features identified herein have significantly reduced the economic and developmental impacts of preferential programs. Although it is difficult to calculate empirical estimates of trade effects, a number of econometric studies shed light on the aggregate economic effects of GSP schemes. Many of these empirical studies suggest that that GSP has produced at best a "modest" increase in beneficiary state exports, with some of these gains resulting from trade diversion rather than trade creation.[74]

Finally, a number of more recent studies have found that GSP schemes are associated with negative economic effects. For example, Özden and Reinhardt found that the U.S. GSP is not associated with an increase in trade.[75] A more recent study found that in the absence of GATT–WTO membership or a regional trade agreement, preference programs increase trade between states by 41 percent; however, if states have one of these other trade relationships, then the granting of preferences appears to benefit the importing state and harm the exporting state.[76] Similar counterintuitive results were reached in a recent study using quite different data and econometric techniques.[77] Hence, the general consensus is that the economic effects of preference programs have been, at best, disappointing; a more pessimistic account concluded that "[b]eyond some relative success stories, the picture is dismal."[78]

---

[73] See Olarreaga and Özden, supra note 71, 65–75.

[74] Craig R. MacPhee and Victor Iwuagwu Oguledo, "The Trade Effects of the U.S. Generalized System of Preferences," *Atlantic Economic Journal* 19 (1991): 19–26; Drusilla K. Brown, "Trade and Welfare Effects of the European Schemes of the Generalized System of Preferences," *Economic Development and Cultural Change* 37 (1989): 757; John Whalley, "Non-Discriminatory Discrimination: Special and Differential Treatment under the GATT for Developing Countries," *The Economic Journal* 100 (1990): 1318; André Sapir and Lars Lundberg, "The U.S. Generalized System of Preferences and its Impacts," in Anne O. Krueger and Robert E. Baldwin (eds.), *The Structure and Evolution of Recent US Trade Policy* (Chicago: University of Chicago Press, 1984), 191.

[75] Çaglar Özden and Eric Reinhardt, "The Perversity of Preferences: GSP and Developing Country Trade Policies, 1976–2000," *Journal of Development Economics* 78 (2005): 1.

[76] Judith L. Goldstein et al., "Institutions in International Relations: Understanding the Effects of the GATT and the WTO on World Trade," *International Organization* 61 (2007): 37. The authors characterize this finding as "implausible" and as a "mystery left to be solved."

[77] See, e.g., Bernhard Herz and Marco Wagner, Do the World Trade Organization and the Generalized System of Preferences Foster Bilateral Trade? (Universitat Bayreuth Diskussionspapier 01–07, 2007). The authors observe that "We find a significantly negative effect of the Generalized System of Preferences of around –16 % on bilateral trade."

[78] "Trade Preferences," supra note 69, x.

I hasten to add that the studies summarized here should not be understood as conclusive arguments against preferential schemes. First, empirically identifying the effects of preferences is extraordinarily difficult, because researchers must separate out the specific impacts of preferences as opposed to other factors.[79] In addition, the studies do not always carefully separate out the effects of different preference schemes; for example, studies that focus on the effect of GSP programs may be seriously misleading because GSP programs have been supplemented over time by a variety of programs affording more preferential treatment, such as CBI, AGOA, and Everything But Arms.[80] Moreover, it should be noted that the literature here is vast, and different studies generate different results. Hence, although a majority of published studies suggest that preferences have limited – or even negative – economic effects, other studies, using different assumptions and methodologies, find more positive results.[81] Finally, the disappointing effects of preference schemes can be understood more as an argument for their reform than an argument for their elimination.[82] However, notwithstanding these important qualifications, the conventional wisdom – shared by both developing and developed states – is that preference programs have produced only modest benefits.

[79] For example, it is difficult for empirical analysis to address the so-called endogeneity effect. Imagine that the United States extended preferential tariff treatment to goods from a particular developing state just as that state was emerging from a protracted civil war. It would be empirically quite difficult to determine how much of a hypothetical boost in exports would be related to reduced tariffs and how much to the end of the fighting.

[80] For example, a more useful, albeit more complex, approach is to look at the size, utilization, and value of all nonreciprocal trade preference programs. For one such effort see Judith M. Dean and John T. Wainio, "Quantifying the Value of US Tariff Preferences for Developing Countries" (World Bank Policy Research Working Paper No. 3977, 2006).

[81] Ibid.; Garth Frazer and Johannes Van Biesebroeck, "Trade Growth under the African Growth and Opportunity Act" (University of Toronto Department of Economics Working Paper No. 289, 2007, finding that AGOA has had "a large and robust impact" on African exports to the United States); Christopher Stevens and Jane Kennan, *Comparative Study of G8 Preferential Access Schemes for Africa* (Sussex, U.K.: Institute of Development Studies, 2004); Judith M. Dean, "Do Preferential Trade Agreements Promote Growth?: An Evaluation of the Caribbean Basin Economic Recovery Act" (USITC Office of Economics Working Paper No. 2002–07-A, 2002).

[82] For recent and thoughtful efforts to prompt a debate over reform along these lines, see Keck and Low, supra note 62; Peter Kleen and Sheila Page, *Special and Differential Treatment of Developing Countries in the World Trade Organization* (Report for the Ministry of Foreign Affairs, Sweden, 2004); Claire Melamed, "Doing 'Development' at the World Trade Organization: The Doha Round and Special and Differential Treatment," *IDS Bulletin* 34 (2003): 12–23; T. Ademola Oyejide, "Special and Differential Treatment," in Bernard Hoekman et al. (eds.), *Development, Trade and the WTO: A Handbook* (Washington, D.C.: World Bank, 2002), 504–508.

Evaluating preference programs on moral terms tends to obscure these cold economic realities – and their uncomfortable political implications. Of course, reviewing the weight of empirical evidence on preference programs raises an intriguing puzzle. Developing state demands for greater market access to developed state markets moved to the center of the agenda during GATT's early years,[83] and have remained there ever since. The contrast between the high political salience of preferences and their disappointing economic results is striking: If preferential treatment generates limited economic benefits, why do developing states continue to advocate for these programs?

iv. TURNING THE DISTRIBUTIVE JUSTICE DEBATE INSIDE OUT

We might approach the puzzle posed by the disjunction between the high political salience and low economic impact of preference programs by returning to the claim that the arguments for preferences rest upon moral claims. I have suggested that this argument is inaccurate as a descriptive and historical matter; we might also explore whether the claim introduces a conceptual map of distributive justice debates that is misleading, if not inside-out.

As Chin Leng Lim's contribution to this volume properly notes, Robert Hudec's magisterial study of the history of developing state arguments for preferential treatment remains a seminal work.[84] In *Developing Countries in the GATT System*, Hudec advanced an interesting and controversial claim. He argued that the economic performance of a developing state is influenced more by its domestic policies than by developed state trade policy; in his words, "a government's own trade-policy decisions are the most important determinant of its own economic welfare."[85]

Hudec's claim rested on political economy grounds, but empirical evidence is starting to emerge that provides support for Hudec's conjecture. Voices from diverse positions on the political spectrum lend support to the claim that both growth and development have much more to do with internal economic and political reforms than with tariff rates in developed states. Thus, a major World Bank review of economic growth during the past decade comes to this conclusion: "All in all, while external factors played a role, explanations

[83] Hudec – *Developing Countries*, supra note 17, 41.
[84] See Chin Leng Lim, "The Conventional Morality of Trade," in this volume. I have examined and critiqued Hudec's writings on this topic in Jeffrey L. Dunoff, "Dysfunction, Diversion and the Debate over Preferences: (How) Do Preferential Trade Policies Work?," in Chantal Thomas and Joel Trachtman (eds.), *Essays on Developing States in the WTO* (Cambridge: Cambridge University Press, 2009), 45, and I draw upon that discussion here.
[85] Hudec – *Developing Countries*, supra note 17, 159.

of performance must be sought primarily in developing countries' domestic policies."[86] From a very different perspective, an UNCTAD report reaches a similar conclusion,[87] and philosopher Thomas Pogge suggests much the same point:

> Even truly free markets would probably not bring rapid economic growth to areas where basic infrastructure is lacking and where the physical and mental development of prospective employees is irreparably impaired through disease, malnutrition and illiteracy. . . . It is only after people have access to adequate food and shelter, vaccines, safe water, basic sanitation [and] health services, and primary education [that the poorest areas will attract significant private investment that can propel growth].[88]

A large literature explores whether the determinants of developing state growth have more to do with domestic political features such as meaningful political representation, individual liberties, independent judiciaries, the rule of law, and institutional and legal infrastructure, or with economic infrastructure.[89] A related literature involves a debate between "macro" development economists, who emphasize the importance of fiscal and other macroeconomic policies, and "micro" development economists who highlight the importance of education, health, and related social programs.[90] For current purposes, it is less important to evaluate the merits of the various positions in these literatures than to note that virtually all of the scholarship foregrounds the critical importance of domestic institutions.[91]

---

[86] See *Economic Growth in the 1990s: Learning from a Decade of Reform* (Washington, D.C.: World Bank, 2005), 9.

[87] UNCTAD, *The African Growth and Opportunity Act: A Preliminary Assessment*, UNCTAD/ITCD/TSB/2003/1 (2003).

[88] Thomas W. Pogge, "Priorities of Global Justice," in Thomas W. Pogge (ed.), *Global Justice* (Oxford: Blackwell, 2001), 6, 12–13.

[89] See, e.g., Robert J. Barro, *Determinants of Economic Growth: A Cross-Country Empirical Study* (Cambridge, MA: MIT Press, 1998); Philippe Aghion and Steven Durlauf (eds.), *Handbook of Economic Growth* (New York: Elsevier, 2005).

[90] See, e.g., Dani Rodrik, "The New Development Economics: We Shall Experiment, But How Shall We Learn?" (available at http://ksghome.harvard.edu/~drodrik).

[91] Douglass North defines institutions as "the rules of the game in a society, or, more formally, . . . the humanly devised constraints that shape human interaction." Douglass C. North, *Institutions, Institutional Change, and Economic Performance* (New York: Cambridge University Press, 1990), 3. See also Douglass C. North, *Structure and Change in Economic History* (New York: Norton, 1981); Daron Acemoglu and James Robinson, "The Role of Institutions in Growth and Development, Commission on Growth & Development" (Commission on Growth and Development Working Paper No. 10, 2008).

Indeed, it is highly unlikely that a definitive or generic answer to the determinants of growth can be found. Even a cursory review of the trajectory of ideas about development suggests that there is no universal answer regarding how best to promote development and growth.[92] The only orthodoxy that emerges from a review of development studies is that there is no orthodoxy – a position that has moved from heterodox to orthodox in recent years. Thus, the "Washington Consensus" has been widely discredited,[93] and much recent (and painful) experience suggests that a one-size-fits-all approach to development is unwarranted and unwise. The divergent nature of success stories in Botswana, China, Hong Kong, Singapore, Taiwan, Turkey, and Vietnam illustrates that there are many paths to development. They also provide substantial empirical support for the claim that the road to development runs inside-out. That is, that the primary determinants of development lie "inside," with developing state policies, rather than "outside," in terms of developed-state tariff policies.

If this inside-out approach to development is correct, then we might consider whether the lengthy and contentious debate over preferences has diverted diplomatic and scholarly attention from the most efficacious approach to the developing world's growth and progress, whether the creation and elaboration of a conceptual geography that has accompanied and fueled the preferences debate has directed our attention to issues of secondary importance, and whether an undue focus on the debate over preferences has obscured more important issues related to domestic reform in developing states.[94] Most importantly, we should consider whether turning the debate inside-out can point us toward concrete policies that are more likely to fuel the development necessary to make any progress on global distributive justice.

It is important to be clear about the implications of these claims. The arguments developed in this chapter should not be understood as a claim that

---

[92] For influential elaborations of this idea see William Easterly, *The Elusive Quest for Growth: Economists' Adventures and Misadventures in the Tropics* (Cambridge, MA: MIT Press, 2001); Lant Pritchett and David Lindauer, "What's the Big Idea? Three Generations of Development Advice," *Economia* 3 (2002): 1–39.

[93] Dani Rodrik, "Goodbye Washington Consensus, Hello Washington Confusion? A Review of the World Bank's Economic Growth in the 1990s: Learning from a Decade of Reform," *Journal of Economic Literature* 44 (2006): 973.

[94] To be sure, this argument does not exclude the possibility that the relative importance of domestic policy exists precisely because existing preference policies have been poorly designed and unevenly applied. See, e.g., Frank J. Garcia, "Beyond Special and Differential Treatment," *Boston College International and Comparative Law Review* 27 (2004): 291.

expanding trade is irrelevant to developing state growth[95] or that WTO rules have little impact on volumes or patterns of international trade.[96] Nor should this contribution be understood as an argument against efforts to reform the trade system or to challenge certain developed-state trade policies. It may well be true that changes to existing trade rules can do much to address global poverty,[97] and there can be little doubt that much more should and can be done to improve duty-free access for products from developing states, lower developed-state tariff peaks and tariff escalation in products of particular importance to developing states, and reduce developed state producer support. In particular, trade-distorting agricultural support in OECD states remains unacceptably high, negatively impacting the prospects for developing-country agriculture.[98] Similarly, although developed states complain bitterly about limited developing-state liberalization in services trade, they often maintain barriers with respect to activities where developing states enjoy a comparative advantage, such as labor-intensive activities that require either temporary entry or work permits.

Along the same lines, several initiatives at the WTO that address distributive justice concerns deserve support. For example, the Enhanced Integrated Framework for Trade Related Technical Assistance (EIF) undertaking is potentially valuable, and recent improvements to its governing structure are welcome.[99] However, the amounts pledged to the EIF Trust Fund to date are

[95] International trade's capacity to promote growth has long been recognized. See, e.g., Bela Balassa, "Exports and Economic Growth: Further Evidence," *Journal of Developmental Economics* 5 (1978): 181.

[96] A large literature debates the trade effect of the GATT–WTO system. See, e.g., Andrew K. Rose, "Do We Really Know that the WTO Increases Trade?," *American Economic Review* 94 (2004): 98; Michael Tomz et al., "Do We Really Know that the WTO Increases Trade? – Comment," *American Economic Review* 97 (2007): 2005–2018; Arvind Subramanian and Shang-Jin Wei, "The WTO Promotes Trade, Strongly but Unevenly," *Journal of International Economics* 72 (2007): 151–175.

[97] Thomas Pogge, "The Role of International Law in Reproducing Massive Poverty," in Samantha Besson and John Tasioulas (eds.), *The Philosophy of International Law* (Oxford: Oxford University Press, 2010), 417–435.

[98] Developing states have started to challenge developed state agricultural subsidies in WTO dispute settlement. See, e.g., *United States – Subsidies on Upland Cotton*, WT/DS267/AB/R (2005); *European Communities – Export Subsidies on Sugar*, WT/DS265/AB/R, WT/DS266/AB/R, WT/DS283/AB/R (2005).

[99] The Integrated Framework for Trade-Related Technical Assistance to least-developed countries (LDCs) is a process established in 1997 to support LDC governments in trade capacity building and integrating trade issues into overall national development strategies. Through it, participating agencies (IMF, ITC, UNCTAD, UNDP, World Bank, and the WTO) combine their efforts with those of LDCs and their other development partners to respond to LDC trade development needs.

unlikely to be sufficient to adequately support the faster integration of least developed countries into the global trade system. Other initiatives, including Aid-for-Trade,[100] are likewise potentially promising and deserve support.

At the same time, we should be realistic about the limits of these programs. World trade has grown rapidly in the new millennium – export volumes grew at an average rate of 8 percent per annum during the 2002–2007 period – but developing states as a whole have seen their share of global exports rise by only about 10 percent between 1995 and 2006. Moreover, much of this increase reflects phenomenal growth rates in a handful of developing states, such as China, India, and Brazil. For least developed states, the picture is far more troubling. This group accounted for 0.42 percent of global exports in 1995; excluding oil, they accounted for 0.38 percent of global exports in 2006.[101] Moreover, during this time, many developing states have become even more dependent upon a narrow range of export products. Increased export concentration is a major source of macroeconomic volatility and is detrimental to long-term growth prospects. Moreover, increased participation in global trade patterns can exacerbate inequality in developing states as the poor are asked to absorb the adjustment costs associated with increased import competition while those with greater economic clout exploit export opportunities.

For example, Madagascar enjoyed a surge in textile and apparel exports starting in the late 1990s. This development created substantial employment opportunities for skilled workers, but it did little for unskilled workers and resulted in rising inequality and only a modest impact upon poverty. Similarly, both Kenya and Zambia have enjoyed increased exports of fruits and vegetables, but most of this growth has been concentrated in large, capital-intensive farms. Brazil is now the world's fourth largest agricultural exporter, but a handful of commercial farms and agribusiness dominates these markets

---

[100] Although the volume of aid for trade-related technical assistance and capacity building has been increasing steadily since the launch of the Doha Development Round in December 2001, the need for further assistance has been widely recognized. In December 2005, at the 6th WTO Ministerial Conference in Hong Kong, the WTO Ministerial Declaration endorsed the enhancement of the Integrated Framework and created a new WTO work program on Aid-for-Trade. Aid-for-Trade aims to help developing countries, particularly least-developed countries, develop the trade-related skills and infrastructure that is needed to implement and benefit from WTO agreements. The success of the initiative depends on creating closer cooperation in national capitals between trade, finance, and development officials of WTO member governments. It is to be matched by close cooperation at the international and regional level among intergovernmental organizations, as well as enhanced reporting and verification. For a detailed analysis of Aid-for-Trade initiatives, see Phoenix X.F. Cai, "Aid for Trade: A Roadmap for Success," *Denver Journal of International Law & Policy* 36 (2008): 283.

[101] Millennium Development Goals Gap Task Force, *Delivering on the Global Partnership for Achieving the Millennium Development Goals* (New York: United Nations, 2008), 24.

and over 10 million people in rural areas live under the poverty line. A number of other developing states have similarly experienced only a weak link between export growth and human development. In short, increased export earnings by themselves may do little to alter underlying the balance of power in a society or the political dysfunctionalities that produce gross inequalities, and hence are no guarantee of progress on the distributive justice front.[102] Thus, "even if developing country governments succeed in gaining all the market access concessions they desire, without gaining more, these concessions may not yield meaningful economic and social progress."[103]

This is also not to argue for a new or revised Washington Consensus. As already noted, different states will take different paths to growth and development. The bottom line is to recognize that although trade can play an important role in development, we should not focus on trade policy in a way that diverts attention from other policy interventions that can be more helpful, and that are necessary prerequisites for preferential treatment to be economically meaningful.

Finally, this is not an argument that seeks to ascribe responsibility for economic inequality and underdevelopment to poor states. The "blame game" is politically popular, although it is rarely productive. In any event, there should be little doubt that many developing states have suffered egregious historical injustices, or that certain features of contemporary international institutions may exacerbate existing inequalities of wealth, power, and resources. This contribution undertakes to move beyond efforts to attribute blame. More importantly, it represents an effort to advance a comparativist – and not a transcendentalist – approach to global distributive justice, and to suggest concrete steps that can help advance the global justice agenda.

v. CONCLUSION

Scholarly attention to global justice is flourishing. Some scholars approach justice issues through critical philosophical reflection and the construction of idealized moral principles; others employ rigorous political analysis; and still others use empirically based social critique. Despite substantial diversity in methodological and substantive approaches, we should understand all of this work as contributing to the common enterprise of understanding and

---

[102] This point has been forcefully argued by Daron Acemoglu in Daron Acemoglu et al., "Institutional Causes, Macroeconomic Symptoms: Volatility, crises and growth," *Journal of Monetary Economics* 50 (2003): 49.

[103] Chantal Thomas, "Poverty Reduction, Trade, and Rights," *American University International Law Review* 18 (2003): 1399, 1410.

advancing debates over global justice. Although I welcome this intellectual diversity, I have suggested that the conceptual geography used in some of this scholarship can highlight some aspects of the global justice problematique but elide other aspects that deserve our attention. That is, some of the arguments are upside down, or backwards, in the sense that they point us in the wrong direction. One important corrective would be to turn these arguments inside out.

7   The Death of Doha? Forensics of Democratic
     Governance, Distributive Justice, and Development
     in the WTO

     Chantal Thomas

The Development Agenda of the 2001 Ministerial Conference of the World
Trade Organization in Doha represents an attempt to achieve greater distributive
justice among WTO members by enhancing the prospects for development
through trade among poorer countries. Development and democratic
governance (as between states)[1] intertwine here: Because developing countries
represent the majority of WTO members, more democratic and broader
participation by developing countries also entails a policy emphasis on redistribution.

The Doha Ministerial Declaration "strongly reaffirm[s] commitment to
the objective of sustainable development" and declares an intention to place
developing-country "needs and interests at the heart of the Work Programme"
for negotiations.[2] For example, developed-country agricultural markets, subject
to disproportionately and stubbornly high trade barriers despite the WTO's
overall success in trade liberalization, formed a preeminent focal point for
redistributive policy in the Doha Work Programme as they held significant
export interest for developing countries. As another example, developing countries
called for strengthening the Principle of Special and Differential Treatment
("SD") which provided for a range of trade policies designed to act as
a corrective for their lesser economic capacity, *inter alia*: the adoption by

---

[1] There are many problems with conceiving of governments as individuals and this metaphor
might break down. However, because the WTO is still a "Member-driven organization," largely
barred to the participation of non-state actors (except for the submission of amici curiae and
some public participation), the conventional view of states as unitary actors in the international
realm holds to some degree here.
[2] Paragraphs 2, 6, WTO Ministerial Declaration, WT/MIN(01)/DEC/1, 20 November 2001
(Adopted on 14 November 2001).

I offer sincere thanks to Chios Carmody, Frank Garcia, and John Linarelli for their invitation
to present this contribution and to the American Society of International Law for hosting the
Symposium on which this book is based.

developed countries of non-reciprocal tariff preferences benefiting developing countries, the allowance of comparatively higher trade barriers for developing economies, and the extension or exemption of implementation requirements. (A more general backgrounder to Doha is briefly provided in Section I for those unfamiliar with the relevant organizational history.)

Efforts to pursue the Doha Declaration's Work Programme have proceeded slowly and with great difficulty: The 2003 Ministerial Conference in Cancun ended abruptly, and subsequent efforts to revive negotiations in the 2005 Ministerial and subsequent gatherings stumbled badly. As a consequence, over the years since its adoption, commentators have tolled the death knell for the Doha Development Agenda.[3] In spring 2011, former U.S. Trade Representative Susan Schwab joined many others in urging, "It's time for the international community to recognize that the Doha Round is doomed,"[4] though WTO Director-General Pascal Lamy continued through mid-2011 to call for renewed efforts to finalize at least parts of the Doha Agenda.[5]

As Section II shows, many of the problems confronting the Doha Agenda can be described as institutional–collective action problems that undermine the benefits of coordination of state behavior potentially available from international institutions. Section III argues that underlying and perhaps exacerbating these coordination difficulties lie deep normative contradictions. These contradictions were perhaps easier to overlook with a smaller set of key players of earlier trade rounds; in the broader negotiations following Doha, they are much harder to ignore.

With these difficulties facing attempts at democratic governance in the WTO, perhaps it would be easier to eschew the time-consuming, logistically complicated scenario of negotiations in favor of some kind of substantive principle that could be more easily implemented from a top-down perspective – that is, a constitutionalism of development. The Framework Agreement on Special and Differential Treatment proposed by some developing countries, for example, has featured in the Doha negotiations as one such project.[6]

---

[3] See, e.g., Paul Krugman, "Dead Doha," New York Times Online, July 30, 2008 (http://krugman.blogs.nytimes.com/2008/07/30/dead-doha/?scp=1&sq=&st=nyt); Martin Jacques, "The Death of Doha Signals the Demise of Globalization," *The Guardian*, July 13, 2006 (http://www.guardian.co.uk/commentisfree/2006/jul/13/comment.globalisation).

[4] Susan C. Schwab, "After Doha: Why the Negotiations Are Doomed and What We Should Do About It," *Foreign Affairs*, May/June 2001, p. 104.

[5] WTO Press Release, 22 June 2011; Lamy urges members to start negotiating to put together a December package (http://www.wto.org/english/news_e/news11_e/tnc_infstat_22jun11_e.htm).

[6] See World Trade Organization Communication from Cuba, Dominican Republic, Honduras, India, Indonesia, Kenya, Malaysia, Pakistan, Sri Lanka, Tanzania, Uganda, and Zimbabwe: Proposal for a Framework Agreement on Special and Differential Treatment, September 19,

Section IV expresses skepticism about this project, however, addressing various kinds of uncertainties about SD. First, the incorporation of SD into WTO decisions in the dispute settlement system may not produce the outcomes developing-country governments would anticipate. The *EC-Tariff Preferences* case, in which India complained that the imposition by the EC of policy conditionalities on GSP benefits ran counter to SD, is discussed as an example of the implications of "judicializing" SD. Second, even if an interpretation of SD in conformity with the developing-country governments' traditional position could be assured, this would not necessarily adhere to their benefit. As a matter of trade economics, not only in theory but also as indicated by historical experience, SD-type policies have sometimes and sometimes not produced economic growth in developing countries. SD, it turns out, may be no more infallible as an approach to trade policy than a neoclassical imperative to liberalize.

Finally, Section V turns to recent contributions from moral philosophy regarding the potential structure of distributive justice in the WTO: Frank Garcia's Rawlsian argument for SD, and Carol Gould's case for human rights as a foundation for development. Both are noteworthy interventions, and yet ultimately cannot avoid the conundrums of trade and development that will require ultimately overt decision making on behalf of redistribution. The chapter ends with a conclusion that, despite myriad flaws and shortcomings, the efforts to reach negotiated agreements in the Doha Round represent a crucial step forward. The challenges and obstacles confronting those efforts should be confronted directly, and indeed can only be resolved by doing so.

I. A BRIEF BACKGROUNDER TO THE DOHA DEVELOPMENT AGENDA

The "Development Round" was intended to address concerns of developing-country governments that they had been underrepresented by the Single Undertaking of the Uruguay Round. The Uruguay Round Agreements had moved away from the strong endorsement of the Principle of Special and Differential Treatment for developing countries that had been a centerpiece of trade and development policy from the 1970s onward, when it was embedded in the GATT's adoption of a permanent waiver for developed countries to adopt trade preferences that were "generalized, non-reciprocal, and non-discriminatory" for developing countries. This Generalized System

2001. The Doha Declaration referenced the Framework proposal; see Doha Declaration at paragraph 44.

of Preferences in turn reflected a bid by developing countries to challenge and address the structural inequality of the international economic order reflected in colonial arrangements.

Yet the Uruguay Round downplayed the Special and Differential Treatment principle in the new agreements, emphasizing uniform trade rules with comparatively minimal exceptions for developing countries – an important example being the Agreement on Trade Related Intellectual Property Rights, which established no substantive exemptions, but rather only adopted more generous implementation timeframes, based on developmental status. The conventional wisdom was that developing-country governments acceded to these more rigorous trade disciplines in exchange for the prospect of liberalizing sectors of the developed-country markets that had long been resiliently protectionist, such as agriculture. By the 2001 Doha Ministerial Conference, however, frustration was increasing with the one-size-fits-all approach of the Uruguay Round, as well as with the slow progress on agriculture negotiations. The result was a round intended to address these concerns – to make significant progress on agriculture and to revisit the question of Special and Differential Treatment in a number of contexts, including agriculture and intellectual property.

In addition to these substantive issues, the Doha negotiations may have also been a response to the success of the new dispute settlement system that had been put in place with the Uruguay Round. Many lauded the Dispute Settlement Body's effects of "legalization" and "judicialization" of the trade regime, but others may have seen these dynamics as moving the regime away from its proper function as a member-driven organization ultimately reflective of the political choices of sovereign states. Certainly, with the WTO Appellate Body's decision in *Shrimp-Turtle II*, endorsing a United States unilateral prohibition on shrimp imports that was designed to protect endangered sea turtles, criticism grew that the AB was overly swayed by the governments and nongovernmental organizations of the North. The Doha talks were also designed to shift the balance away from the "judicial" branch of the WTO and toward the "legislative" branch.

In doing so, the Doha Round also adopted a more inclusive approach to the conduct of negotiations. This, too, was designed as a corrective to the trade regime's history of exclusivity in negotiations. The regime had run, for most of its history, according to a "club model" in which important policies and decisions were dictated by the powerful elite of participating states.[7] The

---

[7] Robert O. Keohane and Joseph S. Nye, "The Club Model of Multilateral Cooperation and Problems of Democratic Legitimacy," in Roger B. Porter et al. (eds.), *Efficiency, Equity,*

limitations of the club model, and the challenges it posed to the WTO's legitimacy, came to light during the "Battle in Seattle," which occurred during the WTO's 1999 Ministerial Conference.[8] Since Seattle, the WTO has struggled to find new ways of including developing-country government participation.

Thus, the Doha talks were intended to address both *substantive* and *institutional* issues. Substantively, they were intended to focus on developing-country concerns such as agricultural market access in developed markets, and SD. Institutionally, they were supposed to distribute decision-making power more evenly among participating states, creating a stronger role for developing-country governments in negotiations.

Doha has not been, as some commentators might imply, a total failure. In some cases, such as intellectual property, important gains such as the WTO decisions on public health and access to medicines have been made.[9] In other cases, however, such as agricultural negotiations, no clear reform has emerged and they appear to be irreparably stalled. Schwab's recent essay gives an accurate sense of the reason for the stalemate. Put simply, the developed countries chafed under the constraint of granting non-reciprocal concessions in agriculture. The agricultural negotiations, in keeping with the Doha agenda, centrally reflected an endorsement of SD, with many exemptions for developing countries. The already fragile commitment of the developed countries to liberalize this most sensitive of sectors broke down under not only the global recession, but also the clear competitiveness of the largest developing economies such as China, Brazil, and India. Notwithstanding the fact that these countries are still in the bottom half of the Human Development Index, the sheer size of their economies ranks them toward the top end of global exports.

II. COORDINATION PROBLEMS THAT SURFACED DURING THE DOHA NEGOTIATIONS

At the 1999 Seattle Ministerial Conference, developing countries decisively objected to the traditional green-room model of WTO negotiations in which deals were hashed out first by a small group of large economies and only then were other countries consulted.

Legitimacy: The Multilateral Trading System at the Millennium, 264–294 (Washington, D.C.: Brookings Institute, 2001).

[8] See, e.g., Lori Wallach and Michelle Sforza, *Whose Trade Organization? Corporate Globalization and the Erosion of Democracy* (Washington, D.C.: Public Citizen, 1999), 138.

[9] *WTO Declaration on TRIPS and Public Health*, WT/MIN(01)/DEC/2 (November 20, 2001), which was followed by the *Decision on the Implementation of Paragraph 6 of the Doha Declaration on the TRIPS Agreement and Public Health*, WT/L/540 (September 2, 2003).

The Doha negotiations thus involved an unprecedented inclusiveness of developing-country governments and their interests. At the same time, a variety of challenges have emerged over the course of the Doha negotiations. Some of these, such as the increase in numerical scale and the expansion of substantive scope (II.A), follow somewhat automatically from the move to greater inclusion. Others, such as the breakdown of developing-country solidarity (II.B), may or may not have been caused by the Doha negotiations directly, but the focus of the negotiations has nevertheless brought them to light. Still others, such as the rise of parallel regional and bilateral trade agreements (II.C), result not from inherent or preexisting factors but from concerted reactions to the Doha negotiations themselves.

A. *Increases in Numerical Scale and Substantive Scope*

In theory, WTO members seek to develop ground rules for the governance of world trade in order to generate efficiency gains from the coordination of state behavior[10] and from the harmonized regulation of the global economy. Yet such efforts face a wide range of transaction costs[11] which impede the WTO's institutional effectiveness.

WTO membership now exceeds many times over the small group of fewer than thirty governments who participated in the GATT's inception. The sheer increase in numerical scale entailed by the WTO's shift from the traditional green-room model, in which the powerful Northern countries cut the deal for everybody else, to a more inclusive approach in recent years, as arguably essential as it is to do so, multiplies the transaction costs inherent in the negotiation process. Transaction costs are those impediments preventing parties from reaching the best agreement. They include include specification costs (the time and effort required to bring all parties to agreement about specific language), strategic holdout costs (the risk that some negotiating states will act opportunistically to refrain from providing their anticipated consent, in order to wring additional concessions from counterparties anxious to gain closure),

---

[10] See, e.g., Robert O. Keohane and Joseph S. Nye, "Introduction," in Joseph S. Nye and John D. Donahue (eds.), *Governance in a Globalizing World* (Washington, D.C.: Brookings Institute, 2000), 19.

[11] See Joel Trachtman, *The Economic Structure of International Law* (Princeton, NJ: Harvard University Press, 2008). Applying insights from institutional economics, Trachtman has demonstrated how international law making can be understood by focusing on transaction costs that freight the negotiation of rights and obligations. See Joel Trachtman, "Economic Analysis of Prescriptive Jurisdiction," *Virginia Journal of International Law* 42 (2001): 1, 51 (stating that rules cost more to develop than standards); see also Joel Trachtman, "The Domain of WTO Dispute Resolution," *Harvard International Law Journal* 40 (1999): 333, 350–356.

"ordering" costs (skewing of negotiations that reflect the order in which preferences are expressed),[12] and capture (costs resulting from suboptimal rules that skew to a particular set of interests within the negotiating state's territory, thereby skewing overall negotiations).

Two particular sources of impediments to negotiations are worth emphasizing. First, information costs (the effect that gaps in information and capacity have in producing suboptimal rules) are particularly at issue for developing-country governments, whose difficulties stemming from scarce institutional resources and other forms of low institutional capacity issues have been extensively noted in trade law scholarship and policy.[13]

Second, the greater role of developing-country governments in the Doha negotiations has also entailed a focus on substantive issues of interest to them but of political sensitivity to developed countries, such as agriculture. This expansion of scope has increased the difficulty of negotiations in particular because of the resistance to negotiators facing political unpopularity at home. There is in other words a politically generated deadweight on agriculture and other touchy issues in developed-country home markets.

B. Fragmentation of Developing Countries as a Political Bloc

The premise of collective action has been a fundamental tenet of developing-country political strategy, crystallizing in such strategic efforts as the Non-Aligned Movement. In international economic law, a solidaristic approach has defined developing-country reform efforts, as with the New International Economic Order and the GATT's Generalized System of Preferences. Indeed, a prevailing argument for the GSP at the time of its adoption was that it did not permit differentiation among developing-countries, thereby attempting to move the global economy out of a neocolonial structure in which trade moved in center-periphery networks reflecting colonial preferences. But the premise of solidarity among developing countries, if always fragile, has been challenged to a greater degree than perhaps at any time since the era of postwar decolonization. To the extent that developing-country governments have sought bargaining power through collective action as a political bloc in

---

[12] See, e.g., Kenneth Arrow, "A Difficulty in the Concept of Social Welfare," *Journal of Political Economy* 58 (1958): 328–346. Arrow's possibility theorem proves this to be true even without the assumption of structural bias in the ranking and order of recognition of country preferences that would apply in the WTO context of developed country versus developing country.

[13] See, e.g., Gregory Shaffer, "Can WTO Technical Assistance and Capacity Building Serve Developing Countries?" *Wisconsin International Law Journal* 23 (2006): 643–686.

the negotiations, several challenges have emerged for the plausibility of that strategy.

Over the course of the Doha talks, the very notion of a category called "developing countries" which would exert political solidarity and bloc bargaining power in negotiations has come into question, even though the Doha Declaration was built on this idea.

To begin with, differences in income level and quality of life among what are considered developing countries are considerable, so that, for example, statistical publications such as the UN Human Development Index now employ three internal differentiations within the overall category of "developing," separating developing countries across "high human development" (Mauritius, Mexico), "medium human development" (Grenada, Guyana), and "low human development" (Nepal, Nigeria).[14]

Doha trade negotiations also reflect such differentiations. In the WTO agriculture negotiations, for instance, talks over the parameters of the "development box" have featured proposals for a more relaxed, open-ended SD provision that would not draw distinctions that are based on level or type of development. Others have proposed additional protections for least developed countries, or for countries deemed to be particularly vulnerable for one reason or another to liberalized agricultural trade. Small-island developing states in the WTO have articulated a collective position emphasizing preferential, nonreciprocal tariffs for developing countries over generalized market liberalization. This emphasis stems from the reliance of many small-island developing economies on Generalized System of Preferences (GSP) trade preference schemes and the like.[15] In this respect, the position on SD articulated by the Caribbean Community (CARICOM) countries[16] (as small-island developing states) contradicts, for example, that of the larger developing economies that

---

[14] See, e.g., *U.N. Human Development Report 2007/2008.*

[15] World Trade Organization, *WTO Agriculture Negotiations: The Issues, and Where We Are Now* (2004), 61–62:

> Many developing countries complain that their exports still face high tariffs and other barriers in developed countries' markets and that their attempts to develop processing industries are hampered by tariff escalation (higher import duties on processed products compared to raw materials). They want to see substantial cuts in these barriers.
>
> On the other hand, some smaller developing countries have expressed concerns about import barriers in developed countries falling too fast. They say they depend on a few basic commodities that currently need preferential treatment (such as duty-free trade) in order to preserve the value of their access to richer countries' markets. If normal tariffs fall too fast, their preferential treatment is eroded, they say.

[16] See "Negotiating Proposal on Behalf of Members of the Caribbean Community (CARICOM)," WTO Doc. G/AG/NG/W/100 (January 15, 2001). The CARICOM countries are Antigua and Barbuda, Barbados, Belize, Dominica, Grenada, Guyana, Jamaica, St. Kitts and Nevis, St. Lucia, St. Vincent and the Grenadines, Trinidad and Tobago, and Suriname.

participate in the Cairns Group, a coalition that spans the developed country–developing country divide.[17]

A related phenomenon has been the emergence of developing-country governments that are heavyweight players in the negotiations, contrasting starkly with the rest. In the spectrum from the old club model to a one-state, one-vote model, this scenario amounts to a slightly more inclusive club:

> The proliferation of coalition representation in the green room has improved some aspects of the internal transparency of WTO decision-making, but far from all. Indeed, since the conclusion of the July Package in 2004 much of the focus of consensus building has shifted to small group discussions between the G-6 (EU, US, Japan, Australia, India and Brazil) and the G-4 (EU, US, India and Brazil), excluding the vast majority of developing countries and their coalitions. These developments seem to affirm . . . earlier claims that the key challenge for WTO decision-making will continue to centre on an "insider-outsider" divide, rather than a "North-South" divide, whereby only a handful of developed and major developing countries are included in key deliberations.[18]

In some ways, the new negotiations format has strengthened the hand of developing-country collective action: With a scenario in which most governments are content to be excluded from talks and to take cues from the leaders, it is easier to hold the line. Indeed, developed-country trade representatives have complained of the stubbornness of the developing-country bloc in holding to central demands related to opening developed-country markets.[19] At the same time, the fractures in the developing-country position as described above

---

[17] Initiated in 1986, the Cairns Group has grown from fourteen to nineteen members: Argentina, Australia, Bolivia, Brazil, Canada, Chile, Colombia, Costa Rica, Guatemala, Indonesia, Malaysia, New Zealand, Pakistan, Paraguay, Peru, Philippines, South Africa, Thailand, and Uruguay. See *Background on the Cairns Group and the WTO Doha Round*, Cairns Group website (http://cairnsgroup.org/Pages/wto_negotiations.aspx). For an example of Cairns Group intervention in WTO negotiations, see *Cairns Group Negotiating Proposal – Export Competition*, WTO Doc. G/AG/NG/W/11, 35 and 93 (June 16, 2000).

[18] Mayur Patel, "New Faces in the Green Room" (Global Trade Governance Project, GEG Working Paper No. 19, 2007; available at http://www.globaleconomicgovernance.org; internal citations omitted).

[19] Susan C. Schwab, "After Doha: Why the Negotiations Are Doomed and What We Should Do About It," *Foreign Affairs*, May/June (2001): 104, at 108. Schwab, the former U.S. trade representative, criticizes the leaders of the developing-country bloc, large emerging economies such as Brazil, China, India, and South Africa (sometimes referred to in the trade and development literature as "BRICSA"), for avoiding the need to make their own market-opening concessions, which might be warranted given their export power, by "hiding behind" the more general developing-country position. Schwab also notes that some developing countries, many of whom are for example in the Cairns Group, have attempted to pursue a stance more favorable to market-opening concessions by developing countries, only to be "ignored or harshly criticized" by BRICSA.

are evident to developed-country trade negotiators, probably contributing to the current stalemate.

C. Parallel Negotiations in Bilateral and Regional North–South Agreements

While Doha negotiations have stalled in part due to the tensions described above, their likelihood of ultimate success has been further winnowed by the proliferation of parallel tracks for trade negotiations in bilateral and regional agreements.

The rise of regional and bilateral trade agreements has become a widely observed phenomenon. Thus, one commentator has written, "124 bilateral and regional trade agreements were concluded in the 48-year GATT regime and 196 bilateral and regional trade agreements have been concluded since during the first eleven years of the WTO regime. . . . Nearly 40 percent of total global trade now takes place under bilateral and regional trade agreements."[20]

The difficulty that such parallel tracks would pose for collective action is manifest. Any preexisting imbalance in power that could be corrected through collective action in a multilateral setting may be exacerbated in a bilateral or regional context.[21]

Intellectual property negotiations also provide a good example of this dynamic. In the WTO context, developing-country governments, led by the African Group coalition, were able to achieve a clarification of the Agreement on Trade-Related Aspects of Intellectual Property Rights, known as the TRIPS Agreement, that supports a more relaxed and open-ended interpretation of its compulsory licensing provisions. These negotiation efforts resulted in the Doha Declaration on TRIPS and Public Health – one of the few concrete outcomes of the Doha Round – and a further clarification of in the WTO General Council's 2003 decision on Paragraph 6 of the Doha Declaration.[22] By comparison, bilateral and regional trade agreements between developed and developing countries often feature what are known as TRIPS-Plus provisions, which are more restrictive than those found in the WTO regime.

The TRIPS-Plus example also indicates that fragmentation need not be the only consequence of collective action problems manifest in bilateral and

---

[20] Larry Crump, "Global Trade Policy Development in a Two-Track System," *Journal of International Economic Law* 9 (2006): 488 (hereinafter *Crump*).

[21] See, e.g., Andrew T. Guzman, "Why LDCs Sign Treaties That Hurt Them: Explaining the Popularity of Bilateral Investment Treaties," *Virginia Journal of International Law* 38 (1997): 639 (hereinafter *Guzman*).

[22] See *Crump*, supra note 20, 504.

regional trade agreements. Indeed, harmonization might be a result of "carving off" individual or groups of developing countries – a dynamic that some commentators have also observed with respect to investor protection clauses in bilateral investment treaties (BITs).[23]

III. NORMATIVE CONTRADICTIONS DESTABILIZING THE DOHA NEGOTIATING ENVIRONMENT

The foregoing section identified impediments to the Doha negotiations in language of institutional economics, describing a range of transaction costs. Yet a purely quantitative analysis does not suffice to understand the problem fully. Even beyond particular impediments to agreement in Doha lie fundamental normative contradictions. This section identifies two sets of contradictions, which are described as *internal* and *external* to the trade regime. The *internal* contradiction arises from the clash between motivating ideologies of comparative advantage on the one hand, and mercantilism and reciprocity on the other. The external contradiction arises from the dissonance between the WTO trade context in which all members supposedly belong to the same club, and a larger geopolitical context which has for the last decade often emphasized national security and border control against external threats.

These contradictions are generally outside the realm of any explicit agenda items or issues, but form part of the discourse within which negotiations occur. Before proceeding to describe them in more detail, however, it may be necessary to make the case from social science for why considerations of discourse are far from frivolous but rather deeply relevant to understanding the dilemma of Doha.

To begin with, institutional economists themselves have identified the role of "ideas and ideologies" in shaping, and distorting, the environments in which institutions operate.[24] The insight follows a long tradition in social science – Weber, for example, famously stated, "ideas have, like switchmen, determined the tracks along which action has been pushed by the dynamic of interest."[25]

---

[23] See *Guzman*, supra note 21, 644–655 (describing the reemergence of the Hull Rule in BITs). But see United Nations Conference on Trade and Development, "Bilateral Investment Treaties 1959–1999," UNCTAD Doc. ITE/IIA/2 (December 15, 2000, finding enormous variation among investor protection clauses in BITs).

[24] "Ideas and ideologies matter, and institutions play a major role in determining just how much they matter. Ideas and ideologies shape the subjective mental constructs that individuals use to interpret the world around them and make choices." Douglass C. North, *Institutions, Institutional Change, and Economic Performance* 111 (New York: Cambridge University Press, 1990).

[25] Max Weber, "Essays in Sociology," in M. Weber et al. (eds.), *From Max Weber* (Oxford: Oxford University Press, 1958), 280.

From Weber onward, institutional legitimacy has been identified as a key aspect of institutional functionality.[26] In other words, legitimacy forms the ground on which an institution operates.

This observation points to a methodological directive. If perceptions of legitimacy affect institutional effectiveness, then social analysis that can identify the sources of, or obstacles to, institutional legitimacy becomes very useful. Social perceptions of institutions, in this sense, directly affect their authoritativeness. If social perceptions are a form of "shared knowledge," then institutional structures are channels for, and manifestations of, the distribution of social knowledge and ideas.[27]

Against the traditional dichotomy in international relations of idealism and interest-based realism, constructivist analysis holds that ideas are not opposed to, but rather *constitutive* of, power and interest in the determination of state and interstate behavior.[28] Constructivism looks for how institutional function rests partially on how power and interest within that institution are conceived. A constructivist analysis of challenges to negotiations in the WTO would consequently look into the discursive construction of the institution's goals and actors. A passage in Alexander Wendt's canonical *Social Theory of International Politics* offers a useful starting point:

> When Neorealists offer multipolarity as an explanation for war, inquire into the discursive conditions that constitute the poles as *enemies rather than friends*. When Liberals offer economic interdependence as an explanation for peace, inquire into the discursive conditions that *constitute states with identities that care about free trade and economic growth*.[29]

What follows is an exposition of the ways in which the current context for international economic law strays from the "liberal" vision in which states are "friends" who "care about free trade." Instead, contradictions abound, both within the WTO and in the international environment more generally, that destabilize these cornerstones of institutional culture.

If shared deliberation is to form a central basis for legitimacy, then discourse must also be shared.[30] The argument presented herein is that these subtexts

[26] Thomas M. Franck, "Legitimacy in the International System," *American Journal of International Law* 82 (1988): 705, 709.

[27] Alexander Wendt, *Social Theory of International Politics* (Cambridge: Cambridge University Press, 1999), 20 (hereinafter Wendt).

[28] Ibid., 135.

[29] See *Wendt*, supra note 27, 135 (emphasis added).

[30] Jürgen Habermas, *Between Fact and Norms: Contributions to a Discourse Theory of Law and Democracy*, translated by William Rehg (Cambridge, MA: MIT Press, 1996), 299, 300 (hereinafter Habermas); ("democratic will-formation has the exclusive function of legitimating the

undermine the implicit assumptions that must support trade negotiations, namely that there is some tolerable level of friendliness and commitment to free trade across state participants.

If globalization inheres in "the intensification of social relations which link distant bodies in such a way that local happenings are shaped by events occurring many miles away and vice versa,"[31] according to "one of the most influential definitions of globalization in the literature on the subject,"[32] then the basis for concerns about legitimacy become clear. The more abstract or remote the institution, the more attenuated the basis for trust in it – what Giddens calls "ontological security."[33] Thus, if private international economic law (*lex mercatoria*) features a paradoxical proliferation of legal normativity and validity without institutions,[34] then public international economic law in the WTO may arguably feature the precise converse: highly salient institutions without a corresponding perception of valid legal normativity. Normative contradictions underlying WTO discourse inhibit the fostering of "ontological security" necessary to form shared vocabularies.

A. Internal Normative Contradictions from Mercantilism and Reciprocity: Do WTO Members Care About Free Trade?

The principle of special and differential treatment is often presented, and misunderstood, as contradictory to the overall focus of the WTO on free trade. Yet the case for free trade from economics, the economics of comparative advantage in particular, holds that countries benefit from trade efficiencies if they *unilaterally* open markets.[35] Since SD would liberalize open developed-country markets, even though it would also allow developing countries to maintain non-reciprocal market protections, it is *consistent* with rather than contradictory to the economic case for gains from trade. If WTO members were driven by the economics that theoretically undergird free trade, then

exercise of political power.... the procedures and communicative presuppositions of demo-cratic opinion- and will-formation function as the most important sluices... for discursive rationalization ...").

[31] Anthony Giddens, *The Consequences of Modernity* (Cambridge: Polity Press, 1990), 64 (here-inafter Giddens).

[32] Justin Rosenberg, *The Follies of Globalization Theory* (London: Verso, 2000), 118.

[33] See Giddens, supra note 31, 92–113.

[34] Gunther Teubner, "'Global Bukowina': Legal Pluralism in the World Society," in Gunther Teubner (ed.), *Global Law Without a State* (Aldershot: Dartmouth, 1997), 3, 15.

[35] Michael Trebilcock and Michael Fishbein, "International Trade: Barriers to Trade," in *Research Handbook in International Economic Law*, Andrew T. Guzman and Alan O. Sykes eds. (Cheltenham, UK: Edward Elgar, 2007), 1–61.

developed countries would be much less averse to, and arguably favorable to, SD.

The normative contradictions to free trade lie not with SD, but with another and much more centrally powerful driver of trade negotiations, namely the concept of reciprocity and the economic mercantilism that undergirds it. The willingness of states to make reciprocal trade concessions is accepted as a necessary component of what makes the trade regime work. As a political and perhaps even psychological matter, negotiators are much less willing to grant trade concessions if equivalent concessions are not forthcoming from their counterparties.

The principle of comparative advantage in any case ranks among the more counterintuitive in economics because it counsels governments that domestic social gain will result from increasing the presence of foreign competitors. Governments who truly commit to comparative advantage should presumably be content with unilateral trade liberalization. However, GATT–WTO trade negotiations have always insisted on reciprocity, and they have even imbued the concept of reciprocity with moral overtones. The unwillingness of developing countries to make reciprocal concessions, even where not cast them in judgmental language, certainly been presented as the basis for their continued marginalization in the WTO.[36]

Contradictions in the Discursive Structure of WTO Debates

	Consistent with liberal economics for free trade		Inconsistent with liberal economics for free trade
Economic	Comparative Advantage	versus	Mercantilism
Political	Special & Differential Treatment	versus	Reciprocity

Such objections ultimately convey ambivalence by the leading states about the validity of the presuppositions that support the WTO. That ambivalence must in turn affect the willingness of developing-country states to embrace identities that "care about free trade," in Wendt's formulation above, since it is far from clear whether developed countries care about free trade rather than mercantilism.

While always a problematic undercurrent to the trade regime, these contradictions have perhaps never come to the surface as explicitly as during the

[36] See, e.g., Robert E. Hudec, *Developing Countries in the GATT Legal System* (Aldershot, Hampshire, U.K.; Brookfield, Vt., USA: Gower, for the Trade Policy Research Center, London, 1987); see also Robert E. Hudec, *Developing Countries in the GATT Legal System* (New York: Cambridge University Press, 2010).

Doha negotiations. Doha's focus on liberalizing developed-country markets starkly presents both the neoclassical case for the gains from trade in terms of consumer prices, and the neoclassical case of political protectionism.

The priority of free trade comes into serious question by the protectionism of developed-country governments on issues of domestic or strategic importance, such as agriculture. From tariff peaks limiting imports, to subsidies promoting exports, developed-country practices on agricultural protection fly in the face of WTO norms; indeed, they constitute textbook examples of mercantilist trade policy. Although virtually all governments act inconsistently in trade policy, the contradictions are glaring from the founding states of the GATT–WTO, and those contradictions have managed to survive decades after that founding.

Such contradictions manifest themselves even more strongly considering that agricultural trade liberalization in developing countries comparatively outdoes that in developed countries, whether through promotion through regional or bilateral trade agreements (as in the case of the North American Free Trade Agreement and Mexico) or through structural adjustment advised by international financial institutions (as in the case of the International Monetary Fund and Jamaica). The sheer volume of involved trade magnifies the impact of this contradiction.

The position of developed-country states on agriculture therefore calls into question the validity of their own "identities" as "states ... that care about free trade" according to Wendt's definition given earlier. The centrality of reciprocity and the existence of massive and long-term "carveouts" generate powerful countervailing signals. The legitimacy of the WTO as an institutional system must struggle with this widespread evidence of mercantilism in the form of efforts to game negotiations so that import liberalization is minimized and export supports are maximized. In short, the goals of the system are constantly thrown into question, destabilizing the ground for institutional advancement and legitimacy.

B. *External Normative Contradictions from National Security: Are WTO Members Friends or Enemies?*

In some ways the Doha Agenda was hastened by fears of terrorism. Mere weeks after the attacks on the U.S. World Trade Center and Pentagon, U.S. Trade Representative Robert Zoellick explicitly linked the two in a *Washington Post* editorial, "Countering Terror with Trade."[37] The shifting

---

[37] Robert B. Zoellick, "Countering Terror with Trade," *Washington Post*, September 20, 2001, at A35.

geopolitics of fear brought developing countries' demands into a new register, in which the WTO was part of the obligation of the international community to provide developing countries with "economic hope to counter internal threats."[38]

Yet at a deeper level, Zoellick's rally for free trade as necessary to the support of "America's political, economic and military vitality" foreshadowed the normative contradiction between economic openness and counterterrorist militarism.

Wendt's formulation described above contrasts a war relationship, in which hostile states are constructed as enemies rather than friends, with a peacetime economic relationship in which states are implicitly constructed as friends rather than enemies. Nevertheless, this construction, too, is contradicted by mixed signals generated by developed-country states.

Particularly after 9/11, international affairs have become heavily influenced by a "friend–enemy" distinction[39] that ranges from Samuel Huntington's explicit "clash of civilizations"[40] to the somewhat more subtle distinction by liberal international relations theory between democratic and nondemocratic states.[41] The friend–enemy distinction as a basis for action also directly contradicts the implicit constraints on sovereignty and emphasis on international rule of law that are signified by multilateral institutions. If state action is determined by the identification of friends or enemies, then this determination becomes the basis for sovereignty and necessitates the capacity to contradict or disobey established principle.[42]

The rise of border control measures in the Global North underscores the centrality of this friend–enemy distinction[43] in shaping the perception of the Global South as a source of threat rather than a friendly co-participant in economic interdependence. "Fortress Europe," the increasingly enthusiastic use by U.S. immigration authorities of bioinformatics, the steadily growing difficulty that nationals from the Global South face in procuring travel or business visas to the Global North – all of these create a context that, although certainly not on the table at WTO negotiations, must necessarily form part of

---

[38] Ibid.

[39] Tracy B. Strong, "Foreword," in Carl Schmitt, *Political Theology*, translated by George Schwab (Chicago: University of Chicago Press, 2005), xx (hereinafter Schmitt).

[40] Samuel Huntington, *The Clash of Civilizations and the Remaking of World Order* (New York: Simon & Schuster, 1998).

[41] See, e.g., Andrew Moravcsik, "Taking Preferences Seriously: A Liberal Theory of International Politics," *International Organization* 51(4) (1997): 513.

[42] See *Schmitt*, supra note 39.

[43] Peter Andreas, "U.S.–Mexico: Open Markets, Closed Borders," *Foreign Policy* 103 (1996): 51.

the background. That background reveals a dichotomy between open markets and closed borders that belies a destabilizing absence of trust.[44]

Wendt observes, "[t]he daily life of international politics is an on-going process of states taking identities in relation to Others, casting them into corresponding counter-identities, and playing out the result."[45] If perceived gains from trade with those "others" are heavily counterbalanced by concerns about sovereignty and security from external threat, then the viable constitution of power and interest within a model of interdependence that could provide the heavy support for difficult, protracted, and complex negotiations is limited.

This normative climate has been noted within the international community. Perhaps without coincidence, the United Nations initiated a High-Level Dialogue on Migration and Development. As part of the United Nations General Assembly session inaugurating the dialogue, Secretary General Jan Eliasson made the observation:

> The *free movement* of people, ideas – and merchandise, of course – is important and has contributed enormously to the positive change in the recent decade. *But* if that *outside world* also, to many, is seen as a *threat*, the political forces are fishing in murky waters and looking at *migration and crime and so forth coming from that dangerous outside*, then we are in trouble.[46]

Eliasson's remarks picked up on the contradiction between open markets, peace and commerce, on the one hand, and closed borders, hostilities and conflict on the other. This conceptual binary does not always hold in reality: Wars have been fought to open borders, for example. Nevertheless, it does constitute the reigning discourse and the oscillation between these oppositional categories may well have negatively affected the willingness of negotiators to communicate openly and to move toward compromise. These mixed signals necessarily must undermine the ontological security that can be attributed to the meta-discourses of trade law.

IV. LEGAL AND ECONOMIC UNCERTAINTIES REGARDING THE SPECIAL AND DIFFERENTIAL TREATMENT PRINCIPLE

Whereas some commentators would argue for a "constitutionalization" of free-trade principles in the WTO, in fact the central goals of the GATT–WTO system have never been articulated in terms of free trade per se. Both the

[44] Ibid.

[45] See *Wendt*, supra note 27, 21.

[46] See Jan Eliasson, The Progress of UN Reform, Speech to Carnegie Council (June 7, 2006, as part of the A Fairer Globalization series; emphasis added).

GATT and the WTO Preambles stress that the goals of the trading regime are *social welfare outcomes* rather than particular economic policies:

> [R]elations in the field of trade and economic endeavour should be conducted with a view to raising standards of living, ensuring full employment and a large and steadily growing volume of real income and effective demand.[47]

Although the particular arrangements detailed under the WTO set out to reduce national policy space in favor of free trade, then, the restraint in endorsing free trade as such is notable. It means, effectively, that at the end of the day the particular balance between free trade and redistributive trade *is still open for discussion*.

A. Open-Endedness in Law: Equality Jurisprudence[48] in the WTO

In their efforts to advocate the adoption of SD, developing-country governments pressed a substantive conceptualization of sovereign equality. Formal differences in policy designed to correct structural economic inequality would further the principle of sovereign equality rather than detract from it, in this view.[49] This substantive equality view informed the NIEO movement and the adoption of the Generalized System of Preferences. The principle of substantive equality was tested in the *EC-Tariff Preferences* case in which India argued the view, widespread among developing-country governments, that the GSP was intended to bar any differentiation within developing countries as a group.

Had the WTO Dispute Settlement Body adopted this view, the conditionalities imposed by the European Communities on certain GSP benefits (including compliance with labor and environmental standards and also anti-drug trafficking measures, the latter of which formed the actual basis for the *EC-Tariff Preferences* decision) would have been ruled WTO-inconsistent. Instead, although the WTO Panel Report upheld India's view, the WTO Appellate Body ultimately rejected it and held that such conditionalities were in principle not WTO-inconsistent (though in their particular implementation by the EC they ran afoul of procedural requirements).

---

[47] See Preamble, General Agreement on Tariffs and Trade, October 30, 1947, 61 Stat. A-11, T.I.A.S. 1700, 55 U.N.T.S. 194 and Preamble, Agreement Establishing the World Trade Organization, April 15, 1994, 1867 U.N.T.S. 154, 33 I.L.M. 1125.

[48] The term jurisprudence is used here even though the WTO Dispute Settlement System is not precisely a judicial system. Indeed, the "judicialization" of the WTO is a dynamic deeply controversial within the WTO, as the rest of the Section indicates.

[49] Mohammed Bedjaoui, *Towards a New International Economic Order* (Paris: UNESCO, 1979).

This section relates the *EC-Tariff Preferences* decision to the emergence of "equality jurisprudence" in the GATT–WTO Dispute Settlement System. It is argued here that the elaboration by the WTO Appellate Body of the principle of substantive equality reflects a logic characteristic of a judicial legal system, rather than a specific set of policy commitments. WTO decisions will not and, it is argued, *cannot* endorse (without an explicit mandate to do so) a particular set of trade policy arrangements.

In *EC-Tariff Preferences*, the Appellate Body embraced at an abstract level the principle of substantive equality that historically informed developing-country government mobilization efforts for reform of the international economic order.[50] In the particulars of the case, however, this principle was ambiguous: Should it be held, as India argued, to mandate a GSP in which developing countries as a whole would receive trade preferences as a group from the developed world, or, as the EC argued, to allow for differentiations among developing countries? The AB upheld the EC's view, deciding that special conditionalities in the EC's GSP arrangements were WTO consistent as long as "similarly situated beneficiaries" were "not treated differently."[51]

The *Tariff Preferences* case builds on a jurisprudential trend at work in a variety of decisions that the Appellate Body constructs into a substantive notion of equality. For example, the Appellate Body asserted equality reasoning forcefully in its *Shrimp – Turtle I* decision, holding that the purpose of the GATT Article XX chapeau was to ensure that similarly situated countries ("countries where the same conditions prevail") would be treated similarly.[52] Although *Shrimp – Turtle I* did not focus on SD directly in the way that *Tariff Preferences* did, the concept of SD clearly animated the question of whether the complainant countries in that case should be required to adopt the same relatively costly devices as producers elsewhere with relatively more resources at their disposal.

The emergence of equality as a central concept in driving decisions is a product of the *relative* shift from a "pragmatic" trade regime in which political diplomacy was paramount to a "legalistic" trade regime in which some trade disputes must be decided through a judicial mechanism. While incomplete,

[50] Professor Lim makes this point in his contribution to this volume. See Chin Leng Lim, "The Conventional Morality of Trade."
[51] *European Communities – Conditions for the Granting of Tariff Preferences to Developing Countries*, WT/DS246/AB/R, para. 173 (April 7, 2004).
[52] *United States – Import Prohibition of Certain Shrimp and Shrimp Products*, WT/DS58/AB/R (October 12, 1998).

this shift has been facilitated by the establishment of the DSB and has created a forum in which claims must be articulated and decided in legal terms.

The Appellate Body's conscious adoption of a legalistic approach was evident in its rejection of the EC's argument in the *Bananas* case for a more "pragmatic" interpretation of the provisions in question. The EC had unsuccessfully sought to persuade the Appellate Body that the deal cut during the Marrakesh negotiations created a political understanding that should override any narrower interpretation that might be supported by a stricter attention to text.[53]

In a similar way, the *EC–Bananas* case reveals the *systematization of law* propelled by the WTO's establishment of an adjudicatory mechanism. A desire to maintain integrity in the WTO as a legal system[54] requires that claims be articulated and decided in jurisprudential terms. The concept of horse-trading represented by the reciprocity in trade negotiations has no real anchor in law's understanding of itself. Therefore, although reciprocity is not only non-controversial but is actually the central driver of negotiations among WTO members, it is untenable as a criterion for disposing of legal claims. Hence, in the *Bananas* case the Appellate Body rejected the EC's claim animated by reciprocity (effectively arguing that its arrangement reflected the political deal cut in Marrakesh with the finalization of the Uruguay Round negotiations) in favor of an interpretation animated by the jurisprudential principle of equality.

The emergence of equality jurisprudence consolidates the transformation of WTO dispute settlement proceedings from a power-orientation model to a rule-orientation model.[55] The transformation reflected the establishment of the WTO DSB as a self-conscious *legal* system.[56]

---

[53] *European Communities – Regime for the Importation, Sale and Distribution of Bananas*, WT/DS27/R/ECU, para. 4.104 (May 22, 1997). This argument was successful at the panel level, see ibid. at para. 7.110, but was reversed by the Appellate Body, *European Communities – Regime for the Importation, Sale and Distribution of Bananas*, WT/DS27/AB/R, paras. 179–188 (September 9, 1997).

[54] Niklas Luhmann, *A Sociological Theory of Law*, translated by Elizabeth King and Martin Albrow (Boston: Routledge & Kegan Paul, 1985); Gunther Teubner (ed.), *Autopoietic Law: A New Approach to Law and Society* (New York: de Gruyter, 1988; hereinafter Teubner).

[55] John Jackson, *The World Trading System: Law and Policy of International Economic Relations* (Cambridge, MA: MIT Press, 1994), 127.

[56] Autopoietic analysis of law focuses on the law's self-referentiality and recursivity – the way in which legal structures are always and only justified by legal acts, and vice versa. "[T]he circular relationship between legal acts and legal norms . . . replaces extra-legal foundations of law." Teubner, "Introduction to *Autopoietic Law*," in *Teubner*, supra note 54, 4.

Legal sociologists such as Niklas Luhmann and Gunther Teubner have taken up the special qualities of legal systems as systems.[57] Systems theory holds that law essentially cannot understand political or social facts as such; rather, those facts must be metabolized in the language of accepted jurisprudential concepts. For example, arguments for outcomes on the basis of economic policy or political theory cannot be absorbed by the WTO DSB in those terms. Because of this encompassing framework of reasoning through legal concepts, legal systems are not directly open to direct claims for political justice. Such claims can only be addressed in terms of their articulation in jurisprudential terms. They will ultimately be determined not by their political objectives but by their legal framing. Thus, systems theory holds that law is *normatively closed* to claims for political or economic justice in and of themselves.

Teubner gives as a prime example of legal autopoiesis the "equality clause" in which "reasonable criteria" must be established to determine the applicability.[58] Consequently, the enterprise of law becomes an endless process of differentiation between circumstances that produce a ruling of "equal" versus those that produce a ruling of "unequal."[59]

The *Tariff Preferences* case would seem to support a systems theory view. Although the substantive equality model *was* adopted as a jurisprudential framework by the EC, that adoption did not correlate with a holding in favor of India. Thus, the emergence of a substantive equality test hardly constitutes a clear victory for the "structuralist" agenda for reform of the New International Economic Order[60] propounded by developing-country governments in the 1970s when the GSP was established. Ironically, although the principle of substantive equality drove the argument by developing-country governments for a GSP back then, in the *Tariff Preferences* case the substantive equality argument was adopted by the EC as respondent.

"Normatively closed" does not mean determinate or fixed.[61] However, *jurisprudential* approach to distributive justice will remain indeterminate in securing specific policies. Rather, the institutional need to view the legal system as valid has necessitated the replacement of "extra-legal foundations"

[57] Niklas Luhmann, *A Sociological Theory of Law*, translated by Elizabeth King and Martin Albrow (Boston: Routledge & Kegan Paul, 1985); in *Teubner*, supra note 54.

[58] Gunther Teubner, "Self-Subversive Justice: Contingency or Transcendence Formula of Law?," *The Modern Law Review* 72(1) (2008): 1, 11.

[59] Ibid.

[60] Raúl Prebisch, *The Economic Development of Latin America and Its Principal Problems* (New York: United Nations, 1950).

[61] Ibid.

with legal concepts within the dispute settlement jurisprudence. From this perspective, it is not surprising that it is *substantive* equality, rather than a more formalistic concept of equality, that has emerged as a central concept. Whereas a formalistic approach would render the process of adjudication relatively more technocratic, the need to parse the concept of substantive equality requires the primacy of jurisprudential tools and analysis.

B. *Open-Endedness in Economics: The Need for Contextual Policies in Trade and Development*

SD is a claim for redistribution of the gains from trade in the global economy. As a redistributive concept, it might mistakenly be analogized to tax-and-transfer socioeconomic entitlements within domestic economies from richer individuals to poorer individuals. However, such entitlements provide concrete benefits that accrue directly to individuals. By contrast, SD identifies governmental practices that shape the conditions for economic production and trade. There is a gap between these regulatory practices and any particular concrete distribution of benefits and costs, and the open-ended implications of that gap will be taken up in this section.

It could be argued that SD is the closest thing to social and economic entitlements in the trading system: SD would support the creation of monies (through increased market access for exports, tariffs, or quota-related price increases for imports) that could be used to target business development, poverty reduction, or both. However, there is no guarantee that those monies will be used in that fashion. Increasing tariff revenues or producer profits does not ensure social and economic benefits for the larger population.

This is *not* to advance the familiar argument against government intervention that might be found in the writing of Milton Friedman or Robert Hudec.[62] Governments are always involved in shaping markets, and the question is what kind of intervention is optimal. SD might be optimal in some cases, but not in others.

Where the conditions exist to generate economic growth through trade, SD in the form of preferential tariffs for exports, and tolerance of higher tariffs and trade barriers for imports, should form part of a larger tailored policy for growth. In others, where the conditions exist to transform such protections

---

[62] Milton Friedman, *Capitalism and Freedom* (Chicago: University of Chicago Press, 1962); Robert E. Hudec, *Developing Countries in the GATT Legal System* (Aldershot, Hampshire, U.K.; Brookfield, Vt., USA: Gower, for the Trade Policy Research Center, London, 1987); see also Robert E. Hudec, *Developing Countries in the GATT Legal System* (New York: Cambridge University Press, 2010).

into classic rent-seeking behavior that harms business development or poverty reduction, SD should not be used.

If the decision is between a broad, open-ended SD framework that would provide sufficient policy autonomy to individual governments to make these tailored decisions, on the one hand, and a total denial of such autonomy on the other, then policy autonomy is preferable for the reasons just stated. Examples in which policy autonomy is important include intellectual property and balance-of-payments restrictions.

The argument just applied to caution against focusing on strengthened SD would apply just as equally to a neoliberal argument for eliminating SD altogether. There is enough historical evidence pointing to the indeterminate gains from trade to question the efficacy of a simplistic free-trade approach in every context. This uncertainty about the relationship between economic policies and social welfare is the basis for Rawls's initial reluctance to identify "core" values in economic and social principles beyond the stated social goals put forward by the difference principle.

Trade liberalization does *not* always equate to economic growth; the experience of the East Asian countries stands as a testament to the possible benefits of an infant-industry approach.[63] However, an infant industry, which would benefit from a nonreciprocal, preferential trade policy at the multilateral level, can also backfire. In short, the benefits of a nonreciprocal or preferential trade policy may be too indeterminate at the abstract level, without examining particular instances.

Take the example of just one developing country, Egypt, which unfortunately seems to have undergone trade liberalization where it would create widespread social harm and foregone trade liberalization where it would generate widespread social gain: The leveling of textile trade preferences for Egypt has dislocated massive small-scale local manufacturers; at the same time, a continuing protection of a domestic steel monopoly has increased housing costs beyond affordability.

In the former case, Egypt received diffuse benefits from the principle of SD; in the latter case, the same principle has worked to exacerbate domestic rents and corruption. The latter scenario certainly bolsters the anti-SD view of trade scholars such as Hudec and many economists. In their view, such mechanisms create too many opportunities for rent seeking and corruption,

---

[63] See, e.g., Alice H. Amsden and Wan-wen Chu, *Beyond Late Development: Taiwan's Upgrading Policies* (Cambridge, MA: MIT Press, 2003); Stephan Haggard, *Pathways from the Periphery: The Politics of Growth in the Newly Industrializing Countries* (Ithaca, NY: Cornell University Press, 1995).

and they strain the overall legitimacy of the system in the Global North as well as the Global South.

In short, we simply do not yet know the optimal arrangement for trade – even if the benefits of trade are universally recognized. If this is true, then a dialogic model may remain important in the ongoing determination of optimal trade policy.

v. PHILOSOPHICAL CONUNDRUMS OF DISTRIBUTIVE JUSTICE

Joining the open-endedness in legal interpretation and economic outcomes described in the previous section is perhaps a more fundamental open-endedness in theoretical underpinnings of distributive justice. This section briefly reviews two leading efforts from philosophy to theorize the implications of distributive justice for the global economy, Frank Garcia's Rawlsian argument for SD, and Carol Gould's argument for social and economic rights. Both are powerful examples of the contributions of political philosophy to reasoning about global justice. Both ventures, however, ultimately lead back to the necessity for political decision making. With the myriad uncertainties described above characterizing the political decision-making process in the WTO, these efforts seem to end by underscoring rather than resolving some of the key conundrums facing distributive justice in the WTO.

A. Frank Garcia's Rawlsian Argument for SD

In applying Rawlsian theory to the international trading regime, Frank Garcia has argued that SD can operate as "a partial fulfillment of the redistributive obligations that Justice as Fairness dictates for wealthier states in response to inequality."[64] Garcia illustrates that the global economy remains deeply shaped by structural inequality, and his account persuasively argues that pursuing global justice requires a serious consideration of the regulatory reforms at every level that would be required to correct this inequality. Garcia's work follows the lead of other global justice philosophers who criticized Rawls for his reluctance to apply his "difference principle" to the international scale,[65] and his argument for SD applies an "international difference principle."

---

[64] Frank Garcia, "Trade and Inequality," *Michigan Journal of International Law* 21 (2000): 1023–1024.

[65] See Thomas Pogge, *Realizing Rawls* (Ithaca, NY: Cornell University Press, 1989), 211–272; Robert Hockett, "The Limits of Their World," *Minnesota Law Review* 90 (2006): 1720; Robert Hockett, "The Deep Grammar of Distribution: A Meta-Theory of Justice," *Cardozo Law Review* 26 (2005): 1179. Rawls's more limited theory of justice in a global setting, set forth

At the same time, Garcia has not fully addressed Rawls's own preference for procedure over substance as a mechanism for distributive justice *even where the difference principle applies*. In *A Theory of Justice*, Rawls elaborated the "veil of ignorance" that would provide a mechanism for a just society.[66] A just society would be created through its determining of the "constitutional essentials," many of which amounted to procedural fairness and what we would identify as civil and political rights.[67]

With respect to social and economic policy, Rawls avoided a specific redistributive approach. Rather, he concluded that the optimal arrangements are still too uncertain and too unknown to maintain enough confidence to constitutionalize them in any form.[68] Consequently, what is required for social rights is ongoing political dialogue as to their proper scope and application.[69] A "central feature of this conception of distributive justice," Rawls wrote, "is that it contains a large element of *procedural justice*."[70]

---

in *The Law of Peoples*, has received significant criticism from philosophers of global justice. See, e.g., Thomas Pogge, "An Egalitarian Law of Peoples," Vol. 23(3), *Philosophy & Public Affairs*, pp. 195–224 (July 1994); see also Simon Caney, "Cosmopolitanism and the Law of Peoples," *Journal of Political Philosophy*, vol. 10 (1), 95–123 (March 2002).

[66] John Rawls, *A Theory of Justice* (Cambridge, MA: Harvard University Press, 1971; hereinafter Rawls). Rawls's social contract is ratified in a condition of perfect equality: The contract is composed of the principles that rational and free persons concerned to further their own interests would accept in an initial position of equality as defining the fundamentals of the terms of their association, according to two basic principles. "First: each person is to have an equal right to the most extensive basic liberty compatible with a similar liberty for others." Ibid., 60. Second, "Social and economic inequalities are to be arranged so that they are both: a) to the greatest benefit of the least advantaged, and b) attached to offices and positions open to all under conditions of fair equality of opportunity." Ibid.

[67] John Rawls, *Political Liberalism* (New York: Columbia University Press, 1993).

[68] See *Rawls*, supra note 66 (discussing distributive justice and political economy). In the context of domestic U.S. jurisprudence, the constitutional scholar Frank Michelman has reviewed Rawlsian justice to determine whether it calls for the establishment of any specific minimum entitlement. Michelman concludes that it does not:

> The point for Rawls is this: A sufficient, legitimating constitutional agreement has to provide fully firm, strict, and reliable substantive guarantees of compliance with what he calls the central ranges of the basic negative liberties – freedoms of conscience and expression, for example. Regarding the rest of social citizenship, the requirement is a looser one. What we need, and all we need, is assurance that, whenever political and legislative choices bear upon the basic structural conditions of social citizenship, those choices will be approached by all who take part in them under what Rawls calls a constraint of public reason.

Frank Michelman, "The Constitution, Social Rights, and Liberal Political Justification," *International Journal of Constitutional Law* 1 (2003): 32 (hereinafter *Michelman*).

[69] *Rawls*, supra note 66.   [70] Ibid., at 267 (emphasis added).

It is certainly possible to critique this proceduralist account of distributive justice as simply an artifact of Rawls's liberal political commitments.[71] Nonetheless, in the context of international trade, the gaps between theory and practical consequence on *both* sides of the spectrum often seem quite stark.

B. *Carol Gould's Human Rights Approach*

In *Globalizing Democracy and Human Rights*, Carol Gould gives a sophisticated argument for developing a framework for the implementation of human rights and democratic governance on a global scale. Gould seeks to develop a stronger basis on which human rights can be required by a theory of justice than would be found in other accounts.[72]

Gould notes that many prevailing theories of justice, including those of Rawls and Habermas, establish a certain circularity between democracy and justice: On the one hand, democracy is desirable because it will lead to just outcomes; on the other, justice can be identified primarily because it is the result of a democratically deliberative decision-making process.

Consequently, there is no independent basis for identifying justice,[73] and these theorists seek to address the obvious concerns about bias by stipulating ideal conditions for deliberation: Rawls's "veil of ignorance" and Habermas's "ideal speech situation."[74] By contrast, Gould argues that adopting

---

[71] See, e.g., Alasdair MacIntyre, *After Virtue* (Notre Dame, IN: University of Notre Dame Press, 1981).

[72] Carol Gould, *Globalizing Democracy and Human Rights* (Cambridge: Cambridge University Press, 2004), 31 (hereinafter Gould).

[73] Ibid. at 15:

> [S]everal theories of justice have themselves framed the principles of justice in terms of some consensus (e.g., Rawls, Habermas), which may seem to put these principles themselves in the context of a quasi-democratic decision procedure. If that is the case, then rights entailed by or derived from these principles of justice might themselves ultimately be social constructs internal to, or constituted by, a democratic or quasi-democratic process and thus not independent of such procedures. It would not be clear, then, why the results of one democratic procedure would have the normative authority to constrain another.

[74] Rawls and Habermas build on the moral principle of reciprocity between human beings and its universalization into general, abstract norms that form the basis of a just society. For Rawls the "veil of ignorance" conceals the norm projections of individual rational actors from their particular circumstances and induces them to design fair political institutions. In Habermas's "ideal speech situation," formal procedures are supposed to guarantee the undistorted reciprocal expression of individual interests as well as their universalization into morally just norms. See *Teubner*, supra note 58.

human rights as a *prior* justice commitment would avoid this problem of circularity.[75]

Gould must address in her own rights-based account the problems of power imbalances and other "differentiations" that would shadow a proceduralist account of justice.[76] She resolves this problem by calling for a "concrete universality"[77] that would recognize the social relationships that both constitute and differentiate individuals and that would depend on "intersociative norms emerging from . . . an interaction"[78] of "peoples and cultures."

Nevertheless, this view also contains its own circularity: Rights are an important precursor to effective democracy, but only an effective democracy can ultimately determine the most just definition of rights.

To be sure, Gould offers a rich conception of deliberative decision making. By proposing a "care model of democratic community," Gould introduces concepts of empathy, cooperative reciprocity, and solidarity that would seem to provide important ballast to her proposal for a "universalizing consensus."[79] The ultimate point, though, remains: If we reject the possibility of deriving a meaning for justice, or rights, from some a priori perspective because we recognize the boundedness of any given vantage point, then some dialogic, deliberative, proceduralist conception of justice is necessary to create acceptable content for itself. This quickly brings us back to the "constitutional circle" that Gould recognized in her critique of earlier accounts. The only way out of this circularity seems to be to posit certain values that are clearly historically specific and therefore not favored in this consciously universalistic approach.[80]

The open-endedness of human rights principles thus leads to the need to point to some *prior* set of values for guiding the process of reasoning principles through to conclusions. In the U.S. legal academy, those embracing an antifoundationalist liberal or progressive perspective have ended up stressing

---

[75] "But if we grant that a democratic procedure, however justified, may still arrive at an unjust outcome, then there must be some independent criterion of justice, the appeal to which cannot be, circularly, to a democratic or quasi-democratic procedure in turn." *Gould*, supra note 72, 32.

[76] Ibid. at 61 ("Certainly, there is the important recognition that the interrelations among individuals or groups often have been characterized not by equality among participants but instead by one-sided relations of domination, superiority, or oppression").

[77] Ibid. at 62 ("a conception of concrete universality that emphasizes networks of social relationships and engagements, where these may involve relations of domination or oppression").

[78] Ibid. at 63.

[79] Ibid. at 45 ("It is further evident that the concept of democratic community, particularly in view of the care model, goes beyond the traditional and thinner notion of democracy as simply a matter of political representation and equal voting rights.")

[80] See, e.g., Michael Dorf, "The Coherentism of Democracy and Distrust," *Yale Law Journal* 114 (2005): 1237, 1246–1250.

the need for democratic deliberation[81] – particularly on economic and social rights.[82]

vi. CONCLUSION

This chapter investigated the continued breakdowns in the Doha talks, mining below the surface to unearth faults in the deep structure of the multilateral trading regime. Those causes have to do not only with clashes of material interests and coordination challenges (Section I), but also with an underlying lack of trust that is revealed and reinforced by a discourse that constitutes state participants in the negotiations as enemies rather than friends (Section II).[83]

This chapter also endeavored to show why, from a normative perspective, the parameters of development law and policy in the WTO have not been unproblematically answered by salient interventions from law, economics, and philosophy (Section III). Far from opening the door to nihilism, recognition of the indeterminacy of distributive justice implies the need for continued deliberation.[84]

Better democratic governance in the WTO requires further reforming its negotiating and legislative processes to allow for broader and more meaningful inclusion of developing-country governments.[85] Ideally, democratization reforms would comprise two components: first, sovereign equality in state participation, such as one state, one vote; and second, sufficient technical assistance and capacity building so as to make voting meaningful for all states.

Between this ideal and contemporary reality, of course, many gradations exist. Short of one-state, one-vote procedural equality, greater support may be required for government negotiation coalitions to assert their interests effectively in negotiations and for a broader range of states to be included at earlier stages in negotiations.

Over the past decade, such networks of coalitions have formed in the WTO, both among developing-country governments and between developed and developing countries. Technical assistance programs for developing-country

---

[81] Michael Dorf, "Legal Indeterminacy and Institutional Design," *New York University Law Review* 78 (2003): 875; Roberto M. Unger, *Democracy Realized: A Progressive Alternative* (London: Verso, 2000; concluding that an "anti-necessitarian" account of law calls for "democratic experimentalism"; hereinafter *Unger*).

[82] See *Michelman*, supra note 68.

[83] See *Schmitt*, supra note 39.   [84] See *Habermas*, supra note 30.

[85] See Peter Sutherland, "The Doha Development Agenda: Political Challenges to the World Trading System – A Cosmopolitan Perspective," *Journal of International Economic Law* 8 (2005): 363; see also Jeffery Atik, "Democratizing the WTO," *George Washington International Law Review* 33 (2001): 451.

negotiators have become programmatized by a variety of actors including the WTO, bilateral donors, and nongovernmental organizations. Developing-country governments have participated much more extensively in negotiations.

These efforts at inclusiveness have fallen far short of the mark. Large gaps in capacity still exist among WTO members. Negotiations most assuredly do not reflect an equitable representation of the range of views among the membership. Even though these increases in inclusiveness have been limited, however, they have still been associated with a freezing up of negotiations.

Like many international institutions, the perceived legitimacy of the WTO has been called into question by the widespread increase in the salience of globalization in the social consciousness.[86] This increased awareness also happened to correlate with an actual expansion of the multilateral trade regime's substantive and institutional power by means of the Uruguay Round, causing some to wonder whether the democratic deficit so decried in the European context might also inhibit the legitimacy of international trade law.[87]

The emphasis on participatory decision making runs contrary to a very strong preference in economic law and policy for "expertise" – so-called technocracy over democracy, as it were.[88] The welfare effects of specific configurations in trade law and policy, it is argued, remain sufficiently unknown so as to call for "democratic experimentalism" rather than constitutionalism.[89]

The state–actor focus deemphasizes a large swath of argumentation for modes of democratization that transcend the traditional venue of interstate relations defined by formal sovereign equality. Such alternative conceptions of democratization include greater transparency and accountability by the WTO to the global public at large,[90] broader incorporation of civil society into the WTO,[91] conditioning a state's participation in the WTO on the state's

---

[86] Arguably the change has not been as great as perceived, and certainly not for developing countries.

[87] Robert Howse, "The Legitimacy of the World Trade Organization," in Jean-Marc Coicaud and Veijo Heiskanen (eds.), *The Legitimacy of International Organizations* (Tokyo: UNU Press, 2001), 355 at 361; Chantal Thomas, "Constitutional Change and International Government," *Hastings Law Journal* 52 (2000): 1.

[88] For a more detailed account of literature on constitutionalizing the WTO, see Chantal Thomas, "Popular Constitutionalism" (2008; manuscript on file with author).

[89] See *Unger, supra* note 81, 10.

[90] Robert Howse, "From Politics to Technocracy and Back Again: The Fate of the Multilateral Trading System," *American Journal of International Law* 96 (2002): 94; Gráinne De Búrca, "Developing Democracy beyond the State," *Columbia Journal of Transnational Law* (2008): 221.

[91] Daniel D. Bradlow, "'The Times They Are A-Changin': Some Preliminary Thoughts on Developing Countries, NGOs and the Reform of the WTO," *George Washington International Law Review* 33 (2001): 503; see *Guzman, supra* note 21.

domestic democratization,[92] and the bypassing of the WTO altogether to form alternative institutional configurations.[93]

With full respect to these approaches, democratic governance among states also constitutes a worthy goal, and one that could reshape WTO policies in the direction of egalitarian redistribution. However, as this chapter showed, opening up WTO decision making to more democratic processes will not necessarily bring about a clear shift in the direction of a particular approach to development policy, or SD. Even if developing-country governments were to gain a clear majoritarian position in WTO governance, complexity in policy decisions on trade and development would continue.

This complexity, however, is precisely why a proceduralist account remains necessary. In the absence of universal policy directives, an open-ended dialogue may allow for the greatest possible consideration of disparate views and varied sources of information. Although a democratized negotiation procedure in the WTO may be far from ideal, it may nevertheless provide the surest – and perhaps the only – path to decisions that reflect some semblance of distributive justice for developing countries.

This idea of a proceduralist theory of distributive justice is both normative and explanatory. The complexity of trade policy, especially in relationship to economic development, problematizes an agenda of "constitutionalization" – whether the substantive principles at issue are conventional disciplines of the GATT–WTO, its regime of SD, or social and economic rights. The complexity of trade policy and the still attenuated legitimacy of the multilateral regime also help to explain why the WTO is now in the very process of attempting to democratize governance among its members – and why that process has been so fraught with difficulty. A proceduralist theory of distributive justice allows for a focus on the basic legitimacy of the regime.

[92] See Gregory Fox and Brad Roth (eds.), *Democratic Governance and International Law* (Cambridge: Cambridge University Press, 2000).
[93] Thomas Pogge, "An Egalitarian Law of Peoples," *Philosophy and Public Affairs* 23 (1994): 195 (arguing for a "Global Resources Dividend" or GRD).

CRITICAL RESPONSES TO CONTEMPORARY THEORIZING ABOUT JUSTICE AND INTERNATIONAL ECONOMIC INSTITUTIONS

8 Global Justice and Trade

Fernando R. Tesón and Jonathan Klick

I. INTRODUCTION

Virtually everyone agrees that world poverty is a major scourge and that alleviating it should be a priority of international law and national policies of developed and developing nations alike.[1] People disagree, however, about the best way to do this; in particular, they disagree about the role of trade in combatting poverty. In this chapter we claim that free trade is *required* by justice. Protectionist laws are indefensible on two grounds. First, they are indefensible in *principle* because they coercively redistribute resources in favor of persons who are not deserving beneficiaries under any plausible theory of domestic or international justice. Second, protectionist laws have objectionable *consequences* because they undermine economic growth and, in doing so, harm persons generally – in particular, the poor. In presenting our argument, we criticize recommendations from the philosophical literature on global justice. We conclude that those recommendations are deficient precisely because they

[1] For a general survey of the magnitude of the problem, see World Commission on the Social Dimension of Globalization, "A Fair Globalization: Creating Opportunities for All" (International Labour Organization, 2004; available at http://www.ilo.org/public/english/standards/relm/ilc/ilc92/pdf/adhoc.pdf; accessed on February 27, 2007).

We thank several people who heard earlier versions of this chapter and made valuable comments: Matthew Brown; Matt Zwolinski; the faculty of the Social Philosophy and Policy Center, Bowling Green State University; participants in the Georgetown Law School International Law Workshop, especially Carlos Vázquez and Steve Charnowitz; participants in the Duke Global Law Workshop, especially Jost Pauwelyn and student comments; participants in the Conference on Global Justice at the University of Virginia, in particular Loren Lomasky, Allen Buchanan, Peter Boetke, and Julia Mahoney; Eduardo Rivera López of the Universidad Torcuato Di Tella; Marcelo Alegre, of the Universidad de Palermo; and the participants in the American Society of International Law Symposium on International Economic Justice, Washington, D.C., especially Joel Trachtman, Carol Gould, and Jeffrey Dunhoff.

overlook the role of trade in alleviating poverty – a role underscored, with little dissent, by reliable economic research.[2]

Philosophers overlook and even sometimes reject the crucial finding that, generally, free trade *helps* the poor. Because free movement of goods, services, and persons will likely reduce world poverty, any theory of global justice should encourage and promote the establishment of free trade and the reduction of barriers to immigration. However, none of the major scholars on global justice or human rights, that is, those *concerned with poverty*, recommend unrestricted trade,[3] and some of them even claim that free trade *hurts* the world's poor.[4] Instead, these scholars typically propose various global redistributive schemes comprising universal aid and including, in some versions, a global regulatory agency that would transfer resources collected through universal taxation from the rich to the poor. They also recommend global regulatory standards (on labor, health, and the environment) restrictive of trade.[5]

Unfortunately, this neglect is not just a scholarly failure. The antiglobalization movement leads a worldwide struggle against free trade partly in the name of protecting the poor.[6] This academic and political hostility to free trade aggravates, we think, the harm that protectionism, and the rent-seeking activities that almost invariably accompany it, inflict on the world's most vulnerable population.[7]

---

[2] We also believe that liberalizing immigration would likely have similar beneficial effect on poverty, but a full defense of that claim requires a separate article.

[3] Surprisingly, the United Nations General Assembly, not known for its sympathies to economic or political liberalism, has taken a better view of the issue. See U.N. Millennium Project, "Investing in Development: A Practical Plan to Achieve the Millennium Development Goals, Overview" (United Nations Development Programme, 2005), xiii (available at http://www.unmilleniumproject.org/documents/overviewEngi-1LowRes.pdf), proposing to fight poverty by, *inter alia*, "[d]evelop[ing] further an *open* rule-based, predictable, non-discriminatory trading and financial system ([which] includes a commitment to good governance, development and poverty reduction – nationally and internationally)" (emphasis added; last accessed on February 12, 2007).

[4] See infra, Section VI.

[5] For a defense of the WTO's pro-trade functions and a criticism of proposals to establish a global regulatory agency, see John O. McGinnis and Mark L. Movsesian, "The World Trade Constitution," *Harvard Law Review* 114 (2000): 511.

[6] See, e.g., Jerry Mander, Debi Baker, and David Korten, *Does Globalization Help the Poor?* (San Francisco, CA: International Forum on Globalization, 2001) (available at http://www.thirdworldtraveler.com/Globalization/DoesGlobalizHelpPoor.html; last accessed on April 26, 2006). For cogent answers, see Jay Mandle, *Globalization and The Poor* (Cambridge: Cambridge University Press, 2003), 100, 121–132 (explaining the economic misconceptions underlying much of the antiglobalization movement), and Jagdish Bhagwati, *In Defense of Globalization* (Oxford: Oxford University Press, 2004), 51–72 (claiming that globalization helps the poor). See also the discussion infra, Section IV, point 1.

[7] We do not discuss international trade lawyers here. Although, in general, their views tend to be more sympathetic to free trade, they do not entirely do justice to the economic literature. For

Our argument is in several parts. We first define the problem as the need to improve the situation of the world's poor as a class. We then review the *status quaestionis* on the effects of trade liberalization on growth, especially on the poor, as it stands in mainstream international economics. Joining a nearly unanimous literature, we conclude that trade liberalization creates global and national growth and generally helps the world's poor. For this reason, any philosophical proposal concerned with the poor should embrace a global system designed to eliminate the barriers to trade, and in particular to curb the influence of concentrated interest groups that benefit from protectionism, and in so doing harm the poor.[8] The exceptions to this general proposition rely on very specific factual assumptions that are unlikely to obtain in the real world of national trade policy. It is fair to say, then, that the condition of the world's poor would most likely improve if governments would allow them fully to participate in the global market as producers and consumers. We show how philosophers approach the question of poverty. Because they neglect economic theory, these scholars misdiagnose world poverty and recommend ineffectual, insufficient, or counterproductive solutions. Finally, we respond to two arguments against free trade: the stolen-goods argument and the pauper-labor argument.

II. DEFINING THE PROBLEM: POVERTY, EQUALITY, AND EFFICIENCY

We must carefully define the problem we are addressing. This chapter is concerned with the predicament of the world's poor. We take as the proper object of moral concern a group defined in some quantifiable way as those who have the lowest real income per capita, across nations.[9] This approach has several corollaries. First, we are not addressing the problem of economic

example, a leading trade legal scholar, John J. Jackson, cautions against embracing unrestrained trade because he thinks that states may legitimately pursue "non-economic" policies. See John J. Jackson, *The World Trading System: Law and Policy of International Economic Relations* (Cambridge, MA: MIT Press, 1997), 18–25. In this chapter, however, we assume that any trade policy *should* enhance the welfare of the poor. Whether in Jackson's term this goal is economic or noneconomic is a semantic choice.

[8] See McGinnis and Movsesian, "The World Trade Constitution," supra note 5.

[9] We bypass the difficult issue of how to measure poverty and, consequently, how to count the poor. We assume, however, that this can be done accurately and impartially. For contrasting views, see "World Bank Development Report 2000/1," 2001 (available at http://www.worldbank.org/wdr/2000/fullreport.html; last accessed April 26, 2006); and Sanjay G. Reddy and Thomas W. Pogge, "How *Not* to Count the Poor," April 21, 2003 (available at http://www.socialanalysis.org; last accessed April 26, 2006).

inequality per se.[10] Many people think that inequality is a serious problem, but it is not the subject of this chapter. We assume either that there is no injustice in disproportionate gains by rich countries or persons if the result is to lift the world's poor from their current predicament,[11] or that if inequality is an injustice, reducing it is a less urgent priority than alleviating poverty in absolute terms. This proviso is important, because it is often the case that a discussion about the effects of trade shifts imperceptibly from the question of whether trade helps the poor to the question of whether trade increases or reduces inequality.[12] Although alleviating world poverty has the potential to reduce inequality, our defense of free trade here does not assume this. We do not take a stance on whether trade reduces or accentuates inequality. Because world poverty is an especially urgent problem, we assume instead that the proper moral concern is to help the world's poor, and we argue that free trade will do this, whatever the effects are on the gap between rich and poor countries, groups, or individuals. Furthermore, precisely because world poverty is so awful, the view that reducing inequality should have moral *priority* over helping the poor in absolute terms is implausible.

Second, this article takes as the proper object of moral concern the world's poor *as a class*. This concept requires elaboration. Philosophers' distrust of free markets stems in great part from their rejection of (utilitarian or Paretian) efficiency as a goal of political arrangements.[13] The argument against utilitarian efficiency is well known: Efficient economic arrangements are indifferent to distribution along the efficiency frontier, so if free trade increases wealth and is thus efficient in this sense but worsens the lot of the poor, then it is morally unacceptable. This is captured by the common wisdom in political philosophy that political and economic arrangements should be attentive to distributional

[10] We assume that any defensible system of international ethics must include a principle of *moral* equality, such as that every person in the globe deserves to be treated with equal concern and respect. See generally Fernando R. Tesón, *A Philosophy of International Law* (Boulder, CO: Westview Press, 1998; defending a Kantian theory of international law). In what follows, the term "inequality" denotes inequality of income or resources.

[11] Here we draw on John Rawls's famous assertion that "there is no injustice in greater benefits earned by a few provided that the situation of persons not so fortunate is thereby improved." John Rawls, *A Theory of Justice*, 2nd ed. (Cambridge, MA: Harvard University Press, 1999), 13.

[12] See, e.g., George F. De Martino, *Global Economy, Global Justice: Theoretical Objections and Policy Alternatives to Neoliberalism* (London: Routledge, 2000), 10–11 (objecting to "neoliberalism" because of its lack of commitment to equality).

[13] For a discussion of the normative objections to standard notions of efficiency, see Daniel M. Hausman and Michael S. McPherson, *Economic Analysis and Moral Philosophy* (Cambridge: Cambridge University Press, 1996), 84–100.

issues.[14] At first sight, Pareto efficiency fares better from the standpoint of the poor, because it forbids worsening their situation for the sake of aggregate gains. However, critics of efficiency point out that Pareto efficiency unduly forbids institutional arrangements that improve the poor at the expense of the rich. That seems unacceptable from the standpoint of a theory of justice that focuses on the poor.

We sidestep those criticisms because we provisionally agree with their normative premise. We endorse neither a standard of utilitarian efficiency nor a standard of Paretian efficiency, although we believe that, all things being equal, efficiency and economic growth are important instrumental values. Economic growth is valuable for many reasons, but for the purposes of this chapter it is valuable *because* it has a positive effect in the alleviation of poverty.

But who are the "world's poor" for the purposes of a theory of global justice? We suggest that an international economic arrangement should benefit *the poor as a class, across countries*. Every economic arrangement involves trade-offs among persons. Hence, whether free trade is desirable from a moral standpoint should be determined by whether it helps the world's poor *as a whole*, even if trade worsens the situation of *some* poor persons. If free trade has that effect, then it is no longer open to the criticisms that have been leveled against efficiency as a goal of distributive justice. A theory that recommends free trade on the grounds that it helps the poor is appropriately qualified from the distributional point of view. It focuses on improving the condition of the world's poor. It does not focus on improving each and every individual person, for the good reason that no policy, national or international, could possibly do that.[15] A philosophical objection to free trade, then, is a denial that trade helps the world's poor as a class.

To make our case, we briefly review the economic literature on trade, growth, and poverty. The survey will show that free trade not only increases global and national welfare (something that is rarely disputed) but also that given reasonably good domestic institutions, free trade has good distributional effects, that is, effects that are morally superior to the distributional effects of maintaining trade barriers. What is more, even in the *absence* of reasonably good domestic institutions, protectionism tends to compound the problem of poverty. Trade liberalization and freer immigration generally help the world's

---

[14] The literature is vast. For an excellent survey, see Will Kymlicka, *Contemporary Political Philosophy*, 2nd ed. (Oxford: Oxford University Press, 2002), 10–52.

[15] Thus, e.g., establishing universal health care will help many poor persons, but it may harm other poor persons by drawing from social resources to fight other manifestations of poverty, such as homelessness and hunger.

poor; protectionism anywhere (that is, in rich and poor countries alike) tends to hurt them.

A. Some Caveats

We offer four caveats to our argument in this chapter. First, we do not have a moral disagreement with those who are the targets of our critique. We assume, as they do, that persons, governments, and institutions have some duty (the basis for which we do not address here) to contribute to poverty relief. Rather, we differ on the means to discharge that duty. Philosophers think that the way to do this is to universalize foreign aid (perhaps by creating a global redistribution agency.) We, in contrast, think that the condition of the world's poor would dramatically improve if nations abolished all barriers to trade.

Second, because free trade alleviates poverty, we agree with those who have defended the role of the World Trade Organization (WTO) in enforcing the trade nondiscrimination rule that in turn has resulted in a dramatic lowering of tariffs and other trade barriers in the past fifty years or so, with the corresponding global economic growth.[16] Nevertheless, although the current WTO regime is preferable to a generalized protectionist regime, it has a number of imperfections from the standpoint of justice and efficiency. On the one hand, current arrangements allow governments to overprotect, thus hampering the chances that the poor will participate in the world economy. One problem with the WTO treaty, therefore, is that it *does not liberalize trade enough.*[17] On the other hand, although generally structured to gradually lower trade barriers, the WTO regime is partly predicated on outdated mercantilist notions: Governments seek to secure foreign markets access for exporters, thus treating access to *their* markets as a bargaining "chip."[18] Because imports benefit consumers, the notion that granting access to one's markets is a *concession* to other countries is false; lowering one's tariffs helps one's citizens.

---

[16] See McGinnis and Movsesian, "The World Trade Constitution," supra note 5, at 529–547.

[17] For an earlier appraisal of the protectionist features of the WTO (then the GATT), see Jagdish Bhagwati, "Protectionism," in *The Concise Encyclopedia of Economics* (1988), 9–15 (available at http://www.economlib.org; last accessed on January 2, 2007). Our criticism of the WTO, therefore, is diametrically opposed to the criticism by the antiglobalization forces: The latter blame the WTO for being too biased toward free trade, whereas we believe it does too little to advance free trade principles.

[18] See Kyle Bagwell and Robert W. Staiger, "The WTO as a Mechanism for Securing Market Access Property Rights: Implications for Global Labor and Environmental Issues," *Journal of Economic Perspectives* 15 (2001): 70. Professors Bagwell and Staiger still believe that the WTO can be defended on nonmercantilist grounds. See Kyle Bagwell and Robert W. Staiger, *The Economics of the World Trading System* (Cambridge, MA: MIT Press, 2002), 57–70.

So, although current vocal criticisms of the WTO should be rejected, the organization is suboptimal from the standpoint of global justice. The WTO is certainly inferior to more liberal alternatives, like unrestricted trade,[19] yet however bad the present system may be, protectionism is worse. Current critics of the WTO, in contrast, while criticizing protectionism in rich countries, seem to assume, usually *sub silentio*, that developing nations can help their economies by enacting protectionist measures. The institutional solution that could bring the world closer to the ideal of unrestricted trade is a WTO-like organization whose sole purpose is to ensure that nations liberalize trade. Nonetheless, excessive international regulation *restrictive* of trade, even if meant to address a market failure, may often be counterproductive with regard to the poor.[20]

Third, free trade does not necessarily mean total absence of regulation. We define "free trade" simply as the absence of barriers to trade. These barriers include, on the one hand, tariffs, quotas, and subsidies; on the other, they include government procurement, quality, sanitary, fiscal, health, environmental, and labor rules where the protectionist effect is not justified by the underlying rationale, or market failure, that these rules attempt to address. We do not object in principle to regulations that may be valid responses to genuine market failures (such as, perhaps, international regulations to curb emissions that cause global warming), although we recognize that those measures often conceal protectionist designs.

Our fourth caveat is that free trade is not a sufficient condition for growth and, consequently, not a sufficient condition for the alleviation of world poverty. Nations need, in addition to open trade, good domestic institutions.[21] More specifically, in order to grow, nations need, at the very least, well-defined property institutions and, arguably, good contract institutions. Nonetheless, we are agnostic about what *other* government programs should accompany trade liberalization.

For example, consider the issue of how to address the situation of workers hurt by trade liberalization. Liberal egalitarians support government retraining programs to help those who suffer from trade liberalization.[22] Libertarians, in

---

[19] *See* Amartya Sen, "How to Judge Globalism," *The American Prospect* 2 (2002): A2–A6 ("Global interchange is good; but the present set of global rules needlessly hurts the poor").

[20] See McGinnis and Movsesian, "The World Trade Constitution," supra note 5.

[21] See the discussion in the paragraphs that follow.

[22] For example, Amartya Sen has recommended various forms of government intervention to help workers hurt by trade, but he (like many others) explicitly warns that protectionism is a bad remedy. See Amartya Sen, *Development as Freedom* (Oxford: Oxford University Press, 2000), 121 (calling protectionist measures, in contrast to nonprotectionist government intervention in

contrast, suggest that the costs of trade readjustment should be borne by workers and producers of the inefficient, formerly protected industries.[23]

Our argument is consistent with either view. It simply rests on the proposition that *whatever else* government can or should do to aid the poor or help those hurt by trade liberalization, enacting protectionist laws is a bad remedy. Free traders do not simply claim that the benefits of capitalism will "trickle down" to the poor. Rather, they accept that, depending on the circumstances, free trade may be consistent with some role of government both in stimulating growth and making public expenditures, on social programs and similar schemes, to alleviate the plight of the poor – as long as these measures do not impair private property rights to a degree incompatible with growth. This is very important, because if the argument in this chapter is right, then free trade *should be supported by defenders of the welfare state (as long as they support property rights) and of laissez-faire economics alike.* An important corollary of our argument is that protectionist laws are indefensible, not just under a classical-liberal view of politics, but under *any* plausible moral-political theory.

III. THE ECONOMICS OF TRADE AND POVERTY ALLEVIATION

A. *Trade, Growth, and Poverty*

It is not possible to work responsibly on global justice without knowing how international markets work and what effects trade has on different social groups, especially on the poor. Plainly, before proposing ways to alleviate world poverty, we must get our social theories and facts right. Thus, we briefly examine what international economists have to say about the effects of trade liberalization on growth and poverty. The literature has a theoretical and an empirical component, which we summarize in turn in the paragraphs that follow.

Modern economic models of international trade generally fall into three categories: (1) the law of comparative advantage, which in turn has two versions, the original Ricardian version and the Heckscher–Olin version; (2) the model

markets, "precapitalist"). In the United States, the training of workers hurt by trade is federally subsidized. See Trade Adjustment Assistance Reform Act, 19 U.S.C.S. § 2401 et seq. (2002).

[23] A classic locus for this position is Gary S. Becker, "Investment in Human Capital: A Theoretical Analysis," *Journal of Political Economics* 70 (1962): 9. For a reply, see R. S. Eckaus, "Investment in Human Capital: A Comment," *Journal of Political Economics* 71 (1963): 501–504. For a more recent survey of the literature, see Mark A. Loewenstein and James R. Spletzer, "Dividing the Costs and Returns to General Training," *Journal of Labor Economics* 16 (1998): 142–171.

based on increasing returns; and (3) the endogenous growth model. The first two models broadly support the view that liberalized trade is good for general economic growth, as well as creating benefits for the poor in particular. The endogenous growth model includes a version of the infant-industry argument and constitutes the strongest theoretical case for (sometimes) supporting trade barriers in the name of helping the poor. For reasons of space, we will limit our discussion to the first and third categories: the comparative advantage model (favorable to free trade) and the endogenous growth model (permissive of some trade restrictions).

B. Comparative Advantage

David Ricardo formalized the idea that nations trade because technological differences lead each to specialize in the production of the good in which it has a comparative advantage.[24] In a model of two countries and two goods, Ricardo demonstrates that even if a country can produce one of the goods more cheaply than the other country, it still may import that good if doing so frees up its resources to produce a good in which its trading partner has an even greater cost disadvantage.[25] Extensions of the Ricardian model increase the

---

[24] David Ricardo, *On the Principles of Political Economy and Taxation*, 3rd ed., § 7.15 (1821; available at http://www.econlib.org/library/Ricardo/ricP.html).

[25] Country 1 has a comparative advantage in the production of Good A relative to Country 2 if its opportunity cost of producing Good A (i.e., how many units of Good B it can no longer produce if it produces an additional unit of Good A for a given stock of resources) is lower than Country 2's opportunity cost of producing Good A. Or, more succinctly, Country 1's marginal rate of transformation between Good A and Good B is lower than that of Country 2. Ricardo offers an example in which England and Portugal both produce wine and cloth. If it takes 100 English workers one year to produce quantity x of cloth and 120 English workers one year to produce quantity y of wine, and it takes 90 Portuguese workers to produce x units of cloth and 80 Portuguese workers to produce y units of wine in the same time period, then Ricardo claims that Portugal will import its cloth from England and export wine to the country. To see this, if Portugal allocates its 90 cloth workers to wine making, in principle, it can ship units of wine to England. In turn, England can now allocate its wine workers to cloth production, sending units of cloth in return to Portugal. After this trade, employing the same total amount of workers as before, Portugal has 20 percent more cloth than it previously produced (and the same amount of wine), and England has 12.5 percent more wine than it previously produced (and the same amount of cloth).

   While the exact split of the surplus generated by the trade will differ depending on the relative demands for wine and cloth in the two countries, in Ricardo's example both countries have the potential to expand their consumption of both goods without using more resources. Joint consumption of both goods across the two countries is guaranteed to rise even though Portugal can produce both goods more cheaply than England can. That is, economic growth occurs even if Portugal has an absolute advantage in the production of both goods. Earlier, Adam Smith

number of countries, increase the number of goods traded,[26] and include transportation costs and tariffs.[27] In general, for all of these extensions, the theory's predictions are robust: Trade continues to increase welfare among the trading partners in the way we already observed.

Whereas the Ricardian model relies on differing technology to ground the concept of comparative advantage, the Heckscher–Ohlin model relies on differential factor abundance to generate trade among countries. In the simplest form of the model, two factors of production are assumed (labor and capital) to be used in the production of two different goods. One of the goods is assumed to be capital intensive and the other is assumed to be labor intensive, meaning that the marginal product of capital for Good A exceeds the marginal product of capital for Good B, while the marginal product of labor for Good B exceeds the marginal product of labor for Good A. Production functions are identical across countries, but one of the countries has a relative abundance of labor while the other has a relative abundance of capital.[28]

Before trade takes place (i.e., in a state of autarky), the domestic price of the capital-intensive good will be lower in the country with an abundance of capital. Because the Heckscher–Ohlin model assumes perfect competition, the price of the capital-intensive good will be competed down because of its relatively large supply owing to the abundance of capital in the country. The same will be true of the domestic price of the labor-intensive good in the labor-abundant country. When trade is opened up, the capital-abundant country will be induced to export the capital-intensive good by the relatively high price of the good in the labor-abundant country and vice versa.

In welfare terms, trade in the Ricardian model is Pareto efficient at the microlevel. That is, all individuals in the trading countries are left no worse off after moving from autarky to trade (and many are made better off). The movement to free trade in the Heckscher–Ohlin model, however, is merely

had argued the case for free trade when a nation has the opportunity to trade with a country exhibiting an absolute advantage in desired goods. In terms of modern microeconomic tools, by specializing in the good in which its comparative advantage lies, trade effectively allows both countries to shift their production possibility frontiers outward.

[26] In fact, the Ricardian model is extended to encompass a continuum of goods in R. Dornbusch et al., "Comparative Advantage, Trade, and Payments in a Ricardian Model with a Continuum of Goods," *American Economic Review* 67 (1977): 823.

[27] For a formal presentation of all of these extensions, see Jagdish Bhagwati, Arvind Panagariya, and T. N. Srinivasani, *Lectures on International Trade* (Cambridge, MA: MIT Press, 1998), chapter 4.

[28] Robert Feenstra, *Advanced International Trade: Theory and Evidence* (Princeton, NJ: Princeton University Press, 2004), 32.

Kaldor–Hicks efficient at the microlevel. That is, although some individuals are left worse off after the change, the gains to the winners are large enough to offset the losses experienced by the owners of the relatively scarce factor of production. Whether the relevant compensation ever takes place is determined outside the trade model.[29]

Both comparative advantage models (Ricardian or Heckscher–Olin) imply an aggregate gain from trade liberalization. In the more refined versions there are important distributional consequences. Given the aggregate gains, however, if a country has well-functioning institutions, everyone could be made better off as a result of trade through redistribution. Obviously, throughout the developing world, the assumption of well-functioning institutions is not trivial. Nevertheless, in the absence of redistributive institutions, many of the refined models actually imply that the poor are the most likely to benefit from trade. As implied by the Stolper–Samuelson theorem, because the poor are most likely to be the owners of the abundant resource in developing countries (i.e., labor), liberalizing trade will increase the return to the poor in those countries.

C. Endogenous Comparative Advantage

Although most supporters of the endogenous growth models do not dispute that free trade is likely to improve growth and welfare,[30] they are concerned that trade, under some circumstances, could effectively displace growth-enhancing research and development. That is, if comparative advantage induces a country to specialize in a low-technology industry, there may be fewer technological spillovers emanating from the research that would have been carried out in the country had it not specialized. This view was first formalized by Paul Krugman.[31] Others have challenged this view, however, by observing that

---

[29] This criticism of the Kaldor–Hicks efficiency criterion has been advanced virtually since the criterion was developed in Nicholas Kaldor, "Welfare Propositions of Economics and Interpersonal Comparisons of Utility," *Economics Journal* 49 (1939): 549, and J. R. Hicks, "The Foundations of Welfare Economics," *Economics Journal* 49 (1939): 696. See, e.g., William Baumol, "Community Indifference," *Review of Economic Studies* 14 (1946): 44, 45. For trade to benefit the poor, however, a country needs to have reasonably good domestic institutions; see the discussion in the paragraphs that follow.

[30] See Philippe Aghion and Peter Howitt, *Endogenous Growth Theory* (Cambridge, MA: MIT Press, 1998), 392.

[31] Paul Krugman, "The Narrow-Moving Band, the Dutch Disease, and the Competitive Consequences of Mrs. Thatcher: Notes on Trade in the Presence of Dynamic Scale Economies," *Journal of Development Economics* 27 (1987): 41.

increased scale occasioned by *trade* can generate increased opportunities for research and development as well as for learning by doing, and these cumulative effects could be very large over time.[32]

Much of the work in this area relies heavily on specific assumptions regarding the patterns of specialization. For example, Ben-David and Loewy offer an open-economy endogenous growth model with knowledge accumulation that builds from the standard neoclassical growth model.[33] In their model, knowledge accumulation is determined by the extent of trade among countries. Even if a country liberalizes trade unilaterally, all countries subsequently improve their steady state (that is, their dynamic equilibrium path or the stable rate of economic growth). Moreover, the growth is most pronounced in the liberalizing country[34] (an insight that contradicts the folk belief, inexplicably adopted by much of the global justice literature,[35] that the country that liberalizes unilaterally is the "sucker" in the international trade game).

However, under different assumptions concerning the form and extent of knowledge accumulation, the predictions of the endogenous growth theory about the effect of trade liberalization can be reversed. For example, the long tradition of the infant-industry rationale for protectionism stems from the idea that in developing countries protected industries will improve in productivity over time, eventually becoming competitive on the world market. If the long-term improvement in growth yielded by developing a comparative advantage in the previously protected industries is large enough, it could justify the short-run loss in efficiency generated by forsaking free trade.[36]

Although at a broad level these arguments are theoretically plausible, implementing an infant-industry policy presents numerous obstacles. First, it requires planners to be able to predict which industries will in fact generate large long-term gains, without falling victim to the special interests engaged in rent seeking. Further, there is some question whether firms within the protected industries will have an incentive to improve their productivity. Lastly, protected industries may not be able to develop the scale necessary to

[32] Luis Rivera-Batiz and Paul Romer, "Economic Integration and Endogenous Growth," *Quarterly Journal of Economics* 106 (1991): 531–556.

[33] Dan Ben-David and Michael Loewy, "Knowledge Dissemination, Capital Accumulation, Trade, and Endogenous Growth," *Oxford Economic Papers* 52 (2000): 637.

[34] Ibid. at 646.

[35] See, e.g., Thomas Pogge's views in the paragraphs that follow.

[36] See, e.g., Murray Kemp, "The Mill-Bastable Infant-Industry Dogma," *Journal of Political Economics* 68 (1960): 65.

maximize productivity.[37] Beyond those purely economic concerns, there is significant tension in trading off current costs (that is, forgone current benefits of trade) with uncertain future benefits (that is, the potential for achieving a higher long-run growth rate by developing a different comparative advantage). Perhaps as a result of these problems, or perhaps as a result of uncertainty regarding the ways in which knowledge accumulation is affected by trade and protectionism, the empirical evidence on the growth effects of infant-industry protection is mixed.[38] Rather than reviewing the huge theoretical literature on infant-industry models of economic growth, we will focus on a specific innovative model in this tradition. Greenwald and Stiglitz offer a so-called infant-economy rationale for protection in which they develop a simple model of an economy with two sectors: industrial (or modern) and agricultural (or traditional).[39] Their model hinges on four assumptions: (1) the industrial sector generates positive externalities for the agricultural sector in the form of knowledge spillovers; (2) knowledge spillovers are limited geographically such that Country A's agricultural sector cannot learn from Country B's industrial innovations; (3) industrial sector innovations have a larger relative effect on industrial productivity; and (4) innovations and their spillover effect are a function of the scale of the industrial market.

Under these conditions, the free-trade equilibrium will involve developing countries specializing in the traditional sector. Because there is no innovation in the traditional sector, developing economies stagnate and fall increasingly behind the developed world in economic growth rates, given the innovation that occurs in the industrial sectors of the developed world. To avoid this undesirable equilibrium, Greenwald and Stiglitz suggest that developing countries can use protectionist measures, such as bans or significant tariffs on industrial inputs. Under such policies, the developing countries would no longer specialize in the traditional sector, generating knowledge spillovers that lead to a higher-growth equilibrium in the long run. The authors concede that these policies generate costs in the short term.

From this model, Greenwald and Stiglitz suggest that developing countries should adopt broad-based industrial tariffs rather than trying to identify the

---

[37] *See* Mitsuhiro Kaneda, "Policy Designs in a Dynamic Model of Infant Industry Protection," *Journal of Development Economics* 72 (2003): 91, 115 at note 4.

[38] See Dani Rodrik, "Trade and Industrial Policy Reform," in Hollis Chenery and T. N. Srinivasan (eds.), *Handbook of Development Economics*, Vol. 3 (New York: North-Holland, 1995), 2925–2982.

[39] Bruce Greenwald and Joseph E. Stiglitz, "Helping Infant Economies Grow: Foundations of Trade Policies for Developing Countries" (Columbia University Working Paper No. d, 2006; available at http://www2.gsb.columbia.edu/faculty/jstiglitz/download/Helping_Infant_Economies_Grow.pdf; last accessed on March 7, 2006).

infant industry that will eventually prove to be the "best" sector in which to develop a comparative advantage. They argue that this broad-based policy both avoids the uncertainty problems involved with picking the right industry and does not involve the creation of narrow special interests. In support of the welfare conclusions and policy prescriptions of the model, Greenwald and Stiglitz point to the success of such broad-based industrial tariffs in generating later growth for the European Economic Community, as well as many of the Asian economies. They even argue that this policy of high, uniform industrial import tariffs characterizes the early history of the United States.

As mentioned before, this model's implications change significantly if the underlying assumptions are changed. At the very least, the trade-off between current losses caused by restricted trade and higher future growth rates becomes increasingly unattractive for infant-economy protection as the assumptions are changed. If innovations are not country specific (that is, if developing countries can learn from innovations in developed countries) and trade facilitates communication between developing and developed countries, then the import tariffs could retard long-run growth. Further, if innovations can occur in the traditional sector, the case for industrial import tariffs is weakened.

Greenwald and Stiglitz argue that their assumptions are reflective of reality because industrial production is more likely to generate innovations given the larger scale and increased stability observed in the industrial sector. Further, they argue that innovations do tend to be area specific, limiting the ability of developing countries to learn from foreign innovations.[40]

However, others challenge these claims. Perhaps most important, Coe and Helpman present a model in which a country's productivity is influenced by the knowledge accumulated by its trading partners.[41] That is, in the language of the Greenwald and Stiglitz model, knowledge spillovers are *not* limited geographically. Country A can benefit (learn) from the innovations created in Country B as long as there are trade linkages between A and B. Coe and Helpman present results that indicate a country's productivity is positively associated with foreign research and development, and the effect is larger when a country is more open to foreign trade.[42] The Coe and Helpman

---

[40] Ibid. at 10–11.
[41] David T. Coe and Elhanan Helpman, "International R&D Spillovers," *European Economic Review* 39 (1995): 859.
[42] Ibid. at 875.

empirical results have been the subject of some debate,[43] but they at least cast some doubt over the infant-economy model.

As indicated by this limited review of dynamic comparative advantage or endogenous growth models of trade, their results are driven by fairly specific assumptions about the ways innovations occur in an economy. Assuming that long-run growth and welfare are desirable, the wisdom of trade restrictions will depend on the relative importance of domestic vis-à-vis international innovations. If countries can learn a substantial amount from outside innovations, trade restrictions will hamper domestic productivity. If however, domestic innovations are significantly more important and those innovations primarily occur in sectors outside of a country's initial comparative advantage, trade will reduce long-term growth.

However, under almost any plausible set of assumptions, short-term economic performance is harmed by trade restrictions. About this, essentially none of the theorists disagrees. The relevant policy decision then involves trading off short-term losses (caused by forgone trade) against predicted future improvements (from having a "better" comparative advantage as a result of nurtured innovations) based on assumptions that are subject to dispute.

The upshot of the foregoing analysis is that under some of the trade models, everyone who owns a factor of production (capital, land, or labor) benefits from open trade; and, under the more complex (although not necessarily more

[43] See, e.g., Chihwa Kao, Min-Hsien Chiang, and Bangtian Chen, "International R&D Spillovers: An Application of Estimation and Inference in Panel Cointegration," *Oxford Bulletin of Economics and Statistics* 61 (1999): 691 (suggesting that more general models do not support the inference that foreign R&D improves domestic productivity, but these models do support the Greenwald and Stiglitz assumption that domestic R&D does improve domestic productivity generally); Chris Edmond, "Some Panel Cointegration Models of International R&D Spillovers," *Journal of Macroeconomics* 23 (2001): 241 (presenting evidence suggesting that the Coe and Helpman results are not robust to different specifications); Wolfgang Keller, "Are International R&D Spillovers Trade-Related? Analyzing Spillovers among Randomly Matched Trade Partners," *European Economic Review* 42 (1998): 1469 (presenting Monte Carlo results that suggest that if international R&D improves domestic productivity, trade openness might not be a necessary condition to benefit from international spillovers). However, a number of subsequent studies have also found support for Coe and Helpman's model. See, e.g., Frank Lichtenberg and Bruno van Pottelsberghe de la Potterie, "International R&D Spillovers: A Comment," *European Economic Review* 42 (1998): 1483 (reanalyzing Coe and Helpman's econometric model correcting for various biases, and finding support for the idea that trade openness determines whether or not a country benefits from international innovations); Tamim Bayoumi, David T. Coe, and Elhanan Helpman, "R&D Spillovers and Global Growth," *Journal of International Economics* 47 (1999): 399 (providing evidence from simulation exercises supporting the Coe and Helpman model); Gwanghoon Lee, "International R&D Spillovers Revisited," *Open Economic Review* 16 (2005): 249 (supporting the Coe and Helpman model by using more sophisticated panel data techniques that allow for cointegration).

accurate) models, such as the Heckscher–Ohlin framework, the owners of the
more abundant factor, which for developing countries will be labor (owned
primarily by the poor), will benefit from liberalized trade. Even under the
models that are less favorable to trade liberalization (that is, the endogenous
comparative advantage models), it is generally recognized that trade liberalization will improve current economic conditions, whereas protectionists policies
have the potential to improve conditions at some undetermined point in the
future if some fairly restrictive assumptions hold and policy makers make the
right decisions about which industries to protect.

Generally speaking, most economists accept that trade is beneficial for
development, even if they do not view it as a panacea for countries with bad
institutions. If economists do deviate from support for free trade, their reasons
are more complex and narrow in scope than the protectionist arguments given
by politicians and scholars who are not economists.

Under the models discussed here, when trade opens between nations, in all
practical situations joint gains occur and no country loses. In most situations,
the gains of trade are split, so each of them gains. Therefore, not only does trade
enhance aggregate wealth (that is, the wealth of both nations added together)
but, in virtually every case, it also enhances the national wealth of each nation.
This improvement occurs because the resources in each country are used more
efficiently. Long-run effects may be different in the endogenous comparative
advantage models, but even in these models restraints on trade generate short-
term losses. Moreover, under those models long-term gains from the restraints
are highly uncertain and depend on a high degree of foresight and predictive
ability on the part of government actors. In particular, those models overlook
the potential susceptibility of such actors to rent-seeking activities on the part
of those industries seeking protection.[44]

The prediction that trade is a positive-sum game when nations are considered as units is of great importance, because it contradicts the claim that the
country that protects helps itself and hurts only or mainly its trade partner
who (perhaps foolishly) liberalizes trade. This claim is commonly advanced
by scholars not trained in economics, and it is based on a serious economic
mistake: that exports are good and imports are bad. The view is the centerpiece of mercantilism.[45] Mercantilism views trade as a zero-sum game: One
country's gains come at the expense of other countries. It rests on the false

---

[44] Note that when this point was formalized in Gene Grossman and Elhanan Helpman, "Protection for Sale," *American Economic Review* 84 (1994): 833–850, they characterized their
rent-seeking model as a new way to look at trade policy (ibid. at 848).

[45] Mercantilism was refuted more than 200 years ago. See generally Adam Smith, *The Wealth of
Nations* (1776) and David Ricardo, supra note 24.

assumption that a surplus in international trade must be a deficit for other countries.[46] Mercantilists claim that exports, believed to benefit domestic producers, should be encouraged, whereas imports, believed to hurt domestic producers, should be discouraged.[47] However, national well-being is based on present and future increased consumption. Exports are valuable only indirectly; they provide the income to buy products to consume.[48] This insight is central to an assessment of the effects of trade on the poor: Independent of whether the poor are able to export (that is, independently of whether or not foreign markets are open to the goods they produce), the poor *benefit from having a wider variety of available imported goods to consume,* either because the product was not available domestically or because trade lowers the price of the product, bringing it within the reach of the poor.

So far, the theoretical prediction is that freer trade causes global and national growth in *aggregate terms.* Nevertheless, nations must be disaggregated to find out who wins and who loses with open trade. Critics of free trade have long argued that the beneficial aggregate effect of trade is consistent with the bad effect of leaving the poor out, because it is possible that the gains of trade fall on the rich or the middle class of both trading partners.[49] In this view, when we take *persons or families* as units, free trade may well lead to losses for the poor.[50]

It is true that *if* open trade would hurt the poor and protectionist policies would be necessary to alleviate poverty, then free trade would be objectionable

[46] See Thomas A. Pugel and Peter H. Lindert, *International Economics,* 11th ed. (New York: McGraw-Hill, 2000), 33.

[47] Ibid.

[48] Thus, "imports are part of the expanding national consumption that a nation seeks, not an evil to be suppressed." Ibid. Equally problematic is the claim that imports reduce domestic employment. See Laura LaHayes, "Mercantilism," *Concise Encyclopedia of Economics* (available at http://www.econlib.org; accessed on February 8, 2007).

[49] This is what critics of globalization mean by the cliché that "trade helps big business." Even philosophers of the stature of John Rawls echo such sentiments. Here Rawls refers to the European Union:

> The large open market including all of Europe is the aim of the large banks and the capitalist business class whose main goal is simply larger profit. The idea of economic growth, onwards and upwards, with no specific end in sight, fits this class perfectly. If they speak about distribution, it is [al]most always in terms of trickle down. The long-term result of this – which we already have in the United States – is a civil society awash in a meaningless consumerism of some kind.
>
> Letter of John Rawls to Philippe van Parijs, June 23, 1998, published in
> "Autour de Rawls," *Revue de Philosophie Economique* vol. 7 (2003): 7–20.

[50] John Rawls and Phillipe van Parijs, "Three Letters on The Law of Peoples and the European Union," *Revue de Philosophie Economique* 8 (2003): 7, 9. Phillipe van Parijs calls this passage Rawls's "most explicitly 'anti-capitalist' text."

and protectionism would be desirable. However, the factual premise of the argument – that open trade hurts the poor – is supported neither by the theory nor by the evidence.[51] A scientific analysis of the effect of trade on poverty centers on a simple two-step argument: Trade enhances growth, and growth reduces poverty.[52] Even if openness to trade *at first blush* does not help the poor, why assume that the poor will end up worse than before? When a country grows, two things happen. First, more industries are created, more jobs are available, and so the opportunities for the poor expand. Second, when a country grows, so do government resources that can be used to alleviate poverty. Indeed, this is the assumption that lawyers make when they condition the obligation of governments to implement social and economic rights to the country's resources.[53] The assumption is that the more resources a country has, the more resources the government will have. In turn, the more resources the government will have, the more effectively it will address the country's poverty. So whether a country's economic policies are laissez-faire or redistributive policies, the poor will benefit from access to global markets as a producer and as a consumer.

D. *The Importance of Institutions*

There is a growing consensus that domestic institutions themselves have important effects on economic growth. Trade models generally do not consider the importance of institutions in channeling the gains from trade into actual welfare improvements for a country's residents. But if, for example, people in a country *do not* own a factor of production (such as slaves who do not own

---

[51] See, inter alia, L. Alan Winters, "Trade and Poverty: Is There a Connection?" (2000; available at http://www.wto.org/English/news_e/presoo_e/pov3_e.pdf); T. N. Srinivasan and Jessica S. Wallack, "Globalization, Growth, and the Poor," *Journal of Economic Literature* 152 (2004): 251; David Dollar and Aart Kraay, "Growth Is Good for the Poor" (World Bank Policy Research Working Paper No. 2587, 2001; arguing that as economies grow, the income going to the bottom quintile of the population rises proportionately). Because one source of growth is expanded trade, trade is likely to lead to income growth among the poor.

[52] The evidence for this proposition is overwhelming. For a nontechnical account, see Jagdish N. Bhagwati, *Globalization*, supra note 6, at 51–67. For a more rigorous analysis, see Neil McCulloch et al., *Trade Liberalization and Poverty: A Handbook* (Washington, D.C.: Centre for Economic Policy Research, 2001), and Jagdish Bhagwati and T. N. Srinivasan, "Trade and Poverty in the Poor Countries," *American Economic Review* 92 (2002): 180. As these authors show, the arguments that free trade helps the poor are static (freer trade should help in the reduction of poverty in the poor countries that use their comparative advantages to export labor-intensive goods), and dynamic (trade promotes growth and growth reduces poverty).

[53] See, e.g., International Covenant on Economic, Social, and Cultural Rights, opened for signature December 16, 1966, Art. 2, 993 U.N.T.S. 3 (entered into force January 3, 1976).

their own labor), then they will not benefit from trade. By the same token, if a country's fiscal or regulatory policies (such as confiscatory taxes or rigid labor laws) prevent the owners of factors of production from selling it in the global market, then those affected by these policies will not benefit from trade. This shows how crucial it is to control for government failure and institutional quality when evaluating the welfare effects of trade.[54]

Modern scholarship on the importance of economic institutions for long-run economic performance is largely associated with Douglass North, although the importance of institutions has been recognized least since Adam Smith. Although North's early work stressed that institutions would evolve efficiently, leading to economic growth,[55] his later work moves away from this efficiency explanation for institutional change and instead argues that institutions are adopted by self-interested rulers and that there is no reason to believe that such institutions would be efficient or lead to maximum economic growth.[56] Building on this theory, North argues that inefficient institutions that are adopted in the interest of the ruler or ruling elite may result in path dependence in economic and institutional development that generates effects that outlive the ruler's tenure.[57]

Later research complements North's emphasis on the importance of studying institutions. De Soto argues that economic development in poor countries is hindered by excessive regulation and bureaucracy that raises transactions costs so high that it prevents entrepreneurial activities, leading to stagnation.[58] He also argues that poor countries lack the foundations of market economies, including a clear system of property rights, such as the systems that rich

---

[54] For example, recent work suggests that when institutions are appropriately controlled for, trade openness is not directly important for economic development; however, trade openness does increase the likelihood that development-friendly institutions will be adopted. See Dani Rodrik et al., "Institutions Rule: The Primacy of Institutions over Geography and Integration in Economic Development," *Journal of Economic Growth* 9 (2004): 131. Thus, trade might have an important "externality" not accounted for in the trade models, namely increasing demand for "good" institutions; see ibid. In a different paper, the relative effects of trade and institutions are reversed, with both mattering quite a bit for long-term growth but trade mattering more in the short run. See David Dollar and Aart Kraay, "Institutions, Trade, and Growth," *Journal of Monetary Economics* 50 (2003): 133. Both sets of results suggest that the short- and long-term effects of trade on development are affected by, and likely affect, institutions.

[55] See, e.g., Douglass C. North and Robert Thomas, *The Rise of the Western World: A New Economic History* (Cambridge: Cambridge University Press, 1973).

[56] See, e.g., Douglass C. North, *Structure and Change in Economic History* (New York: Norton, 1981).

[57] Douglass C. North, *Institutions, Institutional Change and Economic Performance* (Cambridge: Cambridge University Press, 1990).

[58] Hernando De Soto, *The Other Path: The Invisible Revolution in the Third World* (New York: HarperCollins, 1989).

countries developed in the nineteenth century. The absence of such clear institutional underpinnings prevents individuals in poor countries from exploiting
their informal, or extralegal, property holdings, limiting economic growth in
general and the condition of the poor in particular.[59]

More recently, economists have begun efforts to examine the effects of institutions on growth empirically. Acemoglu, Johnson, and Robinson investigate
how preexisting conditions impact the establishment of institutions in European colonies and how institutions impact long-run growth in those former
colonies.[60] Their work takes exception with the argument of Jeffrey Sachs and
others who claim that immutable factors such as disease, environment, and
climate directly consign some areas to poor economic performance today.[61]
Instead Acemoglu et al. argue that economic institutions, such as property
rights, which may have originally been influenced by natural conditions, are
in fact the primary determinants of economic performance today.

Studies of the effect of institutions on growth, however, have the potential to
suffer from reverse causality problems. Although many papers[62] show a strong
correlation between economic freedom and growth, it is difficult to determine causality. Acemoglu et al. address this in their papers by developing new
instruments for economic institutions – variables that are associated with institutions, but that cannot themselves be thought to directly impact growth,
thus avoiding the problems of reverse causality. Other scholars find that
institutions are a primary determinant of economic growth.[63] Even Dani
Rodrik (a critic of free trade) concludes "the quality of institutions trumps
everything else" when it comes to growth.[64]

---

[59] Hernando De Soto, *The Mystery of Capital: Why Capitalism Triumphs in the West and Fails
Everywhere Else* (New York: Basic Books, 2000).

[60] Daron Acemoglu, Simon Johnson, and James A. Robinson, "The Colonial Origins of Comparative Development: An Empirical Investigation," *American Economic Review* 91(5) (2001):
1369–1401, and Daron Acemoglu, Simon Johnson, and James A. Robinson, "Reversal of Fortune: Geography and Institutions in the Making of the Modern World Income Distribution,"
Quarterly Journal of Economics 17 (2002): 1231–1294.

[61] See, e.g., Jeffrey D. Sachs, "Institutions Don't Rule: Direct Effects of Geography on Per Capita
Income" (NBER Working Paper No. 9490, 2003).

[62] For a literature review, see Niclas Berggren, "The Benefits of Economic Freedom," *Independent Review* 8(2) (2003): 193–211.

[63] Easterly and Levine find evidence suggesting that institutions are the fundamental cause
of long-run economic performance. William Easterly and Ross Levine, "Tropics, Germs, and
Crops: How Endowments Influence Economic Development," *Journal of Monetary Economics*
50 (2003): 3–39.

[64] Dani Rodrik, Arvind Subramanian, and Francesco Trebbi, "Institutions Rule: The Primacy of
Institutions Over Geography and Integration in Economic Development," *Journal of Economic
Growth* 9 (2004): 131–165 at 135.

Nonetheless, although institutions may be of primary importance for economic growth, exactly which institutions are important and why is still open to debate. Acemoglu and Johnson identify two types of institutions that reasonably could be thought to be important for economic growth: property rights institutions and contracting institutions.[65] They identify property rights institutions as those that determine how secure property is from expropriation by the state or governmental entities. Contracting institutions are identified as those that govern the security of contracts signed by individual economic agents and how well those contracts are enforced. To address problems with endogeneity, they use colonial mortality as the instrument for property rights and indicators for the origins of the country's legal system as the instrument for the contracting regime.[66]

This analysis reveals a strong relationship between property rights institutions and economic performance. However, once these are controlled for, contracting institutions have no statistically significant impact on growth. The authors hypothesize that, in an environment of secure property rights, economic agents will be able to develop sufficient mechanisms, such as reputation monitoring, to overcome shortcomings from a country's contracting rules.

These results suggest that, in addition to free trade, other political and social institutions will also be important determinants of overall growth in general. These institutions also are likely to have important implications for the plight of the poor specifically, as suggested by De Soto.

E. Conclusions Regarding the Economic Literature

Although free trade is a positive-sum game when nations are concerned, it will of course produce individual winners and losers, and many of those losers will be poor.[67] However, as we saw, our claim here is not that the position of

---

[65] Daron Acemoglu and Simon Johnson, "Unbundling Institutions," *Journal of Political Economics* 113(5) (2005): 949–995.

[66] The intuition and data for these instruments come from Rafael La Porta, Florencio Lopez-de-Silanes, Andrei Shleifer, and Robert W. Vishny, "Legal Determinants of External Finance," *Journal of Finance* 52(July) (1997): 1131–1150; Rafael LaPorta, Florencio Lopez-de-Silanes, Andrei Shleifer, and Robert W. Vishny, "Law and Finance," *Journal of Political Economics* 106(4) (1998): 1113–1155; and Simeon Djankov, Rafael LaPorta, Florencio Lopez-de-Silanes, and Andre Shleifer, "The Regulation of Entry," *Quarterly Journal of Economics* 117 (2002): 1–37.

[67] A more complete treatment of the theoretical and particularly the empirical literature on the relationship among trade, growth, and poverty is available in the working-paper version of the article (available at http://ssrn.com/abstract=1022996).

each poor person will improve as a result of trade liberalization; in fact, no policy can do that. The claim is that, in virtually every instance, the position of the poor as a class will improve. More specifically, trade liberalization can affect the welfare of the poor by changing prices of tradable goods and improving access to new products; changing the relative wages of skilled and unskilled labor and the cost of capital; affecting government revenue; changing incentives for investment and innovation; and affecting the vulnerability of an economy to negative external shocks.[68] On the issue of cost of goods, trade liberalization will help the poor in the same way it helps all consumers: by lowering prices of imports and keeping the prices of substitutes for imported goods low, thus increasing people's real incomes. On the question of wages, the evidence seems to show a number of things. Labor markets require flexibility in order to adjust to comparative advantages. If firms are too constrained by labor laws from reducing their work forces, then the poor may suffer as a result. This is ironic, given that supporters of strict labor regulations claim to act on behalf of the poor.[69] In addition, the gap between the wages of skilled and unskilled workers may increase,[70] but this is hardly an objection to the claim that the poor as a class benefit from trade liberalization. The objection that liberalizing trade will reduce government revenues, and thus its ability to fight poverty, is also misplaced because it ignores the dynamic effects of trade liberalization. If trade liberalization produces growth then taxable incomes will grow as well, and government revenues will grow with them.[71]

In sum, trade liberalization (1) increases aggregate wealth, that is, wealth measured aggregately in both trade partners; (2) increases wealth in each of the trade partners; and (3) *at the very least*, within each trade partner, such growth is most often shared by the poor in various ways. Nevertheless, the claim is *not* that trade liberalization reduces inequality among trade partners or among different groups or individuals within the trade partners.

[68] See Geoffrey J. Bannister and Kamau Thugge, "International Trade and Poverty Alleviation," *Finance and Development* (December 2001): 48.

[69] Thus, e.g., critics of "sweatshops" claim that, partially as a result of lax work conditions, "clothing companies benefit from free trade through BIG profits, and garment workers lose out." See http://www.sweatshopwatch.org/index.php?s=36 (last accessed February 2, 2007).

[70] See Elias Dinopoulos and Paul Segerstrom, "A Schumpeterian Model of Protection and Relative Wages," *American Economic Review* 89 (1999): 450–472.

[71] See Bannister and Thugge, supra note 68, at 49. There are a number of combinations to maintain government revenues at an acceptable level, for example, replacing nontariff barriers with tariffs. Ibid.

IV. THE PHILOSOPHERS

A. *The Failure to Recognize the Importance of Trade*

An important part of the international ethics literature is concerned with global justice.[72] What moral duties do wealthy nations and their citizens owe to poor nations and their citizens? What global economic arrangements are required by justice, especially in the light of the pressing problem of world poverty? Many (but by no means all) who currently write on cosmopolitan justice have argued that current restrictions of nations and borders are arbitrary, at least from the perspective of helping the world's poor.[73] For some, preference for compatriots is objectionable; for others, such preference is appropriate but it does not rule out duties to foreigners, and in particular help to the world's poor. That help may assume various forms: private charity, including aid through nongovernmental organizations, or, more often, governmental aid. Most writers favor governmental aid with the familiar argument that governmental measures solve a collective action problem. A few influential philosophers reject cosmopolitanism and argue that justice makes sense only within the state, but even they agree that there is a duty to do something about world poverty based on elementary notions of humanity.[74] Most global justice philosophers, however, recommend either extensive foreign aid or massive redistribution by a global welfare agency financed through a universal tax. Thomas Pogge's proposal for a "Global Resources Dividend" is typical:

> [S]tates and governments shall not have full libertarian property rights with respect to the natural resources in their territory, but can be required to share

---

[72] Book-length treatments include the following: Andrew Altman and Christopher Heath Wellman, *A Liberal Theory of International Justice* (Oxford: Oxford University Press, 2010); Darrel Moellendorf, *Cosmopolitan Justice* (Boulder, CO: Westview Press, 2002); Kok-Chor Tan, *Justice without Borders* (Cambridge: Cambridge University Press, 2004); Kok-Chor Tan, *Toleration, Diversity, and Global Justice* (University Park: Pennsylvania State University, 2000); Charles K. Jones, *Global Justice* (Oxford: Oxford University Press, 1999); Thomas Pogge, *World Poverty and Human Rights* (Cambridge: Polity Press, 2002); Simon Caney, *Justice beyond Borders* (Oxford: Oxford University Press, 2005), chapter 5; Pablo De Grieff and Ciaran Cronin (eds.), *Global Justice and Transnational Politics* (Cambridge, MA: MIT Press, 2001); and Allen Buchanan, *Justice, Legitimacy, and Self-Determination: Moral Foundations of International Law* (Oxford: Oxford University Press, 2004), chapter 4.

[73] See, e.g., Pogge, supra note 72 at 118–145; and Moellendorf, supra note 72 at 36–44.

[74] In this sense, see Thomas Nagel, "The Problems of Global Justice," *Philosophy and Public Affairs* 33 (2005): 113, 119–120. This article elicited various replies. See Joshua Cohen and Charles Sabel, "Extra Republicam Nulla Justitia?," *Philosophy and Public Affairs* 34 (2006): 147; and A. J. Julius, "Nagel's Atlas," *Philosophy and Public Affairs* 34 (2006): 176.

a small part of the value of any resources they decide to use or sell. Proceeds from the GRD are to be used toward ensuring that all human beings can meet their own basic needs with dignity.[75]

In this chapter we do not take sides on whether a defensible system of international ethics countenances a *thick* notion of distributive justice, or if, on the contrary, we only have *thin* obligations of aid toward foreigners. We do not decide, that is, whether the duty to address world poverty stems from basic notions of humanity (as Thomas Nagel claims), or whether that duty is required instead by justice (as Nagel's critics claim[76]). We only assume that, under any appropriate system of international ethics, alleviating poverty should be a major goal of international economic institutions. This approach is consistent with either of the views just described.

With that goal in mind, in the light of our discussion so far, it seems reasonably clear that anyone concerned with global poverty must address the issue of free trade. Philosophers, however, either overlook trade almost entirely, or reject free trade, or recommend "equitable" trade. None of the major works on global justice draws on the relevant economic literature, the general consensus of which recommends, as we saw, free trade as a way to enhance global and national wealth and thus benefit the poor. The omission is truly perplexing,[77] especially because the question of whether justice requires free markets or government regulation is (at least sometimes) part of the debate on *domestic* issues. Nonetheless, despite the strong consensus of economists on this point, philosophers and politicians continue to claim or imply that attempts to liberalize trade are objectionable because they often result in "inequitable" terms of trade. A brief review of the philosophical literature will help us see the pervasiveness of this problem.

Thomas Pogge, one of the leading philosophers of global justice, addresses the question of world poverty. He mounts a scathing criticism of the policies of developed nations as well as of current economic institutions such as the

---

[75] Pogge, supra note 72, at 196–197. See also Tan, supra note 72, at 158–159.

[76] See Cohen and Sabel, supra note 74. See also Julius, supra note 74, at 176.

[77] As an example, in a book entirely devoted to international distributive justice (Charles Jones, *Global Justice*, supra note 72), one searches in vain for any discussion of international trade as a possible way to help the world's poor. The closest reference that we found was hostile to trade: an indictment (justified, for all we know) of transnational corporations who sell baby-milk powder. See ibid., at 71–72. Likewise, in Altman and Wellman, supra note 72, the word "trade" does not appear on the index. In his book on international ethics, *The Law of Peoples* (Cambridge, MA: Harvard University Press, 1999), John Rawls does not discuss trade. There is evidence, however, that his views were quite hostile to free trade and globalization. See van Parijs and Rawls, "Three Letters on The Law of Peoples and the European Union, supra note 50.

WTO. His main argument is that, given the gravity and urgency of world poverty, rich nations are guilty of criminal neglect by not doing the things they could do to alleviate it.[78] Pogge scores some important points in his multifaceted attack against current global institutions, as in his criticism of the international borrowing privilege (i.e., the prerogative of governments, especially in developing countries, to access large sums of money), which fosters corruption and other evils that end up aggravating poverty.[79]

However, given Pogge's concern for the plight of the world's poor, one would have expected a thorough treatment of the question of trade, including a state-of-the-art discussion of the relevant economic research. Not so. To be sure, Pogge says he would favor free trade under different conditions. His opposition to the present state of affairs is "no reason to oppose any and all possible designs of an integrated global market economy under unified rules of universal scope."[80] However, on the same page he describes the relative trade liberalization that has occurred in the past couple of decades as the "brutal path of economic globalization which our governments have chosen to impose." After indicting globalization in this way (thus implying that it, and not the bad policies of the often inefficient, dictatorial, and corrupt régimes in developing countries, are to blame for poverty), he nowhere mentions the law of comparative advantage.

Further, he does not mention the harm that protectionist measures in developing nations inflict on the poor. His only concession to mainstream economics is his condemnation of the protectionist policies of rich countries. In fact, his references to trade are scarce and, for the most part, erroneous. He writes, for example, that the WTO system is unjust because "it opens *our* markets *too little* and thereby gains for us the benefits of trade while withholding them from the global poor."[81] Pogge does not expressly say that protectionist barriers are good for the country that erects them. However, this silence is precisely the problem we identify in this chapter. The same theory (standard economic trade theory) that condemns protectionist barriers erected by rich countries condemns protectionist barriers erected by developing countries, and any responsible study of trade and poverty should mention this fact. This general position is reminiscent of the discredited theories behind mercantilism, the view that the country that erects protectionist barriers gains and that the country that liberalizes loses (unless the trading partner also liberalizes).[82]

---

[78] See Pogge, supra note 72, at 1–26. [79] Ibid., at 113–115.

[80] Ibid., at 19–20. [81] Ibid. (emphasis in the original.)

[82] In written communication distributed at the University of Virginia Conference on Global Justice, held in November 2006 (on file with the author), Thomas Pogge says, in response to the criticism in the text, that he did not suggest "that protectionist barriers are good for the

Trade protection by rich countries is wrong, not only because it hurts producers in poor countries (as Pogge correctly observes) but also because it hurts *its
own* people. When the United States enacts the Farm Bill, it does not "gain"
for the United States the "benefits of trade," as Pogge says. It hurts American
consumers, perhaps especially the poor, by (among other things) raising the
prices of agricultural products.

Some authors suggest that, directly or indirectly, rich nations bear the main
responsibility for world poverty and thus for alleviating it.[83] Here we do not
address the plausibility of this claim in its general form. However, such emphasis on the responsibility of rich nations obscures the crucial fact that bad governments and bad institutions are a major cause of poverty in developing nations.
One manifestation (albeit not the most evident or egregious) of bad government is protectionism. Protectionism *by poor countries* is self-destructive. One
can ask why, then, governments erect trade barriers. We speculate that this is
not a cognitive mistake – an ignorance of standard economics.[84] Rulers know
well that the trade-restrictive measures they enact hurt their people, but they
persist because those measures *benefit them, the agents of the governments.*

Trade barriers are generally responses to lobbying by powerful local monopolies that, in turn, help those governments remain in power. The irony here
is that because protectionist measures are justified by nationalist rhetoric, and
because the law of comparative advantage is opaque and counterintuitive, the
poor cannot *see* that their own predicament is caused to some extent by those
measures. Politicians trade on the public's rational ignorance.[85] What these
laws do is to consolidate local monopolies at the expense of *local consumers*,
that is, at the expense of everyone else in the country (because everyone is,
of course, a consumer).[86] In addition, protectionist laws create incentives for
misdirecting economic resources toward inefficient activities, thus causing

country erecting them," and added that "there is no general answer to this question." Our main
disagreement, then, is on this last point: We believe there *is* a general answer to that question.

[83] See, e.g., Tan, supra note 72, at 29–32 (arguing that the current economic order, sustained by
rich nations, perpetuates world poverty); see also Pogge, supra note 72, esp. chapter 4 (arguing
that ignoring world poverty amounts to criminal neglect).

[84] In a recent book, Bryan Caplan claims that governments and citizens make cognitive mistakes
when they support bad policies. See Bryan Caplan, *The Myth of the Rational Voter* (Princeton,
NJ: Princeton University Press, 2008). We agree that citizens err, but we do not agree that
governments err when they adopt these bad policies: They know very well what they are doing.
Our reasons for this are found in Guido Pincione and Fernando Tesón, *Rational Choice and
Democratic Deliberation* (Cambridge: Cambridge University Press, 2006).

[85] The public's ignorance is rational because the informational costs are high. For a full treatment
of this phenomenon and how it distorts democratic deliberation, see ibid.

[86] See Robert Cooter, "2005 Madd Lecture: Law, Innovation, and the Poverty of Nations," *Florida
State University Law Review* 33 (2005): 373, 392–393.

a reduction in aggregate welfare and loss of jobs in the (now discouraged) efficient industries – those where the country enjoys a comparative advantage. Protectionist policies are worse than simple transfers of resources from consumers, foreign producers, and unprotected industries to producers and workers in the protected industries. Those policies, in addition, produce deadweight losses, economic losses that no one else recoups. They are games in which some gain, but in which losers lose more than the winners gain.

Protectionist policies are often the result of political rent seeking and other forms of predatory behavior.[87] Well-organized protected industries hire powerful lobbyists who essentially "buy" the protectionist legislation from politicians interested in incumbency. Given this, and contrary to Pogge's claims, world poverty is not caused only (and often, not mainly) by globalization or by the protectionist policies of rich nations.[88] Instead, poverty is largely the result of bad policies and practices pursued by the governments of developing nations who allow or practice predatory behavior. More generally, bad policies include protectionist measures, which, as we saw, hurt all consumers in that society; political corruption and other forms of unproductive public spending; lack of respect for civil and political rights; lack of appropriate transfer policies; failure of the rule of law; lack of protection of private property and freedom of contract; inept and predatory fiscal policies; and a deficient educational system. Although Pogge acknowledges some of these forms of government failure, by failing to reject mercantilism he implicitly endorses some of the policies that aggravate poverty.[89]

Allen Buchanan adopts a similar but more moderate stance in his otherwise good work on the moral foundations of international law. In one chapter, Buchanan addresses the role of distributive justice. Against Rawls and others, he argues that distributive justice should apply to the international "basic structure," and consequently that rich nations have a duty to help poor nations. Although he concedes that at present the international system is relatively incapable of enforcing these principles of distributive justice, he also believes

[87] The political dynamics of protectionism is well summarized in McGinnis and Movsesian, supra note 5, at 521–531. See also Gene Grossman and Elhanan Helpman, "Protection for Sale," supra note 44, and Thomas A. Pugel and Peter H. Lindert, *International Economics*, supra note 46, 61–78.

[88] Whether protectionist measures hurt foreign producers depends on the size of the market. If producers in developing countries can sell their goods elsewhere, then protectionism barriers in Europe and the United States are less certain to be harmful. Nonetheless, we happily agree that protectionist barriers in developed nations are objectionable.

[89] Pogge's criticism of the WTO régime (pp. 15–19) amounts to the simple point that unilateral protectionism of agriculture by rich nations (allowed by the WTO) has caused more poverty than the alternative regime of free trade for all, a point which is undoubtedly correct.

international law could further distributive justice. These measures include "promoting more equitable trade relations, labor standards, environmental regulation, aid for development, and endeavors to preserve global commons."[90] A call for equitable trade means presumably a call to reduce protectionist measures by rich countries so that poor countries can compete in those markets. However, supporting "equitable" trade is not the same as supporting free trade. As we saw, if rich Country A and poor Country B are both *equally and strongly protectionist*, then that would be equitable but nevertheless catastrophic for B (and, as we saw, bad for A too). Buchanan, too, never mentions or implies the well-tested truth that *the government that protects hurts its own people*.[91] That omission leads him to propose specific measures *restrictive* of trade: global wage standards, environmental regulations, and obligation of aid. We are not suggesting here that these measures are always, or often, misguided. What we observe, however, is that economic development depends on governments securing things that Buchanan does *not* mention: reducing barriers to trade and protecting private property rights and freedom of contract so as to attract investment – in short, economic liberties. Alleviation of poverty will not be achieved primarily by aid. Rather, poverty will be considerably alleviated by allowing poor people to exchange in the global market the things they produce for the things they need.

Buchanan's failure to support free trade may stem from his rejection of classic liberal or libertarian views about distributive justice (which he calls "anti-distributive").[92] Because defense of free trade is associated with classic liberalism or libertarianism, those who reject libertarianism may be hostile to free trade as a result of this association. However, opposing free trade on these grounds is a non sequitur. Buchanan could safely reject libertarianism as a theory of *domestic* justice and support free trade as a justified *international* arrangement calculated to help the world's poor. As we saw, whereas in our defense of free international trade we insist that nations should have healthy domestic institutions that sufficiently protect property and contract, we remain agnostic about which *other* domestic redistributive policies governments should enact to combat poverty. We simply claim that, whatever those measures may be, they do not include protectionist measures. So a state may implement worker-training programs, generous welfare programs, or universal

---

[90] Buchanan, supra note 72, at 193.

[91] See Jagdish Bhagwati, "Protectionism," supra note 17.

[92] Ibid. at 222–223. The use of the term "antidistributive" is already biased. Free markets also distribute resources and, moreover, they do so based on the choices of the agents, not of the government. The outcome may not please philosophers, but that does not mean that under free trade there is no redistribution of resources.

health care as ways to help the poor, while allowing free trade of goods and services with the rest of the world. This chapter does not take a position on that, except by observing that government failure aggravates the plight of the poor.[93] Government failure not only includes things that Buchanan recognizes, such as the failure to respect civil and political rights, but it comprises, in addition, excessive tax levels, lack of the rule of law, lack of independence of the judiciary, and the failure to protect private property, contract, and investment.

One way to encapsulate the mistake that Buchanan, Pogge, and many others (including the general public) make about trade is this. They see protectionism as an unsuccessful coordination game, implicitly saying, "[o]ur country must protect because we know *they* will protect. If only they made a credible commitment to repeal their protectionist laws, we would do the same." However, protectionism might be more accurately seen as a successful rent-seeking game: Industries affected by foreign competition seek and obtain protection from their governments in exchange for political support and other benefits. Two further facts explain the political success of protection notwithstanding the well-known fact that open trade is beneficial to the great majority of the population. First, the groups that benefit from free trade, such as consumers, are *diffuse* and have high organizational costs.[94] Second, although trade theory predicts that in the long run many of the workers and firms now hurt by foreign competition will be better off because free trade creates higher-paying jobs and higher returns to capital, workers and owners often cannot easily see these prospects.[95]

Given comparative advantage, if a country's trade partner protects, then that country is better off *not* protecting. Therefore, protectionist laws cannot be the result of a failed coordination game. The government erects trade barriers not because it believes that the trade partner will do the same, but, more likely, because local inefficient producers got the government to secure a domestic monopoly in their favor.[96] The government is not "protecting" its citizens; it is protecting itself and its friends.

---

[93] Buchanan not only fails to recognize government failure as a cause for poverty: Following Christiano, he *praises* the state as an agent of justice.

[94] See Mancur Olson, *The Logic of Collection Action* (Cambridge, MA: Harvard University Press, 1965).

[95] See McGinnis and Movsesian, "The World Trade Constitution," supra note 5, at 525.

[96] Adam Smith put it this way more than 200 years ago: "By restraining, either by high duties or by absolute prohibitions, the importation of such goods from foreign countries as can be produced at home, the monopoly of the home market is more or less secured to the domestic industry employed in producing them." See Smith, supra note 45, at Book IV, chapter 2.

Mercantilists not only misunderstand economics; they overlook the problem of agency costs inherent in modern government. If we assume that part of the government's job is to benefit the people (improve the welfare of its citizens in an appropriately distributive way), then, in the light of the foregoing discussion, government should reduce trade barriers, even unilaterally.[97] But this is not what happens. Instead, a minority of citizens who want to be sheltered from competition succeed, through lobbying, bribes, and similar modes of influence, in securing protectionist laws in their favor. The government caves in because doing so is in *its* interest. The principal (the people) pays for the self-interested behavior of the agent (the government).

In a lengthy discussion of distributive justice, the philosopher Simon Caney unfortunately neglects relevant economic analysis. After surveying the philosophical literature, he proposes the principle that "everyone, without any discrimination, has the right to equal pay for equal work."[98] He then adds that this principle "no doubt condemns much of international trade," because under conditions of trade, wages are determined, he thinks, by the morally irrelevant fact of nationality. However, lower pay is not determined by nationality; it is determined by supply and demand for labor. Caney's principle relies on obsolete theories of just prices, wrongly assuming that the price of labor is not the result of the intersection between the labor supply and demand curves, but that each kind of work should receive an ideally just remuneration. More importantly, if Caney's principle were adopted then many developing nations would collapse, because much of their comparative advantage depends on offering competitive labor in the global market. Because of his neglect of standard economics, Caney, like Buchanan and Pogge, ends up endorsing universal aid and not trade liberalization.[99]

Other philosophers are openly hostile to free trade. In a book almost entirely devoted to international economic justice, Kok-Chor Tan declares that one main reason why globalization has failed the poor is "neoliberal ideology."[100] Tan endorses the main tenets of mercantilism: Free trade is bad because the playing field is "uneven" and thus "competition is never truly free, nor, importantly, fair."[101] Trade liberalization has failed to help the worst-off population, Tan thinks, and this is evidence that capitalism is the wrong way

---

[97] See generally Jagdish Bhagwati (ed.), *Going Alone: The Case for Relaxed Reciprocity in Trade Liberalization* (Cambridge, MA: MIT Press, 2002).

[98] Caney, *Justice beyond Borders*, supra note 72, 123. He adopts the language from Article 23 (2) of the Universal Declaration of Human Rights.

[99] Ibid. at 139.

[100] See Tan, *Justice without Borders*, supra note 72, at 32–33.

[101] Ibid. at 31.

to go.[102] For this proposition he cites not a single mainstream international economist. (He does cite Amartya Sen for a variety of views about the relationship between poverty and inequality, but he omits saying that Sen *supports* free trade.[103]) Tan's rejection of free trade not only disregards mainstream economics, but it also fails to control for important variables such as bad institutions and other forms of government failure, including protectionism in rich and poor countries alike.

Could philosophers concede that free trade may improve aggregate wealth, yet insist that protectionism is somehow required for *moral* reasons? This is highly unlikely. Protectionism is unlikely to serve the public good or any other plausible moral goal. Because individuals cannot make all the things they use, their standard of living will depend on their chances of exchanging the product of their labor with others, especially if they are poor.[104] Trade barriers are attempts by politicians to undercut this freedom of the poor, the freedom to exchange the goods they produce for cheaper and better imported goods. They need this freedom to escape poverty. Such coercion can hardly be justified by anything even remotely approaching fairness or justice.

What other moral argument can possibly justify protectionism? Philosophers do not explain just what value, or what right, a protectionist measure in a developing country is supposed to realize. One reason frequently heard in public debate is that trade barriers can be justified as attempts to protect workers in developing nations from layoffs caused by foreign competition.[105]

---

[102] See, e.g., p. 31 ("neoliberal economic principles cannot meet the basic human and developmental needs of the word's poorest sector"). In passing, we object to the use of the term "neoliberalism," a loaded word used by demagogues and others to deride capitalism and free markets and devoid of any serious scientific meaning.

[103] See Amartya Sen, "How to Judge Globalism," supra note 19.

[104] See James Bovard, "The Morality of Protectionism," *New York University Journal of International Law and Politics* 25 (1992–1993): 236.

[105] See, e.g., Moellendorf, supra note 72, at 61. He does suggest, however, that global mobility is a better remedy than tariffs. Ibid. Other philosophers do not address this point. That silence, we suggest, is precisely the problem: The consensus is that trade *increases* the employment rate in the long run. See Steven Matusz, "International Trade, the Division of Labor, and Unemployment," *International Economic Review* 37 (1996): 71. In contrast, the argument from job protection is popular in the political arena. A campaign advertisement for Senator Sherrod Brown (D-Ohio) read as follows:

> They said that NAFTA would be good for America, but nearly 50,000 Ohio jobs have gone to Mexico. CAFTA, the trade agreement with Central America, will cost us even more. Our trade policy with China has cost our country over a million jobs, huge trade deficits, and it's risking the transfer of sensitive military technology. I voted against all of these deals; my opponent voted for them. I'm Sherrod Brown; I approve this message; it's time to put Americans first.

Indeed, the vivid harm suffered by these workers is a crucial factor in the public defense of protectionism.[106] But such argument lacks philosophical and economic sophistication. To begin with, one should ask whether one has a moral right to keep a job that one currently holds. Having a job is not like having a piece of property. My employment stems from a contractual relation. My employers produce things that consumers demand and they hire me to help them produce those things. If consumers no longer demand the product (because they prefer the cheaper foreign product), it is hard to see what principle of justice authorizes my employers to enlist the government in force-feeding their products to consumers. Nor do I retain a right to my job, given that my employers do not need me anymore. It is hard to see what moral principle can justify the state's using coercion to help people produce things that consumers no longer want.

The protectionist could reply that workers have acquired certain expectations that the government must try to preserve. It is not the workers' fault, the protectionist may argue, that their industry is now inefficient. They got these jobs, started a family, bought a home, and, in short, made life plans that are now frustrated by events they cannot control. They are proper beneficiaries of societal help. In this view, trade barriers are justified, not so much to enrich the local employer (although it does that), but to preserve jobs. Furthermore, it is appropriate for consumers to pay for this: Society (the consuming public) subsidizes fellow citizens (the workers of the affected industries) who are suffering hardship. It is no different from other forms of wealth redistribution.

There are many replies to this argument, but we will mention three. First, this argument can only get off the ground if it is part of a noncosmopolitan theory of justice. If these trade barriers protect the local workers at the expense of the world's poor then they are unjustified under any cosmopolitan view, unless the protected workers happen to be part of the world's poor. Second, and what is more important, when a government protects an industry, it *hampers the creation of jobs in other industries*. This occurs because the economy is not able to adjust to the efficiencies of production. Resources are artificially directed to the less efficient endeavors. If this is so, what should we say about the person who is now unemployed *because those new industries* have not been created as a result of the strangling effect of protectionist laws? Seen in this light, beneficiaries of protection in developing countries are not particularly

---

Available at http://www.citizen.org/trade/articles.cfm?ID=15892 (accessed February 19, 2007).

[106] For an account of vividness, see the classic treatment in Richard Nisbett and Lee Ross, *Human Inference: Strategies and Shortcomings of Social Judgement* (Englewood Cliffs, NJ: Prentice-Hall, 1980), 45.

deserving, because protection is harming *other* persons in that society. Because those persons are the unemployed, they are worse off than the protected workers. Just as the firms obtaining protection get rich at the expense of foreign firms, so the workers in protected industries keep their jobs at the expense of the poor *in their own developing countries* – that is, the poorest persons in the world. Protectionist laws harm the poor directly by reducing their choice set as consumers. In addition, they harm the poor *indirectly* because they abort the creation of new industries and jobs. This harm is opaque, hard to see, a circumstance that facilitates the popularity of protectionist views among the general public. Finally, even if this argument is plausible and the state can legitimately aid workers hurt by trade, erecting trade barriers is a bad remedy. Domestic transfer policies such as industrial retraining are more efficient and fair ways to help those workers.

B. The Problem of Stolen Goods

International trade takes place mostly between private agents. A private producer in state A attempts to sell his product to private consumers in state B but the government of state B interferes by placing trade barriers, thus raising the cost for the consumers. Governments, we have argued, should not interfere with these voluntary transactions. But sometimes this voluntariness has been vitiated. Trade presupposes legitimate ownership over the traded goods, but sometimes the traded goods are stolen. How should the international trade system address the problem of stolen goods? The view that condemns trading in stolen goods has two versions: the Imperialist Thesis and the Dictator-Thief thesis. According to the Imperialist Thesis, rich people in developed nations presently hold resources that they obtained in the past from people in developing countries through theft, force, and deception. Trading with the poor the very resources that the owner stole from them is deeply wrong. According to the Dictator-Thief thesis, despots stole resources from their subjects and sold them to foreigners (usually in rich nations) mostly to advance the despots' own interests and power. Both theses recommend corrective measures even before opening trade. We must return the stolen goods to their rightful owners; only then we could start talking about free trade. I discuss each thesis separately.

We have two replies to the Imperialist Thesis. The first is simply that its factual premises are, for the most part, wrong. The reasons why some nations are rich and others are poor have little to do with theft. Rather, they have to do with different equilibria between productive and predatory forces in society, as reflected in the quality if institutions and in particular on the success or failure of market-friendly practices. But there are surely some instances (some colonial cases comes to mind) where perhaps some of the resources currently held by persons in rich countries are ill-gotten. However, even if ideally compensation would be sometimes justified, the practical difficulties of determining what part of the current wealth held by individuals should be returned to their rightful owners would be daunting. Surely not all wealth, not even its greatest part, is stolen.

But the Imperialist Thesis is misconceived in another sense. It recommends *not* liberalizing trade on the grounds that rich countries have no title over the goods they trade. Yet international institutions should help *reduce poverty, here and now.* If corrective measures are infeasible either because the theft took place too far back in time, or because we cannot possibly know the percentage of wealth that was stolen, or because the amount of coercion needed to restore the *status quo ante* is morally prohibitive, or simply because international politics pose insurmountable practical obstacles, or for some other reason, then that should not be a reason to refuse to liberalize trade, here and now, as a way to alleviate the world's poverty.

The Dictator-Thief thesis is harder to answer.[107] A defense of free trade rests on the moral worth and beneficial effects of voluntary transactions. Yet dictators in some developing countries often appropriate the resources from the people and then sell them to foreigners, most of the time for their own enrichment. In these cases the international transaction was *coerced* at some point, namely when the tyrant appropriated the resources at gunpoint. The case evinces an egregious failure of *domestic* institutions, aggravated by a defective rule of international law – the so-called principle of effectiveness.[108] Under international law, whoever politically controls the country has a right to sell its resources. This rule is obviously unjust, not only from the standpoint

---

[107] The argument is made by Mathias Risse, "Justice in Trade I: Obligations from Trading and the Pauper-Labor Argument," *Politics, Philosophy, and Economics* 6 (2007): 356, and more fully by Leif Wenar, "Property Rights and the Resource Curse," *Philosophy & Public Affairs* 36 (2008): 2.

[108] Under traditional international law, any government (with some exceptions) with effective political control over a territory is deemed to be, internationally, the legitimate government of the state. Moreover, international law is generally indifferent about how the resources of the state are internally distributed: They may be in private hands, or they may have been expropriated by the government in whole or in part. See, e.g., UN General Assembly, *Declaration of Principles of International Law Concerning Friendly Relations and Co-operation Among States in Accordance with the Charter of the United Nations,* 24 October 1970, available at: http://www.unhcr.org/refworld/docid/3dda1f104.html [accessed 25 April 2011], especially the principle that (e) "Each State has the right freely to choose and develop its political, social, economic and cultural systems." This rule allows governments to expropriate private property and do exactly what Wenar criticizes: sell them. Even more explicit are the principles in the Declaration on Permanent Sovereignty over Natural Resources, G.A. res. 1803 (XVII), 17 U.N. GAOR Supp. (No.17) at 15, U.N. Doc. A/5217 (1962), cited approvingly by Wenar:

of basic human rights, but from the standpoint of market rules themselves. The result is objectionable in principle because it countenances the sale of stolen goods, and in terms of its consequences because it aggravates poverty, since the tyrant does not utilize the resources to benefit the people but to increase his own power and wealth. Because the gains from trade are achieved at the expense of the victims of theft and oppression, these persons arguably have a fairness complaint against the trading partner, that is, the buyer of stolen goods.[109] An evaluation of free trade from the standpoint of justice must therefore recommend, as Leif Wenar does, abolishing the rule of effectiveness and substituting the principle that resources belong to the rightful owners and not to the rulers.[110] I think, therefore, that Wenar's general point is essentially correct and that the international trade system should be reformed to require that exported goods belong to their rightful owners.

There are a couple of difficulties with the argument, however. Wenar claims that material resources *collectively* belong to the people. This principle, he says, is compatible with either private or public ownership of the resources. According to Wenar, for the government to be legitimately entitled to sell the resources, the process of public acquisition must meet democratic strictures.[111] But the idea of the *people* collectively owning the resources does not sit well with private property rights. The farm belongs to the farmer, not to the people. Wenar attempts to solve this problem by requiring that any transfer of resources to the government be sanctioned by democratic procedures. Yet many formally democratic governments are not very different from our Dictator-Thief. The majority is no more entitled than the dictator to steal from the private owner *just because it is a majority*. So, in order to specify the rightful owners of the traded goods, Wenar must add a plausible *substantive* theory of justice that shows when the government may redistribute resources in its favor (or in its friends' favor). This is not the place to discuss this large issue in political philosophy. Suffice it to say that grotesque dictators are not the only ones who steal resources from their rightful owners. Many democratically elected

---

4. Nationalization, expropriation or requisitioning shall be based on grounds or reasons of public utility, security or the national interest which are recognized as overriding purely individual or private interests, both domestic and foreign.

[109] Risse, supra n. 107, p. 362.
[110] This same point was made by Thomas Pogge, "Recognized and Violated By International Law: The Human Rights of the Global Poor," *Leiden Journal of International Law* 18 (2005): 717; Peter Singer, *One World: The Ethics of Globalization* (New Haven: Yale University Press, 2004): 96–105; and, in general terms (not specifically in reference to the trade system) in Fernando R. Tesón, *A Philosophy of International Law*, supra n. 10, pp. 1–2.
[111] Wenar, supra n. 107, pp. 20–21.

governments (governments that would satisfy Wenar's proviso) systematically steal from their citizens as well.

Moreover, dictators of the world believe that placing the collective ownership on "the people" entitles them, the dictators, to dispose of the resources. As we indicated, the standard interpretation of the international instruments that Wenar cites (such as the Declaration on the Permanent Sovereignty of Natural Resources) endorses the governments' power to expropriate resources. This is why dictators support the principle that the "people" collectively own the natural resources: They claim to represent the people, *l'état, c'est moi!* In other words: Wenar's interpretation of the principle of permanent sovereignty over natural resources departs from the (objectionable) common understanding in international law that undemocratic governments, too, are deemed to represent the people. This means that Wenar cannot just invoke the people's ownership of natural resources without adding a theory of international representativeness that is diametrically opposed to (although of course better than) the theory presupposed by the international instruments on which he relies.

Finally, it is entirely unclear that the government in the country where the prospective buyers reside will cure this injustice by erecting protectionist barriers. The Dictator-Thief problem dramatically underscores the fact that most injustices are homegrown, as we have indicated. While opening international trade alone will not remedy those injustices, closing trade will not do the job either. Here as elsewhere, protectionism is an ill-suited remedy to cure the problem. Something different is required, namely establishing a corrective procedure for restoring the stolen goods to their owners while maintaining free trade. The Dictator-Thief objection accurately identifies a problem in international trade, the problem of predatory rulers. *This* problem, however, cannot be solved by protectionist laws.

These difficulties are not fatal to Wenar's thesis. He can simply claim that the global trade system must address the difficulty of stolen goods, *whatever* our thesis may be about when the goods are in fact stolen. Yet, the fact remains that, grotesque cases aside, liberal egalitarians will often disagree with classical liberals about when traded goods are indeed stolen goods.

C. The Pauper-Labor Argument

Some authors believe that domestic workers in rich countries are entitled to protection if the imported goods arrive in our shores, not through oppression or theft, but as a result of lower labor standards in the countries of origin. This is the Pauper-Labor argument, usually advanced with considerably stridency in labor circles. Mathias Risse has given a qualified defense of this argument.

For him, if labor laws in rich countries are established for moral reasons, then for the sake of consistency workers harmed by imports deserve compensation from the government.[112] The idea is that the moral reasons that underlie labor standards are universal, so while the government cannot enforce those in the country of origin, it should acknowledge the universality of those reasons by compensating domestic workers harmed by imports. The domestic workers' competitive disadvantage is the direct result of a morally objectionable act.

It is doubtful, however, that many labor standards are always or often enacted for moral reasons. The overwhelming evidence is that governments enact them for a host of political reasons, including protectionist reasons.[113] However, perhaps labor standards are *supported* by moral reasons, even if the government had other reasons for enacting the standards. This will largely depend on the labor standard in question. Take minimum wages: It is unlikely that high wages in rich countries are supported by moral reasons. These salaries are the result of self-interested bargaining by workers, either individually or through unions, at a time where world labor markets were highly segmented. With the rise of globalization, it became obvious that labor in developing countries was more competitive. Labor leaders and politicians in rich countries speak of sweatshops and slave labor, thus implying that workers in developing countries are in the same moral category as the oppressed, that they are coerced into working for miserly salaries, almost at gunpoint.[114] This rhetoric conceals the fact that unionized workers in rich countries have been simply out-competed. Assuming voluntary relationships, including a right to terminate the contract, one does not have a right to an ongoing high wage if the employer finds someone that can perform the same work at a lower wage.[115] In fact, our intuition is exactly the opposite to Risse's: Domestic workers in rich countries are acting *immorally* when they demand protection against cheaper imports, because in doing so they are knowingly enlisting the state in the aggravation of world poverty.[116]

[112] Risse, supra n. 107, pp. 366–369.

[113] See Risse's example of the 1930 U.S Tariff Act, ibid. p. 367. Horacio Spector has identified labor standards precisely along these dimensions, and concluded that most of them do *not* reflect moral principles but rather rent-seeking, desire to avoid competition, etc. See Horacio Spector, "Philosophical Foundations of Labor Law," *Florida State University Law Review* 33 (2006): 1119.

[114] For a refutation of these arguments, see Matt Zwolinski, "Sweatshops, Choice, and Exploitation," *Business Ethics Quarterly* 17 (2007): 689–727.

[115] Of course, parties must abide by their contracts, so employers could be contractually committed to paying higher wages even if cheaper labor is available elsewhere.

[116] Quite apart from this, the evidence does not support the view that trading with developing countries has depressed wages in rich countries. Rather, trade with poor countries may well have improved wages, in the sense that it has moderated the decline that might have occurred due to

But perhaps *some* labor standards, such as occupational safety rules, are morally required in the sense that the workers have a *right* to those standards.[117] Even then, Risse's argument fails for two reasons. If workers in a developing country have a right to a labor standard, the employer who denies it harms those workers. It is entirely unclear why workers in the *rich* country should be entitled to compensation, especially considering that the taxpayers of the rich country, who have done nothing wrong, must foot the bill. Maybe the argument is that the failure of the developing country to secure the standard creates a "right" by workers in the rich country that their government ban the import (or place trade barriers against it). This has the peculiar effect of enriching parties who were not wronged (were not denied the labor standard in question) and who are already much better off by global standards, while at the same time harming the people who have already suffered the alleged injustice.[118] Surely this cannot be right.

Further, the argument assumes that labor standards are *inalienable*. This is highly dubious. Imagine that the government of a developing country offers a choice to workers in a particularly successful industry. The government offers to enforce the standards, but workers have to understand that this would make their product more expensive and hence less competitive overseas. Because the market for this particular product is largely foreign, enforcement of the labor standards will adversely affect the workers' own welfare. Alternatively, the government offers to relax the standards to keep the industry internationally competitive and thus continue to benefit workers. If the workers accept this offer, they *consent* to lower standards in exchange for their overall economic welfare. They trade the risk of a workplace injury or illness for their enhanced prosperity. I cannot see why this would be objectionable unless one thinks, implausibly, that individuals are morally forbidden from making trade-offs of this kind. Accepting a higher occupational risk in exchange for a better economic prospect seems far removed from the standard cases of inalienability, such as consenting to being tortured, or even selling an organ. In this case workers in rich countries have no claim to protection.[119]

---

non-trade factors, such as labor-saving technological change. Jagdish Bhagwati, *Globalization*, supra n. 6, pp. 124–125.

[117] We are even unsure about the claim that safety standards are morally required. Why not think of different levels of safety as labor benefits offered by businesses, so that workers can freely choose between various combinations of accident risk and economic welfare? But we do not pursue the matter.

[118] We owe this point to Matt Zwolinski.

[119] Matt Zwolinski and Ben Powell make a similar point in "The Ethical and Economic Case for Sweatshop Labor: A Critical Assessment" (unpublished, 2011). Here again, the evidence does not support the much feared "race to the bottom," i.e., the view that allowing imports

D. Trade and Human Rights

We can put our moral critique of protectionism into the form of a dilemma. Either a government enacts trade barriers as a response to lobbying and other forms of rent seeking, or it enacts them, as it should, out of a sincere desire to promote the public good. In the first case, protection is morally objectionable for obvious reasons: Having more lobbying or bribing power is hardly a characteristic that makes people deserving of a transfer of resources in their favor. If, in contrast, the government protects for public reasons (and not as a response to lobbying), it is hard to see what public reason can identify producers and workers of inefficient industries as deserving of a transfer of resources from (1) consumers and (2) those persons who remain unemployed because of the reduction in general welfare caused by protection (we are not considering here the harm done to foreign producers). In other words, any theory of justice concerned with the poor should have the poor as the rightful beneficiary of transfer of resources. However, the group "owners and workers of inefficient industries" is not coextensive with "the poor," and it is therefore an inappropriate beneficiary of redistribution – an inappropriate object of moral concern.

Liberal cosmopolitans tend to ground their views on human rights.[120] Standard lists of those rights include civil and political rights on the one hand and socioeconomic rights on the other. In view of the findings of the economic literature on the relationship between market institutions, growth, and the alleviation of poverty, we propose to reinterpret the principle that states must respect socioeconomic rights. We suggest that governments have a prima facie duty to alleviate poverty (understood in an aggregative measurable sense) in their territories. This is the domestic version of the international duty we mentioned at the outset of this chapter. The international community has a moral obligation to design international economic institutions and policies with an aim to alleviate world poverty in general. Our proposal, then, excludes the view that *each* individual has a right to a certain amount of food, or to a house, or to health care. But our view reaffirms the main thrust of socioeconomic rights. Nations must try to alleviate poverty.

---

from countries with low standards will cause governments to relax theirs, thus creating a desperate race to lower production costs. Rather, the evidence shows exactly the opposite, a race to the *top*. As incomes rise in poor countries, their growing middle class expects and demands improvements in the workplace conditions. See Bhagwati, *Globalization*, supra n. 6, pp. 127–134.

[120] See, e.g., Fernando R. Tesón, "The Kantian Theory of International Law," *Columbia Law Review* 92 (1992): 53; and Allen Buchanan, supra note 72, at 118–190.

In addition, we suggest rethinking the law and philosophy of human rights. An improved, economically literate version of human rights law should move away from the dichotomy of civil-political–socioeconomic rights and put forth instead a *trilogy* of recommendations. First, states should respect civil and political rights. The reasons for this are many and obvious, and they include the fact that enjoyment of civil and political rights facilitates development.[121] Second, states have a prima facie obligation to alleviate poverty. Discharging this obligation requires making trade-offs and establishing priorities among various development needs. Whether the fight against poverty requires laissez-faire politics or, on the contrary, government intervention in the economy (provided it respects property and contract) is an issue of institutional design that depends on context and cannot be decided in advance. Third, states should secure economic *liberties*.[122] In other words, they should not interfere with rights to private property and freedom of contract to such a degree that would create significant disincentives to productive activities and economic growth.

E. Protectionist Fallacies

The hostility that many people have to free markets blinds them in inexplicable ways. For example, objectors rarely notice that some of the bad effects of free markets are the result of *government* failure, not of the workings of markets. For example, those who criticize free trade by citing the predatory behavior of transnational firms in developing countries overlook the fact that, in those cases, transnational firms *bribed* corrupt governments, often to secure cheap labor.[123] This appalling behavior would be banned in a global *free* market system. The system we propose would use coercion (supervised, perhaps, by appropriate international institutions) only to make sure that exchanges are *voluntary*. Free trade is based on free exchanges, and there is nothing free about a firm's bribing a government to secure slave labor.

---

[121] Amartya Sen, supra note 22, chapters 1–3.

[122] See generally James W. Nickel, "Economic Liberties," in Victoria Davion and Clark Wolf (eds.), *The Idea of Political Liberalism* (Lanham, MD: Rowman & Littlefield, 2000), 155–175; and Loren Lomasky, "Liberalism without Borders," *Social Philosophy and Policy* 24 (2007): 206, 213–217 (the main cause of poverty is bad institutions, including the lack of economic liberties).

[123] See, e.g., *Doe v. Unocal Corp.*, 963 F. Supp. 880, 883–85 (D.C. Cal. 1997) (recounting the factual setting where the transnational firm allegedly obtained slave labor from the Government of Burma); *Doe v. Unocal Corp.*, 27 F. Supp. 2d 1174, 1178–79 (D.C. Cal. 1998) (same); *Doe v. Unocal Corp.*, 395 F.3d 932, 936–43 (9th Cir. 2002) (same).

Defending free trade faces another difficulty. As a proposal to address world poverty, the recommendation to liberalize trade suffers from a rhetorical disadvantage against its two rivals, namely protectionism and global redistribution. This occurs in two ways. On the one hand, the merits of free trade rely on opaque, impersonal workings of the market. For free traders, the poor will improve, not as a result of individuals and governments engaging in altruistic acts of charity, but by allowing them to advance their self-interest through voluntary exchanges. In contrast, proposals for international aid are vivid; they look like acts of charity imbued with the right altruistic intent. By implementing aid, for example by establishing a global agency to redistribute resources, we are giving things to people who need them. It looks as if we are discharging our justice-based duty. Of course, this does not mean that politicians who support international aid are necessarily acting out of duty. There are good reasons to believe politicians react to electoral incentives, which may favor aid, at least relative to trade. A politician who supports trade is at a rhetorical disadvantage because she advocates transactions from which the rich will also benefit. Given the vivid views that the public has, voters might not see moral worth in trading with the poor, even if the poor are thereby made much better off, because the trader is simply acting out of self-interest.

At the end of the day, philosophers recommend to people in power (governments, international institutions) that they do things, here and now, that discharge the justice-based duty toward the poor in a vivid way. That may be why foreign aid, and not trade, is important to them. Aiding a poor person looks like a lofty way of implementing our justice-based duty to that person. Trading with this person does not, *even if the poor as a class are better off with widespread trade than with widespread aid*. Free trade rests on self-interest, and this, we believe, is one of the reasons why philosophers overlook free-trade institutions as a way to help the poor. Promoting trade, for them, is not a sufficiently *lofty* way to discharge our duties based on justice.

This approach is deeply mistaken, an instance of Kantianism gone awry. If we care about helping the poor, we should care about designing institutions that do just that – help the poor. We should not support institutions that help the poor inefficiently, simply because the intent of the actors is, arguably, more pure.[124] The justice-based duty to help the poor has a *consequentialist* structure. It enjoins us to do those things that alleviate poverty, not those things that are subjectively pure yet counterproductive or insufficient. If trading with

---

[124] For a skeptical view on the possibility that those political proposals may be defended on account of their *symbolic* value, see Guido Pincione and Fernando R. Tesón, "Self-Defeating Symbolism in Politics," *Journal of Philosophy* 98 (2001): 636.

the poor helps them more than giving them things for nothing, then trading is morally preferable to aiding.[125]

There is another reason why supporters of free trade tend to lose in the political arena. It stems from the rhetoric of protectionism. Protectionists rely on the imagery of nationalism. We need to protect "us" against "them"; our local industries against the invading products; our culture against immigrant invasion.[126] This is an instance of the use of vivid imagery for political purposes. To see the advantages of trade, people need to see that the country that protects *hurts its own people* because protection hurts consumers. This is concealed by the notion of "protecting" something that is ours, in our country, against something that comes from the outside. Because that "something" is alien, external, politicians and rent seekers can easily portray it as a threat. All one can say is a trivial truth: The government can protect *specific* workers by protecting the industry from foreign competition. However, trade barriers do not "protect" the employment rate in one's country because of their high opportunity costs (that is, they prevent the creation of new industries by artificially divesting resources toward the protected sector). Trade barriers do not "protect" the real value of wages; and they positively harm consumers, reducing general welfare particularly among the poor. When the rhetorical smoke clears, trade barriers "protect" weak producers by giving them the chance to prey on even weaker consumers.[127] Particularly hidden are the opportunity costs of protectionism, that is, the harmful effects of protection in other sectors of the economy, including reduced job creation in those other sectors. Workers in industries yet to be created do not have lobbyists (nor philosophers, it seems) to champion their cause.

v. CONCLUSIONS

We have addressed the surprising lack of attention philosophers pay to liberalized trade as a mechanism for improving the condition of the poor. Our discussion can be summarized as follows:

---

[125] Fernando Tesón and Guido Pincione call the rhetoric we criticize in the text "the moral turn." This is defending a public policy on nonconsequentialist grounds and thus ignoring the policy's unpalatable consequences, when it is unreasonable to do so (that is, when unpalatable consequences *should* reasonably be taken into account). See Pincione and Tesón, supra note 84, chapter 6.

[126] This rhetorical argument was criticized more than a hundred years ago by Henry George, *Protection or Free Trade: An Examination of the Tariff Question, with Special Regard to the Interests of Labor* (1886), chapter 6 (*available at* the Library of Economics and Liberty, http://www.econlib.org/library/YPDBooks/George/grgPFT6.html; last accessed February 19, 2007).

[127] Bovard, supra note 104, at 238.

1. Persons and governments have a prima facie duty to try to alleviate poverty. We remain agnostic as to whether this duty stems from principles of justice or from elementary considerations of humanity.
2. Those duties are owed to the world's poor as a class, not to individuals or states.
3. For empirical reasons, liberalizing trade and immigration are likely to go a long way toward implementing those duties.
4. Protectionist measures are morally indefensible both because they harm the poor and because they benefit undeserving persons.
5. In order for trade to benefit the poor, nations need to have good institutions; in particular, they must respect civil and political rights, property, and contracts.
6. What other policies governments may pursue to reduce poverty is left as an open question (thus we are not committed to the view that whatever distribution results from the market is ideally just).
7. Free trade is required by *any* plausible theory of international justice.

This chapter identifies a serious omission in the global justice literature. Scholars in this area ignore the theoretical claims and empirical evidence of economists suggesting that liberalized trade is likely to improve the condition of the poor. The benefits from trade to the poor are denied both by protectionist measures in developed countries and by local monopolies and foreign interests allied with those in power in developing nations. Few things have done as much to cause the economic stagnation in the developing world as the policies of import substitution and similar protectionist devices (perhaps only *political* failure ranks higher in the list of such causes).[128]

Developed countries have chosen to protect their inefficient industries – notably, but not only, agriculture. They deserve scorn for not opening their markets to products made by the world's poor. Ruling elites in developing nations deserve scorn for allowing bad institutions and political practices, including misguided protectionism. Realizing these facts, rather than engaging in cheap talk about socioeconomic rights, global taxes, and ineffectual treaties, will help the poor. International reform, then, should try to *create those effectively functioning institutions* that best help the poor. Because trade relies on mutual advantage and not on altruism, there is little doubt in our

---

[128] For the effect of import substitution policies in Latin America, see Joseph L. Love, "The Rise and Decline of Economic Structuralism in Latin America: New Dimensions," *Latin American Research Review* 40 (2005): 105 ("it is universally agreed that ISI has not been a viable policy for some time"). For a useful account of the debate, see generally Henry J. Burton, "A Reconsideration of Import Substitution," *Journal of Economic Literature* 36 (1998): 903 (acknowledging that the pro-trade view has carried the day but suggesting a more nuanced view).

mind that liberalizing global voluntary exchanges, trade and immigration, will go a long way toward that goal. Critics of free trade simply do not believe that the poor can compete in world markets. They conjure up the image of poor and uneducated peasants immersed into a whirlwind of overwhelming economic forces that they cannot possibly shape or control. When we advocate that these poor peasants be allowed to participate freely in a global free market, we propose to endow them with freedoms they *do not* currently have: the freedoms to produce, work, trade, and emigrate at will. The poor peasants are the victims not of free trade but of one or more of the following: oppressive political conditions, in particular denial of human rights; collusion of the government with local monopolies or foreign producers; lack of protection of property and contract; lack of labor mobility; and stifling cultural structures. These failures cause poverty, not the other way around. Poor persons in developing countries could participate in the world economy, if only they would be given the chance to do so by those who hold an extraordinary amount of power over them.

9   Jam Tomorrow: A Critique of International Economic Law

Barbara Stark

"I'm sure I'll take *you* with pleasure!" the Queen said. "Twopence a week, and jam every other day."
Alice couldn't help laughing, as she said, "I don't want you to hire *me* – and I don't care for jam."
"It's very good jam," said the Queen.
"Well, I don't want any *to-day*, at any rate."
"You couldn't have it if you *did* want it," the Queen said. "The rule is, jam to-morrow and jam yesterday – but never jam *to-day*."
"It *must* come sometimes to 'jam to-day,'" Alice objected.
"No, it can't," said the Queen. "It's jam every *other* day: to-day isn't any *other* day, you know."

– Lewis Carroll, Through the Looking Glass and
What Alice Found There (1871)[1]

"Distributive justice" is an ambiguous goal. If we simply mean "more fair than what we've got now," "distributive justice" is within easy reach, because we could hardly do worse. As a recent UN study explains, global wealth is distributed "as if one person in a group of ten takes 99% of the total pie and

[1] "Socialists often used to ridicule the capitalist system as offering the empty promise of 'jam tomorrow.'" As Labour politician Tony Benn said in 1969, "Some of the jam we thought was for tomorrow, we've already eaten." See http://www.phrases.org.uk/meanings/211400.html.

I am deeply grateful to Tim Sellers, Frank Garcia, Chi Carmody, John Linarelli, and Sheila Ward for organizing this Symposium and inviting me to participate. Warm thanks to the other participants at Tillar House, especially Jeanne Woods, Jeff Dunoff, and Chantal Thomas, and to Tom Cady, Jim Friedberg, Anne Lofaso, Marjorie McDiarmid, Mike Risch, Caprice Roberts, John Taylor, and Grace Wigal for their helpful comments and to Debbie Swiney for her expert research assistance and manuscript preparation. A longer version of this chapter, "Distributive Justice and the Limits of International Economic Law," appears in *Boston College Third World Law Journal* 30 (2010): 3.

the others share the remaining 1%."[2] The assets of the world's richest three individuals exceed the combined gross national products of *all* of the least developed countries (LDCs), with a population totaling 600 million people.[3] The chasm between the rich and the poor has become unfathomable.

Although the number of people living in poverty has increased by almost 100 million,[4] there are more billionaires than ever before,[5] people who, as Barack Obama put it, "make more in 10 minutes than a worker makes in 10 months."[6] Simply rolling back some of the generous deregulation and outright gifts that have brought us here would be a start, and may indeed have already begun – but how much more is required for actual distributive "justice"?

I take as a starting point the relatively modest objective of the Millennium Development Goals (MDGs)[7] – to halve the number of people living in extreme poverty, namely the 1.1 billion humans subsisting on less than $1 a day, by 2015. As economist and Director of the MDGs Jeffrey Sachs points out, the wealth is there.[8] It is just a matter of moving it around.

My thesis here is that this is not going to happen under the aegis of international economic law, or the neoliberal economic order as presently constituted, for two reasons. First, the neoliberal economic order does not want this to happen. Indeed, it is inconsistent with the basic objectives and fundamental values of neoliberalism, including free markets and individual autonomy.[9] This argument draws on Karl Marx, especially his notion of ideology, to show that the neoliberal economic order does not support the redistribution of wealth. Second, even if the political will were there, it would not happen because "international economic law" is not a coherent legal subject with the

[2] Anthony Shorrocks et al., *Pioneering Study Shows Richest Two Percent Own Half the World's Wealth* (available at www.wider.unu.edu/research/2006–2007). UNU World Institute for Development Economies Research (WIDER), The World Distribution of Household Wealth (2006), 4.
[3] Peter Singer, *One World: The Ethics of Globalization*, 2nd ed. (Yale University Press, New Haven, CT: 2004), 81 (citing 1999 Human Development Report).
[4] The number of people living in poverty has increased, even as total world income has increased by 2.5 percent. Joseph Stiglitz, *Globalization and Its Discontents* (New York: Norton, 2003), 5.
[5] Eric Konisberg, "A New Class War: The Haves vs. the Have Mores," N.Y. *Times*, November 19, 2006 (explaining that the "superrich" – the $20 million a year households – "are getting richer almost twice as fast as the rich" – the top 1 percent with an average income of $940,000).
[6] Jeff Zeleny, "Obama Proposes Tax Cut for Middle Class and Retirees," N.Y. *Times*, September 19, 2007, at A22.
[7] U.N. Millennium Development Goals, available at www.un.org/millenniumgoals.
[8] Jeffrey Sachs, *The End of Poverty* (New York: Penguin Press, 2005).
[9] A crucial aspect of these fundamental values, as Carol Gould points out, is a human rights framework that persistently neglects basic economic and social rights. Carol Gould, "Approaching Global Justice through Human Rights: Elements of Theory and Practice," in this volume.

capacity to make it happen.[10] This argument draws on postmodern theory to show that the metanarrative of development is not coherent.

By the "neoliberal economic order," I refer more specifically to a cluster of premises known as the "Washington Consensus." According to Kerry Rittich, these premises include the following:

> That the implementation of efficiency enhancing rules is an uncontentious goal, that everyone stands to gain from free trade, that property and contract rights are the paramount legal entitlements, and that rule-based regimes "level the playing field" and ensure fairness among otherwise unequal parties.[11]

The Washington Consensus has been widely criticized and its success has been decidedly mixed.[12] The current global economic crisis, moreover, renders it increasingly problematic. It remains the dominant paradigm, however, if only by default.[13]

I. A MARXIST CRITIQUE

> "Face it: Marx was partly right about capitalism."
> – Rowan Williams, the Archbishop of Canterbury[14]

My first argument draws on Karl Marx – not as an economist, but as a political theorist – to explain how redistributive justice is inconsistent with the basic objectives and fundamental values of neoliberalism, including free markets and individual autonomy. Marx has been many things to many people.[15] I draw on Marx here because, as Tony Judt has pointed out, "from first to last, Marxism's strongest suit was ... the moral seriousness of Marx's conviction that the destiny of our world as a whole is tied up with the condition of its

[10] This paper relies on critical and postmodern approaches that some commentators, perhaps prudently, eschew in this context. See, e.g., John Linarelli, "What Do We Owe Each Other in the Global Economic Order? Constructivist and Contractual Accounts," *Journal of Transnational Law and Policy* 15 (2006): 181, 184 ("[n]o critical or postmodern approaches are undertaken").

[11] Kerry Rittich, "Enchantments of Reason/Coercions of Law," *University of Miami Law Review* 57 (2003): 727, 739–740.

[12] See, e.g., Sanjay Reddy and Antoine Heuty, *The End of Poverty?* (available at http://www.columbia.edu/~sr793/endofpoverty.pdf; noting that Sachs fails to adequately question the questionable orthodox prescription for economic development).

[13] Aaron James suggests a fundamental shift in this paradigm, to "structural fairness." See Aaron James, "Global Economic Fairness: Internal Principles," in this volume.

[14] Rowan Williams, *Face It: Marx Was Partly Right About Capitalism*, The Spectator, Sept. 24, 2008.

[15] For an original and provocative perspective, see Carol C. Gould, *Marx's Social Ontology* (Cambridge, MA: MIT Press, 1978), xi (proposing a new approach to Marx as a "great systemic philosopher in the tradition of Aristotle, Kant, and Hegal").

poorest and most disadvantaged members."[16] In addition, as Judt further notes, "Marxism . . . is now once again, largely for want of competition, the common currency of international protest movements."[17]

According to Marx, "The ruling ideas of each age have ever been the ideas of its ruling class."[18] As a corollary, those ideas support, justify, and further enrich that class. Today, the "ruling class" is made up of those who drive the neoliberal economic order, including industrialized states and transnational corporations. As Peter Singer notes,

> One hundred and fifty years ago, Karl Marx gave a one sentence summary of his theory of history: "The hand mill gives you society with the feudal lord; the steam mill, society with the industrial capitalist." Today he could have added: "The jet plane, the telephone, and the Internet give you a global society with the transnational corporation and the World Economic Forum."[19]

As Susan Marks explains, from a Marxist perspective international law in general has long supported the ruling class. She cites Anthony Anghie's early work showing how colonial powers shaped international law. According to Anghie, Francisco de Victoria "framed a conception of sovereignty that helped to legitimate Spanish conquest and dispossession in the Americas by defining the peoples of the region as non-sovereign."[20] Later, in the 1920s, the Russian jurist E. B. Pashukanis described how capitalist states banded together, dividing the world into "civilized" states and those that were not civilized. The former included those that had adopted the capitalist mode of production and were entitled to the protection of international law; the latter, "the remainder of the world," were "considered as a simple object of their completed transactions."[21]

As others have shown, the liberal ideology of "development" has similarly benefited the West more than it has benefited the underdeveloped countries that are its erstwhile focus. As Arturo Escobar argues, beginning with the "discovery" of poverty after World War II,[22] liberal ideology has shaped

---

[16] Tony Judt, "Goodbye to All That?," *New York Review of Books* 53 (2006): 9. The limits of Marxist critique are well known. As Judt observes, "the predictive powers of Marxian economics have long been discounted even by the left" (citing Joseph A. Schumpeter, *Capitalism, Socialism, and Democracy*, 1942). For a rigorous and compelling analysis of the challenge of attaining *both* distributive justice and democratic governance, see Chantal Thomas, "The Death of Doha? Forensics of Democratic Governance, Distributive Justice, and Development in the WTO," in this volume.

[17] Judt, supra note 16, at 11.

[18] Karl Marx and Fredrick Engels, "Manifesto of the Communist Party," in *The Marx–Engels Reader*, edited by Robert C. Tucker (New York: Norton, 1978), 489.

[19] Singer, supra note 3, at 10.

[20] Susan Marks, "Empire's Law," *Indiana Journal of Global Legal Studies* 10 (2003): 449, 458.

[21] Ibid. at 456.

[22] Arturo Escobar, *Encountering Development: The Making and Unmaking of the Third World* (Princeton, Princeton University Press 1994), 21 (describing the "discovery" of mass poverty in Asia, Africa, and Latin America after World War II).

development discourse. A brief review of three distinct but overlapping eras of development shows how, somehow, the West consistently profits from development at the expense of the less developed countries.

First, during the Cold War (1950–1990s), aid was used to buy political support for the West. The West provided aid to a brutal lineup of dictators and crooks whose only redeeming virtue was their opposition to the Soviets. These included Pinochet, Mobutu, and the apartheid regimes in South Africa. As Nobel-prize-winning economist Joseph Stiglitz notes, although most dictators are gone now, their people are left with their "odious debts."[23] Under Mobutu, for example, then-Zaire took on $8 billion in debt while its leader amassed a fortune estimated to be between $5 and 10 billion.[24] As a result, as Stiglitz observes, "Chileans today are repaying the debts incurred during the Pinochet regime, South Africans the debt incurred during apartheid."[25]

The second development era, during the 1980s–1990s, was a time of significant lending. Credit was extended, but always on terms set by the creditor (i.e., the International Monetary Fund).[26] Thus, loans were conditioned on rigid structural adjustment plans under which borrowing states were required to tighten their belts and slash social safety nets.[27] Equally damaging, risks remained with the borrower. Thus, if exchange rates or interest rates changed, the borrowing state still had to meet its obligation. Indeed, because most loans were payable on demand, those obligations often became due precisely when they were hardest to pay.[28]

Third, and finally, the current system of global reserves is an ongoing source of low-cost loans for the West, especially for the United States, and a formidable obstacle to investment in infrastructure for LDCs. After the credit crises in Asia and Latin America during the 1990s, LDCs began to hold reserves to back their currencies. Before the 1970s, the conventional wisdom was that states needed gold to back their currencies. Now, the idea is that they need "confidence," which can be grounded in a strong currency such as the U.S. dollar.

LDCs used to hold reserves worth three to four months of imports; now, they generally hold reserves worth up to eight months of imports.[29] China has $900 billion, mostly in U.S. Treasury bills. These are low-interest reserves, and

---

[23] Joseph Stiglitz, *Making Globalization Work* (New York: Norton, 2007), 238–241.
[24] Ibid. at 229.   [25] Ibid.
[26] Ibid. at 217.
[27] But see Paul Collier, *The Bottom Billion: Why the Poorest Countries Are Failing and What Can Be Done About It* (Oxford: Oxford University Press, 2007), 67 (arguing that the "Western left... conflated the limited reforms being urged on the governments of the bottom billion [with the domestic policies of Reagan and Thatcher].... As a result, reforms that should have been popular with all except corrupt elites became toxic").
[28] Stiglitz, *Making Globalization Work*, supra note 23 at 218–219.
[29] Ibid. at 247.

more importantly, they represent capital that China cannot invest in its own infrastructure.[30] If an Asian enterprise borrows $100 million from a U.S. bank, the state adds $100 million to reserves.[31] The loans, accordingly, are a wash because the state has to have currency reserves equal to the debt. As Stiglitz concludes, the "global financial system is not working well . . . especially for developing countries. Money is flowing uphill, from the poor to the rich. The richest country in the world, the U.S., borrow[s] . . . $2 billion a day from poorer countries."[32] This $2 billion is part debt repayment and part global reserves.

Development schemes developed by the very Western neoliberals who rely on these low-cost loans are not going to reverse this flow. Marks urges "those studying globalization . . . to consider the ways in which globalizing processes intersect with and reproduce pre-existing forms of exploitation and exclusion. To fail to do that is to carry forward the long and inglorious tradition in international legal scholarship, noted by both Pashukanis and Anghie, of covering up for international law (whether intentionally or not)."[33] Several scholars, including Rittich and others cited in this chapter, rigorously challenge the ways in which "globalizing processes intersect with and reproduce pre-existing forms of exploitation and exclusion." However, the institutions that shape these globalizing processes are unlikely to incorporate their critiques. Rather, neoliberal ideology continues to determine the policies of the institutions, including the International Monetary Fund, the World Bank, the World Trade Organization,[34] and, most recently, the MDGs, which purport to restrain it.[35]

Several commentators have pointed out that the ongoing viability of neoliberalism itself may well hinge on the rescue of the "bottom billion."[36] Surely liberalism's longevity is attributable, in part, to its ability to co-opt or placate its

---

[30] Ibid. at 248. But see David Barboza, "China Unveils Sweeping Plan for Economy," *N.Y. Times,* November 9, 2008, at 1 (describing China's plan to invest $586 billion in infrastructure over the next two years).

[31] Stiglitz, *Making Globalization Work,* supra note 23 at 249.

[32] Ibid. at 245.   [33] Ibid. at 465.

[34] A discussion of trade is beyond the scope of this chapter, although I argue elsewhere that the same critiques apply in that context. Stark, "Distributive Justice and the Limits of International Economic Law," *Boston College Third World Law Journal* 30 (2010): 16–18. For a thought-provoking defense of free trade, see Fernando Tesón, in this volume. For a rigorous analysis, see Chios Carmody, "A Theory of WTO Law," *Journal of International Economic Law* 11 (2008): 1. For a comprehensive and groundbreaking critique, see Frank J. Garcia, *Trade, Inequality, and Justice: Toward a Liberal Theory of Just Trade* (Amsterdam: Hotei, 2003).

[35] Arturo Escobar, *Encountering Development: the Making and Unmaking of the Third World* (Princeton, NJ: Princeton University Press, 1995), 72 (explaining how the Bretton Woods institutions supported the private sector by expanding domestic and foreign markets).

[36] Collier, supra note 27 at 99. The "bottom billion" refers to the roughly 980 million people living in what Collier calls "trapped" countries, i.e., the world's poorest countries, where the life expectancy is fifty and one in seven children die before the age of five.

detractors. However, the kind of risky, expensive, multifaceted aid that would be necessary, but perhaps insufficient, to enable the world's poorest to climb out of their crippling poverty is a hard sell under the best of circumstances. It is doubtful whether any liberal politician would even consider it in the current economic climate. As Audre Lourde put it, "The master's tools will never dismantle the master's house."[37]

II. A POMO CRITIQUE

Like Marxists, postmodernists challenge the metanarrative of development. Two major arguments are pertinent here. First, as Jean-François Lyotard defines it, "Postmodernism is incredulity toward metanarratives."[38] Second, as Frederic Jameson suggests, "Postmodernism is the cultural logic of late capitalism."[39] The first argument exposes the theoretical flaws of the metanarrative of development, while the second shows how the flawed metanarrative actually plays out in contemporary global culture.

A. Incredulity toward Metanarratives

For postmodernists, it is not that liberalism is the wrong metanarrative, but that *all* metanarratives – including Marxism, liberalism, religion, and the Enlightenment itself – are suspect. Marxism, like liberalism, is just another Enlightenment metanarrative. As Judt observes, "[t]he Marxist project ... was one strand in the great progressive narrative of our time: it shares with classical liberalism, its antithetical historical twin, that narrative's optimistic, rationalistic account of modern society and its possibilities."[40] All metanarratives have their own "will to power."[41] They all tell us more about their proponents than about the objective world they purport to explain.

---

[37] Audre Lourde, "The Master's Tools Will Never Dismantle the Master's House," in Cherrie Moraga and Gloria Anzaldua (eds.), *This Bridge Called My Back* (Watertown, MA: Persephone Press, 1981), 98.
[38] Jean-Francois Lyotard, *The Postmodern Condition: A Report on Knowledge*, translated by Geoff Bennington and Brian Massumi (Minneapolis: University of Minnesota Press, 1984), xxiv.
[39] Fredric Jameson, *Postmodernism, or the Cultural Logic of Late Capitalism* (Durham, NC: Duke University Press, 1991).
[40] Judt, supra note 16, at 8.
[41] The phrase is Nietzsche's. See Gillian Rose, *The Melancholy Science: An Introduction to the Thought of Theodor W. Adorno* (London: Macmillan, 1978), 19. ("Nietzsche, according to Adorno, refused 'complicity with the world' which ... comes to mean rejecting the prevalent norms and values of society on the ground that they have come to legitimise a society that in no way corresponds to them – they have become 'lies'" [citations omitted]). This includes those who view "universalism," or secular *Western* universalism, as a Western "will to power" or quest for hegemony.

Liberalism's "universal" subject turns out to be a Western white man.[42] As Pierre Schlag explains, "postmodernism questions the integrity, the coherence, and the actual identity of the humanist individual self. . . . For postmodernism, this humanist individual subject is a construction of texts, discourses, and institutions. The promise that this particular human agent would realize freedom, autonomy, etc. has turned out to be just so much Kant."[43]

Reason and science do not inevitably lead to progress and human good. Indeed, some have noted the role of the Enlightenment in the Holocaust.[44] After all, the "final solution" was not a barbarian rampage, but an orderly, systematic, "scientific" program of genocide – bureaucratic and perversely "rational."[45]

Like any other metanarrative, the metanarrative of development demands close analysis. As economist Bob Sutcliffe suggests, the metanarrative of development is perhaps best captured in the metaphor of a journey – nation-states start from roughly the same place, but at different times.[46] Thus, the less developed countries are today where Europe was in the fourteenth century. The "form of travel is characterized by the transfer of labor from low-productivity agriculture to higher productivity industry and modern services."[47] However, everyone ends up at the same place, with high consumption matching high productivity. Economic progress brings electricity, toilets, education, urbanization, medical services, longer lives, democracy, and human rights – in short, modernization.

According to Sutcliffe, the metanarrative of development has given rise to three major critiques. First, as set out in the "polarization critique," Europe

---

[42] See, e.g., Hilary Charlesworth, "Feminist Methods in International Law," *American Journal of International Law* 93 (1999): 379, 383 ("[i]nternational law asserts a generality and universality that can appear strikingly incongruous in an international community made up of almost two hundred different nationalities and many more cultural, religious, linguistic and ethnic groups").

[43] Pierre Schlag, *Laying Down the Law: Mysticism, Fetishism, and the American Legal Mind* (New York: New York University Press, 1996), 24.

[44] See Theodor Adorno and Max Horkheimer, *Dialectic of Enlightenment*, translated by John Cummings (New York: Herder and Herder, 1972).

[45] See James C. Scott, *Seeing Like a State: How Certain Schemes to Improve the Human Condition Have Failed* (New Haven, CT: Yale University Press, 1998; arguing that states seek to make the life of society "legible" in order to make it controllable by political power).

[46] Bob Sutcliffe, "The Place of Development in Theories of Imperialism and Globalization," in Ronaldo Munck and Dennis O'Hearn (eds.), *Critical Development Theory: Contributions to a New Paradigm* (London: Zed Books, 1999), 135.

[47] Ibid. Varun Gauri, Senior Economist at the World Bank, suggests that now the transfer of labor is from low-productivity agriculture to high-productivity agriculture. Comment of Varun Gauri, Tillar House Symposium, mentioned in the acknowledgment to this chapter.

developed, and as a result, nations polarized into developed and underdeveloped states. This polarization was set and unalterable by the end of the nineteenth century. As Sutcliffe colorfully describes it, "[u]nderdevelopment is, like Dorian Gray's portrait, development's alter ego."[48] The underdeveloped states can never catch up, in part because of all the trash the developed states have left in their way, from toxic waste to historical baggage.

The second critique is the attainability critique, namely that it is physically impossible for the whole world to reach the destination, to enjoy the level of consumption enjoyed by those in the West. Rather, greenhouse gases, contaminants, and nonrenewable resources "cannot be generalized... without causing an apocalypse."[49] As one critic observes, "[i]f all countries 'successfully' followed the industrial model, five or six planets would be needed to serve as mines and waste dumps."[50] That is, Western-style development is simply unsustainable.

Third, and finally, the multiple "desirability critiques" suggest that not everyone aspires to such levels of consumption. These critiques are very diverse, ranging from those living off the land, or off the grid, to those who seek to develop sustainable urban living. What these critiques have in common is their rejection of high consumption and high productivity. They see "[rich developed states] full of needy, oppressed and unfulfilled people."[51]

The metanarrative of development fails, accordingly, because it is grounded in an erroneous premise – that Western-style development is what the world wants. Thus, in the context of development, postmodern incredulity toward metanarratives reframes the question: If development is not the objective, what is? Who says?

B. The Cultural Logic of Late Capitalism

The second argument suggested by postmodernism draws on cultural critic Jameson's characterization of postmodernism as the "cultural logic of late capitalism."[52] One consequence of this, for Jameson, is the commodification of *everything*, including art. As Schlag points out, "ours is a world... where the value of freedom implies at once the downfall of the Berlin Wall and the imbibing of Pepsi."[53]

---

[48] Sutcliffe, supra note 46 at 136.
[49] Ibid. at 138. Daniel Butt suggests a sensible response to this critique with his notion of "sufficientarianism." Daniel Butt, "Global Equality of Opportunity as an Institutional Standard of Distributive Justice," in this volume.
[50] Jan Nederveen Pieterse, "Critical Holism and the Tao of Development," in *Critical Development Theory*, supra note 46 at 63, 73.
[51] Sutcliffe, supra note 46 at 138.   [52] Jameson, supra note 39.
[53] Schlag, supra note 43, at 47.

One of the most striking recent examples of this phenomenon is the commodification of charity. Until the recent crisis of the global economic system, charity had become the "must-have" commodity of the hyper-rich.[54] As journalist Alessandra Stanley observed, "[a]fter 25 years of ever-escalating exorbitance, the pendulum has swung towards conspicuous nonconsumption. Extravagance is measured not by how much is spent, but by how much is given away."[55] Bono has enlisted companies such as Dell and The Gap to market lines that donate a portion of their profits to aid Africa.[56] MTV aired a new documentary special on the Poverty Crisis in Africa, starring Angelina Jolie.[57]

The MDGs make a moral pitch to the philanthropists and celebrities whose support they seek. Getting photographed with African children makes them look "good." It also distracts the public from negative publicity.[58] Just as conspicuous consumption became a status system in Theodore Veblen's day,[59] conspicuous philanthropy has become a status symbol in ours. The idea that the extremely well-off should give some of their wealth to the needy has become part of the zeitgeist, the air we breathe and the coffee we drink.[60] As a recent article in *Fortune* explained, "leaders of the hedge fund world have banded together to fight poverty – taking gobs of money from the rich . . . and making philanthropy cool among the business elite."[61] The almost 65 billion dollars pledged by Buffet and Gates[62] dwarf the contributions of many donor states,[63] and they do not come with the same strings. As Professor Singer

[54] See, e.g., James Traub, "The Celebrity Solution," N.Y. *Times Magazine*, March 9, 2008, at 38 (explaining how "Hollywood celebrities have become central players on deeply political issues like development aid").
[55] Alessandra Stanley, "Humble Celebrity and Eager Newsman," N.Y. *Times*, June 22, 2006.
[56] Ron Nixon, "Bottom Line for (Red)," N.Y. *Times*, February 6, 2008, at C1.
[57] *The Diary of Angelina Jolie and Dr. Jeffrey Sachs in Africa*, September 14, 2006.
[58] See, e.g., Cate Soty, "Who's the Most Charitable of Us All? Celebrities Don't Always Make the List," N.Y. *Times*, September 10, 2007 at C7 (noting Angelina's acknowledgment that her charitable work distracts the public from her "colorful" personal life).
[59] Theodore Veblen, *The Theory of the Leisure Class* (New York: Penguin Classics, 1994; originally published 1899).
[60] See, e.g., Starbucks Ad, N.Y. *Times*, August 27, 2006, at N17 (describing its clean-water campaign to raise $10 million, partnering with "non-governmental organizations to bring clean water, improved sanitation, and hygiene education to villages in need").
[61] See Andy Serwer, "The Legend of Robin Hood," *Fortune*, September 18, 2006, at 102.
[62] Peter Singer, "What Should a Billionaire Give – and What Should You?," N.Y. *Times*, December 17, 2006, at 58, 60. Adjusted for inflation, the contributions of Gates and Buffet are "more than double the lifetime total [of Carnegie and Rockefeller combined]." Ibid.
[63] The "consequences" are generally imposed on recipient states. See, e.g., UN, Millennium Development Goals Report 2007 at 30 (describing program under which LDCs can obtain debt relief after meeting "certain criteria"). Donor states, in contrast, merely face an increasingly disappointed Ban Ki-Moo, U.N. Secretary General, when they fail to meet promised goals. Ibid.

observes, "Unconstrained by diplomatic considerations or the desire to swing votes at the United Nations, private donors can more easily avoid dealing with corrupt or wasteful governments. They can go directly into the field, working with local villages and grass-roots organizations."[64] Private charity may well be more effective than public rights, especially if the former means billions of dollars and the latter means empty promises.

But the cultural logic of late capitalism does not lead to redistributive justice. Although charity can be a force for good, it is not a particularly dependable force, as shown by the impact of the current global economic crisis on international donors.[65] No one is more vulnerable to shifting mores than the poor.[66] Nor does charity sensibly distribute costs or benefits,[67] or provide an antidote for donor fatigue.

The main reason that the cultural logic of late capitalism does not lead to redistributive justice is that that is not its purpose; its purpose is to perpetuate capital and to benefit those who control it. Thus, Angelina, Gates, and hedge fund managers can use their obscene wealth to buy virtue. If, in the face of a global economic crisis, virtue becomes too expensive, they can change their minds. The real purpose of late capitalism is most glaringly revealed, however, in the notion that global poverty can be constructively dealt with by *shopping*, that is, by the very overconsumption that perpetuates it. Red companies spent as much as $100 million in advertising to raise $18 million for Africa.[68] As consumers stop spending, of course, the Red companies stop giving.[69]

at 3. See also Celia Dugger, "U.S. Agency's Slow Pace Endangers Foreign Aid," N.Y. *Times*, December 7, 2007, at 1 (noting that the Millennium Challenge Corporation, a federal agency established almost four years ago, has spent only $155 million of the $4.8 billion approved for aid projects).

[64] Singer, supra note 62, at 62.

[65] See, e.g., Stephanie Strom, "Bracing for Lean Times Ahead," N.Y. *Times*, November 11, 2008, at F1 (asking whether philanthropy, "like the housing and financial markets, [was] riding a bubble that has finally burst?"). But see Matthew Bishop, "A Tarnished Capitalism Still Serves Philanthropy," N.Y. *Times*, November 11, 2008 (arguing that "philanthrocapitalists" will simply become more efficient).

[66] See Thomas Pogge, *World Poverty and Human Rights: Cosmopolitan Responsibilities and Reforms* (Cambridge: Polity Press, 2002), 2. Hopefully, some of these pledges have already been paid, in cash. Louise Story, "Hedge Funds' Steep Fall Sends Investors Fleeing," N.Y. *Times*, October 23, 2008, at 1 (noting that hedge funds, which defined "the era of Wall Street hyper-wealth," have lost $180 billion in the last three months).

[67] Stephanie Strom, "Big Gifts, Tax Breaks, and a Debate on Charity," N.Y. *Times*, September 6, 2007 (noting that "roughly three-quarters of charitable gifts of $50 million and more . . . went to universities, private foundations, hospitals and art museums").

[68] Nixon, supra note 56.

[69] David Leonhardt, "Buying Binge Slams to a Halt," N.Y. *Times*, November 12, 2008, at A1.

III. WHAT ABOUT TODAY?

This is a question that neither Marx nor the postmodernists deign to answer, for similar reasons. For Marx, any answer is subject to the "false consciousness" that inspires it; that is, the futile hope that there is a possibility of authentic "species-life" within capitalism. For the postmodernists, the question shows the questioner's inability to abandon the questions of the Enlightenment. Surely reason and science, pumped up by our unprecedented ability to generate and manipulate data, will lead to a solution. Alice just cannot stop arguing with the Queen.

Perhaps, this chapter suggests, she is wasting her time. As Schlag observes, "[o]ne might think that destruction is inherently bad and construction inherently good . . . but it all depends on what is being destroyed and what is being constructed."[70] To question the Enlightenment is not necessarily to embrace nihilism. As Roy Boyne and Ali Rattansi point out, there is a "postmodernism of 'resistance' as well as a postmodernism of reaction.'"[71]

You do not have to be a Marxist to share Marx's conviction that "the destiny of our world as a whole is tied up with the condition of its poorest and most disadvantaged members."[72] You do not have to accept the metanarrative of development to believe that the existing distribution of global wealth is absurd and that the lives of the poorest should, and can, be better. Indeed, it may be necessary to abandon that metanarrative, or "turn it inside out" as Jeffrey Dunoff urges,[73] to even imagine what might really improve their lives.

Section I of this chapter suggests that the Washington Consensus does more for Washington than it does for the ostensible target of its concern. Section II questions the objective of the Washington Consensus, namely development itself. The rejection of the Washington Consensus or "development" would not be "inherently bad." Rather, it might make it possible to "create space for local alternatives," as Rittich argues, reminding us that the "intuition behind the norm of self-determination is that important . . . legal reforms . . . should be made by those who will have to live with the consequences."[74]

---

[70] Schlag, supra note 43 at 68.
[71] Roy Boyne and Ali Rattansi, "The Theory and Politics of Postmodernism," in Roy Boyne and Ali Rattansi (eds.), *Postmodernism and Society* (London: Palgrave Macmillan, 1990), 10, 29.
[72] Judt, supra note 16, at 9.
[73] See Jeffrey Dunoff, "The Political Geography of Distributive Justice," in this volume.
[74] Rittich, supra note 11, at 738.

10 Doing Justice: The Economics and Politics of International Distributive Justice

Joel P. Trachtman

I. INTRODUCTION

This chapter argues that the project of distributive justice is interdisciplinary. Philosophical arguments alone cannot tell us what to do to effect distributive justice.

Philosophical arguments help us to determine what should be done, but they have four salient limitations. First, they are not necessarily dispositive and convincing to all ("limited consensus"). Second, philosophical arguments are often surprisingly dependent on a clear view of existing circumstances and causal relationships ("limited knowledge of causation"). Third, even assuming that philosophical arguments can define distributive justice, they cannot provide a complete answer to the question of how to implement distributive justice ("limited knowledge of remedies"). Fourth, although certainly under some circumstances better arguments can persuade individuals to alter their positions, they cannot provide a complete answer to the question of how to develop the political will to do justice ("limited inducement").

The following table lists each of these limitations alongside a reference to the main disciplinary expertise that can address the limitation, the main question asked in relation to the limitation, the relationship between the referenced limitation and other limitations, and the remedy that might overcome the limitation. The rest of this chapter is devoted to spelling out these topics in more detail.

I am grateful to participants in the American Society of International Law Symposium on Distributive Justice and International Law, including especially Daniel Butt, Frank Garcia, Carol Gould, and Fernando Tesón for comments, as well as to Lionel McPherson for advice. Errors are mine.

Limitation	Main Expertise	Main Question	Relation to Other Limitations	Remedy
Limited consensus	Philosophy	What does distributive justice require?	Failure to agree on requirements causes limited inducement.	Stronger public philosophy debate
Limited knowledge of causation	Economics and Law	How and why does the world as it is fail to measure up to the requirements of distributive justice?	Limited knowledge of causation causes limited consensus, limited knowledge of remedies, and limited inducement.	Stronger interdisciplinary collaboration with economists and lawyers
Limited knowledge of remedies	Economics and Law	What alternative measures would result in compliance with the requirements of distributive justice?	Limited knowledge of remedies causes limited inducement.	Stronger interdisciplinary collaboration with economists and lawyers
Limited inducement	Political Science; Sociology; Psychology	What would induce individuals to support compliance with the requirements of distributive justice in individual or political action?	Causes no other limitation	Stronger interdisciplinary collaboration with political scientists, sociologists, and psychologists

The practice of philosophy addresses the problem of limited consensus, although it has not yet overcome it, at least in the field of distributive justice. The expert skills of philosophers are insufficient by themselves to overcome the other limitations. These are areas in which the practical expertise of lawyers and the theoretical and empirical expertise of political scientists, sociologists, social psychologists, and economists are critical inputs.

Furthermore, these four limitations are related to one another in important ways. Limited consensus, limited knowledge of causation, or limited knowledge of remedies may result in limited inducement. Each of these limitations alone is thus sufficient to stymie efforts to do justice. I evaluate these four limitations in Sections II through IV, evaluate some examples of particular justice issues in Section V, and conclude in Section VI.

II. LIMITED CONSENSUS

There does not seem to be a consensus position among philosophers regarding the demands of international distributive justice. It is likely that there never will be consensus, and that philosophy will continue as a marketplace of ideas, the currency of which is argument, with varying degrees of consensus. Despite that, a consensus on the basic practical demands of justice could be developed. An appropriate goal for public philosophy may be to negotiate a practical consensus from theoretical diversity. Achieving this goal would be a philosophical microcosm of policy making in a liberal society, in which practical action must be forged from diverse preferences and perspectives.

However, it is clear that the degree of dissensus among philosophers will significantly impair the implementation of principles of justice in a political setting. Indeed, implementation puts pressure both on consensus and on the degree of specificity of consensus.

This is not the place for me to attempt to articulate a definition of international distributive justice. Much attention by people more skilled than I am has been devoted to that project. Furthermore, much of my argument is independent of the adopted definition of distributive justice.

However, to show how limited consensus may impede the distributive justice project, I wish to highlight one of the fundamental problems in distributive justice viewed from an international perspective: the question of the appropriate site for doing justice. From one perspective, the central question in international distributive justice is the cross-border question: Do we as individuals or as citizens have distributive justice obligations to foreign individuals or states, or is the state the appropriate vertical site of justice? As Barbara Stark's chapter in this volume suggests, without consensus on the site of distributive justice, distributive justice may not be done.

One response to this vertical site problem is to formulate a practical response that recognizes the duty to do distributive justice, but that also recognizes the factual implications of different contexts. This practical response might be understood as a kind of "justice subsidiarity," because it would seek to allocate authority and responsibility according to some parameter or parameters of appropriateness. Parameters of appropriateness in this context would relate to the particular advantages or disadvantages of doing justice at different vertical sites. The existence of the state would be one factor to be considered among other parameters of appropriateness. One type of parameter of appropriateness in this context might evaluate problems of incentive structures or moral hazard. For example, does the possibility of international aid increase the likelihood of need for international aid by imposing soft constraints on governments? Another parameter of appropriateness is the practical ability to induce action. Does national allegiance and solidarity play an important role in inducing action to implement justice? This may be simply a behavioral artifact of human anthropology, or it may have to do with the ability to police reciprocity so as to make actions to implement justice more desirable than they otherwise would be. A third parameter may simply be, in the pure spirit of subsidiarity, to protect local autonomy regarding the desirable social structure.

Prior to the question of the appropriate vertical governmental site for the effectuation of distributive justice is the question of whether distributive justice is a government function at all, either on the giving end or on the receiving end. This, too, can be understood as a question of justice subsidiarity. Still, good behavioral, if not philosophical, reasons exist to involve government on the giving end. First, collective action problems might reduce the incentives for any one individual to implement justice where there was uncertainty regarding the contributions of others. For instance, the power to tax is best explained by the need to overcome collective action problems in the production of public goods. Second, economies of scale might make it more efficient to act collectively.

What about the receiving end, however? Should the targets of distributive justice be states or their citizens? Again, the response is likely to be driven by practical considerations. Will the state serve as an altruistic and efficient intermediary, or is it likely to divert benefits? Which target is likely to be most appealing in inducing political support for action to effect justice?

In addition to the vertical unit of analysis problem just discussed, a functional unit of analysis problem is also present. In functional terms, where is justice to be done? Is it best done in an income tax, as some law and economics scholars argue, in trade rules – and if so, in which trade rules in particular, in the international financial architecture, in the law of the sea, or in other areas or all areas?

The concept of justice subsidiarity, as applied to both the vertical unit of analysis problem and the functional unit of analysis problem, recognizes that it is unlikely to be appropriate to effect justice by every institution or every act, but it insists that justice be effected somewhere. It is unlikely to be appropriate to do justice in every act, simply because some vertical or functional areas will be more efficient or effective areas in which to do justice than others.

From a natural law standpoint, it might be posited that the law, as a tool of implementation, simply conforms to the requirements of justice. However, this would still leave a question of specifics: How particularly does philosophy answer questions of implementation of law? To what extent does a vision of justice give us a vision of the details of tax codes, tort law, criminal law, or antidumping law? What is the level of granularity at which philosophy works? Even more devastating to the natural law position is the problem of dissensus discussed in earlier paragraphs: Without consensus on what justice requires, it is impossible to take the position that the requirements of justice are ipso facto transmuted into natural law. So, without first reaching consensus, it would be democratically illegitimate to move directly from a vision of justice to implementation in law. Of course, the force of this argument depends on the hierarchical relationship between democratic legitimacy and substantive justice. That is, if my vision of substantive justice supervenes my vision of democratic legitimacy, then I am likely to impose my vision of justice on others regardless of its democratic pedigree.

In contrast, in a positive law, or realist, world, justice does not determine law. Rather, a political connection, a bridge, or a filter is required to establish the relationship between justice and international law. Section V of this chapter examines the political connection between distributive justice and international law and attempts to mark out the domain of this type of bridge or filter.

Thus, in a world of policy complexity and unintended consequences, an understanding of the requirements of justice does not necessarily determine specific policy measures. Nor does an understanding of the requirements of justice help us in diagnosing the causes of injustice. Indeed, it would be strange if philosophers could dominate the world of public policy through philosophy alone, just as it would be strange if philosophers could dominate the world of automotive design, of pharmaceutical research, or of any other scientific or practical domain. How can justice interact with economics?

III. LIMITED KNOWLEDGE OF CAUSATION AND OF REMEDIES: JUSTICE ≠ ECONOMICS

Once a workable definition of justice is established, we must examine what causes injustice, and how justice is implemented. Why are the causes of injustice important? From one perspective, they are necessary in order to assign responsibility for injustice. However, another analytical perspective, and one that I prefer, is not dependent on causation. Duties of justice should not depend on culpability or causation, which are neither necessary nor sufficient to give rise to a duty of justice. Instead, causation is important as a guide to remediation: as a means to help determine how best to do justice.

Whereas economics, like other social sciences, focuses on the positive analysis of the relationship between causes and effects, philosophy operates largely in the determination of desirable effects. However, philosophers seem to have little to contribute to the analysis of causation. Economists and other social scientists simply spend more time, and operate with more analytical care, skepticism, and detachment with relation to the analysis of causal relationships, than philosophers seem to do. Philosophers seem to fall into the empirical errors of juxtaposition and correlation. Frequently, they move, without analysis, from identification of a problem to assertion of a solution. Tesón and Klick have done a fine job of explaining this in the trade area.[1]

Philosophers should therefore cede the territory of empirical analysis of circumstances, and of causation of circumstances, to economists and other social scientists. Assessment of circumstances can be quite complex, involving, for example, needs to develop metrics of comparison of diverse goods and lifestyles. Economists are skilled at interrogating narratives and designing sophisticated inquiry in order to separate false from true causal links.

Nevertheless, the determination of desirable effects – preferences – is generally agreed to be outside the realm of economic analysis. Economists generally take preferences as exogenous, including preferences for distributive outcomes.[2] A frontier area of economics, however, examines the possibility and the implications of endogenous preferences. This frontier area has much in common with international relations constructivism. As I discuss in the paragraphs that follow, it is possible that philosophy might assist individuals in evaluating and in modifying their preferences. Furthermore, philosophy might have something to say not just about ends but also about means, by suggesting limits on the types of means that could be used to achieve desirable ends.

---

[1] Fernando Tesón and Jonathan Klick, "Global Justice and Trade: A Puzzling Omission" (working paper dated October 2007, available at http://papers.ssrn.com/sol3/papers.cfm?abstract_id= 1022996).

[2] An important part of welfare economics examines the optimal method of implementing exogenously determined distributive goals. See William Vickrey, *Agenda for Progressive Taxation* (New York: Ronald Press, 1947); James A. Mirrlees, "An Exploration in the Theory of Optimum Income Taxation," *Review of Economic Studies* 38 (1971): 175.

IV. LIMITED INDUCEMENT: JUSTICE ≠ POLITICS

It is unclear how a philosophical determination of the requirements of justice would result in political action. Nonetheless, work by philosophers on the definition of justice – overcoming limitations of consensus – is important because a lack of consensus regarding the requirements of justice can be expected to affect the ability to implement justice in political action.

In this section, however, I follow a liberal perspective that accepts that individuals may differ in their conceptions of justice. Although I hasten to acknowledge that justice is not simply a matter of taste, or even of preference, it seems reasonable to recognize that in the world as it is there is no consensus on the requirements of justice, and that it seems inappropriate for me simply to impose my vision of justice on you. I also hasten to add that individuals are not necessarily willing to comply with the dictates of justice, even when they understand them. Instead, it is necessary to examine the extent to which knowledge of the dictates of justice influences behavior, rather than to assume that it determines behavior.[3]

We would expect that, within political discourse, individuals would try to implement their own vision of justice by advancing it and attempting to convince others that they should support it. Constructivist theories focus on the role of ideas and on the social construction of meaning as an influence on behavior. It seems that philosophy will have its greatest effect through the social construction of meaning, through the development of perceptions regarding what doing justice means, and regarding the duty to do justice. As already noted, an economist might understand this within the context of endogenous preferences. Economics increasingly accepts that individuals might change their preferences, and that a number of different types of inputs would influence these changes.

Economic theory, including normative individualism, is hospitable to the possibility that philosophers would advise us regarding our preferences. "Preferences" is simply an economist's word for tastes, aspirations, and felt duties. In the liberal economic model, philosophers contribute to the global justice project through preference modification: Their job is to help the rest of us to formulate our preferences – more specifically, to help us to understand our duties. It is something of a feat of levitation that we hire them, that we have a preference to improve our own preferences. Perhaps we also

---

[3] See Klaus R. Scherer, "Issues in the Study of Justice," in K. R. Scherer (ed.), *Justice: An Interdisciplinary Perspective* (Cambridge: Cambridge University Press, 1992), 1–15.

hire them to improve the preferences of others, as agents of meddlesome preferences.

Kaplow and Shavell have argued that adding concerns for fairness or justice to social policy analysis necessarily (and tautologically) reduces welfare except insofar as individual preferences include a "preference" for fairness or justice.[4] This economic perspective may not have practical implications; Kaplow and Shavell importantly and correctly accept justice and fairness as inputs through individual preferences. Furthermore, one might extend their analysis by suggesting that individuals, in implementing their preference for fairness or justice, may delegate the task of assessing what is fair or just to judges, legislators, treaty writers, or other agents. Welfare economics would therefore accept the possibility that such actors may appropriately include fairness or justice in their deliberations.

v. EXAMPLES OF POSSIBLE SITES FOR DISTRIBUTIVE JUSTICE

In this section, I utilize the framework developed herein to briefly evaluate the degree of leverage that distributive justice analysis seems to provide in connection with five archetypical international distributive contexts. Of course, these are not the only sites to be considered. In fact, it may make sense to devise a wholly new international institution by which to effect distributive justice. Justice subsidiarity suggests that not every site of international governance must be a site of distributive justice. The central question is how best to effect distributive justice. In domestic society, it may be best to use a tax and transfer system and a system of equal opportunity in order to effect distributive justice while avoiding considerations of distributive justice in the contract or tort system. Similarly, in international society, it would be appropriate to select the optimal mechanisms by which to effect distributive justice.

In contrast, framing or other devices may be appropriate under some circumstances to overcome problems of limited inducement. This may suggest the use of otherwise suboptimal devices in order to effect distributive justice.

A. *Right to Health and TRIPS*

It is clear that the Trade-Related Aspects of Intellectual Property Rights, or TRIPS, deal has imposed significant costs on poor countries and on poor

---

[4] Louis Kaplow and Steven Shavell, *Fairness versus Welfare* (Cambridge, MA: Harvard University Press, 2002).

people. Viewed independently, TRIPS was a bad deal for poor countries. It may be that even as part of the Uruguay Round package, TRIPS was a bad deal for poor countries because it resulted in a transfer of wealth from poor to wealthy countries. However, the problem for poor countries, and more specifically of poor people, in relation to TRIPS is not the rules of TRIPS themselves, but the poverty of these individuals. One strategy that some people have explored to seek to reduce the costs of AIDS and other medicines and to relieve the burden of TRIPS on poor people is to argue for the modification or termination of TRIPS. One basis for doing so in diplomatic discourse, and perhaps in judicial discourse, is the application of the right to health. If all other things remained equal, this would redistribute wealth from the wealthy to the poor (or would reverse the redistribution from the poor to the wealthy effected by the original TRIPS). However, it would change the global level of intellectual property protection.

Economists have failed to develop a consensus view regarding the efficient global level of intellectual property protection. However, in ideal circumstances, the efficient global level of intellectual property protection – whatever that may be – should not be modified to provide greater access to medicines for the poor. It would be much more efficient, if we had the institutional infrastructure to do so, simply to transfer resources to the poor to enable them to acquire needed medicines on their own.

Thus, it appears that the TRIPS–AIDS problem might be optimally addressed by a redistribution of financial resources. However, we lack effective institutions for redistribution. Under these circumstances, there may be stronger arguments to modify TRIPS obligations themselves, or even to use human-rights-based arguments to procure effective redistribution through abrogation of intellectual property rights. However, we should be clear that this technique amounts to a global expropriation of the existing ownership rights of pharmaceutical companies, as well as a modification of the incentives of these companies to develop the next round of AIDS treatments. Thus, philosophical arguments alone seem insufficient to determine the best method of addressing the problem of essential medicines. This is a problem of limited knowledge of remedies.

In this context, a particular crisis, such as the HIV–AIDS epidemic, perhaps combined with rights-based discourse, can help to overcome the problem of limited inducement. In addition, it may be that this type of crisis can help to overcome problems of limited consensus, insofar as a concrete crisis may serve as the practical basis for consensus where theoretical consensus is otherwise unachievable.

B. *International Tort: Bhopal*

Should a catastrophic tort serve as an occasion for redistribution? We might say that Bhopal, like AIDS, serves as a good occasion to effect redistribution that is otherwise appropriate, insofar as it presents a crisis that may overcome problems of limited inducement and limited consensus. However, recall the structure of the Bhopal legal context. The Indian subsidiary of a U.S.-based company, Union Carbide, caused a disaster in India, with great suffering and loss of life among Indians. The main substantive question, masked behind technical legal arguments regarding jurisdiction and the doctrine of forum non conveniens, was whether Indian victims should benefit from a standard of recovery applicable in the United States with respect to U.S. victims of U.S. torts.

From the standpoint of basic principles of equality, we might ask, "How can an Indian life be worth less than a U.S. life?" Standards of recovery might be viewed as a matter of local public policy, and it might well be that an artificially high standard of recovery applicable in India would chill investment and economic growth in India. If investors were required to value Indian life at a level higher than the actual value to poor Indians, then they might be deterred from investing in circumstances in which Indians would desire their investment: in circumstances in which accepting the investment, even with the unappealing local level of valuation of human life, would be better than the alternatives available.

Therefore, the emergence of the justice issue in connection with Bhopal, like that in connection with AIDS, seems to be somewhat opportunistic. I do not mean this in a pejorative sense – there is no reason not to be opportunistic in the cause of justice. It does seem that by linking claims for justice to particular crises, we may be missing the larger claim for systemic justice. In both the AIDS context and in the Bhopal case, the systemic problem is the poverty of Africans and Indians, not the particular context of disease or disaster. Furthermore, by linking claims to particular crises, as in the AIDS context, we may be undermining these claims by subjecting them to reasonable arguments regarding efficiency or burden sharing that would not be applicable in connection with a broader program of international distributive justice.

Again, limited knowledge of causation and limited knowledge of remedies may result in claims or arguments that would be counterproductive or excessively limited in scope. Although crises may provide a specific case in order to form a casuist basis for consensus, and although they may assist in inducement to do justice, they may not result in a broadly satisfactory, or efficient, program of distributive justice.

C. Special and Differential Treatment at the World Trade Organization

Philosophers writing about international distributive justice, such as Thomas Pogge, sometimes claim that poverty in poor countries is caused by particular activities of wealthy countries, or by the international economic system. On this basis, they argue for modifications of the international economic system. Although we may ask whether causation is necessary in order to establish a duty, these arguments also generally suffer from limited knowledge of causation and limited knowledge of remedies.

The quasi-legal concept of special and differential treatment (S&D) for developing countries that has been a mantra of the international trade system is sometimes advanced by philosophers as a way of complying with the duty of distributive justice.[5] Although S&D still features prominently in the Doha Development Agenda, it appears that, at least as applied so far, it has limited utility. S&D is a complex phenomenon – some aspects of S&D are undoubtedly beneficial. S&D includes several specific rules and approaches that can be placed in three categories: nonreciprocity, preferential market access, and permissive protection.

First, S&D includes the concept, initially expressed in the mid-1960s, that poor countries will not be expected or requested to make reciprocal concessions in trade negotiations. This vague principle was later incorporated in Part IV of the General Agreement on Tariffs and Trade. However, those who are not required to reciprocate often find that few concessions are accorded to them – even under conditions of most favored nation. This lack of reciprocity is because, of course, the products of export interest to developing countries often differ from those of interest to other countries, and so they are not included in the give and take of negotiation over concessions.

Second, S&D includes the aspiration to provide enhanced market access to developing-country products. Partly because of the principle of nonreciprocity, this aspiration was often ignored. The area in which S&D has had its greatest effect is in connection with the Generalized System of Preferences (GSP), which provides for reduced tariff treatment for certain developing-country products. Although the GSP has provided modest benefits, it has not been applied to provide greater market access for many of the most important poor country products, and the United States and European Union have imposed substantial conditions on access to their GSP programs. "Graduation" policies including ceilings on eligible exports have also diminished the utility of GSP.

[5] For critiques of S&D, see the chapters by Chin Leng Lim and Jeffrey Dunoff in this volume.

Furthermore, as developed-country tariffs have decreased to an average of less than 5 percent, and with the formation of more free-trade areas and customs unions, the preferences under the GSP have been greatly eroded and will be further eroded in future. The magnitude of the "differential" has declined substantially. If benefits are unstable and are a wasting asset, they cannot form a sound basis for investment that would allow poor countries to actually achieve market access. Furthermore, the principle of nonreciprocity, as implemented through the GSP, seems to have the effect of diminishing incentives for liberalization by beneficiary countries.

Third, S&D includes greater permission for protection, in particular under Articles XII and XVIII of the General Agreement on Tariffs and Trade, relating to balance of payments. For much of the past twenty years, a consensus – part of the "Washington Consensus" – developed that poor countries would benefit from liberalization of their domestic markets. The debate about whether protection of domestic markets is good or bad for poor countries has recently been revived. However, solid reasons still exist for poor countries to liberalize at some point in their development path. Furthermore, there would seem to be little basis for questioning liberalization as to goods and services, such as financial and telecommunications services, that provide infrastructure for other productive activities.

So, there is certainly no consensus among economists that either (1) the failure of S&D has somehow caused poverty, or (2) any of the features of S&D have been beneficial for poor people. Indeed, it seems equally likely that the S&D mindset has resulted in actions that would reduce the welfare of poor people.

Again, in this context, it appears that philosophers should either (1) seek greater information and assistance from economists to help them to overcome limited knowledge of causation and limited knowledge of remedies, or (2) abstain from analysis that is dependent on information regarding the causation and remedies for poverty.

D. Regulation of Foreign Direct Investment

Some philosophers have criticized regimes, such as the North American Free Trade Agreement or various bilateral investment treaties, that require developing countries to liberalize market access for foreign direct investment, or that protect foreign direct investment from discrimination or expropriation. Although the concerns they express seem largely immaterial or specious, economists seem to broadly agree that investment can assist significantly in growth. To recommend for or against investment treaties, one would need to evaluate any adverse effects and compare those effects to the beneficial ones in inducing investment. These are complex questions of cost–benefit analysis that are not susceptible to the tools deployed by philosophers.

Again, it appears that philosophers should either (1) seek greater information and assistance from economists to help them to overcome limited knowledge of causation and limited knowledge of remedies, or (2) abstain from analysis that is dependent on information regarding the causation and remedies for poverty.

E. World Bank–International Monetary Fund Conditionality

Conditionality, the practice by which international financial organizations establish conditions for the availability of their lending, is a form of intervention, and some call it a form of neocolonialism. Conditionality certainly reduces the bundle of autonomous state rights known as "sovereignty." Sovereignty, in the form of absolute state control over its own affairs, has been oversold to poor small states, and, more specifically, to citizens. Local control does not benefit individuals when it is in the hands of predatory or incompetent governments; we must be open to a post-postcolonial possibility of intervention in cases of failed domestic governance. If predatory governments can be disciplined through a regime of analysis, transparency, and conditionality, then their citizens' daily lives may be improved.

It may seem strange to be advancing greater international intervention and conditionality at a time when the policies underlying World Bank and International Monetary Fund (IMF) conditionality have been hotly criticized. Although international governance is quite imperfect to the extent that it can engage in a policy dialogue with poor countries, useful measures may result and will prove less imperfect than the alternatives. Mechanisms have to be created to ensure and facilitate reasoned dialogue based on agreed principles, rather than diktat.

How should philosophers respond to conditionality? Some philosophers have written in support of humanitarian intervention, so why not support appropriate conditionality as a less intrusive form of intervention? Again, philosophers may experience problems of limited knowledge of facts and limited knowledge of remedies. Many evaluations of World Bank and IMF actions and conditionality have been performed, and these programs have been revised extensively. Therefore, distinguishing between good and bad conditionality requires careful and very specific evaluation by use of social scientific tools in place of philosophical tools.

VI. CONCLUSION: JUSTIFYING RULES AND INSTITUTIONS

Many of the problems that confront international distributive justice are complex, both in terms of their causation and in terms of their solution. Limited consensus, limited knowledge of causation, limited knowledge of remedies, and limited inducement interact with one another in important ways, limiting the influence of philosophical understandings on the practice of distributive justice. Developing a greater philosophical consensus will enhance the influence of these understandings. The development of this consensus will be assisted by efforts to overcome problems of limited knowledge of causation and limited knowledge of remedies, based on the best description and analysis of the existing problems. As a result, a more coherent interdisciplinary analysis may be able to establish arguments for distributive justice, specify appropriate remedies, and, therefore, overcome limited inducement. It is only through a more coherent interdisciplinary program, engaging economists, political scientists, social psychologists, and lawyers, that the greatest social effects may be attained.

Conclusion: An Agenda for Research and Action

Chios Carmody, Frank J. Garcia, and John Linarelli

We began this volume with three interrelated aims. First, there is the need to more closely integrate political theory on distributive justice matters into the study, critique, and reform of international economic law doctrine and institutions. The global justice debate has made it abundantly clear that the ready assumption that economic theory and political realism would together resolve all relevant normative issues in international economic law is now untenable (if it ever was tenable). Second, we recognize that political theory, for all its normative power, will ultimately fail to realize its full transformative potential without a more thorough and nuanced accounting of how institutions and rule systems – in all their messy human splendor – actually work. That is where justice will actually take place. Finally, we want to see how a closer conversation between international law and political theory might contribute to a clearer and more powerful analysis of global justice and its relationship to international economic law, thus strengthening both fields.

In practice, this has resulted in a series of challenging and innovative papers – conversations, really – linked together by their cumulative exploration of the following questions: How can the justice of global economic relations be enhanced and safeguarded by international economic law? What substantive or procedural principles of justice should organize our efforts to improve the efficiency and social welfare of the international economic law system? What limits do we discover in prevailing accounts of global justice when we explore their claims and implications through the complexity of international economic law systems as we find them? What limits within international economic law scholarship does the global justice debate highlight?

The first section of the book advances several specific arguments on the nature of distributive justice and its relationship to global economic systems. Gould, Butt, and Hockett all offer egalitarian principles of justice, from within a broadly cosmopolitan perspective, and argue for their implementation through international law.

This raises a fundamental question central to the project of this book: If we take both global justice and the complex, stubborn reality of international institutions and their politics seriously, how can we acknowledge the often radically egalitarian principles and implications of political theory in a way that offers practical, realizable guidance toward global justice? Our authors collectively identify and employ three different types of answers to this question.

The first approach, employed by both Gould and Butt, is to offer a set of intermediate principles or mechanisms as bridging tools between political theory and institutional reality. For Gould, the key is human rights, but human rights understood as a set of benchmarks, prioritizing changes within domestic and international institutions rather than mandating radical redistribution. This results in a set of recommendations familiar to anyone conversant with the global justice literature, such as the use of human rights impact assessments, but with a difference. Instead of a facile laundry list of changes, such prescriptions are grounded in a comprehensive theory of equal positive freedom, with human rights as an intermediate set of organizing principles rather than as an imagined shortcut to implementation.

Similarly, Butt argues for a robust cosmopolitan principle – the principle of equality of opportunity – while fully recognizing the gulf between the implications of this theory and contemporary global socioeconomic reality. In Butt's case, rather than offer human rights to bridge the gap, he suggests careful attention to three sets of intermediate issues critical to the implementation of any normative principles by actual institutions: their normative desirability, practicality, and popular legitimacy. Recognizing that the specific nature of distinct institutions, and the particular socioeconomic context of the people they affect, influences the sorts of actions that can and should be taken toward global justice at different levels, Butt reminds us that global equality of opportunity does not require equal material conditions, just the conditions of equal substantive opportunity in the relevant society.

Thus we see two philosophers advocating ambitious theories, but within a framework that recognizes that implementation will be progressive, evolutionary, and grounded in the specific nature of actual institutions, the societies they affect, and the larger context of domestic and international politics. The corrective, if you will, against disengaged theorizing or facile prescription is through intermediate mechanisms – whether human rights principles or mediating concepts – that take into account the contextual reality of their target institutions.

Hockett, by contrast, offers us a different kind of corrective mechanism. He too pursues a broadly cosmopolitan principle of justice – that of fair distribution based on equal-opportunity-grounded welfare – but his focus is on the traps we create for ourselves within our own theoretical discourse. Arguing that all maximization models are distributive, equalizing–disequalizing, and reductive, but generally along the wrong criteria, he tries to make us self-conscious and critical of the assumptions in our formulae and their unexpected implications. The need for this kind of internal housecleaning for global justice theory may only become apparent as we try to apply it to concrete institutions and decisions.

These three theorists all operate through the same basic structure: Develop the broadest, most powerful principle of justice you can, then work out the issues that arise when you proceed to argue for its implementation through law and institutions. Their contribution is to suggest mechanisms whereby the application can be more gradual, nuanced, and in keeping with institutional and political realities. In contrast, what if we approach the issue from an entirely different perspective, one that does away with the need for such complex attempts at mediation? What if we looked for principles of justice *within* the systems and institutions we are studying, instead of outside them? That is the premise behind James' intriguing alternative approach to global justice theorizing offered in our fourth chapter.

According to James, rather than engage in traditional political theory we should focus on internal principles of justice, namely principles tied to the internal structure of actual economic arrangements themselves. Within international economic relations, he identifies internal principles of fairness, which he calls principles of structural equity. These internal principles of justice depend for their normative force on an underlying shared social practice of market reliance, rather than an overarching theory of distributive justice. The promise of this approach is that it does away with the need for intermediate mechanisms, because the theory comes from within the institutional arrangements themselves, thus improving the fit between theory and social reality. Insofar as it begins with a close analysis of the structure and operation of international economic law institutions themselves, James' work is itself a type of bridge between the more explicitly normative offerings of the other theorists and the institutional context in which global justice reforms must occur.

Taken together, the work of these four theorists suggests the need for more careful, formal attention to the relationship between normative theory and social facts *from the theoretical side*. In the case of external principles of justice, this can mean employing mediating structures such as human rights, but in a more nuanced or open structure as Gould does; or exploring in a philosophically rigorous manner the practical implications of mediating concepts, as with Butt's account of popular legitimacy; or critically monitoring the institutional implications of our own theoretical language, as Hockett urges. Alternatively, one can follow James and locate the normative project entirely within the social context by seeking internal principles of justice and thereby obviating the need for mediation. Whatever approach one takes, what is essential is that theorists help do the extra work of bringing their ideas across the practical threshold – it cannot be left solely to those approaching the issues from the institutional or doctrinal side.

For their part, those coming from within the institutional perspective have their distinctive contribution to, and responsibility for, the overall success of the enterprise as well, as is typified by the authors in our second section. All three academic lawyers are, characteristically, deeply immersed in the nuanced particularity of international economic law and its institutions. Together, they raise a second fundamental question for this project: If we agree on the priority of global justice, what is the most effective way for us as theorists and lawyers to integrate the messy contingency of human life and political reality within our efforts to articulate and pursue normative aims in an institutional context? Too many theorists are content to resolve the matter with gestures toward "nonideal" conditions, and too many academic lawyers seem to disdain theory or mistakenly assume that facts can refute ideas. What distinguishes these three offerings from much other scholarship – in addition to their careful and sophisticated use of normative theory – is their shared assumption that the best normative analysis, and therefore the best avenue toward increased justice, is *through* this particularity, not over or around it.

Drawing on a meticulous review of the debate over trade preferences, Lim argues that although moral claims within institutions are messy, complicated things that need different treatment than normative claims in ideal theory, with much more care taken to characterize their social, historical, and political context, they are moral claims nonetheless. Lim calls this "middle-level" theorizing, reminiscent of Blake's institutional theory.[1] In contrast, Dunoff looks at the same debate and the same history but reaches opposite conclusions, questioning whether developing countries have in fact been making moral claims at all, or rather adopting strategic positions for historically contingent political and economic reasons. For Dunoff, arguments in favor of trade preferences should be evaluated empirically, strategically, and contextually, because what matters most is not the moral language in which a claim is

---

[1] Michael Blake, "Distributive Justice, State Coercion and Autonomy," *Philosophy and Public Affairs* 30 (2002): 257, 261–266.

made, but whether the sought-for policy actually works to achieve the stated goals.

The dialogue between Lim and Dunoff reminds us that specific claims have specific histories and strategic implications in the fora within which they are raised, and they demand specific policy responses in those fora. Injustice takes place in specific concrete instances of time, place, and person, and so justice and the remediation of injustice must be similarly specific and grounded. Both Lim and Dunoff, in their different ways, agree that states' moral claims are to be taken seriously, and that means contextually. And yet, we cannot easily dismiss the concern raised by Dunoff (echoing generations of realists) that states employ moral language for a variety of tactical reasons, and the mere use of moral language or justification should not settle any policy arguments. However, to remain with the example raised by both Lim and Dunoff, it cannot be that the simple existence of strategic realities affecting state positions with respect to trade preferences would by itself eliminate or render superfluous the moral claims that states do make, or (even more importantly) the moral significance of the positions they take. Our concern over the justice or injustice of the global trading system is not exhausted by the claims that states happen to make or not make, nor is it settled by the concrete results states accept or contest.

It is this process of claim, counterclaim, and contestation by states that is at the heart of Thomas' contribution to the volume. Thomas argues that distributive justice is best approached through democratized governance procedures. She reminds us that the discourse of states in the World Trade Organization, like anywhere else, is complex and contradictory and makes broad substantive aims and programs difficult if not suspect. Add transaction costs and the reality of both policy differentiation among least developed countries and the proliferation of trade fora, and you get an idea of the complexity of the politics of trade and the coordination problems that states face.

Adopting a procedural approach to substantive reform is one very lawyerly response to the complex realities Thomas catalogues. An intelligent use of historical and empirical data is another way to more effectively mesh theory with institutional reality, as both Dunoff and Lim suggest. Taken together, all three of our academic lawyers suggest a second important principle: When theorizing institutional reform, normative theory must undergo a "step change" or downshift if it is to effectively integrate with the very institutional realities it seeks to reform. This argues for a much more cautious and contextual approach to normative theorizing about institutional reform along global justice lines, reflecting both political theory and concrete differences in politics, resources, and conceptions of equality.

All of this assumes that our normative language is an effective tool through which to identify injustice and prescribe remedies. This brings us to the third set of contributors, each of whom in their different ways pose the third major question of this volume: Is the normative project of global justice as currently defined sustainable or even coherent?

Tesón and Klick argue that much contemporary philosophy on the global justice question misses the mark on trade policy and distributive justice, because it ignores empirical reality in favor of ideal theory. Insofar as empirical work demonstrates that free trade is the most effective approach to alleviating world poverty, then free trade should be the policy prescription behind which all theories of global justice line up. The fact that it is not, and that free trade is often the target for global justice theorists, suggests to Tesón and Klick a dangerous level of confusion, disingenuousness, or worse.

That "worse" is what Stark's contribution is all about. She is deeply skeptical of the transformative capacity of contemporary global justice theory and its sincerity, but for different reasons. In her view, trade theory and international economic law cannot deliver justice because they are both fatally embedded in the neoliberal political, moral, and economic system, which is class-based and essentially opposed to wealth redistribution. Moreover, the whole narrative of "development" is flawed for similar reasons. All a reformer can hope to do is expose these ideological constructs for what they are, opening up the possibility for something more honest to take its place.

Trachtman also finds contemporary global justice theory to be lacking, but not on the basis of its ideological underpinnings. Instead, he analyzes the problem in terms of the methodological limits of the discipline, leading philosophers to overpromise and the rest of us to overrely on normative theory beyond what it is capable of delivering. However, because all the other disciplines involved in the global justice inquiry – economics, law, and psychology to name three – have their own complementary blind spots, the solution when it comes to global justice lies in a consistent commitment to interdisciplinarity. In this way, each discipline working on global justice can support and reinforce the others.

In an interesting way, the chapters in this section reflect three of the most salient positions on the larger debate concerning globalization itself. One tends to find that global opinion concerning the fairness problems in globalization divides itself into three camps. On one end of the spectrum, there are those who would agree with Tesón and Klick (Bhagwati foremost among them[2]) that the failures of globalization are attributable in large part to an inadequate

[2] Jagdish Bhagwati, *In Defense of Globalization* (Oxford: Oxford University Press, 2007).

commitment to liberalism – we need more free trade, not less, and the problem is well on the way to being solved. At the other end of the spectrum are those who would agree with Stark (Bourdieu is perhaps the most striking exponent[3]) that the problems of globalization cannot be fixed because globalization works exactly how those in power want it to, namely by enhancing the returns to capital on a global scale. In the middle are those of a more technocratic or policy-oriented nature (Stiglitz comes to mind[4]), who both see the problems and believe they can be fixed but would suggest (as does Trachtman) that it is a matter of "getting it right" – better policy *can* lead to fairer globalization.

Whatever your view of this globalization debate or the three contributions to this section, one can at least agree that they each offer important cautionary tales as we set about addressing the manifest suffering of the global many. Together, their injunctions constitute a third principal theme of this volume: When theorizing global justice and institutional reform, pay close attention to empirical theory, whatever one thinks of the politics associated with it; acknowledge the reality and limits of one's own ideology and the pervasive effects of power inequalities; and avoid disciplinary hubris.

This brings us to the conclusion of the conclusion. In our view the chapters in this volume underscore, despite their differences, that on matters of global justice the discourse is not so much confused with regard to what justice would look like, at least in its rough contours, as it is overwhelmed by the degree of injustice and the seeming intractability of current institutions and politics when it comes to real reform. Together, the offerings in this volume argue that rather than remain embarrassed at the audacity of the claims of justice, our often feeble responses, and the seeming impossibility of the obstacles, we can and should form a clear, coherent, and multidisciplinary agenda of research and action.

First, we need several clear, powerful, well-argued principles or ideas that can inspire, animate, and organize our efforts toward a more just global economic system. This is the preeminent task of political theory. We need several of these ideas, not just one, because as Sen reminds us in *The Idea of Justice*, seeking a single triumphant idea of justice can be both a delusion and a dangerous distraction. When over 26,000 children die each day, as Dunoff points out, we must move ahead as best we can with the tools we have.

The theoretical contributions in this volume amply illustrate this potential and its realization. Both external and internal principles of justice all have a

---

[3] Pierre Bourdieu, *Acts of Resistance: Against the Tyranny of the Market*, translated by Richard Nice (New York: The New Press, 1998).

[4] Joseph E. Stiglitz, *Globalization and Its Discontents* (New York: Norton, 2003).

place in the larger normative conversation, each playing a vital role in generating important mutually reinforcing policy prescriptions – no comprehensive approach to global justice is complete without both approaches. Political theorists must examine, critique, and develop these ideas among themselves on the basis of a number of formal, aesthetic, and disciplinary criteria that are of fundamental importance to the quality and strength of their ideas, but that will never be a major preoccupation of academic lawyers and policy makers.

Second, on the basis of such foundational principles, we need detailed intermediate models for reforming core rules, policies, and procedures in each key functional area of international economic law. Substantively, we need models and structures for the gamut of justice-oriented policy innovations affecting both substantive rules and legal process: mechanisms for universal welfare rights and benefits, transnational transfer payments, increased participation by least developed countries in governance and negotiation, representation of individuals in international economic governance, and basic procedural rights and safeguards, just to name a few. Formally, these models must draw equally on political theory, economic theory, and a nuanced understanding of the nitty-gritty reality of rules, systems of rules, and institutions. They should rely significantly on mediating concepts when based on external principles of justice, or they should be closely related to internal principles of justice if one begins as James suggests. In either case, this is where academic lawyers and philosophers, together with economists, can have their most fruitful collaboration. Lim, Dunoff, and Thomas remind us of the complexity, contingency, indeterminacy, and contradiction inherent in human social activity, and that academic lawyers are fully capable of analyzing and managing this complexity – it is their strong suit. Essentially, there must be a collaborative effort among philosophers and academic lawyers for each major institution and area of international economic law which may need revision in view of the demands of global justice.

Third, on the basis of these ideas and these policy models, we need a wide range of legal arguments and an equally wide range of political strategies, addressed to each major country, each major institution, and each major stakeholder – as many arguments as possible and in the terms most persuasive with respect to that audience – in support of movement toward a more just global economic system. This is where philosophers and academic lawyers can work fruitfully with others such as political scientists and social psychologists interested in justice issues.

The need for such arguments reflects the fundamental difference, albeit a mutually reinforcing one, between philosophy, law, and policy. All three involve arguments, but the arguments needed for political, legal, and

economic reforms are of a different order than the arguments needed in theoretical discourse or in a court of law. They are not unrelated, but they are more
cousins than siblings. If we are to move ahead in implementing the reforms
that, by and large, we all agree on (even communitarians acknowledge the
most severe abuses and the basic shape of a response),[5] then we need strategies
to persuade (and hold accountable) the entrenched powers and interests that
currently dictate the shape of global economic relations. Philosophers may be
right about justice and lawyers may be right about institutionalized rules and
power, but by themselves neither will be able to bring about any justice without
a concerted effort to develop sophisticated, clear, and compelling arguments
for political change (and accountability). Following Trachtman, we need the
contributions of each discipline, united in a comprehensive policy package
that can be delivered and implemented by political leaders.

Together, this shapes a worthy research agenda for the next generation of
global justice scholarship.

[5] Michael Walzer, *Thick and Thin: Moral Argument at Home and Abroad* (Notre Dame, IN:
University of Notre Dame Press, 1994).

Index

CPSIA information can be obtained at www.ICGtesting.com
Printed in the USA
LVOW05s0843060814

397789LV00008B/104/P